New . . . St. Joseph

SUNDAY MISSAL

PRAYERBOOK AND HYMNAL

For 2020-2021

THE COMPLETE MASSES FOR SUNDAYS, HOLYDAYS, and the SACRED PASCHAL TRIDUUM

With the People's Parts of Holy Mass
Printed in Boldface Type
and Arranged for Parish Participation

IN ACCORD WITH THE THIRD TYPICAL EDITION
OF THE ROMAN MISSAL

WITH THE "NEW AMERICAN BIBLE" TEXT
FROM THE REVISED SUNDAY LECTIONARY,
SHORT HELPFUL NOTES AND EXPLANATIONS,
AND A TREASURY OF POPULAR PRAYERS

Dedicated to St. Joseph
Patron of the Universal Church

CATHOLIC BOOK PUBLISHING CORP.
New Jersey

NIHIL OBSTAT: Rev. Pawel Tomczyk, Ph.D.
Censor Librorum

IMPRIMATUR: ✠ Arthur J. Serratelli, S.T.D., S.S.L., D.D.
Bishop of Paterson

May 28, 2020

Published with the approval of the
Committee on Divine Worship,
United States Conference of Catholic Bishops

The St. Joseph Missals have been diligently prepared with the invaluable assistance of a special Board of Editors, including specialists in Liturgy and Sacred Scripture, Catechetics, Sacred Music and Art.

In this new Sunday Missal Edition the musical notations for responsorial antiphons are by Rev. John Selner, S.S.

(T-2021)

ISBN 978-1-947070-71-4

© 2020 by *Catholic Book Publishing Corp.*, N.J.
catholicbookpublishing.com
Printed in the U.S.A.

PREFACE

IN the words of the Second Vatican Council in the *Constitution on the Liturgy*, the *Mass* "is an action of Christ the priest and of his body which is the Church; it is a sacred action surpassing all others; no other action of the Church can equal its efficacy by the same title and to the same degree" (art. 7). Hence the Mass is a sacred sign, something visible which brings the invisible reality of Christ to us in the worship of the Father.

The Mass is the re-presentation of the Paschal Mystery, which delivers us from sin, death, and the devil and whereby we merit to receive a share in the eternal life of the Resurrected Christ.

"At the Last Supper, on the night when he was betrayed, our Savior instituted the Eucharistic sacrifice of his body and blood. He did this in order to perpetuate the sacrifice of the Cross throughout the centuries until he should come again, and so to entrust to his beloved spouse, the Church, a memorial of his death and resurrection: a sacrament of love, a sign of unity, a bond of charity, a Paschal banquet in which Christ is eaten, the mind is filled with grace, and a pledge of future glory is given to us.

"The Church, therefore, earnestly desires that Christ's faithful, when present at this mystery of faith, should not be there as strangers or silent spectators; on the contrary, through a good understanding of the rites and prayers they should take part in the sacred action conscious of what they are doing, with devotion and full

7

collaboration. They should be instructed by God's word
and be nourished at the table of the Lord's body; they
should give thanks to God; by offering the immaculate
Victim, not only through the hands of the priests but
also with him, they should learn also to offer themselves;
through Christ the Mediator, they should be drawn day
by day into ever more perfect union with God and with
each other, so that . . . God may be all in all" (art. 47-48).

Accordingly, this new Sunday Missal has been edited,
in conformity with the latest findings of modern liturgists,
especially to enable the people to attain the most active
participation.

To insure that "each . . . lay person who has an office
to perform [will] do all of, but only, those parts which
pertain to his office" (art. 28), a simple method of instant
identification of the various parts of the Mass, has been
designed, using different typefaces:

(1) **boldface type**—clearly identifies all people's parts
for each Mass.

(2) lightface type—indicates the Priest's, Deacon's, or
reader's parts.

In order to enable the faithful to prepare each Mass
AT HOME and so participate more actively AT MASS,
the editors have added short helpful explanations of the
new scripture readings, geared to the spiritual needs of
daily life. A large selection of hymns for congregational
singing has been included as well as a treasury of private
prayers.

We trust that all these special features will help
Catholics who use this new St. Joseph Missal to be led—
in keeping with the desire of the Church—"to that full,
conscious, and active participation in liturgical celebrations which is demanded by the very nature of the liturgy.
Such participation by the Christian people as a chosen
race, a royal priesthood, a holy nation, a redeemed people
(1 Pt 2:9; cf. 2:4-5), is their right and duty by reason of
their baptism" (art. 14).

THE ORDER OF MASS TITLES

THE INTRODUCTORY RITES

1. Entrance Chant
2. Greeting
3. Rite for the Blessing and Sprinkling of Water
4. Penitential Act
5. Kyrie
6. Gloria
7. Collect (Proper)

THE LITURGY OF THE WORD

8. First Reading (Proper)
9. Responsorial Psalm (Proper)
10. Second Reading (Proper)
11. Gospel Acclamation (Proper)
12. Gospel Dialogue
13. Gospel Reading (Proper)
14. Homily
15. Profession of Faith (Creed)
16. Universal Prayer

THE LITURGY OF THE EUCHARIST

17. Presentation and Preparation of the Gifts
18. Invitation to Prayer
19. Prayer over the Offerings (Proper)
20. Eucharistic Prayer
21. Preface Dialogue
22. Preface
23. Preface Acclamation
    Eucharistic Prayer
    1, 2, 3, 4
    Reconciliation 1, 2
    Various Needs 1, 2, 3, 4

THE COMMUNION RITE

24. The Lord's Prayer
25. Sign of Peace
26. Lamb of God
27. Invitation to Communion
28. Communion
29. Prayer after Communion (Proper)

THE CONCLUDING RITES

30. Solemn Blessing
31. Final Blessing
32. Dismissal

THE ORDER OF MASS

Options are indicated by A, B, C, D in the margin.

THE INTRODUCTORY RITES

Acts of prayer and penitence prepare us to meet Christ as he comes in Word and Sacrament. We gather as a worshiping community to celebrate our unity with him and with one another in faith.

1 ENTRANCE CHANT `STAND`

If it is not sung, it is recited by all or some of the people.

Joined together as Christ's people, we open the celebration by raising our voices in praise of God who is present among us. This song should deepen our unity as it introduces the Mass we celebrate today.

→ Turn to Today's Mass

2 GREETING (3 forms)

When the Priest comes to the altar, he makes the customary reverence with the ministers and kisses the altar. Then, with the ministers, he goes to his chair. After the Entrance Chant, all make the Sign of the Cross:

Priest: In the name of the Father, and of the Son, and of the Holy Spirit.

PEOPLE: **Amen.**

The Priest welcomes us in the name of the Lord. We show our union with God, our neighbor, and the Priest by a united response to his greeting.

A

Priest: The grace of our Lord Jesus Christ,
and the love of God,
and the communion of the Holy Spirit
be with you all.

PEOPLE: **And with your spirit.**

B —————— OR ——————

Priest: Grace to you and peace from God our Father
and the Lord Jesus Christ.

PEOPLE: **And with your spirit.**

C —————— OR ——————

Priest: The Lord be with you.

PEOPLE: **And with your spirit.**

[Bishop: Peace be with you.

PEOPLE: **And with your spirit.**]

3 RITE FOR the BLESSING and SPRINKLING OF WATER

From time to time on Sundays, especially in Easter Time, instead of the customary Penitential Act, the Blessing and Sprinkling of Water may take place (see pp. 78-81) as a reminder of Baptism.

4 PENITENTIAL ACT (3 forms)

(Omitted when the Rite for the Blessing and Sprinkling of Water [see pp. 78-81] has taken place or some part of the liturgy of the hours has preceded.)

Before we hear God's word, we acknowledge our sins humbly, ask for mercy, and accept his pardon.

Invitation to repent:

After the introduction to the day's Mass, the Priest invites the people to recall their sins and to repent of them in silence:

Priest: Brethren (brothers and sisters), let us acknowledge our sins,

and so prepare ourselves to celebrate the sacred mysteries.

Then, after a brief silence, one of the following forms is used.

A

Priest and **PEOPLE:**

I confess to almighty God
and to you, my brothers and sisters,
that I have greatly sinned,
in my thoughts and in my words,
in what I have done and in what I have
failed to do,

They strike their breast:

through my fault, through my fault,
through my most grievous fault;

Then they continue:

therefore I ask blessed Mary ever-Virgin,
all the Angels and Saints,
and you, my brothers and sisters,
to pray for me to the Lord our God.

B ———————— OR ————————

Priest: Have mercy on us, O Lord.

PEOPLE: For we have sinned against you.

Priest: Show us, O Lord, your mercy.

PEOPLE: And grant us your salvation.

C ———————— OR————————

Priest, or a Deacon or another minister:

You were sent to heal the contrite of heart:
Lord, have mercy.

PEOPLE: Lord, have mercy.

Priest or other minister:

You came to call sinners:
Christ, have mercy.

PEOPLE: Christ, have mercy.

Priest or other minister:

You are seated at the right hand of the
Father to intercede for us:

Lord, have mercy.

PEOPLE: Lord, have mercy.

———————

Absolution:

At the end of any of the forms of the Penitential Act:

Priest: May almighty God have mercy on us,
forgive us our sins,
and bring us to everlasting life.

PEOPLE: Amen.

5 KYRIE

Unless included in the Penitential Act, the Kyrie is sung or said by all, with alternating parts for the choir or cantor and for the people:

℣. Lord, have mercy.

℟. **Lord, have mercy.**

℣. Christ, have mercy.

℟. **Christ, have mercy.**

℣. Lord, have mercy.

℟. **Lord, have mercy.**

6 GLORIA

As the Church assembled in the Spirit we praise and pray to the Father and the Lamb.

When the Gloria is sung or said, the Priest or the cantors or everyone together may begin it:

Glory to God in the highest,
and on earth peace to people of good will.

We praise you,
we bless you,
we adore you,
we glorify you,
we give you thanks for your great glory,
Lord God, heavenly King,
O God, almighty Father.

Lord Jesus Christ, Only Begotten Son,
Lord God, Lamb of God, Son of the Father,
you take away the sins of the world,
    have mercy on us;

you take away the sins of the world,
   receive our prayer;
you are seated at the right hand of the Father,
   have mercy on us.

For you alone are the Holy One,
you alone are the Lord,
you alone are the Most High,
Jesus Christ,
with the Holy Spirit,
in the glory of God the Father.
Amen.

7 COLLECT

The Priest invites us to pray silently for a moment and then,
in our name, expresses the theme of the day's celebration and
petitions God the Father through the mediation of Christ in the
Holy Spirit.

Priest: Let us pray.

→ **Turn to Today's Mass**

*Priest and people pray silently for a while. Then the
Priest says the Collect prayer, at the end of which the
people acclaim:*

PEOPLE: Amen.

THE LITURGY OF THE WORD

The proclamation of God's Word is always centered on Christ, present through his Word. Old Testament writings prepare for him; New Testament books speak of him directly. All of scripture calls us to believe once more and to follow. After the reading we reflect on God's words and respond to them.

As in Today's Mass `SIT`

8 FIRST READING

At the end of the reading: Reader: The word of the Lord.

PEOPLE: Thanks be to God.

9 RESPONSORIAL PSALM

The people repeat the response sung by the cantor the first time and then after each verse.

10 SECOND READING

At the end of the reading: Reader: The word of the Lord.

PEOPLE: Thanks be to God.

11 GOSPEL ACCLAMATION `STAND`

Jesus will speak to us in the Gospel. We rise now out of respect and prepare for his message with the Alleluia.

The people repeat the Alleluia after the cantor's Alleluia and then after the verse. During Lent one of the following invocations is used as a response instead of the Alleluia:

(a) **Glory and praise to you, Lord Jesus Christ!**
(b) **Glory to you, Lord Jesus Christ, Wisdom of God the Father!**
(c) **Glory to you, Word of God, Lord Jesus Christ!**
(d) **Glory to you, Lord Jesus Christ, Son of the Living God!**

16

(e) **Praise and honor to you, Lord Jesus Christ!**

(f) **Praise to you, Lord Jesus Christ, King of endless glory!**

(g) **Marvelous and great are your works, O Lord!**

(h) **Salvation, glory, and power to the Lord Jesus Christ!**

12 GOSPEL DIALOGUE

Before proclaiming the Gospel, the Deacon asks the Priest: Your blessing, Father. *The Priest says:*

May the Lord be in your heart and on your lips, that you may proclaim his Gospel worthily and well, in the name of the Father, and of the Son, ✠ and of the Holy Spirit. *The Deacon answers:* Amen.

If there is no Deacon, the Priest says inaudibly:

Cleanse my heart and my lips, almighty God, that I may worthily proclaim your holy Gospel.

13 GOSPEL READING

Deacon (or Priest):
          The Lord be with you.

PEOPLE: And with your spirit.

Deacon (or Priest):

✠ A reading from the holy Gospel according to N.

PEOPLE: Glory to you, O Lord.

At the end:

Deacon (or Priest):
          The Gospel of the Lord.

PEOPLE: Praise to you, Lord Jesus Christ.

Then the Deacon (or Priest) kisses the book, saying inaudibly: Through the words of the Gospel may our sins be wiped away.

14 HOMILY   SIT

God's word is spoken again in the Homily. The Holy Spirit speaking through the lips of the preacher explains and applies today's biblical readings to the needs of this particular congregation. He calls us to respond to Christ through the life we lead.

15 PROFESSION OF FAITH (CREED) `STAND`

As a people we express our acceptance of God's message in the Scriptures and Homily. We summarize our faith by proclaiming a creed handed down from the early Church.

All say the Profession of Faith on Sundays.

——————— THE NICENE CREED ———————

I believe in one God,
the Father almighty,
maker of heaven and earth,
of all things visible and invisible.

I believe in one Lord Jesus Christ,
the Only Begotten Son of God,
born of the Father before all ages.
God from God, Light from Light,
true God from true God,
begotten, not made, consubstantial with the Father;
through him all things were made.
For us men and for our salvation
he came down from heaven,
and by the Holy Spirit was incarnate of the Virgin
    Mary,   } *bow*
and became man.

For our sake he was crucified under Pontius Pilate,
he suffered death and was buried,
and rose again on the third day
in accordance with the Scriptures.
He ascended into heaven
and is seated at the right hand of the Father.
He will come again in glory
to judge the living and the dead
and his kingdom will have no end.

I believe in the Holy Spirit, the Lord, the giver of life,
who proceeds from the Father and the Son,
who with the Father and the Son is adored and
    glorified,
who has spoken through the prophets.

I believe in one, holy, catholic and apostolic Church.
I confess one Baptism for the forgiveness of sins
and I look forward to the resurrection of the dead
and the life of the world to come. Amen.

OR ——————— APOSTLES' CREED ———————

*Especially during Lent and Easter Time, the Apostles'
Creed may be said after the Homily.*

I believe in God,
the Father almighty,
Creator of heaven and earth,
and in Jesus Christ, his only Son, our Lord,
who was conceived by the Holy Spirit, } *bow*
born of the Virgin Mary,
suffered under Pontius Pilate,
was crucified, died and was buried;
he descended into hell;
on the third day he rose again from the dead;
he ascended into heaven,
and is seated at the right hand of God the Father
    almighty;
from there he will come to judge the living and the dead.

I believe in the Holy Spirit,
the holy catholic Church,
the communion of saints,
the forgiveness of sins,
the resurrection of the body,
and life everlasting. Amen.

16 UNIVERSAL PRAYER   (Prayer of the Faithful)

As a priestly people we unite with one another to pray for today's
needs in the Church and the world.

*After the Priest gives the introduction the Deacon or other
minister sings or says the invocations.*

PEOPLE: Lord, hear our prayer.
(or other response, according to local custom)
At the end the Priest says the concluding prayer:
PEOPLE: Amen.

THE LITURGY OF THE EUCHARIST

17 PRESENTATION AND PREPARATION `SIT` OF THE GIFTS

While the people's gifts are brought forward to the Priest and are placed on the altar, the Offertory Chant is sung.

Before placing the bread on the altar, the Priest says inaudibly:

Blessed are you, Lord God of all creation,
for through your goodness we have received
the bread we offer you:
fruit of the earth and work of human hands,
it will become for us the bread of life.

If there is no singing, the Priest may say this prayer aloud, and the people may respond:

PEOPLE: Blessed be God for ever.

When he pours wine and a little water into the chalice, the Deacon (or the Priest) says inaudibly:

By the mystery of this water and wine
may we come to share in the divinity of Christ
who humbled himself to share in our humanity.

Before placing the chalice on the altar, he says:

Blessed are you, Lord God of all creation,
for through your goodness we have received
the wine we offer you:
fruit of the vine and work of human hands,
it will become our spiritual drink.

If there is no singing, the Priest may say this prayer aloud, and the people may respond:

PEOPLE: Blessed be God for ever.

The Priest says inaudibly:
With humble spirit and contrite heart
may we be accepted by you, O Lord,
and may our sacrifice in your sight this day
be pleasing to you, Lord God.

Then he washes his hands, saying:
Wash me, O Lord, from my iniquity
and cleanse me from my sin.

18 INVITATION TO PRAYER

Priest: Pray, brethren (brothers and sisters),
          that my sacrifice and yours
          may be acceptable to God,
          the almighty Father.   `STAND`

PEOPLE:

**May the Lord accept the sacrifice at your hands
for the praise and glory of his name,
for our good
and the good of all his holy Church.**

19 PRAYER OVER THE OFFERINGS

*The Priest, speaking in our name, asks the Father to
bless and accept these gifts.*

→ `Turn to Today's Mass`

At the end, **PEOPLE: Amen.**

20 EUCHARISTIC PRAYER

We begin the eucharistic service of praise and thanksgiving, the center of the entire celebration, the central prayer of worship. We lift our hearts to God, and offer praise and thanks as the Priest addresses this prayer to the Father through Jesus Christ. Together we join Christ in his sacrifice, celebrating his memorial in the holy meal and acknowledging with him the wonderful works of God in our lives.

21 PREFACE DIALOGUE

Priest: The Lord be with you.
PEOPLE: And with your spirit.

Priest: Lift up your hearts.
PEOPLE: We lift them up to the Lord.

Priest: Let us give thanks to the Lord our God.
PEOPLE: It is right and just.

22 PREFACE

As indicated in the individual Masses of this Missal, the Priest may say one of the following Prefaces (listed in numerical order).

23 PREFACE ACCLAMATION

Priest and **PEOPLE:**
Holy, Holy, Holy Lord God of hosts.
Heaven and earth are full of your glory.
Hosanna in the highest.
Blessed is he who comes in the name of the Lord.
Hosanna in the highest.   `KNEEL`

Then the Priest continues with one of the following Eucharistic Prayers.

EUCHARISTIC PRAYER ....Choice of ten

1	To you, therefore, most merciful Father ..	p. 24
2	You are indeed Holy, O Lord, the fount ...	p. 31
3	You are indeed Holy, O Lord, and all	p. 34
4	We give you praise, Father most holy	p. 39
R1	You are indeed Holy, O Lord, and from ...	p. 44
R2	You, therefore, almighty Father	p. 49
V1	You are indeed Holy and to be glorified ..	p. 53
V2	You are indeed Holy and to be glorified ..	p. 58
V3	You are indeed Holy and to be glorified ..	p. 63
V4	You are indeed Holy and to be glorified ..	p. 68

EUCHARISTIC PRAYER No. 1

The Roman Canon

(This Eucharistic Prayer is especially suitable for Sundays and Masses with proper Communicantes and Hanc igitur.)

[The words within parentheses may be omitted.]

To you, therefore, most merciful Father,
we make humble prayer and petition
through Jesus Christ, your Son, our Lord:
that you accept
and bless ✠ these gifts, these offerings,
these holy and unblemished sacrifices,
which we offer you firstly
for your holy catholic Church.
Be pleased to grant her peace,
to guard, unite and govern her
throughout the whole world,
together with your servant N. our Pope,
and N. our Bishop,
and all those who, holding to the truth,
hand on the catholic and apostolic faith.

Remember, Lord, your servants N. and N.
and all gathered here,
whose faith and devotion are known to you.
For them, we offer you this sacrifice of praise
or they offer it for themselves
and all who are dear to them:
for the redemption of their souls,
in hope of health and well-being,
and paying their homage to you,
the eternal God, living and true.

In communion with those whose memory we
     venerate,
especially the glorious ever-Virgin Mary,
Mother of our God and Lord, Jesus Christ,
† and blessed Joseph, her Spouse,
your blessed Apostles and Martyrs
Peter and Paul, Andrew,
(James, John,
Thomas, James, Philip,
Bartholomew, Matthew,
Simon and Jude;
Linus, Cletus, Clement, Sixtus,
Cornelius, Cyprian,
Lawrence, Chrysogonus,
John and Paul,
Cosmas and Damian)
and all your Saints;
we ask that through their merits and prayers,
in all things we may be defended
by your protecting help.
(Through Christ our Lord. Amen.)

Therefore, Lord, we pray:*
graciously accept this oblation of our service,
that of your whole family;
order our days in your peace,
and command that we be delivered from eternal
     damnation
and counted among the flock of those you have
     chosen.
(Through Christ our Lord. Amen.)

Be pleased, O God, we pray,
to bless, acknowledge,
and approve this offering in every respect;

† * See p. 95 for proper Communicantes and Hanc igitur.

1 make it spiritual and acceptable,
so that it may become for us
the Body and Blood of your most beloved Son,
our Lord Jesus Christ.

On the day before he was to suffer,
he took bread in his holy and venerable hands,
and with eyes raised to heaven
to you, O God, his almighty Father,
giving you thanks, he said the blessing,
broke the bread
and gave it to his disciples, saying:

Take this, all of you, and eat of it,
for this is my Body,
which will be given up for you.

In a similar way when supper was ended,
he took this precious chalice
in his holy and venerable hands,
and once more giving you thanks, he said the
    blessing
and gave the chalice to his disciples, saying:

Take this, all of you, and drink from it,
for this is the chalice of my Blood,
the Blood of the new and eternal covenant,
which will be poured out for you and for many
for the forgiveness of sins.

Do this in memory of me.

Priest: The mystery of faith. *(Memorial Acclamation)*
PEOPLE:

A We proclaim your Death, O Lord,
and profess your Resurrection
until you come again.

B **When we eat this Bread and drink this Cup,
we proclaim your Death, O Lord,
until you come again.**

C **Save us, Savior of the world,
for by your Cross and Resurrection
you have set us free.**

Therefore, O Lord,
as we celebrate the memorial of the blessed Passion,
the Resurrection from the dead,
and the glorious Ascension into heaven
of Christ, your Son, our Lord,
we, your servants and your holy people,
offer to your glorious majesty
from the gifts that you have given us,
this pure victim,
this holy victim,
this spotless victim,
the holy Bread of eternal life
and the Chalice of everlasting salvation.

Be pleased to look upon these offerings
with a serene and kindly countenance,
and to accept them,
as once you were pleased to accept
the gifts of your servant Abel the just,
the sacrifice of Abraham, our father in faith,
and the offering of your high priest Melchizedek,
a holy sacrifice, a spotless victim.

In humble prayer we ask you, almighty God:
command that these gifts be borne
by the hands of your holy Angel
to your altar on high

1 in the sight of your divine majesty,
so that all of us, who through this participation at
    the altar
receive the most holy Body and Blood of your Son,
may be filled with every grace and heavenly
    blessing.
(Through Christ our Lord. Amen.)

Remember also, Lord, your servants *N.* and *N.*,
who have gone before us with the sign of faith
and rest in the sleep of peace.
Grant them, O Lord, we pray,
and all who sleep in Christ,
a place of refreshment, light and peace.
(Through Christ our Lord. Amen.)

To us, also, your servants, who, though sinners,
hope in your abundant mercies,
graciously grant some share
and fellowship with your holy Apostles and
    Martyrs:
with John the Baptist, Stephen,
Matthias, Barnabas,
(Ignatius, Alexander,
Marcellinus, Peter,
Felicity, Perpetua,
Agatha, Lucy,
Agnes, Cecilia, Anastasia)
and all your Saints;
admit us, we beseech you,
into their company,
not weighing our merits,
but granting us your pardon,
through Christ our Lord.

1

Through whom
you continue to make all these good things,
  O Lord;
you sanctify them, fill them with life,
bless them, and bestow them upon us.

(Concluding Doxology)

Through him, and with him, and in him,
O God, almighty Father,
in the unity of the Holy Spirit,
all glory and honor is yours,
for ever and ever.

The people acclaim: **Amen.**

Continue with the Mass, as on p. 72.

EUCHARISTIC PRAYER No. 2

(This Eucharistic Prayer is particularly suitable on Weekdays or for special circumstances.)

STAND

℣. The Lord be with you.
℟. **And with your spirit.**

℣. Lift up your hearts.
℟. **We lift them up to the Lord.**

℣. Let us give thanks to the Lord our God.
℟. **It is right and just.**

It is truly right and just, our duty and our salvation,
always and everywhere to give you thanks, Father
    most holy,
through your beloved Son, Jesus Christ,
your Word through whom you made all things,
whom you sent as our Savior and Redeemer,
incarnate by the Holy Spirit and born of the Virgin.

Fulfilling your will
    and gaining for you a holy people,
he stretched out his hands
    as he endured his Passion,
so as to break the bonds of death
    and manifest the resurrection.

And so, with the Angels and all the Saints
we declare your glory,
as with one voice we acclaim:

Holy, Holy, Holy Lord God of hosts.
Heaven and earth are full of your glory.
Hosanna in the highest.
Blessed is he who comes in the name of the Lord.
Hosanna in the highest.

`KNEEL`

You are indeed Holy, O Lord,
the fount of all holiness.

Make holy, therefore, these gifts, we pray,
by sending down your Spirit upon them like the
    dewfall,
so that they may become for us
the Body and ✠ Blood of our Lord Jesus Christ.

At the time he was betrayed
and entered willingly into his Passion,
he took bread and, giving thanks, broke it,
and gave it to his disciples, saying:

Take this, all of you, and eat of it,
for this is my Body,
which will be given up for you.

In a similar way, when supper was ended,
he took the chalice
and, once more giving thanks,
he gave it to his disciples, saying:

Take this, all of you, and drink from it,
for this is the chalice of my Blood,
the Blood of the new and eternal covenant,
which will be poured out for you and for many
for the forgiveness of sins.
Do this in memory of me.

2 Priest: The mystery of faith. *(Memorial Acclamation)*

PEOPLE:

A We proclaim your Death, O Lord,
and profess your Resurrection
until you come again.

B When we eat this Bread and drink this Cup,
we proclaim your Death, O Lord,
until you come again.

C Save us, Savior of the world,
for by your Cross and Resurrection
you have set us free.

Therefore, as we celebrate
the memorial of his Death and Resurrection,
we offer you, Lord,
the Bread of life and the Chalice of salvation,
giving thanks that you have held us worthy
to be in your presence and minister to you.

Humbly we pray
that, partaking of the Body and Blood of Christ,
we may be gathered into one by the Holy Spirit.

Remember, Lord, your Church,
spread throughout the world,
and bring her to the fullness of charity,
together with N. our Pope and N. our Bishop
and all the clergy.

In Masses for the Dead, the following may be added:
Remember your servant N.,
whom you have called (today)
from this world to yourself.

Grant that he (she) who was united with your Son in a
    death like his,
may also be one with him in his Resurrection.

2

Remember also our brothers and sisters
who have fallen asleep in the hope of the
    resurrection,
and all who have died in your mercy:
welcome them into the light of your face.
Have mercy on us all, we pray,
that with the Blessed Virgin Mary, Mother of
    God,
with blessed Joseph, her Spouse,
with the blessed Apostles,
and all the Saints who have pleased you
    throughout the ages,
we may merit to be coheirs to eternal life,
and may praise and glorify you
through your Son, Jesus Christ.

(Concluding Doxology)

Through him, and with him, and in him,
O God, almighty Father,
in the unity of the Holy Spirit,
all glory and honor is yours,
for ever and ever.

The people acclaim: **Amen.**

Continue with the Mass, as on p. 72.

EUCHARISTIC PRAYER No. 3

(This Eucharistic Prayer may be used with any Preface and preferably on Sundays and feast days.)

KNEEL

You are indeed Holy, O Lord,
and all you have created
rightly gives you praise,
for through your Son our Lord Jesus Christ,
by the power and working of the Holy Spirit,
you give life to all things and make them holy,
and you never cease to gather a people to yourself,
so that from the rising of the sun to its setting
a pure sacrifice may be offered to your name.

Therefore, O Lord, we humbly implore you:
by the same Spirit graciously make holy
these gifts we have brought to you for
    consecration,
that they may become the Body and ✠ Blood
of your Son our Lord Jesus Christ,
at whose command we celebrate these mysteries.

For on the night he was betrayed
he himself took bread,
and, giving you thanks, he said the blessing,
broke the bread and gave it to his disciples,
    saying:

Take this, all of you, and eat of it,
for this is my Body,
which will be given up for you.

In a similar way, when supper was ended,
he took the chalice,

3

and, giving you thanks, he said the blessing,
and gave the chalice to his disciples, saying:

Take this, all of you, and drink from it,
for this is the chalice of my Blood,
the Blood of the new and eternal covenant,
which will be poured out for you and for many
for the forgiveness of sins.

Do this in memory of me.

Priest: The mystery of faith. *(Memorial Acclamation)*

PEOPLE:

A We proclaim your Death, O Lord,
   and profess your Resurrection
   until you come again.

B When we eat this Bread and drink this Cup,
   we proclaim your Death, O Lord,
   until you come again.

C Save us, Savior of the world,
   for by your Cross and Resurrection
   you have set us free.

Therefore, O Lord, as we celebrate the memorial
of the saving Passion of your Son,
his wondrous Resurrection
and Ascension into heaven,
and as we look forward to his second coming,
we offer you in thanksgiving
this holy and living sacrifice.

Look, we pray, upon the oblation of your Church
and, recognizing the sacrificial Victim by whose
   death
you willed to reconcile us to yourself,

3 grant that we, who are nourished
by the Body and Blood of your Son
and filled with his Holy Spirit,
may become one body, one spirit in Christ.

May he make of us
an eternal offering to you,
so that we may obtain an inheritance with your elect,
especially with the most Blessed Virgin Mary,
   Mother of God,
with blessed Joseph, her Spouse,
with your blessed Apostles and glorious Martyrs
(with Saint *N.*: the Saint of the day or Patron Saint)
and with all the Saints,
on whose constant intercession in your presence
we rely for unfailing help.

May this Sacrifice of our reconciliation,
we pray, O Lord,
advance the peace and salvation of all the world.
Be pleased to confirm in faith and charity
your pilgrim Church on earth,
with your servant *N.* our Pope and *N.* our Bishop,
the Order of Bishops, all the clergy,
and the entire people you have gained for your
   own.

Listen graciously to the prayers of this family,
whom you have summoned before you:
in your compassion, O merciful Father,
gather to yourself all your children
scattered throughout the world.

† To our departed brothers and sisters
and to all who were pleasing to you
at their passing from this life,
give kind admittance to your kingdom.

3

There we hope to enjoy for ever the fullness of
    your glory
through Christ our Lord,
through whom you bestow on the world all that
    is good. †

(Concluding Doxology)

Through him, and with him, and in him,
O God, almighty Father,
in the unity of the Holy Spirit,
all glory and honor is yours,
for ever and ever.

The people acclaim: **Amen.**

Continue with the Mass, as on p. 72.

---

† *In Masses for the Dead the following may be said:*

†Remember your servant N.
whom you have called (today)
from this world to yourself.
Grant that he (she) who was united with your Son in a
    death like his,
may also be one with him in his Resurrection,
when from the earth
he will raise up in the flesh those who have died,
and transform our lowly body
after the pattern of his own glorious body.
To our departed brothers and sisters, too,
and to all who were pleasing to you
at their passing from this life,
give kind admittance to your kingdom.
There we hope to enjoy for ever the fullness of your glory,
when you will wipe away every tear from our eyes.
For seeing you, our God, as you are,
we shall be like you for all the ages
and praise you without end,
through Christ our Lord,
through whom you bestow on the world all that is good. †

EUCHARISTIC PRAYER No. 4

℣. The Lord be with you.
℟. **And with your spirit.**

℣. Lift up your hearts.
℟. **We lift them up to the Lord.**

℣. Let us give thanks to the Lord our God.
℟. **It is right and just.**

It is truly right to give you thanks,
truly just to give you glory, Father most holy,
for you are the one God living and true,
existing before all ages and abiding for all eternity,
dwelling in unapproachable light;
yet you, who alone are good, the source of life,
have made all that is,
so that you might fill your creatures with blessings
and bring joy to many of them by the glory of your
    light.

And so, in your presence are countless hosts of
    Angels,
who serve you day and night
and, gazing upon the glory of your face,
glorify you without ceasing.

With them we, too, confess your name in exultation,
giving voice to every creature under heaven,
as we acclaim:

Holy, Holy, Holy Lord God of hosts.
Heaven and earth are full of your glory.
Hosanna in the highest.

**Blessed is he who comes in the name of the Lord.
Hosanna in the highest.**

4

KNEEL

We give you praise, Father most holy,
for you are great
and you have fashioned all your works
in wisdom and in love.
You formed man in your own image
and entrusted the whole world to his care,
so that in serving you alone, the Creator,
he might have dominion over all creatures.
And when through disobedience he had lost your
    friendship,
you did not abandon him to the domain of death.
For you came in mercy to the aid of all,
so that those who seek might find you.
Time and again you offered them covenants
and through the prophets
taught them to look forward to salvation.

And you so loved the world, Father most holy,
that in the fullness of time
you sent your Only Begotten Son to be our Savior.
Made incarnate by the Holy Spirit
and born of the Virgin Mary,
he shared our human nature
in all things but sin.
To the poor he proclaimed the good news of
    salvation,
to prisoners, freedom,
and to the sorrowful of heart, joy.
To accomplish your plan,
he gave himself up to death,
and, rising from the dead,
he destroyed death and restored life.

4 And that we might live no longer for ourselves
but for him who died and rose again for us,
he sent the Holy Spirit from you, Father,
as the first fruits for those who believe,
so that, bringing to perfection his work in the world,
he might sanctify creation to the full.

Therefore, O Lord, we pray:
may this same Holy Spirit
graciously sanctify these offerings,
that they may become
the Body and ✢ Blood of our Lord Jesus Christ
for the celebration of this great mystery,
which he himself left us
as an eternal covenant.

For when the hour had come
for him to be glorified by you, Father most holy,
having loved his own who were in the world,
he loved them to the end:
and while they were at supper,
he took bread, blessed and broke it,
and gave it to his disciples, saying:

Take this, all of you, and eat of it,
for this is my Body,
which will be given up for you.

In a similar way,
taking the chalice filled with the fruit of the vine,
he gave thanks,
and gave the chalice to his disciples, saying:

Take this, all of you, and drink from it,
for this is the chalice of my Blood,
the Blood of the new and eternal covenant,

4

which will be poured out for you and for many for the forgiveness of sins.

Do this in memory of me.

Priest: The mystery of faith. *(Memorial Acclamation)*

PEOPLE:

A We proclaim your Death, O Lord,
and profess your Resurrection
until you come again.

B When we eat this Bread and drink this Cup,
we proclaim your Death, O Lord,
until you come again.

C Save us, Savior of the world,
for by your Cross and Resurrection
you have set us free.

Therefore, O Lord,
as we now celebrate the memorial of our redemption,
we remember Christ's Death
and his descent to the realm of the dead,
we proclaim his Resurrection
and his Ascension to your right hand,
and, as we await his coming in glory,
we offer you his Body and Blood,
the sacrifice acceptable to you
which brings salvation to the whole world.

Look, O Lord, upon the Sacrifice
which you yourself have provided for your Church,
and grant in your loving kindness
to all who partake of this one Bread and one Chalice
that, gathered into one body by the Holy Spirit,

4 they may truly become a living sacrifice in Christ
to the praise of your glory.

Therefore, Lord, remember now
all for whom we offer this sacrifice:
especially your servant N. our Pope,
N. our Bishop, and the whole Order of Bishops,
all the clergy,
those who take part in this offering,
those gathered here before you,
your entire people,
and all who seek you with a sincere heart.

Remember also
those who have died in the peace of your Christ
and all the dead,
whose faith you alone have known.

To all of us, your children,
grant, O merciful Father,
that we may enter into a heavenly inheritance
with the Blessed Virgin Mary, Mother of God,
with blessed Joseph, her Spouse,
and with your Apostles and Saints in your kingdom.
There, with the whole of creation,
freed from the corruption of sin and death,
may we glorify you through Christ our Lord,
through whom you bestow on the world all that
    is good.

(Concluding Doxology)

Through him, and with him, and in him,
O God, almighty Father,
in the unity of the Holy Spirit,
all glory and honor is yours,
for ever and ever.

The people acclaim: **Amen.**

Continue with the Mass, as on p. 72.

EUCHARISTIC PRAYER FOR RECONCILIATION I

STAND

℣. The Lord be with you.

℟. **And with your spirit.**

℣. Lift up your hearts.

℟. **We lift them up to the Lord.**

℣. Let us give thanks to the Lord our God.

℟. **It is right and just.**

It is truly right and just
that we should always give you thanks,
Lord, holy Father, almighty and eternal God.

For you do not cease to spur us on
to possess a more abundant life
and, being rich in mercy,
you constantly offer pardon
and call on sinners
to trust in your forgiveness alone.

Never did you turn away from us,
and, though time and again we have broken your
     covenant,
you have bound the human family to yourself
through Jesus your Son, our Redeemer,
with a new bond of love so tight
that it can never be undone.

Even now you set before your people
a time of grace and reconciliation,
and, as they turn back to you in spirit,
you grant them hope in Christ Jesus
and a desire to be of service to all,

43

R 1

while they entrust themselves
more fully to the Holy Spirit.

And so, filled with wonder,
we extol the power of your love,
and, proclaiming our joy
at the salvation that comes from you,
we join in the heavenly hymn of countless hosts,
as without end we acclaim:

Holy, Holy, Holy Lord God of hosts.
Heaven and earth are full of your glory.
Hosanna in the highest.
Blessed is he who comes in the name of the Lord.
Hosanna in the highest.

KNEEL

You are indeed Holy, O Lord,
and from the world's beginning
are ceaselessly at work,
so that the human race may become holy,
just as you yourself are holy.

Look, we pray, upon your people's offerings
and pour out on them the power of your Spirit,
that they may become the Body and ✠ Blood
of your beloved Son, Jesus Christ,
in whom we, too, are your sons and daughters.

Indeed, though we once were lost
and could not approach you,
you loved us with the greatest love:
for your Son, who alone is just,
handed himself over to death,

and did not disdain to be nailed for our sake
to the wood of the Cross.

But before his arms were outstretched between
   heaven and earth,
to become the lasting sign of your covenant,
he desired to celebrate the Passover with his
   disciples.

As he ate with them,
he took bread
and, giving you thanks, he said the blessing,
broke the bread and gave it to them, saying:

Take this, all of you, and eat of it,
for this is my Body,
which will be given up for you.

In a similar way, when supper was ended,
knowing that he was about to reconcile all things
   in himself
through his Blood to be shed on the Cross,
he took the chalice, filled with the fruit of the
   vine,
and once more giving you thanks,
handed the chalice to his disciples, saying:

Take this, all of you, and drink from it,
for this is the chalice of my Blood,
the Blood of the new and eternal covenant,
which will be poured out for you and for many
for the forgiveness of sins.
Do this in memory of me.

R 1

Priest: **The mystery of faith.** *(Memorial Acclamation)*
PEOPLE:

A We proclaim your Death, O Lord,
and profess your Resurrection
until you come again.

B When we eat this Bread and drink this Cup,
we proclaim your Death, O Lord,
until you come again.

C Save us, Savior of the world,
for by your Cross and Resurrection
you have set us free.

Therefore, as we celebrate
the memorial of your Son Jesus Christ,
who is our Passover and our surest peace,
we celebrate his Death and Resurrection from the
    dead,
and looking forward to his blessed Coming,
we offer you, who are our faithful and merciful
    God,
this sacrificial Victim
who reconciles to you the human race.

Look kindly, most compassionate Father,
on those you unite to yourself
by the Sacrifice of your Son,
and grant that, by the power of the Holy Spirit,
as they partake of this one Bread and one
    Chalice,
they may be gathered into one Body in Christ,
who heals every division.

Be pleased to keep us always
in communion of mind and heart,
together with N. our Pope and N. our Bishop.
Help us to work together
for the coming of your Kingdom,
until the hour when we stand before you,
Saints among the Saints in the halls of heaven,
with the Blessed Virgin Mary, Mother of God,
the blessed Apostles and all the Saints,
and with our deceased brothers and sisters,
whom we humbly commend to your mercy.

Then, freed at last from the wound of corruption
and made fully into a new creation,
we shall sing to you with gladness
the thanksgiving of Christ,
who lives for all eternity.

(Concluding Doxology)

Through him, and with him, and in him,
O God, almighty Father,
in the unity of the Holy Spirit,
all glory and honor is yours,
for ever and ever.

The people acclaim: **Amen.**

Continue with the Mass, as on p. 72.

EUCHARISTIC PRAYER FOR RECONCILIATION II

R 2

℣. The Lord be with you.

℟. **And with your spirit.**

℣. Lift up your hearts.

℟. **We lift them up to the Lord.**

℣. Let us give thanks to the Lord our God.

℟. **It is right and just.**

It is truly right and just
that we should give you thanks and praise,
O God, almighty Father,
for all you do in this world,
through our Lord Jesus Christ.

For though the human race
is divided by dissension and discord,
yet we know that by testing us
you change our hearts
to prepare them for reconciliation.

Even more, by your Spirit you move human hearts
that enemies may speak to each other again,
adversaries join hands,
and peoples seek to meet together.

By the working of your power
it comes about, O Lord,
that hatred is overcome by love,
revenge gives way to forgiveness,
and discord is changed to mutual respect.

Therefore, as we give you ceaseless thanks
with the choirs of heaven,

we cry out to your majesty on earth,
and without end we acclaim:

Holy, Holy, Holy Lord God of hosts.
Heaven and earth are full of your glory.
Hosanna in the highest.
Blessed is he who comes in the name of the Lord.
Hosanna in the highest.

You, therefore, almighty Father,   **KNEEL**
we bless through Jesus Christ your Son,
who comes in your name.
He himself is the Word that brings salvation,
the hand you extend to sinners,
the way by which your peace is offered to us.
When we ourselves had turned away from you
on account of our sins,
you brought us back to be reconciled, O Lord,
so that, converted at last to you,
we might love one another
through your Son,
whom for our sake you handed over to death.

And now, celebrating the reconciliation
Christ has brought us,
we entreat you:
sanctify these gifts by the outpouring of your Spirit,
that they may become the Body and ✠ Blood of
    your Son,
whose command we fulfill
when we celebrate these mysteries.

For when about to give his life to set us free,
as he reclined at supper,
he himself took bread into his hands,

R 2 and, giving you thanks, he said the blessing,
broke the bread and gave it to his disciples, saying:

Take this, all of you, and eat of it,
for this is my Body,
which will be given up for you.

In a similar way, on that same evening,
he took the chalice of blessing in his hands,
confessing your mercy,
and gave the chalice to his disciples, saying:

Take this, all of you, and drink from it,
for this is the chalice of my Blood,
the Blood of the new and eternal covenant,
which will be poured out for you and for many
for the forgiveness of sins.

Do this in memory of me.

Priest: The mystery of faith. *(Memorial Acclamation)*

PEOPLE:

A **We proclaim your Death, O Lord,**
and profess your Resurrection
until you come again.

B **When we eat this Bread and drink this Cup,**
we proclaim your Death, O Lord,
until you come again.

C **Save us, Savior of the world,**
for by your Cross and Resurrection
you have set us free.

Celebrating, therefore, the memorial
of the Death and Resurrection of your Son,
who left us this pledge of his love,
we offer you what you have bestowed on us,
the Sacrifice of perfect reconciliation.

R 2

Holy Father, we humbly beseech you
to accept us also, together with your Son,
and in this saving banquet
graciously to endow us with his very Spirit,
who takes away everything
that estranges us from one another.

May he make your Church a sign of unity
and an instrument of your peace among all people
and may he keep us in communion
with N. our Pope and N. our Bishop
and all the Bishops
and your entire people.

Just as you have gathered us now at the table of
    your Son,
so also bring us together,
with the glorious Virgin Mary, Mother of God,
with your blessed Apostles and all the Saints,
with our brothers and sisters
and those of every race and tongue
who have died in your friendship.
Bring us to share with them the unending banquet
    of unity
in a new heaven and a new earth,
where the fullness of your peace will shine forth
in Christ Jesus our Lord.

(Concluding Doxology)

Through him, and with him, and in him,
O God, almighty Father,
in the unity of the Holy Spirit,
all glory and honor is yours,
for ever and ever.

The people acclaim: **Amen.**

Continue with the Mass, as on p. 72.

V EUCHARISTIC PRAYER FOR USE IN MASSES FOR VARIOUS NEEDS I

STAND

℣. The Lord be with you.
℟. **And with your spirit.**

℣. Lift up your hearts.
℟. **We lift them up to the Lord.**

℣. Let us give thanks to the Lord our God.
℟. **It is right and just.**

It is truly right and just to give you thanks
and raise to you a hymn of glory and praise,
O Lord, Father of infinite goodness.

For by the word of your Son's Gospel
you have brought together one Church
from every people, tongue, and nation,
and, having filled her with life by the power of
    your Spirit,
you never cease through her
to gather the whole human race into one.

Manifesting the covenant of your love,
she dispenses without ceasing
the blessed hope of your Kingdom
and shines bright as the sign of your faithfulness,
which in Christ Jesus our Lord
you promised would last for eternity.

And so, with all the Powers of heaven,
we worship you constantly on earth,
while, with all the Church,
as one voice we acclaim:

V1

Holy, Holy, Holy Lord God of hosts.
Heaven and earth are full of your glory.
Hosanna in the highest.
Blessed is he who comes in the name of the Lord.
Hosanna in the highest.

`KNEEL`

You are indeed Holy and to be glorified, O God,
who love the human race
and who always walk with us on the journey of life.
Blessed indeed is your Son,
present in our midst
when we are gathered by his love
and when, as once for the disciples, so now for us,
he opens the Scriptures and breaks the bread.

Therefore, Father most merciful,
we ask that you send forth your Holy Spirit
to sanctify these gifts of bread and wine,
that they may become for us
the Body and ✠ Blood
of our Lord Jesus Christ.

On the day before he was to suffer,
on the night of the Last Supper,
he took bread and said the blessing,
broke the bread and gave it to his disciples, saying:

Take this, all of you, and eat of it,
for this is my Body,
which will be given up for you.

In a similar way, when supper was ended,
he took the chalice, gave you thanks
and gave the chalice to his disciples, saying:

**V
1**

Take this, all of you, and drink from it,
for this is the chalice of my Blood,
the Blood of the new and eternal covenant,
which will be poured out for you and for many
for the forgiveness of sins.

Do this in memory of me.

Priest: The mystery of faith. *(Memorial Acclamation)*

PEOPLE:

A We proclaim your Death, O Lord,
and profess your Resurrection
until you come again.

B When we eat this Bread and drink this Cup,
we proclaim your Death, O Lord,
until you come again.

C Save us, Savior of the world,
for by your Cross and Resurrection
you have set us free.

Therefore, holy Father,
as we celebrate the memorial of Christ your Son,
    our Savior,
whom you led through his Passion and Death on
    the Cross
to the glory of the Resurrection,
and whom you have seated at your right hand,
we proclaim the work of your love until he comes
    again
and we offer you the Bread of life
and the Chalice of blessing.

Look with favor on the oblation of your Church,
in which we show forth

V 1

the paschal Sacrifice of Christ that has been
    handed on to us,
and grant that, by the power of the Spirit of your
    love,
we may be counted now and until the day of
    eternity
among the members of your Son,
in whose Body and Blood we have communion.

Lord, renew your Church (which is in N.)
by the light of the Gospel.
Strengthen the bond of unity
between the faithful and the pastors of your people,
together with N. our Pope, N. our Bishop,
and the whole Order of Bishops,
that in a world torn by strife
your people may shine forth
as a prophetic sign of unity and concord.

Remember our brothers and sisters (N. and N.),
who have fallen asleep in the peace of your Christ,
and all the dead, whose faith you alone have
    known.
Admit them to rejoice in the light of your face,
and in the resurrection give them the fullness of
    life.

Grant also to us,
when our earthly pilgrimage is done,
that we may come to an eternal dwelling place
and live with you for ever;
there, in communion with the Blessed Virgin Mary,
    Mother of God,
with the Apostles and Martyrs,

**V
1**
(with Saint N.: the Saint of the day or Patron)
and with all the Saints,
we shall praise and exalt you
through Jesus Christ, your Son.

(Concluding Doxology)

Through him, and with him, and in him,
O God, almighty Father,
in the unity of the Holy Spirit,
all glory and honor is yours,
for ever and ever.

The people acclaim: **Amen.**

Continue with the Mass, as on p. 72.

EUCHARISTIC PRAYER FOR USE IN MASSES FOR VARIOUS NEEDS II

V2

STAND

℣. The Lord be with you.
℟. **And with your spirit.**

℣. Lift up your hearts.
℟. **We lift them up to the Lord.**

℣. Let us give thanks to the Lord our God.
℟. **It is right and just.**

It is truly right and just, our duty and our salvation,
always and everywhere to give you thanks,
Lord, holy Father,
creator of the world and source of all life.

For you never forsake the works of your wisdom,
but by your providence are even now at work in our midst.
With mighty hand and outstretched arm
you led your people Israel through the desert.
Now, as your Church makes her pilgrim journey in the world,
you always accompany her
by the power of the Holy Spirit
and lead her along the paths of time
to the eternal joy of your Kingdom,
through Christ our Lord.

And so, with the Angels and Saints,
we, too, sing the hymn of your glory,
as without end we acclaim:

**V
2**
Holy, Holy, Holy Lord God of hosts.
Heaven and earth are full of your glory.
Hosanna in the highest.
Blessed is he who comes in the name of the Lord.
Hosanna in the highest.

KNEEL

You are indeed Holy and to be glorified, O God,
who love the human race
and who always walk with us on the journey of life.
Blessed indeed is your Son,
present in our midst
when we are gathered by his love,
and when, as once for the disciples, so now for us,
he opens the Scriptures and breaks the bread.

Therefore, Father most merciful,
we ask that you send forth your Holy Spirit
to sanctify these gifts of bread and wine,
that they may become for us
the Body and ✠ Blood
of our Lord Jesus Christ.

On the day before he was to suffer,
on the night of the Last Supper,
he took bread and said the blessing,
broke the bread and gave it to his disciples, saying:

Take this, all of you, and eat of it,
for this is my Body,
which will be given up for you.

In a similar way, when supper was ended,
he took the chalice, gave you thanks
and gave the chalice to his disciples, saying:

V 2

Take this, all of you, and drink from it,
for this is the chalice of my Blood,
the Blood of the new and eternal covenant,
which will be poured out for you and for many
for the forgiveness of sins.

Do this in memory of me.

Priest: The mystery of faith. *(Memorial Acclamation)*

PEOPLE:

A We proclaim your Death, O Lord,
   and profess your Resurrection
   until you come again.

B When we eat this Bread and drink this Cup,
   we proclaim your Death, O Lord,
   until you come again.

C Save us, Savior of the world,
   for by your Cross and Resurrection
   you have set us free.

Therefore, holy Father,
as we celebrate the memorial of Christ your Son,
   our Savior,
whom you led through his Passion and Death on
   the Cross
to the glory of the Resurrection,
and whom you have seated at your right hand,
we proclaim the work of your love until he comes
   again
and we offer you the Bread of life
and the Chalice of blessing.

Look with favor on the oblation of your Church,
in which we show forth

V 2 the paschal Sacrifice of Christ that has been
handed on to us,
and grant that, by the power of the Spirit of your
love,
we may be counted now and until the day of
eternity
among the members of your Son,
in whose Body and Blood we have communion.

And so, having called us to your table, Lord,
confirm us in unity,
so that, together with N. our Pope and N. our
Bishop,
with all Bishops, Priests and Deacons,
and your entire people,
as we walk your ways with faith and hope,
we may strive to bring joy and trust into the world.

Remember our brothers and sisters (N. and N.),
who have fallen asleep in the peace of your Christ,
and all the dead, whose faith you alone have
known.
Admit them to rejoice in the light of your face,
and in the resurrection give them the fullness of
life.

Grant also to us,
when our earthly pilgrimage is done,
that we may come to an eternal dwelling place
and live with you for ever;
there, in communion with the Blessed Virgin Mary,
Mother of God,
with the Apostles and Martyrs,
(with Saint N.: the Saint of the day or Patron)

V 2

and with all the Saints,
we shall praise and exalt you
through Jesus Christ, your Son.

(Concluding Doxology)

Through him, and with him, and in him,
O God, almighty Father,
in the unity of the Holy Spirit,
all glory and honor is yours,
for ever and ever.

The people acclaim: **Amen.**

Continue with the Mass, as on p. 72.

V 3 EUCHARISTIC PRAYER FOR USE IN MASSES FOR VARIOUS NEEDS III

STAND

℣. The Lord be with you.
℟. **And with your spirit.**

℣. Lift up your hearts.
℟. **We lift them up to the Lord.**

℣. Let us give thanks to the Lord our God.
℟. **It is right and just.**

It is truly right and just, our duty and our salvation,
always and everywhere to give you thanks,
holy Father, Lord of heaven and earth,
through Christ our Lord.

For by your Word you created the world
and you govern all things in harmony.
You gave us the same Word made flesh as Mediator,
and he has spoken your words to us
and called us to follow him.
He is the way that leads us to you,
the truth that sets us free,
the life that fills us with gladness.

Through your Son
you gather men and women,
whom you made for the glory of your name,
into one family,
redeemed by the Blood of his Cross
and signed with the seal of the Spirit.

Therefore, now and for ages unending,
with all the Angels,

V 3

we proclaim your glory,
as in joyful celebration we acclaim:

Holy, Holy, Holy Lord God of hosts.
Heaven and earth are full of your glory.
Hosanna in the highest.
Blessed is he who comes in the name of the Lord.
Hosanna in the highest.

`KNEEL`

You are indeed Holy and to be glorified, O God,
who love the human race
and who always walk with us on the journey of life.
Blessed indeed is your Son,
present in our midst
when we are gathered by his love
and when, as once for the disciples, so now for us,
he opens the Scriptures and breaks the bread.

Therefore, Father most merciful,
we ask that you send forth your Holy Spirit
to sanctify these gifts of bread and wine,
that they may become for us
the Body and ✠ Blood
of our Lord Jesus Christ.

On the day before he was to suffer,
on the night of the Last Supper,
he took bread and said the blessing,
broke the bread and gave it to his disciples, saying:

Take this, all of you, and eat of it,
for this is my Body,
which will be given up for you.

V 3 In a similar way, when supper was ended,
he took the chalice, gave you thanks
and gave the chalice to his disciples, saying:

Take this, all of you, and drink from it,
for this is the chalice of my Blood,
the Blood of the new and eternal covenant,
which will be poured out for you and for many
for the forgiveness of sins.

Do this in memory of me.

Priest: The mystery of faith. *(Memorial Acclamation)*

PEOPLE:

A We proclaim your Death, O Lord,
and profess your Resurrection
until you come again.

B When we eat this Bread and drink this Cup,
we proclaim your Death, O Lord,
until you come again.

C Save us, Savior of the world,
for by your Cross and Resurrection
you have set us free.

Therefore, holy Father,
as we celebrate the memorial of Christ your Son,
    our Savior,
whom you led through his Passion and Death on
    the Cross
to the glory of the Resurrection,
and whom you have seated at your right hand,
we proclaim the work of your love until he comes
    again
and we offer you the Bread of life
and the Chalice of blessing.

Look with favor on the oblation of your Church,
in which we show forth
the paschal Sacrifice of Christ that has been
    handed on to us,
and grant that, by the power of the Spirit of your
    love,
we may be counted now and until the day of
    eternity
among the members of your Son,
in whose Body and Blood we have communion.

By our partaking of this mystery, almighty Father,
give us life through your Spirit,
grant that we may be conformed to the image of
    your Son,
and confirm us in the bond of communion,
together with N. our Pope and N. our Bishop,
with all other Bishops,
with Priests and Deacons,
and with your entire people.

Grant that all the faithful of the Church,
looking into the signs of the times by the light of
    faith,
may constantly devote themselves
to the service of the Gospel.

Keep us attentive to the needs of all
that, sharing their grief and pain,
their joy and hope,
we may faithfully bring them the good news of
    salvation
and go forward with them
along the way of your Kingdom.

V 3

Remember our brothers and sisters (*N.* and *N.*),
who have fallen asleep in the peace of your Christ,
and all the dead, whose faith you alone have known.
Admit them to rejoice in the light of your face,
and in the resurrection give them the fullness of life.

Grant also to us,
when our earthly pilgrimage is done,
that we may come to an eternal dwelling place
and live with you for ever;
there, in communion with the Blessed Virgin Mary,
   Mother of God,
with the Apostles and Martyrs,
(with Saint *N.*: the Saint of the day or Patron)
and with all the Saints,
we shall praise and exalt you
through Jesus Christ, your Son.

(Concluding Doxology)

Through him, and with him, and in him,
O God, almighty Father,
in the unity of the Holy Spirit,
all glory and honor is yours,
for ever and ever.

The people acclaim: **Amen.**

Continue with the Mass, as on p. 72.

EUCHARISTIC PRAYER FOR USE IN MASSES FOR VARIOUS NEEDS IV

V 4

STAND

℣. The Lord be with you.
℟. **And with your spirit.**

℣. Lift up your hearts.
℟. **We lift them up to the Lord.**

℣. Let us give thanks to the Lord our God.
℟. **It is right and just.**

It is truly right and just, our duty and our salvation,
always and everywhere to give you thanks,
Father of mercies and faithful God.

For you have given us Jesus Christ, your Son,
as our Lord and Redeemer.

He always showed compassion
for children and for the poor,
for the sick and for sinners,
and he became a neighbor
to the oppressed and the afflicted.

By word and deed he announced to the world
that you are our Father
and that you care for all your sons and daughters.

And so, with all the Angels and Saints,
we exalt and bless your name
and sing the hymn of your glory,
as without end we acclaim:

V
4

Holy, Holy, Holy Lord God of hosts.
Heaven and earth are full of your glory.
Hosanna in the highest.
Blessed is he who comes in the name of the Lord.
Hosanna in the highest.

`KNEEL`

You are indeed Holy and to be glorified, O God,
who love the human race
and who always walk with us on the journey of life.
Blessed indeed is your Son,
present in our midst
when we are gathered by his love
and when, as once for the disciples, so now for us,
he opens the Scriptures and breaks the bread.

Therefore, Father most merciful,
we ask that you send forth your Holy Spirit
to sanctify these gifts of bread and wine,
that they may become for us
the Body and ✠ Blood
of our Lord Jesus Christ.

On the day before he was to suffer,
on the night of the Last Supper,
he took bread and said the blessing,
broke the bread and gave it to his disciples, saying:

Take this, all of you, and eat of it,
for this is my Body,
which will be given up for you.

In a similar way, when supper was ended,
he took the chalice, gave you thanks
and gave the chalice to his disciples, saying:

V4

Take this, all of you, and drink from it,
for this is the chalice of my Blood,
the Blood of the new and eternal covenant,
which will be poured out for you and for many
for the forgiveness of sins.

Do this in memory of me.

Priest: The mystery of faith. *(Memorial Acclamation)*

PEOPLE:

A We proclaim your Death, O Lord,
and profess your Resurrection
until you come again.

B When we eat this Bread and drink this Cup,
we proclaim your Death, O Lord,
until you come again.

C Save us, Savior of the world,
for by your Cross and Resurrection
you have set us free.

Therefore, holy Father,
as we celebrate the memorial of Christ your Son,
    our Savior,
whom you led through his Passion and Death on
    the Cross
to the glory of the Resurrection,
and whom you have seated at your right hand,
we proclaim the work of your love until he comes
    again
and we offer you the Bread of life
and the Chalice of blessing.

Look with favor on the oblation of your Church,
in which we show forth

**V
4**

the paschal Sacrifice of Christ that has been
  handed on to us,
and grant that, by the power of the Spirit of your
  love,
we may be counted now and until the day of
  eternity
among the members of your Son,
in whose Body and Blood we have communion.

Bring your Church, O Lord,
to perfect faith and charity,
together with N. our Pope and N. our Bishop,
with all Bishops, Priests and Deacons,
and the entire people you have made your own.

Open our eyes
to the needs of our brothers and sisters;
inspire in us words and actions
to comfort those who labor and are burdened.
Make us serve them truly,
after the example of Christ and at his command.
And may your Church stand as a living witness
to truth and freedom,
to peace and justice,
that all people may be raised up to a new hope.

Remember our brothers and sisters (N. and N.),
who have fallen asleep in the peace of your Christ,
and all the dead, whose faith you alone have
  known.
Admit them to rejoice in the light of your face,
and in the resurrection give them the fullness of
  life.

Grant also to us,
when our earthly pilgrimage is done,
that we may come to an eternal dwelling place
and live with you for ever;
there, in communion with the Blessed Virgin Mary,
    Mother of God,
with the Apostles and Martyrs,
(with Saint *N.*: the Saint of the day or Patron)
and with all the Saints,
we shall praise and exalt you
through Jesus Christ, your Son.

(Concluding Doxology)

Through him, and with him, and in him,
O God, almighty Father,
in the unity of the Holy Spirit,
all glory and honor is yours,
for ever and ever.

The people acclaim: **Amen.**

Continue with the Mass, as on p. 72.

THE COMMUNION RITE

To prepare for the paschal meal, to welcome the Lord, we pray for forgiveness and exchange a sign of peace. Before eating Christ's Body and drinking his Blood, we must be one with him and with all our brothers and sisters in the Church.

24 THE LORD'S PRAYER

STAND

Priest: At the Savior's command
and formed by divine teaching,
we dare to say:

Priest and **PEOPLE**:

**Our Father, who art in heaven,
hallowed be thy name;
thy kingdom come,
thy will be done
on earth as it is in heaven.
Give us this day our daily bread,
and forgive us our trespasses,
as we forgive those who trespass against us;
and lead us not into temptation,
but deliver us from evil.**

Priest: Deliver us, Lord, we pray, from every evil,
graciously grant us peace in our days,
that, by the help of your mercy,
we may be always free from sin
and safe from all distress,
as we await the blessed hope
and the coming of our Savior, Jesus Christ.

PEOPLE: **For the kingdom,**
the power and the glory are yours
now and for ever.

25 SIGN OF PEACE

The Church is a community of Christians joined by the Spirit in love. It needs to express, deepen, and restore its peaceful unity before eating the one Body of the Lord and drinking from the one cup of salvation. We do this by a sign of peace.

The Priest says the prayer for peace:

Lord Jesus Christ,
who said to your Apostles:
Peace I leave you, my peace I give you,
look not on our sins,
but on the faith of your Church,
and graciously grant her peace and unity
in accordance with your will.
Who live and reign for ever and ever.

PEOPLE: **Amen.**

Priest: The peace of the Lord be with you always.

PEOPLE: **And with your spirit.**

Deacon (or Priest):
Let us offer each other the sign of peace.

The people exchange a sign of peace, communion and charity, according to local customs.

26 LAMB OF GOD

Christians are gathered for the "breaking of the bread," another name for the Mass. In Communion, though many we are made one body in the one bread, which is Christ.

The Priest breaks the host over the paten and places a small piece in the chalice, saying quietly:

May this mingling of the Body and Blood
of our Lord Jesus Christ
bring eternal life to us who receive it.

Meanwhile the following is sung or said:

PEOPLE:

> **Lamb of God, you take away the sins of the world,**
>> **have mercy on us.**
> **Lamb of God, you take away the sins of the world,**
>> **have mercy on us.**
> **Lamb of God, you take away the sins of the world,**
>> **grant us peace.**

The invocation may even be repeated several times if the breaking of the bread is prolonged. Only the final time, however, is grant us peace *said.*

KNEEL

We pray in silence and then voice words of humility and hope as our final preparation before meeting Christ in the Eucharist.

Before Communion, the Priest says quietly one of the following prayers:

Lord Jesus Christ, Son of the living God,
who, by the will of the Father
and the work of the Holy Spirit,
through your Death gave life to the world,
free me by this, your most holy Body and Blood,
from all my sins and from every evil;
keep me always faithful to your commandments,
and never let me be parted from you.

———————— **OR** ————————

May the receiving of your Body and Blood,
Lord Jesus Christ,
not bring me to judgment and condemnation,
but through your loving mercy
be for me protection in mind and body
and a healing remedy.

27 INVITATION TO COMMUNION*

The Priest genuflects, takes the host and, holding it slightly raised above the paten or above the chalice, while facing the people, says aloud:

Priest: Behold the Lamb of God,
behold him who takes away the sins of the world.
Blessed are those called to the supper of the Lamb.

Priest and **PEOPLE** (once only):

**Lord, I am not worthy
that you should enter under my roof,
but only say the word
and my soul shall be healed.**

Before reverently consuming the Body of Christ, the Priest says quietly:

May the Body of Christ
keep me safe for eternal life.

Then, before reverently consuming the Blood of Christ, he takes the chalice and says quietly:

May the Blood of Christ
keep me safe for eternal life.

* *See Guidelines on pp. 664-665.*

28 COMMUNION

He then gives Communion to the people.

Priest: **The Body of Christ.** Communicant: **Amen.**
Priest: **The Blood of Christ.** Communicant: **Amen.**

The Communion Psalm or other appropriate chant is sung while Communion is given to the faithful. If there is no singing, the Communion Antiphon is said.

→ **Turn to Today's Mass**

The vessels are purified by the Priest or Deacon or acolyte. Meanwhile he says quietly:

What has passed our lips as food, O Lord,
may we possess in purity of heart,
that what has been given to us in time
may be our healing for eternity.

After Communion there may be a period of sacred silence, or a canticle of praise or a hymn may be sung.

29 PRAYER AFTER COMMUNION   STAND

The Priest prays in our name that we may live the life of faith since we have been strengthened by Christ himself. Our *Amen* makes his prayer our own.

Priest: **Let us pray.**

Priest and people may pray silently for a while unless silence has just been observed. Then the Priest says the Prayer after Communion.

→ **Turn to Today's Mass**

At the end, PEOPLE: **Amen.**

THE CONCLUDING RITES

We have heard God's Word and eaten the Body of Christ. Now it is time for us to leave, to do good works, to praise and bless the Lord in our daily lives.

30 SOLEMN BLESSING STAND

After any brief announcements, the Blessing and Dismissal follow:

Priest: The Lord be with you.

PEOPLE: And with your spirit.

31 FINAL BLESSING

Priest: May almighty God bless you,
the Father, and the Son, ✠ and the Holy Spirit.

PEOPLE: Amen.

On certain days or occasions, this formula of blessing is preceded, in accordance with the rubrics, by another more solemn formula of blessing (pp. 97-105) or by a prayer over the people (pp. 105-110).

32 DISMISSAL

Deacon (or Priest):

A Go forth, the Mass is ended.

B Go and announce the Gospel of the Lord.

C Go in peace, glorifying the Lord by your life.

D Go in peace.

PEOPLE: Thanks be to God.

If any liturgical service follows immediately, the rites of dismissal are omitted.

RITE FOR THE BLESSING AND SPRINKLING OF WATER

If this rite is celebrated during Mass, it takes the place of the usual Penitential Act at the beginning of Mass.

After the greeting, the Priest stands at his chair and faces the people. With a vessel containing the water to be blessed before him, he calls upon the people to pray in these or similar words:

Dear brethren (brothers and sisters),
let us humbly beseech the Lord our God
to bless this water he has created,
which will be sprinkled on us
as a memorial of our Baptism.
May he help us by his grace
to remain faithful to the Spirit we have received.

And after a brief pause for silence, he continues with hands joined:

Almighty ever-living God,
who willed that through water,
the fountain of life and the source of purification,
even souls should be cleansed
and receive the gift of eternal life;
be pleased, we pray, to ✛ bless this water,
by which we seek protection on this your day, O Lord.
Renew the living spring of your grace within us
and grant that by this water we may be defended
from all ills of spirit and body,
and so approach you with hearts made clean
and worthily receive your salvation.
Through Christ our Lord. ℟. **Amen.**

Or:

Almighty Lord and God,
who are the source and origin of all life,

whether of body or soul,
we ask you to ✚ bless this water,
which we use in confidence
to implore forgiveness for our sins
and to obtain the protection of your grace
against all illness and every snare of the enemy.
Grant, O Lord, in your mercy,
that living waters may always spring up for our
    salvation,
and so may we approach you with a pure heart
and avoid all danger to body and soul.
Through Christ our Lord. ℟. **Amen.**

Or (during Easter Time):

Lord our God,
in your mercy be present to your people's prayers,
and, for us who recall the wondrous work of our creation
and the still greater work of our redemption,
graciously ✚ bless this water.
For you created water to make the fields fruitful
and to refresh and cleanse our bodies.
You also made water the instrument of your mercy:
for through water you freed your people from slavery
and quenched their thirst in the desert;
through water the Prophets proclaimed the new
    covenant
you were to enter upon with the human race;
and last of all,
through water, which Christ made holy in the Jordan,
you have renewed our corrupted nature
in the bath of regeneration.
Therefore, may this water be for us
a memorial of the Baptism we have received,
and grant that we may share
in the gladness of our brothers and sisters
who at Easter have received their Baptism.
Through Christ our Lord. ℟. **Amen.**

Where the circumstances of the place or the custom of the people suggest that the mixing of salt be preserved in the blessing of water, the Priest may bless salt, saying:

We humbly ask you, almighty God:
be pleased in your faithful love to bless ✠ this salt
you have created,
for it was you who commanded the prophet Elisha
to cast salt into water,
that impure water might be purified.
Grant, O Lord, we pray,
that, wherever this mixture of salt and water is sprinkled,
every attack of the enemy may be repulsed
and your Holy Spirit may be present
to keep us safe at all times.
Through Christ our Lord. ℟. **Amen.**

Then he pours the salt into the water, without saying anything.

Afterward, taking the aspergillum, the Priest sprinkles himself and the ministers, then the clergy and people, moving through the church, if appropriate.

Meanwhile, one of the following chants, or another appropriate chant is sung.

Outside Easter Time

ANTIPHON 1 Ps 51 (50):9

Sprinkle me with hyssop, O Lord, and I shall be cleansed; wash me and I shall be whiter than snow.

ANTIPHON 2 Ez 36:25-26

I will pour clean water upon you, and you will be made clean of all your impurities, and I shall give you a new spirit, says the Lord.

HYMN Cf. 1 Pt 1:3-5

Blessed be the God and Father of our Lord Jesus Christ, who in his great mercy has given us new birth into a living hope through the Resurrection of Jesus Christ from the dead, into an inheritance that will not perish, preserved for us in heaven for the salvation to be revealed in the last time!

During Easter Time

ANTIPHON 1 Cf. Ez 47:1-2, 9

I saw water flowing from the Temple, from its right-hand side, alleluia: and all to whom this water came were saved and shall say: Alleluia, alleluia.

ANTIPHON 2 Cf. Zeph 3:8; Ez 36:25

On the day of my resurrection, says the Lord, alleluia, I will gather the nations and assemble the kingdoms and I will pour clean water upon you, alleluia.

ANTIPHON 3 Cf. Dn 3:77, 79

You springs and all that moves in the waters, sing a hymn to God, alleluia.

ANTIPHON 4 1 Pt 2:9

O chosen race, royal priesthood, holy nation, proclaim the mighty works of him who called you out of darkness into his wonderful light, alleluia.

ANTIPHON 5

From your side, O Christ, bursts forth a spring of water, by which the squalor of the world is washed away and life is made new again, alleluia.

When he returns to his chair and the singing is over, the Priest stands facing the people and, with hands joined, says:

May almighty God cleanse us of our sins,
and through the celebration of this Eucharist
make us worthy to share at the table of his Kingdom.
℟. **Amen**.

Then, when it is prescribed, the hymn Gloria in excelsis *(Glory to God in the highest) is sung or said.*

PREFACES

PREFACE I OF ADVENT (P 1)

The two comings of Christ

(From the First Sunday of Advent to December 16)

It is truly right and just, our duty and our salvation,
always and everywhere to give you thanks,
Lord, holy Father, almighty and eternal God,
through Christ our Lord.

For he assumed at his first coming
the lowliness of human flesh,
and so fulfilled the design you formed long ago,
and opened for us the way to eternal salvation,
that, when he comes again in glory and majesty
and all is at last made manifest,
we who watch for that day
may inherit the great promise
in which now we dare to hope.

And so, with Angels and Archangels,
with Thrones and Dominions,
and with all the hosts and Powers of heaven,
we sing the hymn of your glory,
as without end we acclaim: → No. 23, p. 23

PREFACE II OF ADVENT (P 2)

The twofold expectation of Christ

(From December 17 to December 24)

It is truly right and just, our duty and our salvation,
always and everywhere to give you thanks,
Lord, holy Father, almighty and eternal God,
through Christ our Lord.

For all the oracles of the prophets foretold him,
the Virgin Mother longed for him
with love beyond all telling,

82

John the Baptist sang of his coming
and proclaimed his presence when he came.

It is by his gift that already we rejoice
at the mystery of his Nativity,
so that he may find us watchful in prayer
and exultant in his praise.

And so, with Angels and Archangels,
with Thrones and Dominions,
and with all the hosts and Powers of heaven,
we sing the hymn of your glory,
as without end we acclaim: → No. 23, p. 23

PREFACE I OF THE NATIVITY OF THE LORD (P 3)

Christ the Light

(For the Nativity of the Lord, its Octave Day and within the Octave)

It is truly right and just, our duty and our salvation,
always and everywhere to give you thanks,
Lord, holy Father, almighty and eternal God.

For in the mystery of the Word made flesh
a new light of your glory has shone upon the eyes of our
    mind,
so that, as we recognize in him God made visible,
we may be caught up through him in love of things invisible.

And so, with Angels and Archangels,
with Thrones and Dominions,
and with all the hosts and Powers of heaven,
we sing the hymn of your glory,
as without end we acclaim: → No. 23, p. 23

PREFACE II OF THE NATIVITY OF THE LORD (P 4)

The restoration of all things in the Incarnation

(For the Nativity of the Lord, its Octave Day and within the Octave)

It is truly right and just, our duty and our salvation,
always and everywhere to give you thanks,
Lord, holy Father, almighty and eternal God,
through Christ our Lord.

For on the feast of this awe-filled mystery,
though invisible in his own divine nature,

he has appeared visibly in ours;
and begotten before all ages,
he has begun to exist in time;
so that, raising up in himself all that was cast down,
he might restore unity to all creation
and call straying humanity back to the heavenly Kingdom.

And so, with all the Angels, we praise you,
as in joyful celebration we acclaim: → No. 23, p. 23

PREFACE III OF THE NATIVITY OF THE LORD (P 5)

The exchange in the Incarnation of the Word

(For the Nativity of the Lord, its Octave Day and within the Octave)

It is truly right and just, our duty and our salvation,
always and everywhere to give you thanks,
Lord, holy Father, almighty and eternal God,
through Christ our Lord.

For through him the holy exchange that restores our life
has shone forth today in splendor:
when our frailty is assumed by your Word
not only does human mortality receive unending honor
but by this wondrous union we, too, are made eternal.

And so, in company with the choirs of Angels,
we praise you, and with joy we proclaim: → No. 23, p. 23

PREFACE I OF LENT (P 8)

The spiritual meaning of Lent

It is truly right and just, our duty and our salvation,
always and everywhere to give you thanks,
Lord, holy Father, almighty and eternal God,
through Christ our Lord.

For by your gracious gift each year
your faithful await the sacred paschal feasts
with the joy of minds made pure,
so that, more eagerly intent on prayer
and on the works of charity,
and participating in the mysteries
by which they have been reborn,

they may be led to the fullness of grace
that you bestow on your sons and daughters.

And so, with Angels and Archangels,
with Thrones and Dominions,
and with all the hosts and Powers of heaven,
we sing the hymn of your glory,
as without end we acclaim: ➨ No. 23, p. 23

PREFACE II OF LENT (P 9)
Spiritual penance

It is truly right and just, our duty and our salvation,
always and everywhere to give you thanks,
Lord, holy Father, almighty and eternal God.

For you have given your children a sacred time
for the renewing and purifying of their hearts,
that, freed from disordered affections,
they may so deal with the things of this passing world
as to hold rather to the things that eternally endure.

And so, with all the Angels and Saints,
we praise you, as without end we acclaim: ➨ No. 23, p. 23

PREFACE I OF EASTER I (P 21)
The Paschal Mystery

(At the Easter Vigil, is said "on this night"; on Easter Sunday and throughout the Octave
of Easter, is said "on this day"; on other days of Easter Time, is said "in this time.")

It is truly right and just, our duty and our salvation,
at all times to acclaim you, O Lord,
but (on this night / on this day / in this time) above all
to laud you yet more gloriously,
when Christ our Passover has been sacrificed.

For he is the true Lamb
who has taken away the sins of the world;
by dying he has destroyed our death,
and by rising, restored our life.

Therefore, overcome with paschal joy,
every land, every people exults in your praise
and even the heavenly Powers, with the angelic hosts,
sing together the unending hymn of your glory,
as they acclaim: ➨ No. 23, p. 23

PREFACE II OF EASTER (P 22)
New life in Christ

It is truly right and just, our duty and our salvation,
at all times to acclaim you, O Lord,
but in this time above all to laud you yet more gloriously,
when Christ our Passover has been sacrificed.

Through him the children of light rise to eternal life
and the halls of the heavenly Kingdom
are thrown open to the faithful;
for his Death is our ransom from death,
and in his rising the life of all has risen.

Therefore, overcome with paschal joy,
every land, every people exults in your praise
and even the heavenly Powers, with the angelic hosts,
sing together the unending hymn of your glory,
as they acclaim: → No. 23, p. 23

PREFACE III OF EASTER (P 23)
Christ living and always interceding for us

It is truly right and just, our duty and our salvation,
at all times to acclaim you, O Lord,
but in this time above all to laud you yet more gloriously,
when Christ our Passover has been sacrificed.

He never ceases to offer himself for us
but defends us and ever pleads our cause before you:
he is the sacrificial Victim who dies no more,
the Lamb, once slain, who lives for ever.

Therefore, overcome with paschal joy,
every land, every people exults in your praise
and even the heavenly Powers, with the angelic hosts,
sing together the unending hymn of your glory,
as they acclaim: → No. 23, p. 23

PREFACE IV OF EASTER (P 24)
The restoration of the universe through the
Paschal Mystery

It is truly right and just, our duty and our salvation,
at all times to acclaim you, O Lord,

but in this time above all to laud you yet more gloriously,
when Christ our Passover has been sacrificed.

For, with the old order destroyed,
a universe cast down is renewed,
and integrity of life is restored to us in Christ.

Therefore, overcome with paschal joy,
every land, every people exults in your praise
and even the heavenly Powers, with the angelic hosts,
sing together the unending hymn of your glory,
as they acclaim: → No. 23, p. 23

PREFACE V OF EASTER (P 25)

Christ, Priest and Victim

It is truly right and just, our duty and our salvation,
at all times to acclaim you, O Lord,
but in this time above all to laud you yet more gloriously,
when Christ our Passover has been sacrificed.

By the oblation of his Body,
he brought the sacrifices of old to fulfillment
in the reality of the Cross
and, by commending himself to you for our salvation,
showed himself the Priest, the Altar, and the Lamb of
    sacrifice.

Therefore, overcome with paschal joy,
every land, every people exults in your praise
and even the heavenly Powers, with the angelic hosts,
sing together the unending hymn of your glory,
as they acclaim: → No. 23, p. 23

PREFACE I OF THE ASCENSION OF THE LORD (P 26)

The mystery of the Ascension
(Ascension to the Saturday before Pentecost inclusive)

It is truly right and just, our duty and our salvation,
always and everywhere to give you thanks,
Lord, holy Father, almighty and eternal God.

For the Lord Jesus, the King of glory,
conqueror of sin and death,

ascended (today) to the highest heavens,
as the Angels gazed in wonder.

Mediator between God and man,
judge of the world and Lord of hosts,
he ascended, not to distance himself from our lowly state
but that we, his members, might be confident of following
where he, our Head and Founder, has gone before.

Therefore, overcome with paschal joy,
every land, every people exults in your praise
and even the heavenly Powers, with the angelic hosts,
sing together the unending hymn of your glory,
as they acclaim: ➔ No. 23, p. 23

PREFACE II OF THE ASCENSION OF THE LORD (P 27)

The mystery of the Ascension
(Ascension to the Saturday before Pentecost inclusive)

It is truly right and just, our duty and our salvation,
always and everywhere to give you thanks,
Lord, holy Father, almighty and eternal God,
through Christ our Lord.

For after his Resurrection
he plainly appeared to all his disciples
and was taken up to heaven in their sight,
that he might make us sharers in his divinity.

Therefore, overcome with paschal joy,
every land, every people exults in your praise
and even the heavenly Powers, with the angelic hosts,
sing together the unending hymn of your glory,
as they acclaim: ➔ No. 23, p. 23

PREFACE I OF THE SUNDAYS IN ORDINARY TIME (P 29)

The Paschal Mystery and the People of God

It is truly right and just, our duty and our salvation,
always and everywhere to give you thanks,
Lord, holy Father, almighty and eternal God,
through Christ our Lord.

For through his Paschal Mystery,
he accomplished the marvelous deed,

by which he has freed us from the yoke of sin and death,
summoning us to the glory of being now called
a chosen race, a royal priesthood,
a holy nation, a people for your own possession,
to proclaim everywhere your mighty works,
for you have called us out of darkness
into your own wonderful light.

And so, with Angels and Archangels,
with Thrones and Dominions,
and with all the hosts and Powers of heaven,
we sing the hymn of your glory,
as without end we acclaim: → No. 23, p. 23

PREFACE II OF THE SUNDAYS IN ORDINARY TIME (P 30)

The mystery of salvation

It is truly right and just, our duty and our salvation,
always and everywhere to give you thanks,
Lord, holy Father, almighty and eternal God,
through Christ our Lord.

For out of compassion for the waywardness that is ours,
he humbled himself and was born of the Virgin;
by the passion of the Cross he freed us from unending death,
and by rising from the dead he gave us life eternal.

And so, with Angels and Archangels,
with Thrones and Dominions,
and with all the hosts and Powers of heaven,
we sing the hymn of your glory,
as without end we acclaim: → No. 23, p. 23

PREFACE III OF THE SUNDAYS IN ORDINARY TIME (P 31)

The salvation of man by a man

It is truly right and just, our duty and our salvation,
always and everywhere to give you thanks,
Lord, holy Father, almighty and eternal God.

For we know it belongs to your boundless glory,
that you came to the aid of mortal beings with your divinity
and even fashioned for us a remedy out of mortality itself,
that the cause of our downfall

might become the means of our salvation,
through Christ our Lord.

Through him the host of Angels adores your majesty
and rejoices in your presence for ever.
May our voices, we pray, join with theirs
in one chorus of exultant praise, as we acclaim:

➜ No. 23, p. 23

PREFACE IV OF THE SUNDAYS IN ORDINARY TIME (P 32)
The history of salvation

It is truly right and just, our duty and our salvation,
always and everywhere to give you thanks,
Lord, holy Father, almighty and eternal God,
through Christ our Lord.

For by his birth he brought renewal
to humanity's fallen state,
and by his suffering, canceled out our sins;
by his rising from the dead
he has opened the way to eternal life,
and by ascending to you, O Father,
he has unlocked the gates of heaven.

And so, with the company of Angels and Saints,
we sing the hymn of your praise,
as without end we acclaim:

➜ No. 23, p. 23

PREFACE V OF THE SUNDAYS IN ORDINARY TIME (P 33)
Creation

It is truly right and just, our duty and our salvation,
always and everywhere to give you thanks,
Lord, holy Father, almighty and eternal God.

For you laid the foundations of the world
and have arranged the changing of times and seasons;
you formed man in your own image
and set humanity over the whole world in all its wonder,
to rule in your name over all you have made
and for ever praise you in your mighty works,
through Christ our Lord.

And so, with all the Angels, we praise you,
as in joyful celebration we acclaim: → No. 23, p. 23

PREFACE VI OF THE SUNDAYS IN ORDINARY TIME (P 34)

The pledge of the eternal Passover

It is truly right and just, our duty and our salvation,
always and everywhere to give you thanks,
Lord, holy Father, almighty and eternal God.

For in you we live and move and have our being,
and while in this body
we not only experience the daily effects of your care,
but even now possess the pledge of life eternal.

For, having received the first fruits of the Spirit,
through whom you raised up Jesus from the dead,
we hope for an everlasting share in the Paschal Mystery.

And so, with all the Angels, we praise you,
as in joyful celebration we acclaim: → No. 23, p. 23

PREFACE VII OF THE SUNDAYS IN ORDINARY TIME (P 35)

Salvation through the obedience of Christ

It is truly right and just, our duty and our salvation,
always and everywhere to give you thanks,
Lord, holy Father, almighty and eternal God.

For you so loved the world
that in your mercy you sent us the Redeemer,
to live like us in all things but sin,
so that you might love in us what you loved in your Son,
by whose obedience we have been restored to those gifts
   of yours
that, by sinning, we had lost in disobedience.

And so, Lord, with all the Angels and Saints,
we, too, give you thanks, as in exultation we acclaim:
    → No. 23, p. 23

PREFACE VIII OF THE SUNDAYS IN ORDINARY TIME (P 36)

The Church united by the unity of the Trinity

It is truly right and just, our duty and our salvation,
always and everywhere to give you thanks,
Lord, holy Father, almighty and eternal God.

For, when your children were scattered afar by sin,
through the Blood of your Son and the power of the Spirit,
you gathered them again to yourself,
that a people, formed as one by the unity of the Trinity,
made the body of Christ and the temple of the Holy Spirit,
might, to the praise of your manifold wisdom,
be manifest as the Church.

And so, in company with the choirs of Angels,
we praise you, and with joy we proclaim: ➡ No. 23, p. 23

PREFACE I OF THE MOST HOLY EUCHARIST (P 47)
The Sacrifice and the Sacrament of Christ

It is truly right and just, our duty and our salvation,
always and everywhere to give you thanks,
Lord, holy Father, almighty and eternal God,
through Christ our Lord.

For he is the true and eternal Priest,
who instituted the pattern of an everlasting sacrifice
and was the first to offer himself as the saving Victim,
commanding us to make this offering as his memorial.
As we eat his flesh that was sacrificed for us,
we are made strong,
and, as we drink his Blood that was poured out for us,
we are washed clean.

And so, with Angels and Archangels,
with Thrones and Dominions,
and with all the hosts and Powers of heaven,
we sing the hymn of your glory,
as without end we acclaim: ➡ No. 23, p. 23

PREFACE II OF THE MOST HOLY EUCHARIST (P 48)
The fruits of the Most Holy Eucharist

It is truly right and just, our duty and our salvation,
always and everywhere to give you thanks,
Lord, holy Father, almighty and eternal God,
through Christ our Lord.

For at the Last Supper with his Apostles,
establishing for the ages to come the saving memorial of
    the Cross,
he offered himself to you as the unblemished Lamb,
the acceptable gift of perfect praise.

Nourishing your faithful by this sacred mystery,
you make them holy, so that the human race,
bounded by one world,
may be enlightened by one faith
and united by one bond of charity.

And so, we approach the table of this wondrous Sacrament,
so that, bathed in the sweetness of your grace,
we may pass over to the heavenly realities here fore-
    shadowed.

Therefore, all creatures of heaven and earth
sing a new song in adoration,
and we, with all the host of Angels,
cry out, and without end we acclaim: → No. 23, p. 23

PREFACE I FOR THE DEAD (P 77)
The hope of resurrection in Christ

It is truly right and just, our duty and our salvation,
always and everywhere to give you thanks,
Lord, holy Father, almighty and eternal God,
through Christ our Lord.

In him the hope of blessed resurrection has dawned,
that those saddened by the certainty of dying
might be consoled by the promise of immortality to come.
Indeed for your faithful, Lord,
life is changed not ended,
and, when this earthly dwelling turns to dust,
an eternal dwelling is made ready for them in heaven.

And so, with Angels and Archangels,
with Thrones and Dominions,
and with all the hosts and Powers of heaven,
we sing the hymn of your glory,
as without end we acclaim: → No. 23, p. 23

PREFACE II FOR THE DEAD (P 78)
Christ died so that we might live

It is truly right and just, our duty and our salvation,
always and everywhere to give you thanks,
Lord, holy Father, almighty and eternal God,
through Christ our Lord.

For as one alone he accepted death,
so that we might all escape from dying;
as one man he chose to die,
so that in your sight we all might live for ever.

And so, in company with the choirs of Angels,
we praise you, and with joy we proclaim: → No. 23, p. 23

PREFACE III FOR THE DEAD (P 79)
Christ, the salvation and the life

It is truly right and just, our duty and our salvation,
always and everywhere to give you thanks,
Lord, holy Father, almighty and eternal God,
through Christ our Lord.

For he is the salvation of the world,
the life of the human race,
the resurrection of the dead.

Through him the host of Angels adores your majesty
and rejoices in your presence for ever.
May our voices, we pray, join with theirs
in one chorus of exultant praise, as we acclaim:
→ No. 23, p. 23

PREFACE IV FOR THE DEAD (P 80)
From earthly life to heavenly glory

It is truly right and just, our duty and our salvation,
always and everywhere to give you thanks,
Lord, holy Father, almighty and eternal God.

For it is at your summons that we come to birth,
by your will that we are governed,
and at your command that we return,
on account of sin,
to that earth from which we came.

And when you give the sign,
we who have been redeemed by the Death of your Son,
shall be raised up to the glory of his Resurrection.

And so, with the company of Angels and Saints,
we sing the hymn of your praise,
as without end we acclaim: → No. 23, p. 23

PREFACE V FOR THE DEAD (P 81)
Our resurrection through the victory of Christ

It is truly right and just, our duty and our salvation,
always and everywhere to give you thanks,
Lord, holy Father, almighty and eternal God.

For even though by our own fault we perish,
yet by your compassion and your grace,
when seized by death according to our sins,
we are redeemed through Christ's great victory,
and with him called back into life.

And so, with the Powers of heaven,
we worship you constantly on earth,
and before your majesty
without end we acclaim: → No. 23, p. 23

PROPER COMMUNICANTES
AND HANC IGITUR

FOR EUCHARISTIC PRAYER I (THE ROMAN CANON)

Communicantes for the Nativity of the Lord
and throughout the Octave

Celebrating the most sacred night (day)
on which blessed Mary the immaculate Virgin
brought forth the Savior for this world,
and in communion with those whose memory we venerate,
especially the glorious ever-Virgin Mary,
Mother of our God and Lord, Jesus Christ,† etc., p. 25.

Communicantes for the Epiphany of the Lord

Celebrating the most sacred day
on which your Only Begotten Son,
eternal with you in your glory,
appeared in a human body, truly sharing our flesh,

and in communion with those whose memory we venerate,
especially the glorious ever-Virgin Mary,
Mother of our God and Lord, Jesus Christ,† etc., p. 25.

Communicantes for Easter

Celebrating the most sacred night (day)
of the Resurrection of our Lord Jesus Christ in the flesh,
and in communion with those whose memory we venerate,
especially the glorious ever-Virgin Mary,
Mother of our God and Lord, Jesus Christ,† etc., p. 25.

Hanc Igitur for the Easter Vigil
until the Second Sunday of Easter

Therefore, Lord, we pray:
graciously accept this oblation of our service,
that of your whole family,
which we make to you
also for those to whom you have been pleased to give
the new birth of water and the Holy Spirit,
granting them forgiveness of all their sins;
order our days in your peace,
and command that we be delivered from eternal damnation
and counted among the flock of those you have chosen.
(Through Christ our Lord. Amen.)   → *Canon*, p. 25.

Communicantes for the Ascension of the Lord

Celebrating the most sacred day
on which your Only Begotten Son, our Lord,
placed at the right hand of your glory
our weak human nature,
which he had united to himself,
and in communion with those whose memory we venerate,
especially the glorious ever-Virgin Mary,
Mother of our God and Lord, Jesus Christ,† etc., p. 25.

Communicantes for Pentecost Sunday

Celebrating the most sacred day of Pentecost,
on which the Holy Spirit
appeared to the Apostles in tongues of fire,
and in communion with those whose memory we venerate,
especially the glorious ever-Virgin Mary,
Mother of our God and Lord, Jesus Christ,† etc., p. 25.

BLESSINGS AT THE END OF MASS AND PRAYERS OVER THE PEOPLE

SOLEMN BLESSINGS

The following blessings may be used, at the discretion of the Priest, at the end of the celebration of Mass, or of a Liturgy of the Word, or of the Office, or of the Sacraments.

The Deacon or, in his absence, the Priest himself, says the invitation: Bow down for the blessing. *Then the Priest, with hands extended over the people, says the blessing, with all responding:* **Amen**.

I. For Celebrations in the Different Liturgical Times

1. ADVENT

May the almighty and merciful God,
by whose grace you have placed your faith
in the First Coming of his Only Begotten Son
and yearn for his coming again,
sanctify you by the radiance of Christ's Advent
and enrich you with his blessing. R̷. **Amen.**

As you run the race of this present life,
may he make you firm in faith,
joyful in hope and active in charity. R̷. **Amen.**

So that, rejoicing now with devotion
at the Redeemer's coming in the flesh,
you may be endowed with the rich reward of eternal life
when he comes again in majesty. R̷. **Amen.**

And may the blessing of almighty God,
the Father, and the Son, ✠ and the Holy Spirit,
come down on you and remain with you for ever. R̷. **Amen.**

2. THE NATIVITY OF THE LORD

May the God of infinite goodness,
who by the Incarnation of his Son has driven darkness from the world
and by that glorious Birth has illumined this most holy night (day),
drive far from you the darkness of vice
and illumine your hearts with the light of virtue. R̷. **Amen.**

97

May God, who willed that the great joy
of his Son's saving Birth
be announced to shepherds by the Angel,
fill your minds with the gladness he gives
and make you heralds of his Gospel. ℟. **Amen.**

And may God, who by the Incarnation
brought together the earthly and heavenly realm,
fill you with the gift of his peace and favor
and make you sharers with the Church in heaven. ℟. **Amen.**

And may the blessing of almighty God,
the Father, and the Son, ✝ and the Holy Spirit,
come down on you and remain with you for ever. ℟. **Amen.**

3. THE BEGINNING OF THE YEAR

May God, the source and origin of all blessing,
grant you grace,
pour out his blessing in abundance,
and keep you safe from harm throughout the year. ℟. **Amen.**

May he give you integrity in the faith,
endurance in hope,
and perseverance in charity
with holy patience to the end. ℟. **Amen.**

May he order your days and your deeds in his peace,
grant your prayers in this and in every place,
and lead you happily to eternal life. ℟. **Amen.**

And may the blessing of almighty God,
the Father, and the Son, ✝ and the Holy Spirit,
come down on you and remain with you for ever. ℟. **Amen.**

4. THE EPIPHANY OF THE LORD

May God, who has called you
out of darkness into his wonderful light,
pour out in kindness his blessing upon you
and make your hearts firm
in faith, hope and charity. ℟. **Amen.**

And since in all confidence you follow Christ,
who today appeared in the world
as a light shining in darkness,

may God make you, too,
a light for your brothers and sisters. ℟. **Amen.**

And so when your pilgrimage is ended,
may you come to him
whom the Magi sought as they followed the star
and whom they found with great joy, the Light from Light,
who is Christ the Lord. ℟. **Amen.**

And may the blessing of almighty God,
the Father, and the Son, ✠ and the Holy Spirit,
come down on you and remain with you for ever. ℟. **Amen.**

5. THE PASSION OF THE LORD

May God, the Father of mercies,
who has given you an example of love
in the Passion of his Only Begotten Son,
grant that, by serving God and your neighbor,
you may lay hold of the wondrous gift of his blessing.
℟. **Amen.**

So that you may receive the reward of everlasting life from
him,
through whose earthly Death
you believe that you escape eternal death. ℟. **Amen.**

And by following the example of his self-abasement,
may you possess a share in his Resurrection. ℟. **Amen.**

And may the blessing of almighty God,
the Father, and the Son, ✠ and the Holy Spirit,
come down on you and remain with you for ever. ℟. **Amen.**

6. EASTER TIME

May God, who by the Resurrection of his Only Begotten Son
was pleased to confer on you
the gift of redemption and of adoption,
give you gladness by his blessing. ℟. **Amen.**

May he, by whose redeeming work
you have received the gift of everlasting freedom,
make you heirs to an eternal inheritance. ℟. **Amen.**

And may you, who have already risen with Christ
in Baptism through faith,

by living in a right manner on this earth,
be united with him in the homeland of heaven. ℟. **Amen.**

And may the blessing of almighty God,
the Father, and the Son, ✠ and the Holy Spirit,
come down on you and remain with you for ever. ℟. **Amen.**

7. THE ASCENSION OF THE LORD

May almighty God bless you,
for on this very day his Only Begotten Son
pierced the heights of heaven
and unlocked for you the way
to ascend to where he is. ℟. **Amen.**

May he grant that,
as Christ after his Resurrection
was seen plainly by his disciples,
so when he comes as Judge
he may show himself merciful to you for all eternity.
    ℟. **Amen.**

And may you, who believe he is seated
with the Father in his majesty,
know with joy the fulfillment of his promise
to stay with you until the end of time. ℟. **Amen.**

And may the blessing of almighty God,
the Father, and the Son, ✠ and the Holy Spirit,
come down on you and remain with you for ever. ℟. **Amen.**

8. THE HOLY SPIRIT

May God, the Father of lights,
who was pleased to enlighten the disciples' minds
by the outpouring of the Spirit, the Paraclete,
grant you gladness by his blessing
and make you always abound with the gifts of the same
    Spirit. ℟. **Amen.**

May the wondrous flame that appeared above the disciples,
powerfully cleanse your hearts from every evil
and pervade them with its purifying light. ℟. **Amen.**

And may God, who has been pleased to unite many
    tongues

in the profession of one faith,
give you perseverance in that same faith
and, by believing, may you journey from hope to clear
    vision. ℟. **Amen.**

And may the blessing of almighty God,
the Father, and the Son, ✠ and the Holy Spirit,
come down on you and remain with you for ever. ℟. **Amen.**

9. ORDINARY TIME I

May the Lord bless you and keep you. ℟. **Amen.**

May he let his face shine upon you
and show you his mercy. ℟. **Amen.**

May he turn his countenance towards you
and give you his peace. ℟. **Amen.**

And may the blessing of almighty God,
the Father, and the Son, ✠ and the Holy Spirit,
come down on you and remain with you for ever. ℟. **Amen.**

10. ORDINARY TIME II

May the peace of God,
which surpasses all understanding,
keep your hearts and minds
in the knowledge and love of God,
and of his Son, our Lord Jesus Christ. ℟. **Amen.**

And may the blessing of almighty God,
the Father, and the Son, ✠ and the Holy Spirit,
come down on you and remain with you for ever. ℟. **Amen.**

11. ORDINARY TIME III

May almighty God bless you in his kindness
and pour out saving wisdom upon you. ℟. **Amen.**

May he nourish you always with the teachings of the faith
and make you persevere in holy deeds. ℟. **Amen.**

May he turn your steps towards himself
and show you the path of charity and peace. ℟. **Amen.**

And may the blessing of almighty God,
the Father, and the Son, ✠ and the Holy Spirit,
come down on you and remain with you for ever. ℟. **Amen.**

12. ORDINARY TIME IV

May the God of all consolation order your days in his peace
and grant you the gifts of his blessing. ℟. **Amen.**

May he free you always from every distress
and confirm your hearts in his love. ℟. **Amen.**

So that on this life's journey
you may be effective in good works,
rich in the gifts of hope, faith and charity,
and may come happily to eternal life. ℟. **Amen.**

And may the blessing of almighty God,
the Father, and the Son, ✠ and the Holy Spirit,
come down on you and remain with you for ever. ℟. **Amen.**

13. ORDINARY TIME V

May almighty God always keep every adversity far from you
and in his kindness pour out upon you the gifts of his
blessing. ℟. **Amen.**

May God keep your hearts attentive to his words,
that they may be filled with everlasting gladness. ℟. **Amen.**

And so, may you always understand what is good and right,
and be found ever hastening along
in the path of God's commands,
made coheirs with the citizens of heaven. ℟. **Amen.**

And may the blessing of almighty God,
the Father, and the Son, ✠ and the Holy Spirit,
come down on you and remain with you for ever. ℟. **Amen.**

14. ORDINARY TIME VI

May God bless you with every heavenly blessing,
make you always holy and pure in his sight,
pour out in abundance upon you the riches of his glory,
and teach you with the words of truth;
may he instruct you in the Gospel of salvation,
and ever endow you with fraternal charity.
Through Christ our Lord. ℟. **Amen.**

And may the blessing of almighty God,
the Father, and the Son, ✠ and the Holy Spirit,
come down on you and remain with you for ever. ℟. **Amen.**

II. For Celebrations of the Saints

15. THE BLESSED VIRGIN MARY

May God, who through the childbearing of the Blessed
    Virgin Mary
willed in his great kindness to redeem the human race,
be pleased to enrich you with his blessing. ℟. **Amen.**

May you know always and everywhere the protection of
    her,
through whom you have been found worthy to receive the
    author of life. ℟. **Amen.**

May you, who have devoutly gathered on this day,
carry away with you the gifts of spiritual joys and heavenly
    rewards. ℟. **Amen.**

And may the blessing of almighty God,
the Father, and the Son, ✠ and the Holy Spirit,
come down on you and remain with you for ever. ℟. **Amen.**

16. SAINTS PETER AND PAUL, APOSTLES

May almighty God bless you,
for he has made you steadfast in Saint Peter's saving
    confession
and through it has set you on the solid rock of the Church's
    faith. ℟. **Amen.**

And having instructed you
by the tireless preaching of Saint Paul,
may God teach you constantly by his example
to win brothers and sisters for Christ. ℟. **Amen.**

So that by the keys of St. Peter and the words of St. Paul,
and by the support of their intercession,
God may bring us happily to that homeland
that Peter attained on a cross
and Paul by the blade of a sword. ℟. **Amen.**

And may the blessing of almighty God,
the Father, and the Son, ✚ and the Holy Spirit,
come down on you and remain with you for ever. ℟. **Amen.**

17. THE APOSTLES

May God, who has granted you
to stand firm on apostolic foundations,
graciously bless you through the glorious merits
of the holy Apostles *N.* and *N.* (the holy Apostle *N.*). ℟.
    Amen.

And may he, who endowed you
with the teaching and example of the Apostles,
make you, under their protection,
witnesses to the truth before all. ℟. **Amen.**

So that through the intercession of the Apostles,
you may inherit the eternal homeland,
for by their teaching you possess firmness of faith. ℟. **Amen.**

And may the blessing of almighty God,
the Father, and the Son, ✚ and the Holy Spirit,
come down on you and remain with you for ever. ℟. **Amen.**

18. ALL SAINTS

May God, the glory and joy of the Saints,
who has caused you to be strengthened
by means of their outstanding prayers,
bless you with unending blessings. ℟. **Amen.**

Freed through their intercession from present ills
and formed by the example of their holy way of life,
may you be ever devoted
to serving God and your neighbor. ℟. **Amen.**

So that, together with all,
you may possess the joys of the homeland,
where Holy Church rejoices
that her children are admitted in perpetual peace
to the company of the citizens of heaven. ℟. **Amen.**

And may the blessing of almighty God,
the Father, and the Son, ✚ and the Holy Spirit,
come down on you and remain with you for ever. ℟. **Amen.**

III. Other Blessings

19. FOR THE DEDICATION OF A CHURCH

May God, the Lord of heaven and earth,
who has gathered you today for the dedication of this
    church,
make you abound in heavenly blessings. ℟. **Amen.**

And may he, who has willed that all his scattered children
should be gathered together in his Son,
grant that you may become his temple
and the dwelling place of the Holy Spirit. ℟. **Amen.**

And so, when you are thoroughly cleansed,
may God dwell within you
and grant you to possess with all the Saints
the inheritance of eternal happiness. ℟. **Amen.**

And may the blessing of almighty God,
the Father, ✠ and the Son, ✠ and the Holy ✠ Spirit,
come down on you and remain with you for ever. ℟. **Amen.**

20. IN CELEBRATIONS FOR THE DEAD

May the God of all consolation bless you,
for in his unfathomable goodness he created the human
    race,
and in the Resurrection of his Only Begotten Son
he has given believers the hope of rising again. ℟. **Amen.**

To us who are alive, may God grant pardon for our sins,
and to all the dead, a place of light and peace. ℟. **Amen.**

So may we all live happily for ever with Christ,
whom we believe truly rose from the dead. ℟. **Amen.**

And may the blessing of almighty God,
the Father, and the Son, ✠ and the Holy Spirit,
come down on you and remain with you for ever. ℟. **Amen.**

PRAYERS OVER THE PEOPLE

*The following prayers may be used, at the discretion
of the Priest, at the end of the celebration of Mass,
or of a Liturgy of the Word, or of the Office, or of the
Sacraments.*

The Deacon or, in his absence, the Priest himself, says the invitation: Bow down for the blessing. *Then the Priest, with hands outstretched over the people, says the prayer, with all responding:* **Amen**.

After the prayer, the Priest always adds: And may the blessing of almighty God, the Father, and the Son, ✠ and the Holy Spirit, come down on you and remain with you for ever. ℟. Amen.

1. Be gracious to your people, O Lord,
   and do not withhold consolation on earth
   from those you call to strive for heaven.
   Through Christ our Lord.

2. Grant, O Lord, we pray,
   that the Christian people
   may understand the truths they profess
   and love the heavenly liturgy
   in which they participate.
   Through Christ our Lord.

3. May your people receive your holy blessing,
   O Lord, we pray,
   and, by that gift,
   spurn all that would harm them
   and obtain what they desire.
   Through Christ our Lord.

4. Turn your people to you with all their heart,
   O Lord, we pray,
   for you protect even those who go astray,
   but when they serve you with undivided heart,
   you sustain them with still greater care.
   Through Christ our Lord.

5. Graciously enlighten your family, O Lord, we pray,
   that by holding fast to what is pleasing to you,
   they may be worthy to accomplish all that is good.
   Through Christ our Lord.

6. Bestow pardon and peace, O Lord, we pray,
   upon your faithful,
   that they may be cleansed from every offense

and serve you with untroubled hearts.
Through Christ our Lord.

7. May your heavenly favor, O Lord, we pray,
   increase in number the people subject to you
   and make them always obedient to your commands.
   Through Christ our Lord.

8. Be propitious to your people, O God,
   that, freed from every evil,
   they may serve you with all their heart
   and ever stand firm under your protection.
   Through Christ our Lord.

9. May your family always rejoice together, O God,
   over the mysteries of redemption they have celebrated,
   and grant its members the perseverance
   to attain the effects that flow from them.
   Through Christ our Lord.

10. Lord God, from the abundance of your mercies
    provide for your servants and ensure their safety,
    so that, strengthened by your blessings,
    they may at all times abound in thanksgiving
    and bless you with unending exultation.
    Through Christ our Lord.

11. Keep your family, we pray, O Lord,
    in your constant care,
    so that, under your protection,
    they may be free from all troubles
    and by good works show dedication to your name.
    Through Christ our Lord.

12. Purify your faithful, both in body and in mind,
    O Lord, we pray,
    so that, feeling the compunction you inspire,
    they may be able to avoid harmful pleasures
    and ever feed upon your delights.
    Through Christ our Lord.

13. May the effects of your sacred blessing, O Lord,
    make themselves felt among your faithful,

to prepare with spiritual sustenance the minds of all,
that they may be strengthened by the power of your
   love
to carry out works of charity.
Through Christ our Lord.

14. The hearts of your faithful submitted to your name,
    entreat your help, O Lord,
    and since without you they can do nothing that is just,
    grant by your abundant mercy
    that they may both know what is right
    and receive all that they need for their good.
    Through Christ our Lord.

15. Hasten to the aid of your faithful people
    who call upon you, O Lord, we pray,
    and graciously give strength in their human weakness,
    so that, being dedicated to you in complete sincerity,
    they may find gladness in your remedies
    both now and in the life to come.
    Through Christ our Lord.

16. Look with favor on your family, O Lord,
    and bestow your endless mercy on those who seek it:
    and just as without your mercy,
    they can do nothing truly worthy of you,
    so through it,
    may they merit to obey your saving commands.
    Through Christ our Lord.

17. Bestow increase of heavenly grace
    on your faithful, O Lord;
    may they praise you with their lips,
    with their souls, with their lives;
    and since it is by your gift that we exist,
    may our whole lives be yours.
    Through Christ our Lord.

18. Direct your people, O Lord, we pray,
    with heavenly instruction,
    that by avoiding every evil
    and pursuing all that is good,
    they may earn not your anger

but your unending mercy.
Through Christ our Lord.

19. Be near to those who call on you, O Lord,
and graciously grant your protection
to all who place their hope in your mercy,
that they may remain faithful in holiness of life
and, having enough for their needs in this world,
they may be made full heirs of your promise for eternity.
Through Christ our Lord.

20. Bestow the grace of your kindness
upon your supplicant people, O Lord,
that, formed by you, their creator,
and restored by you, their sustainer,
through your constant action they may be saved.
Through Christ our Lord.

21. May your faithful people, O Lord, we pray,
always respond to the promptings of your love
and, moved by wholesome compunction,
may they do gladly what you command,
so as to receive the things you promise.
Through Christ our Lord.

22. May the weakness of your devoted people
stir your compassion, O Lord, we pray,
and let their faithful pleading win your mercy,
that what they do not presume upon by their merits
they may receive by your generous pardon.
Through Christ our Lord.

23. In defense of your children, O Lord, we pray,
stretch forth the right hand of your majesty,
so that, obeying your fatherly will,
they may have the unfailing protection
of your fatherly care.
Through Christ our Lord.

24. Look, O Lord, on the prayers of your family,
and grant them the assistance they humbly implore,
so that, strengthened by the help they need,
they may persevere in confessing your name.
Through Christ our Lord.

25. Keep your family safe, O Lord, we pray,
    and grant them the abundance of your mercies,
    that they may find growth
    through the teachings and the gifts of heaven.
    Through Christ our Lord.

26. May your faithful people rejoice, we pray, O Lord,
    to be upheld by your right hand,
    and, progressing in the Christian life,
    may they delight in good things
    both now and in the time to come.
    Through Christ our Lord.

ON FEASTS OF SAINTS

27. May the Christian people exult, O Lord,
    at the glorification of the illustrious members of your
        Son's Body,
    and may they gain a share in the eternal lot
    of the Saints on whose feast day
    they reaffirm their devotion to you,
    rejoicing with them for ever in your glory.
    Through Christ our Lord.

28. Turn the hearts of your people
    always to you, O Lord, we pray,
    and, as you give them the help of such great patrons as
        these,
    grant also the unfailing help of your protection.
    Through Christ our Lord.

"What I say to you, I say to all: 'Watch!'"

NOVEMBER 29, 2020

1st SUNDAY OF ADVENT

ENTRANCE ANT. Cf. Ps 25 (24):1-3   [Hope]

To you, I lift up my soul, O my God. In you, I have trusted; let me not be put to shame. Nor let my enemies exult over me; and let none who hope in you be put to shame.   → No. 2, p. 10 (Omit Gloria)

COLLECT   [Meeting Christ]

Grant your faithful, we pray, almighty God,
the resolve to run forth to meet your Christ
with righteous deeds at his coming,
so that, gathered at his right hand,
they may be worthy to possess the heavenly Kingdom.
Through our Lord Jesus Christ, your Son,
who lives and reigns with you in the unity of the Holy
   Spirit,
one God, for ever and ever. ℟. **Amen.** ↓

111

FIRST READING Is 63:16b-17, 19b; 64:2-7 [God Our Redeemer]

God is our Father. We are sinful, and you, O God, are hidden from our eyes. We are the work of your hands.

A reading from the Book of the Prophet Isaiah

YOU, LORD, are our father,
our redeemer you are named forever.
Why do you let us wander, O LORD, from your ways,
and harden our hearts so that we fear you not?
Return for the sake of your servants,
the tribes of your heritage.
Oh, that you would rend the heavens and come down,
with the mountains quaking before you,
while you wrought awesome deeds we could not hope
for,
such as they had not heard of from of old.
No ear has ever heard, no eye ever seen, any God but
you
doing such deeds for those who wait for him.
Would that you might meet us doing right,
that we were mindful of you in our ways!
Behold, you are angry, and we are sinful;
all of us have become like unclean men,
all our good deeds are like polluted rags;
we have all withered like leaves,
and our guilt carries us away like the wind.
There is none who calls upon your name,
who rouses himself to cling to you;
for you have hidden your face from us
and have delivered us up to our guilt.
Yet, O LORD, you are our father;
we are the clay and you are the potter:
we are all the work of your hands.

The word of the Lord. ℟. **Thanks be to God.** ↓

RESPONSORIAL PSALM Ps 80   [Come To Save Us]

R. Lord, make us turn to you; let us see your face and we shall be saved.

O shepherd of Israel, hearken,
    from your throne upon the cherubim, shine forth.
Rouse your power,
    and come to save us.—R.

Once again, O LORD of hosts,
    look down from heaven, and see;
take care of this vine,
    and protect what your right hand has planted,
    the son of man whom you yourself made strong.—R.

May your help be with the man of your right hand,
    with the son of man whom you yourself made strong.
Then we will no more withdraw from you;
    give us new life, and we will call upon your name.
    —R. ↓

SECOND READING 1 Cor 1:3-9   [Fellowship with Christ]

Jesus gives us faith and the strength to persevere. God
calls his followers into the fellowship of Christ.

A reading from the first Letter of Saint Paul
to the Corinthians

BROTHERS and sisters: Grace to you and peace
from God our Father and the Lord Jesus Christ.
I give thanks to my God always on your account for
the grace of God bestowed on you in Christ Jesus,
that in him you were enriched in every way, with all
discourse and all knowledge, as the testimony to
Christ was confirmed among you, so that you are

not lacking in any spiritual gift as you wait for the revelation of our Lord Jesus Christ. He will keep you firm to the end, irreproachable on the day of our Lord Jesus Christ. God is faithful, and by him you were called to fellowship with his Son, Jesus Christ our Lord.—The word of the Lord. ℟. **Thanks be to God.** ↓

ALLELUIA Ps 85:8   [Mercy and Love]

℟. **Alleluia, alleluia.**
Show us, Lord, your love;
and grant us your salvation.
℟. **Alleluia, alleluia.** ↓

GOSPEL Mk 13:33-37   [On Guard]

Be on guard always. We do not know what time or hour God will come.

℣. The Lord be with you. ℟. **And with your spirit.**
✚ A reading from the holy Gospel according to Mark.
℟. **Glory to you, O Lord.**

JESUS said to his disciples: "Be watchful! Be alert! You do not know when the time will come. It is like a man traveling abroad. He leaves home and places his servants in charge, each with his own work, and orders the gatekeeper to be on the watch. Watch, therefore; you do not know when the lord of the house is coming, whether in the evening, or at midnight, or at cockcrow, or in the morning. May he not come suddenly and find you sleeping. What I say to you, I say to all: 'Watch!' "—The Gospel of the Lord. ℟. **Praise to you, Lord Jesus Christ.**   → No. 15, p. 18

PRAYER OVER THE OFFERINGS   [Eternal Redemption]

Accept, we pray, O Lord, these offerings we make,
gathered from among your gifts to us,

and may what you grant us to celebrate devoutly here
  below
gain for us the prize of eternal redemption.
Through Christ our Lord.
℟. **Amen.**   → No. 21, p. 22 (Pref. P 1)

COMMUNION ANT. Ps 85 (84):13   **[God's Bounty]**
**The Lord will bestow his bounty, and our earth shall
yield its increase.** ↓

PRAYER AFTER COMMUNION   **[Love for Heaven]**

May these mysteries, O Lord,
in which we have participated,
profit us, we pray,
for even now, as we walk amid passing things,
you teach us by them
to love the things of heaven
and hold fast to what endures.
Through Christ our Lord.
℟. **Amen.**   → No. 30, p. 77

Optional Solemn Blessings, p. 97, and Prayers over the People, p. 105

"Prepare the way of the Lord. . . ."

DECEMBER 6

2nd SUNDAY OF ADVENT

ENTRANCE ANT. Cf. Is 30:19, 30   [Lord of Salvation]

O people of Sion, behold, the Lord will come to save the nations, and the Lord will make the glory of his voice heard in the joy of your heart.

→ No. 2, p. 10 (Omit Gloria)

COLLECT   [Heavenly Wisdom]

Almighty and merciful God,
may no earthly undertaking hinder those
who set out in haste to meet your Son,
but may our learning of heavenly wisdom
gain us admittance to his company.
Who lives and reigns with you in the unity of the Holy
   Spirit,
one God, for ever and ever.
℟. **Amen.** ↓

FIRST READING Is 40:1-5, 9-11   [God Is Near]

Make ready the way for the Messiah. Make known the Good News, for God is near.

116

A reading from the Book of the Prophet Isaiah

COMFORT, give comfort to my people,
    says your God.
Speak tenderly to Jerusalem, and proclaim to her
    that her service is at an end,
        her guilt is expiated;
indeed, she has received from the hand of the LORD
    double for all her sins.

    A voice cries out:
In the desert prepare the way of the LORD!
    Make straight in the wasteland a highway for our
        God!
Every valley shall be filled in,
    every mountain and hill shall be made low;
the rugged land shall be made a plain,
    the rough country, a broad valley.
Then the glory of the LORD shall be revealed,
    and all mankind shall see it together;
        for the mouth of the LORD has spoken.

Go up onto a high mountain,
    Zion, herald of glad tidings;
cry out at the top of your voice,
    Jerusalem, herald of good news!
Fear not to cry out
    and say to the cities of Judah:
        Here is your GOD!
Here comes with power
    the Lord GOD,
        who rules by his strong arm;
here is his reward with him,
    his recompense before him.
Like a shepherd he feeds his flock;
    in his arms he gathers the lambs,
carrying them in his bosom,
    and leading the ewes with care.
The word of the Lord. ℟. **Thanks be to God.** ↓

RESPONSORIAL PSALM Ps 85   [God's Salvation]

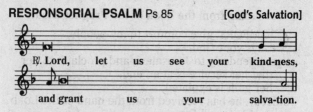

℟. Lord, let us see your kind-ness, and grant us your salva-tion.

I will hear what God proclaims;
    the LORD—for he proclaims peace to his people.
Near indeed is his salvation to those who fear him,
    glory dwelling in our land.—℟.

Kindness and truth shall meet;
    justice and peace shall kiss.
Truth shall spring out of the earth,
    and justice shall look down from heaven.—℟.

The LORD himself will give his benefits;
    our land shall yield its increase.
Justice shall walk before him,
    and prepare the way of his steps.—℟. ↓

SECOND READING 2 Pt 3:8-14   [A New Earth]

There is no counting of time with God. He does not want
anyone to perish. We await a new heaven and earth, relying on the justice of God.

A reading from the second Letter of Saint Peter

DO not ignore this one fact, beloved, that with the
Lord one day is like a thousand years and a thousand years like one day. The Lord does not delay his
promise, as some regard "delay," but he is patient with
you, not wishing that any should perish but that all
should come to repentance. But the day of the Lord will
come like a thief, and then the heavens will pass away
with a mighty roar and the elements will be dissolved by

fire, and the earth and everything done on it will be found out.

Since everything is to be dissolved in this way, what sort of persons ought you to be, conducting yourselves in holiness and devotion, waiting for and hastening the coming of the day of God, because of which the heavens will be dissolved in flames and the elements melted by fire. But according to his promise we await new heavens and a new earth in which righteousness dwells. Therefore, beloved, since you await these things, be eager to be found without spot or blemish before him, at peace.—The word of the Lord. R̸. **Thanks be to God**. ↓

ALLELUIA Lk 3:4, 6   [Prepare the Way]

R̸. **Alleluia, alleluia.**
Prepare the way for the Lord, make straight his paths:
all flesh shall see the salvation of God.
R̸. **Alleluia, alleluia.** ↓

GOSPEL Mk 1:1-8   [Need for Repentance]

John the Baptist announced the coming of Jesus. John called for repentance and promised that the Messiah would baptize in the Holy Spirit.

Y̸. The Lord be with you. R̸. **And with your spirit.**
✠ A reading from the holy Gospel according to Mark.
R̸. **Glory to you, O Lord.**

THE beginning of the gospel of Jesus Christ the Son of God.
As it is written in Isaiah the prophet:
Behold, I am sending my messenger ahead of you;
he will prepare your way.
A voice of one crying out in the desert:
"Prepare the way of the Lord,
make straight his paths."
John the Baptist appeared in the desert proclaiming a baptism of repentance for the forgiveness of sins.

People of the whole Judean countryside and all the inhabitants of Jerusalem were going out to him and were being baptized by him in the Jordan River as they acknowledged their sins. John was clothed in camel's hair, with a leather belt around his waist. He fed on locusts and wild honey. And this is what he proclaimed: "One mightier than I is coming after me. I am not worthy to stoop and loosen the thongs of his sandals. I have baptized you with water; he will baptize you with the Holy Spirit."—The Gospel of the Lord.
℟. **Praise to you, Lord Jesus Christ.**   → No. 15, p. 18

PRAYER OVER THE OFFERINGS   [Our Offering]

Be pleased, O Lord, with our humble prayers and
    offerings,
and, since we have no merits to plead our cause,
come, we pray, to our rescue
with the protection of your mercy.
Through Christ our Lord.
℟. **Amen.**   → No. 21, p. 22 (Pref. P 1)

COMMUNION ANT. Bar 5:5; 4:36   [Coming Joy]

Jerusalem, arise and stand upon the heights, and behold the joy which comes to you from God. ↓

PRAYER AFTER COMMUNION   [Wise Judgment]

Replenished by the food of spiritual nourishment,
we humbly beseech you, O Lord,
that, through our partaking in this mystery,
you may teach us to judge wisely the things of earth
and hold firm to the things of heaven.
Through Christ our Lord.
℟. **Amen.**   → No. 30, p. 77

Optional Solemn Blessings, p. 97, and Prayers over the People, p. 105

"Hail, full of grace! The Lord is with you."

DECEMBER 8

THE IMMACULATE CONCEPTION OF THE BLESSED VIRGIN MARY

Patronal Feastday of the United States of America

Solemnity

ENTRANCE ANT. Is 61:10   [Mary Rejoices in the Lord]

I rejoice heartily in the Lord, in my God is the joy of my soul; for he has clothed me with a robe of salvation, and wrapped me in a mantle of justice, like a bride adorned with her jewels.   → No. 2, p. 10

COLLECT   [Admitted to God's Presence]

O God, who by the Immaculate Conception of the
    Blessed Virgin
prepared a worthy dwelling for your Son,
grant, we pray,
that, as you preserved her from every stain
by virtue of the Death of your Son, which you foresaw,
so, through her intercession,
we, too, may be cleansed and admitted to your presence.

121

Through our Lord Jesus Christ, your Son,
who lives and reigns with you in the unity of the Holy
   Spirit,
one God, for ever and ever. ℟. **Amen.** ↓

FIRST READING Gn 3:9-15, 20   **[Promise of the Redeemer]**

**In the Garden, humankind enjoys an intimacy with God. It
is disrupted by sin, and the free and happy relationship
between humankind and God is broken.**

A reading from the Book of Genesis

AFTER the man, Adam, had eaten of the tree the
Lord God called to the man and asked him, "Where
are you?" He answered, "I heard you in the garden; but I
was afraid, because I was naked, so I hid myself." Then
he asked, "Who told you that you were naked? You have
eaten, then, from the tree of which I had forbidden you
to eat!" The man replied, "The woman whom you put
here with me—she gave me fruit from the tree, and so I
ate it." The Lord God then asked the woman, "Why did
you do such a thing?" The woman answered, "The serpent tricked me into it, so I ate it."

Then the Lord God said to the serpent:
"Because you have done this, you shall be banned
   from all the animals
   and from all the wild creatures;
on your belly shall you crawl,
   and dirt shall you eat
   all the days of your life.
I will put enmity between you and the woman,
   and between your offspring and hers;
he will strike at your head
   while you strike at his heel."

The man called his wife Eve, because she became
the mother of all the living.—The word of the Lord. ℟.
Thanks be to God. ↓

RESPONSORIAL PSALM Ps 98   [God's Salvation]

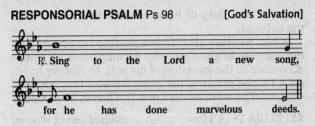

℟. Sing to the Lord a new song, for he has done marvelous deeds.

Sing to the LORD a new song,
  for he has done wondrous deeds;
his right hand has won victory for him,
  his holy arm.—℟.

The LORD has made his salvation known:
  in the sight of the nations he has revealed his justice.
He has remembered his kindness and his faithfulness
  toward the house of Israel.—℟.

All the ends of the earth have seen
  the salvation by our God.
Sing joyfully to the LORD, all you lands;
  break into song; sing praise.—℟. ↓

SECOND READING Eph 1:3-6, 11-12   [God's Saving Plan]

God is praised for revealing his plan of salvation. Whatever God wills he works effectively and surely to accomplish. Let us make his will our will.

A reading from the Letter of Saint Paul to the Ephesians

BROTHERS and sisters: Blessed be the God and Father of our Lord Jesus Christ, who has blessed us in Christ with every spiritual blessing in the heavens, as he chose us in him, before the foundation of the world, to be holy and without blemish before him. In love he destined us for adoption to himself through Jesus Christ, in accord with the favor of his will, for the praise of the glory of his grace that he granted us in the beloved.

In him we were also chosen, destined in accord with the purpose of the One who accomplishes all things according to the intention of his will, so that we might exist for the praise of his glory, we who first hoped in Christ.—The word of the Lord. ℟. **Thanks be to God.** ↓

ALLELUIA Cf. Lk 1:28 [Blessed among Women]

℟. **Alleluia, alleluia.**
Hail, Mary, full of grace, the Lord is with you;
blessed are you among women.
℟. **Alleluia, alleluia.** ↓

GOSPEL Lk 1:26-38 [Mary's Great Holiness]

Mary has received a promise of supreme grace and blessing and accepts it in faith, assenting to God's Word with her "Amen."

℣. The Lord be with you. ℟. **And with your spirit.**
✛ A reading from the holy Gospel according to Luke.
℟. **Glory to you, O Lord.**

THE angel Gabriel was sent from God to a town of Galilee called Nazareth, to a virgin betrothed to a man named Joseph, of the house of David, and the virgin's name was Mary. And coming to her, he said, "Hail, full of grace! The Lord is with you." But she was greatly troubled at what was said and pondered what sort of greeting this might be. Then the angel said to her, "Do not be afraid, Mary, for you have found favor with God. Behold, you will conceive in your womb and bear a son, and you shall name him Jesus. He will be great and will be called Son of the Most High, and the Lord God will give him the throne of David his father, and he will rule over the house of Jacob forever, and of his Kingdom there will be no end." But Mary said to the angel, "How can this be, since I have no relations with a man?" And the angel said to her in reply, "The Holy Spirit will come upon you, and the power of the Most High will overshadow you. Therefore the child to be born will be called holy, the Son of God. And behold, Elizabeth, your relative, has also conceived a son in her old age, and this is the sixth month for her who was called barren; for nothing will be impossible for God." Mary said, "Behold, I am the handmaid of the Lord. May it be done to me according to your word." Then the angel departed from her.—The Gospel of the Lord. ℟. **Praise to you, Lord Jesus Christ.**

➔ No. 15, p. 18

PRAYER OVER THE OFFERINGS
                                    [Helped by Mary's Intercession]

Graciously accept the saving sacrifice
which we offer you, O Lord,
on the Solemnity of the Immaculate Conception
of the Blessed Virgin Mary,
and grant that, as we profess her,
on account of your prevenient grace,
to be untouched by any stain of sin,
so, through her intercession,
we may be delivered from all our faults.
Through Christ our Lord.
℟. **Amen.** ↓

PREFACE (P 58)   [Mary Our Advocate]

℣. The Lord be with you. ℟. **And with your spirit.**
℣. Lift up your hearts. ℟. **We lift them up to the Lord.**
℣. Let us give thanks to the Lord our God. ℟. **It is right and just.**

It is truly right and just, our duty and our salvation,
always and everywhere to give you thanks,
Lord, holy Father, almighty and eternal God.

For you preserved the Most Blessed Virgin Mary
from all stain of original sin,

so that in her, endowed with the rich fullness of your
   grace,
you might prepare a worthy Mother for your Son
and signify the beginning of the Church,
his beautiful Bride without spot or wrinkle.

She, the most pure Virgin, was to bring forth a Son,
the innocent Lamb who would wipe away our offenses;
you placed her above all others
to be for your people an advocate of grace
and a model of holiness.

And so, in company with the choirs of Angels,
we praise you, and with joy we proclaim:

→ No. 23, p. 23

COMMUNION ANT. [Glorious Things Spoken of Mary]

**Glorious things are spoken of you, O Mary, for from
you arose the sun of justice, Christ our God. ↓**

PRAYER AFTER COMMUNION [Heal Our Wounds]

May the Sacrament we have received,
O Lord our God,
heal in us the wounds of that fault
from which in a singular way
you preserved Blessed Mary in her Immaculate
   Conception.
Through Christ our Lord.
℟. **Amen.**

→ No. 30, p. 77

Optional Solemn Blessings, p. 97, and Prayers over the People, p. 105

"I baptize with water; but there is one among you whom you do not recognize."

DECEMBER 13

3rd SUNDAY OF ADVENT

ENTRANCE ANT. Phil 4:4-5   [Mounting Joy]
Rejoice in the Lord always; again I say, rejoice. Indeed, the Lord is near. → No. 2, p. 10 (Omit Gloria)

COLLECT   [Joy of Salvation]
O God, who see how your people
faithfully await the feast of the Lord's Nativity,
enable us, we pray,
to attain the joys of so great a salvation
and to celebrate them always
with solemn worship and glad rejoicing.
Through our Lord Jesus Christ, your Son,
who lives and reigns with you in the unity of the Holy
    Spirit,
one God, for ever and ever.
℞. **Amen.** ↓

FIRST READING Is 61:1-2a, 10-11　　[God's Glad Tidings]

Isaiah has been sent to proclaim glad tidings to those in need. He rejoices in the Lord who will prove that he is the God of justice and peace.

A reading from the Book of the Prophet Isaiah

THE spirit of the Lord GOD is upon me,
　　because the LORD has anointed me;
he has sent me to bring glad tidings to the poor,
　　to heal the brokenhearted,
to proclaim liberty to the captives
　　and release to the prisoners,
to announce a year of favor from the LORD
　　and a day of vindication by our God.

I rejoice heartily in the LORD,
　　in my God is the joy of my soul;
for he has clothed me with a robe of salvation,
　　and wrapped me in a mantle of justice,
like a bridegroom adorned with a diadem,
　　like a bride bedecked with her jewels.
As the earth brings forth its plants,
　　and a garden makes its growth spring up,
so will the Lord GOD make justice and praise
　　spring up before all the nations.
The word of the Lord. ℟. **Thanks be to God.** ↓

RESPONSORIAL PSALM Lk 1　　[God's Mighty Works]

℟. **My soul re-joic-es in my God.**

My soul proclaims the greatness of the Lord;
　　my spirit rejoices in God my Savior,
for he has looked upon his lowly servant.
　　From this day all generations shall call me
　　blessed:—℟.

the Almighty has done great things for me,
    and holy is his Name.
He has mercy on those who fear him
    in every generation.—R⎞.

He has filled the hungry with good things,
    and the rich he has sent away empty.
He has come to the help of his servant Israel
    for he has remembered his promise of mercy.—R⎞. ↓

SECOND READING 1 Thes 5:16-24   [Christian Joy]

Paul admonishes that Christians should rejoice. He prays
that the Christ-bearer will be free from any semblance of
evil, but rather will grow in holiness.

A reading from the first Letter of Saint Paul
to the Thessalonians

BROTHERS and sisters: Rejoice always. Pray without ceasing. In all circumstances give thanks, for
this is the will of God for you in Christ Jesus. Do not
quench the Spirit. Do not despise prophetic utter-
ances. Test everything; retain what is good. Refrain
from every kind of evil.
    May the God of peace make you perfectly holy and
may you entirely, spirit, soul, and body, be preserved blameless for the coming of our Lord Jesus
Christ. The one who calls you is faithful, and he will
also accomplish it.—The word of the Lord. R⎞. **Thanks
be to God.** ↓

ALLELUIA Is 61:1 (cited in Lk 4:18)   [Glad Tidings]

R⎞. **Alleluia, alleluia.**
The Spirit of the Lord is upon me,
    because he has anointed me
to bring glad tidings to the poor.
R⎞. **Alleluia, alleluia.** ↓

GOSPEL Jn 1:6-8, 19-28   [Witness to Christ]

John the Baptist is the forerunner of Jesus. He gives witness to Jesus by his preaching.

℣. The Lord be with you. ℟. **And with your spirit.**
✛ A reading from the holy Gospel according to John.
℟. **Glory to you, O Lord.**

A MAN named John was sent from God. He came for testimony, to testify to the light, so that all might believe through him. He was not the light, but came to testify to the light.

And this is the testimony of John. When the Jews from Jerusalem sent priests and Levites to him to ask him, "Who are you?" he admitted and did not deny it, but admitted, "I am not the Christ." So they asked him, "What are you then? Are you Elijah?" And he said, "I am not." "Are you the Prophet?" He answered, "No." So they said to him, "Who are you, so we can give an answer to those who sent us? What do you have to say for yourself?" He said:

"I am *the voice of one crying out in the desert,*
   '*make straight the way of the Lord,*'
as Isaiah the prophet said." Some Pharisees were also sent. They asked him, "Why then do you baptize if you are not the Christ or Elijah or the Prophet?" John answered them, "I baptize with water; but there is one among you whom you do not recognize, the one who is coming after me, whose sandal strap I am not worthy to untie." This happened in Bethany across the Jordan, where John was baptizing.—The Gospel of the Lord. ℟. **Praise to you, Lord Jesus Christ.** ➜ No. 15, p. 18

PRAYER OVER THE OFFERINGS   [Unceasing Sacrifice]

May the sacrifice of our worship, Lord, we pray,
be offered to you unceasingly,
to complete what was begun in sacred mystery

and powerfully accomplish for us your saving work.
Through Christ our Lord.
℟. **Amen.**   ➜ No. 21, p. 22 (Pref. P 1 or 2)

COMMUNION ANT. Cf. Is 35:4   [Trust in God]

**Say to the faint of heart: Be strong and do not fear.
Behold, our God will come, and he will save us.** ↓

PRAYER AFTER COMMUNION   [Preparation for Christ]

We implore your mercy, Lord,
that this divine sustenance may cleanse us of our faults
and prepare us for the coming feasts.
Through Christ our Lord.
℟. **Amen.**   ➜ No. 30, p. 77

Optional Solemn Blessings, p. 97, and Prayers over the People, p. 105

"Do not be afraid, Mary, for you have found favor with God."

DECEMBER 20

4th SUNDAY OF ADVENT

ENTRANCE ANT. Cf. Is 45:8   [The Advent Plea]

**Drop down dew from above, you heavens, and let the
clouds rain down the Just One; let the earth be opened
and bring forth a Savior.** ➜ No. 2, p. 10 (Omit Gloria)

COLLECT [From Suffering to Glory]

Pour forth, we beseech you, O Lord,
your grace into our hearts,
that we, to whom the Incarnation of Christ your Son
was made known by the message of an Angel,
may by his Passion and Cross
be brought to the glory of his Resurrection.
Who lives and reigns with you in the unity of the Holy
    Spirit,
one God, for ever and ever.
℟. **Amen.** ↓

FIRST READING 2 Sm 7:1-5, 8b-12, 14a, 16 [A King Forever]

**David wishes to build a temple to house the tables of the
Law, but God speaks to him, promising to exalt and secure
the House of David forever. The Lord will bring peace.**

A reading from the second Book of Samuel

WHEN King David was settled in his palace, and the
LORD had given him rest from his enemies on every
side, he said to Nathan the prophet, "Here I am living in a
house of cedar, while the ark of God dwells in a tent!"
Nathan answered the king, "Go, do whatever you have in
mind, for the LORD is with you." But that night the LORD
spoke to Nathan and said: "Go, tell my servant David,
'Thus says the LORD: Should you build me a house to
dwell in?

" 'It was I who took you from the pasture and from the
care of the flock to be commander of my people Israel. I
have been with you wherever you went, and I have
destroyed all your enemies before you. And I will make
you famous like the great ones of the earth. I will fix a
place for my people Israel; I will plant them so that they
may dwell in their place without further disturbance.
Neither shall the wicked continue to afflict them as they
did of old, since the time I first appointed judges over my
people Israel. I will give you rest from all your enemies.

The LORD also reveals to you that he will establish a house for you. And when your time comes and you rest with your ancestors, I will raise up your heir after you, sprung from your loins, and I will make his kingdom firm. I will be a father to him, and he shall be a son to me. Your house and your kingdom shall endure forever before me; your throne shall stand firm forever.'"—The word of the Lord. ℟. **Thanks be to God.** ↓

RESPONSORIAL PSALM Ps 89   [An Eternal Covenant]

℟. For ev - er   I will sing the good-ness of the Lord.

The promises of the LORD I will sing forever;
  through all generations my mouth shall proclaim
    your faithfulness.
For you have said, "My kindness is established for-
    ever";
  in heaven you have confirmed your faithfulness.—℟.

"I have made a covenant with my chosen one,
  I have sworn to David my servant:
forever will I confirm your posterity
  and establish your throne for all generations."—℟.

"He shall say of me, 'You are my father,
  my God, the Rock, my savior.'
Forever I will maintain my kindness toward him,
  and my covenant with him stands firm."—℟. ↓

SECOND READING Rom 16:25-27   [Faith and Obedience]
God has revealed his plan of salvation through the coming
of his Son, Jesus Christ. It is made known to all people that
they may believe and obey.

A reading from the Letter of Saint Paul to the Romans

Bⁱ⁾ROTHERS and sisters: To him who can strength-
  en you, according to my gospel and the procla-

mation of Jesus Christ, according to the revelation
of the mystery kept secret for long ages but now
manifested through the prophetic writings and,
according to the command of the eternal God, made
known to all nations to bring about the obedience of
faith, to the only wise God, through Jesus Christ be
glory forever and ever. Amen.—The word of the Lord.
℟. **Thanks be to God.** ↓

ALLELUIA Lk 1:38   [The Lord's Handmaid]

℟. **Alleluia, alleluia.**
Behold, I am the handmaid of the Lord.
May it be done to me according to your word.
℟. **Alleluia, alleluia.** ↓

GOSPEL Lk 1:26-38   [Mary's Consent]

Gabriel speaks to Mary, announcing that she who is a virgin shall conceive through the Holy Spirit and give birth to
a son. Mary agrees to God's request.

℣. The Lord be with you. ℟. **And with your spirit.**
✠ A reading from the holy Gospel according to Luke.
℟. **Glory to you, O Lord.**

THE angel Gabriel was sent from God to a town of
Galilee called Nazareth, to a virgin betrothed to
a man named Joseph, of the house of David, and the
virgin's name was Mary. And coming to her, he said,
"Hail, full of grace! The Lord is with you." But she
was greatly troubled at what was said and pondered
what sort of greeting this might be. Then the angel
said to her, "Do not be afraid, Mary, for you have
found favor with God.

"Behold, you will conceive in your womb and bear a
son, and you shall name him Jesus. He will be great
and will be called Son of the Most High, and the
Lord God will give him the throne of David his
father, and he will rule over the house of Jacob forever, and of his kingdom there will be no end." But

Mary said to the angel, "How can this be, since I have no relations with a man?" And the angel said to her in reply, "The Holy Spirit will come upon you, and the power of the Most High will overshadow you. Therefore the child to be born will be called holy, the Son of God. And behold, Elizabeth, your relative, has also conceived a son in her old age, and this is the sixth month for her who was called barren; for nothing will be impossible for God." Mary said, "Behold, I am the handmaid of the Lord. May it be done to me according to your word." Then the angel departed from her.—The Gospel of the Lord. ℟. **Praise to you, Lord Jesus Christic.**   → No. 15, p. 18

PRAYER OVER THE OFFERINGS   [Power of the Spirit]

May the Holy Spirit, O Lord,
sanctify these gifts laid upon your altar,
just as he filled with his power the womb of the Blessed
    Virgin Mary.
Through Christ our Lord.
℟. **Amen.**   → No. 21, p. 22 (Pref. P 2)

COMMUNION ANT. Is 7:14   [The Virgin Mother]

Behold, a Virgin shall conceive and bear a son; and his name will be called Emmanuel. ↓

PRAYER AFTER COMMUNION   [Worthy Celebration]

Having received this pledge of eternal redemption,
we pray, almighty God,
that, as the feast day of our salvation draws ever nearer,
so we may press forward all the more eagerly
to the worthy celebration of the mystery of your Son's
    Nativity.
Who lives and reigns for ever and ever.
℟. **Amen.**   → No. 30, p. 77

Optional Solemn Blessings, p. 97, and Prayers over the People, p. 105

The Word is made flesh.

DECEMBER 25

THE NATIVITY OF THE LORD [CHRISTMAS]

Solemnity

AT THE MASS DURING THE NIGHT

ENTRANCE ANT. Ps 2:7   [Son of God]

The Lord said to me: You are my Son. It is I who have begotten you this day.

OR   [True Peace]

Let us all rejoice in the Lord, for our Savior has been born in the world. Today true peace has come down to us from heaven.   → No. 2, p. 10

COLLECT   [Eternal Gladness]

O God, who have made this most sacred night
radiant with the splendor of the true light,
grant, we pray, that we, who have known the mysteries
    of his light on earth,
may also delight in his gladness in heaven.
Who lives and reigns with you in the unity of the Holy
    Spirit,
one God, for ever and ever. ℟. **Amen.** ↓

FIRST READING Is 9:1-6   [The Messiah's Kingdom]

The Messiah is a promise of peace for the world. His reign shall be vast and filled with justice. The power of God is revealed through the weakness of humans.

A reading from the Book of the Prophet Isaiah

THE people who walked in darkness
    have seen a great light;
upon those who dwelt in the land of gloom
    a light has shone.
You have brought them abundant joy
    and great rejoicing,
as they rejoice before you as at the harvest,
    as people make merry when dividing spoils.
For the yoke that burdened them,
    the pole on their shoulder,
and the rod of their taskmaster
    you have smashed, as on the day of Midian.
For every boot that tramped in battle,
    every cloak rolled in blood,
    will be burned as fuel for flames.
For a child is born to us, a son is given us;
    upon his shoulder dominion rests.
They name him Wonder-Counselor, God-Hero,
    Father-Forever, Prince of Peace.
His dominion is vast
    and forever peaceful,
from David's throne, and over his kingdom,
    which he confirms and sustains
by judgment and justice,
    both now and forever.
The zeal of the LORD of hosts will do this!
The word of the Lord. ℟. **Thanks be to God.** ↓

RESPONSORIAL PSALM Ps 96   [Bless the Lord]

℟. Today is born our Sav - ior, Christ the Lord.

Sing to the LORD a new song;
  sing to the LORD, all you lands.
Sing to the LORD; bless his name.

R̰. **Today is born our Savior, Christ the Lord.**

Announce his salvation, day after day.
  Tell his glory among the nations;
  among all peoples, his wondrous deeds.—R̰.

Let the heavens be glad and the earth rejoice;
  let the sea and what fills it resound;
  let the plains be joyful and all that is in them!
Then shall all the trees of the forest exult.—R̰.

They shall exult before the LORD, for he comes;
  for he comes to rule the earth.
He shall rule the world with justice
  and the peoples with his constancy.—R̰. ↓

SECOND READING Ti 2:11-14   [Salvation for All]

  God offers salvation to all people. His way asks us to reject
  worldly desires—to live temperately and justly. He gave us
  his only Son to sacrifice himself to redeem us.

A reading from the Letter of Saint Paul to Titus

BELOVED: The grace of God has appeared, saving
all and training us to reject godless ways and
worldly desires and to live temperately, justly, and
devoutly in this age, as we await the blessed hope, the
appearance of the glory of our great God and savior
Jesus Christ, who gave himself for us to deliver us
from all lawlessness and to cleanse for himself a people as his own, eager to do what is good.—The word of
the Lord. R̰. **Thanks be to God.** ↓

ALLELUIA Lk 2:10-11   [Great Joy]

R̰. **Alleluia, alleluia.**
I proclaim to you good news of great joy:

today a Savior is born for us,
Christ the Lord.
℞. **Alleluia, alleluia.** ↓

GOSPEL Lk 2:1-14   [Birth of Christ]

Caesar Augustus desired a world census. Joseph and Mary
go to Bethlehem where Jesus, the Lord of the universe, is
born in a stable. Glory to God and peace on earth!

℣. The Lord be with you. ℞. **And with your spirit.**
✚ A reading from the holy Gospel according to Luke.
℞. **Glory to you, O Lord.**

IN those days a decree went out from Caesar
Augustus that the whole world should be enrolled.
This was the first enrollment, when Quirinius was gov-
ernor of Syria. So all went to be enrolled, each to his
own town. And Joseph too went up from Galilee from
the town of Nazareth to Judea, to the city of David that
is called Bethlehem, because he was of the house and
family of David, to be enrolled with Mary, his
betrothed, who was with child. While they were there,
the time came for her to have her child, and she gave
birth to her firstborn son. She wrapped him in swaddling clothes and laid him in a manger, because there
was no room for them in the inn.

Now there were shepherds in that region living in
the fields and keeping the night watch over their flock.
The angel of the Lord appeared to them and the glory
of the Lord shone around them, and they were struck
with great fear. The angel said to them, "Do not be
afraid; for behold, I proclaim to you good news of
great joy that will be for all the people. For today in the
city of David a savior has been born for you who is
Christ and Lord. And this will be a sign for you: you
will find an infant wrapped in swaddling clothes and
lying in a manger." And suddenly there was a multi-

tude of the heavenly host with the angel, praising God
and saying:

"Glory to God in the highest
   and on earth peace to those on whom his favor
   rests."

The Gospel of the Lord. ℟. **Praise to you, Lord Jesus
Christ.**
→ No. 15, p. 18

The Creed is said. All kneel at the words and by the Holy
Spirit was incarnate.

PRAYER OVER THE OFFERINGS   [Become Like Christ]

May the oblation of this day's feast
be pleasing to you, O Lord, we pray,
that through this most holy exchange
we may be found in the likeness of Christ,
in whom our nature is united to you.
Who lives and reigns for ever and ever.

℟. **Amen.**
→ No. 21, p. 22 (Pref. P 3-5)

When the Roman Canon is used, the proper form of the
Communicantes *(In communion with those) is said.*

COMMUNION ANT. Jn 1:14   [Glory of Christ]

The Word became flesh, and we have seen his glory. ↓

PRAYER AFTER COMMUNION   [Union with Christ]

Grant us, we pray, O Lord our God,
that we, who are gladdened by participation
in the feast of our Redeemer's Nativity,
may through an honorable way of life become worthy of
   union with him.
Who lives and reigns for ever and ever.

℟. **Amen.**
→ No. 30, p. 77

Optional Solemn Blessings, p. 97, and Prayers over the People, p. 105

AT THE MASS AT DAWN

ENTRANCE ANT. Cf. Is 9:1, 5; Lk 1:33   [Prince of Peace]

Today a light will shine upon us, for the Lord is born for us; and he will be called Wondrous God, Prince of peace, Father of future ages: and his reign will be without end. → No. 2, p. 10

COLLECT   [Light of Faith]

Grant, we pray, almighty God,
that, as we are bathed in the new radiance of your
    incarnate Word,
the light of faith, which illumines our minds,
may also shine through in our deeds.
Through our Lord Jesus Christ, your Son,
who lives and reigns with you in the unity of the Holy
    Spirit,
one God, for ever and ever.
℟. **Amen.** ↓

FIRST READING Is 62:11-12   [The Savior's Birth]

Isaiah foretells the birth of the Savior who will come to
Zion. These people will be called holy and they shall be
redeemed.

A reading from the Book of the Prophet Isaiah

SEE, the LORD proclaims
   to the ends of the earth:
say to daughter Zion,
      your savior comes!
Here is his reward with him,
      his recompense before him.
They shall be called the holy people,
      the redeemed of the LORD,
and you shall be called "Frequented,"
      a city that is not forsaken.
The word of the Lord. ℟. **Thanks be to God.** ↓

RESPONSORIAL PSALM Ps 97   [Be Glad in the Lord]

℟. A light will shine on us this day: the Lord is born for us.

The LORD is king; let the earth rejoice;
  let the many isles be glad.
The heavens proclaim his justice,
  and all peoples see his glory.—℟.

Light dawns for the just;
  and gladness, for the upright of heart.
Be glad in the LORD, you just,
  and give thanks to his holy name.—℟. ↓

SECOND READING Ti 3:4-7   [Saved by God's Mercy]

Christians are saved not because of their own merits but because of the mercy of God. We are saved through baptism and renewal in the Holy Spirit.

A reading from the Letter of Saint Paul to Titus

BELOVED:
  When the kindness and generous love
    of God our savior appeared,
  not because of any righteous deeds we had done
    but because of his mercy,
  he saved us through the bath of rebirth
    and renewal by the Holy Spirit,
  whom he richly poured out on us
    through Jesus Christ our savior,
  so that we might be justified by his grace
    and become heirs in hope of eternal life.
The word of the Lord. ℟. **Thanks be to God.** ↓

ALLELUIA Lk 2:14   [Glory to God]

℟. **Alleluia, alleluia.**
Glory to God in the highest,

and on earth peace to those
on whom his favor rests.
℟. **Alleluia, alleluia.** ↓

GOSPEL Lk 2:15-20   [Jesus, the God-Man]

> The shepherds, the poor of the people of God, come to pay
> homage to Jesus. Mary ponders and prays over the great
> event of God becoming one of us.

℣. The Lord be with you. ℟. **And with your spirit.**

✠ A reading from the holy Gospel according to Luke.

℟. **Glory to you, O Lord.**

W HEN the angels went away from them to heaven,
the shepherds said to one another, "Let us go,
then, to Bethlehem to see this thing that has taken
place, which the Lord has made known to us." So they
went in haste and found Mary and Joseph, and the
infant lying in the manger. When they saw this, they
made known the message that had been told them
about this child. All who heard it were amazed by what
had been told them by the shepherds. And Mary kept
all these things, reflecting on them in her heart. Then
the shepherds returned, glorifying and praising God
for all they had heard and seen, just as it had been told
to them.—The Gospel of the Lord. ℟. **Praise to you,
Lord Jesus Christ.**   → No. 15, p. 18

The Creed is said. All kneel at the words and by the Holy
Spirit was incarnate.

PRAYER OVER THE OFFERINGS   [Gift of Divine Life]

May our offerings be worthy, we pray, O Lord,
of the mysteries of the Nativity this day,
that, just as Christ was born a man and also shone forth
    as God,
so these earthly gifts may confer on us what is divine.
Through Christ our Lord.
℟. **Amen.**   → No. 21, p. 22 (Pref. P 3-5)

When the Roman Canon is used, the proper form of the Communicantes *(In communion with those) is said.*

COMMUNION ANT. Cf. Zec 9:9   [The Holy One]

Rejoice, O Daughter Sion; lift up praise, Daughter Jerusalem: Behold, your King will come, the Holy One and Savior of the world. ↓

PRAYER AFTER COMMUNION   [Fullness of Faith]

Grant us, Lord, as we honor with joyful devotion
the Nativity of your Son,
that we may come to know with fullness of faith
the hidden depths of this mystery
and to love them ever more and more.
Through Christ our Lord.
℟. **Amen.**   → No. 30, p. 77

Optional Solemn Blessings, p. 97, and Prayers over the People, p. 105

AT THE MASS DURING THE DAY

ENTRANCE ANT. Cf. Is 9:5   [The Gift of God's Son]

A child is born for us, and a son is given to us; his scepter of power rests upon his shoulder, and his name will be called Messenger of great counsel.

→ No. 2, p. 10

COLLECT   [Share in Christ's Divinity]

O God, who wonderfully created the dignity of human
   nature
and still more wonderfully restored it,
grant, we pray,
that we may share in the divinity of Christ,
who humbled himself to share in our humanity.
Who lives and reigns with you in the unity of the Holy
   Spirit,
one God, for ever and ever. ℟. **Amen.** ↓

FIRST READING Is 52:7-10   [Your God Is King]

God shows salvation to all people. He brings peace and good news. He comforts his people and redeems them.

A reading from the Book of the Prophet Isaiah

HOW beautiful upon the mountains
    are the feet of him who brings glad tidings,
announcing peace, bearing good news,
    announcing salvation, and saying to Zion,
    "Your God is King!"

Hark! Your sentinels raise a cry,
    together they shout for joy,
for they see directly, before their eyes,
    the LORD restoring Zion.

Break out together in song,
    O ruins of Jerusalem!
For the LORD comforts his people,
    he redeems Jerusalem.

The LORD has bared his holy arm
    in the sight of all the nations;
all the ends of the earth will behold
    the salvation of our God.

The word of the Lord. ℟. **Thanks be to God.** ↓

RESPONSORIAL PSALM Ps 98   [Sing a New Song]

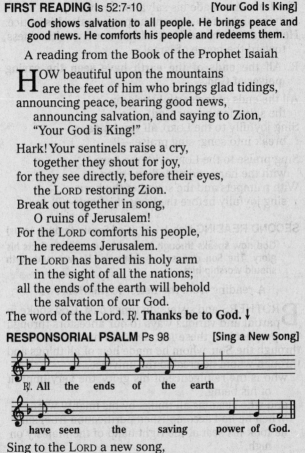

℟. All the ends of the earth have seen the saving power of God.

Sing to the LORD a new song,
    for he has done wondrous deeds;
his right hand has won victory for him,
    his holy arm.—℟.

The LORD has made his salvation known:
in the sight of the nations he has revealed his justice.
He has remembered his kindness and his faithfulness
toward the house of Israel.

℟. **All the ends of the earth have seen the saving power of God.**

All the ends of the earth have seen
the salvation by our God.
Sing joyfully to the LORD, all you lands;
break into song; sing praise.—℟.

Sing praise to the LORD with the harp,
with the harp and melodious song.
With trumpets and the sound of the horn
sing joyfully before the King, the LORD.—℟. ↓

SECOND READING Heb 1:1-6   [God Speaks through Jesus]

God now speaks through Jesus, his Son, who reflects his glory. The Son cleanses us from sin. Heaven and earth should worship him.

A reading from the Letter to the Hebrews

BROTHERS and sisters: In times past, God spoke in partial and various ways to our ancestors through the prophets; in these last days, he has spoken to us through the Son, whom he made heir of all things and through whom he created the universe,
who is the refulgence of his glory, the very imprint of his being,
and who sustains all things by his mighty word.
When he had accomplished purification from sins,
he took his seat at the right hand of the Majesty on high,
as far superior to the angels
as the name he has inherited is more excellent than theirs.

For to which of the angels did God ever say:

You are my son; this day I have begotten you?

Or again:

I will be a father to him, and he shall be a son to me?

And again, when he leads the firstborn into the world, he says:

Let all the angels of God worship him.

The word of the Lord. ℟. **Thanks be to God.** ↓

ALLELUIA   [Adore the Lord]

℟. **Alleluia, alleluia.**

A holy day has dawned upon us.

Come, you nations, and adore the Lord.

For today a great light has come upon the earth.

℟. **Alleluia, alleluia.** ↓

GOSPEL Jn 1:1-18 or 1:1-5, 9-14   [The True Light]

John's opening words parallel the Book of Genesis. Jesus is the Word made flesh, the light of the world, who always was and will ever be.

[If the "Shorter Form" is used, the indented text in brackets is omitted.]

℣. The Lord be with you. ℟. **And with your spirit.**

✛ A reading from the holy Gospel according to John.

℟. **Glory to you, O Lord.**

IN the beginning was the Word,
and the Word was with God,
    and the Word was God.

He was in the beginning with God.

All things came to be through him,
    and without him nothing came to be.

What came to be through him was life,
    and this life was the light of the human race;

the light shines in the darkness,
    and the darkness has not overcome it.

[A man named John was sent from God. He came for testimony, to testify to the light, so that all might believe through him. He was not the light, but came to testify to the light.]

The true light, which enlightens everyone, was coming into the world.

He was in the world,
    and the world came to be through him,
    but the world did not know him.
He came to what was his own,
    but his own people did not accept him.

But to those who did accept him he gave power to become children of God, to those who believe in his name, who were born not by natural generation nor by human choice nor by a man's decision but of God.

And the Word became flesh
    and made his dwelling among us,
    and we saw his glory,
    the glory as of the Father's only Son,
    full of grace and truth.

[John testified to him and cried out, saying, "This was he of whom I said, 'The one who is coming after me ranks ahead of me because he existed before me.'" From his fullness we have all received, grace in place of grace, because while the law was given through Moses, grace and truth came through Jesus Christ. No one has ever seen God. The only Son, God, who is at the Father's side, has revealed him.]

The Gospel of the Lord. ℟. **Praise to you, Lord Jesus Christ.**   → No. 15, p. 18

The Creed is said. All kneel at the words and by the Holy Spirit was incarnate.

PRAYER OVER THE OFFERINGS   [Reconciliation]

Make acceptable, O Lord, our oblation on this solemn
    day,
when you manifested the reconciliation
that makes us wholly pleasing in your sight
and inaugurated for us the fullness of divine worship.
Through Christ our Lord.
℟. **Amen.**   → No. 21, p. 22 (Pref. P 3-5)

When the Roman Canon is used, the proper form of the
Communicantes *(In communion with those) is said.*

COMMUNION ANT. Cf. Ps 98 (97):3   [God's Power]

**All the ends of the earth have seen the salvation of our
God.** ↓

PRAYER AFTER COMMUNION   [Giver of Immortality]

Grant, O merciful God,
that, just as the Savior of the world, born this day,
is the author of divine generation for us,
so he may be the giver even of immortality.
Who lives and reigns for ever and ever.
℟. **Amen.**   → No. 30, p. 77

Optional Solemn Blessings, p. 97, and Prayers over the People, p. 105

Simeon said, "This child is destined for the fall and rise of many in Israel."

DECEMBER 27

THE HOLY FAMILY OF JESUS, MARY AND JOSEPH

Feast

ENTRANCE ANT. Lk 2:16 [Jesus, Mary, and Joseph]
The shepherds went in haste, and found Mary and Joseph and the Infant lying in a manger.

→ No. 2, p. 10

COLLECT [Shining Example]

O God, who were pleased to give us
the shining example of the Holy Family,
graciously grant that we may imitate them
in practicing the virtues of family life and in the bonds
   of charity,
and so, in the joy of your house,
delight one day in eternal rewards.
Through our Lord Jesus Christ, your Son,
who lives and reigns with you in the unity of the Holy
   Spirit,
one God, for ever and ever. ℟. **Amen.** ↓

The following readings (except the Gospel) are optional. In their place, the readings for Year A, pp. 156-158, may be used.

FIRST READING Gn 15:1-6; 21:1-3   [Abraham's Faith]

Abraham believed in God. As a result, God gave him and his wife a son in their old age. The family thus becomes the sign of the faith of human beings and of the love of God.

A reading from the Book of Genesis

THE word of the LORD came to Abram in a vision, saying: "Fear not, Abram! I am your shield; I will make your reward very great." But Abram said, "O Lord GOD, what good will your gifts be, if I keep on being childless and have as my heir the steward of my house, Eliezer?" Abram continued, "See, you have given me no offspring, and so one of my servants will be my heir." Then the word of the LORD came to him: "No, that one shall not be your heir; your own issue shall be your heir." The Lord took Abram outside and said, "Look up at the sky and count the stars, if you can. Just so," he added, "shall your descendants be." Abram put his faith in the LORD, who credited it to him as an act of righteousness.

The LORD took note of Sarah as he had said he would; he did for her as he had promised. Sarah became pregnant and bore Abraham a son in his old age, at the set time that God had stated. Abraham gave the name Isaac to this son of his whom Sarah bore him.—The word of the Lord. ℟. **Thanks be to God.** ↓

RESPONSORIAL PSALM Ps 105   [God's Covenant]

℟. The Lord re-mem-bers his cov-e-nant for ev-er.

Give thanks to the LORD, invoke his name;
  make known among the nations his deeds.
Sing to him, sing his praise,
  proclaim all his wondrous deeds.

℟. **The Lord remembers his covenant for ever.**

Glory in his holy name;
  rejoice, O hearts that seek the LORD!
Look to the LORD in his strength;
  constantly seek his face.—℟.

You descendants of Abraham, his servants,
  sons of Jacob, his chosen ones!
He, the LORD, is our God;
  throughout the earth his judgments prevail.—℟.

He remembers forever his covenant
  which he made binding for a thousand generations
which he entered into with Abraham
  and by his oath to Isaac.—℟. ↓

SECOND READING Heb 11:8, 11-12, 17-19   [Trust God]

Abraham believed God's promises and put his faith in him, living that faith in every phase of his life. And since God is faithful to his promises, faith becomes the source of hope and happiness for his family. We should place our trust in God's promises.

A reading from the Letter to the Hebrews

BROTHERS and sisters: By faith Abraham obeyed when he was called to go out to a place that he was to receive as an inheritance; he went out, not knowing where he was to go. By faith he received power to generate, even though he was past the normal age—and Sarah herself was sterile—for he thought that the one who had made the promise was trustworthy. So it was that there came forth from one man, himself as good as dead, descendants as numerous as the stars in the sky and as countless as the sands on the seashore.

By faith Abraham, when put to the test, offered up Isaac, and he who had received the promises was ready to offer his only son, of whom it was said, "Through Isaac descendants shall bear your name." He reasoned that God was able to raise even from the dead, and he received Isaac back as a symbol.—The word of the Lord. ℟. **Thanks be to God.** ↓

ALLELUIA Heb 1:1-2   [God Speaks]

℟. **Alleluia, alleluia.**

In the past God spoke to our ancestors through the prophets;

in these last days, he has spoken to us through the Son.

℟. **Alleluia, alleluia.** ↓

GOSPEL Lk 2:22-40 or 2:22, 39-40   [God's Anointed One]

Joseph and Mary take Jesus to the temple in Jerusalem to be presented to the Lord. Simeon recognizes him as the Anointed of the Lord and blesses him. The child returns to Nazareth and grows to maturity.

[If the "Shorter Form" is used, the indented text in brackets is omitted.]

℣. The Lord be with you. ℟. **And with your spirit.**

✠ A reading from the holy Gospel according to Luke.

℟. **Glory to you, O Lord.**

WHEN the days were completed for their purification according to the law of Moses, they took him up to Jerusalem to present him to the Lord, [just as it is written in the law of the Lord, *Every male that opens the womb shall be consecrated to the Lord*, and to offer the sacrifice of *a pair of turtledoves or two young pigeons*, in accordance with the dictate in the law of the Lord.

Now there was a man in Jerusalem whose name was Simeon. This man was righteous and devout, awaiting the consolation of Israel, and the Holy Spirit was upon him. It had been revealed to him by the Holy Spirit that he should not see death before he had seen the Christ of the Lord. He came in the Spirit into the temple; and when the parents brought in the child Jesus to perform the custom of the law in regard to him, he took him into his arms and blessed God, saying:

"Now, Master, you may let your servant go
    in peace, according to your word,
for my eyes have seen your salvation,
    which you prepared in sight of all the
    peoples,
a light for revelation to the Gentiles,
    and glory for your people Israel."

The child's father and mother were amazed at what was said about him; and Simeon blessed them and said to Mary his mother, "Behold, this child is destined for the fall and rise of many in Israel, and to be a sign that will be contradicted—and you yourself a sword will pierce—so that the thoughts of many hearts may be revealed." There was also a prophetess, Anna, the daughter of Phanuel, of the tribe of Asher. She was advanced in years, having lived seven years with her husband after her marriage, and then as a widow until she was eighty-four. She never left the temple, but worshiped night and day with fasting and prayer. And coming forward at that very time, she gave thanks to God and spoke about the child to all who were awaiting the redemption of Jerusalem.]

When they had fulfilled all the prescriptions of the law of the Lord, they returned to Galilee, to their own town of Nazareth. The child grew and became strong, filled with wisdom; and the favor of God was

upon him.—The Gospel of the Lord. ℟. **Praise to you,
Lord Jesus Christ.**   → No. 15, p. 18

When this Feast is celebrated on Sunday, the Creed is said.

PRAYER OVER THE OFFERINGS   [Grace and Peace]

We offer you, Lord, the sacrifice of conciliation,
humbly asking that,
through the intercession of the Virgin Mother of God
  and Saint Joseph,
you may establish our families firmly in your grace
  and your peace.
Through Christ our Lord.
℟. **Amen.**   → No. 21, p. 22 (Pref. P 3-5)

When the Roman Canon is used, the proper form of the
Communicantes (In communion with those) *is said.*

COMMUNION ANT. Bar 3:38   [God with Us]
**Our God has appeared on the earth, and lived among
us.** ↓

PRAYER AFTER COMMUNION   [Imitate Their Example]

Bring those you refresh with this heavenly Sacrament,
most merciful Father,
to imitate constantly the example of the Holy Family,
so that, after the trials of this world,
we may share their company for ever.
Through Christ our Lord.
℟. **Amen.**   → No. 30, p. 77

Optional Solemn Blessings, p. 97, and Prayers over the People, p. 105

The following readings from Year A may be used in place of the optional ones given on pp. 151-153.

FIRST READING Sir 3:2-6, 12-14   [Duties toward Parents]

Fidelity to God implies many particular virtues, and among them Sirach gives precedence to duties toward parents. He promises atonement for sin to those who honor their parents.

A reading from the Book of Sirach

GOD sets a father in honor over his children;
a mother's authority he confirms over her sons.
Whoever honors his father atones for sins,
    and preserves himself from them.
When he prays, he is heard;
    he stores up riches who reveres his mother.
Whoever honors his father is gladdened by children,
    and when he prays, is heard.
Whoever reveres his father will live a long life;
    he obeys his father who brings comfort to his mother.

My son, take care of your father when he is old;
    grieve him not as long as he lives.
Even if his mind fail, be considerate of him;
    revile him not all the days of his life;
kindness to a father will not be forgotten,
    firmly planted against the debt of your sins
    —a house raised in justice to you.

The word of the Lord. ℟. **Thanks be to God.** ↓

RESPONSORIAL PSALM Ps 128   [Happiness in Families]

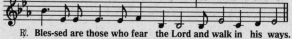

℟. Bles-sed are those who fear the Lord and walk in his ways.

Blessed is everyone who fears the LORD,
    who walks in his ways!

For you shall eat the fruit of your handiwork;
    blessed shall you be, and favored.—R̸.

Your wife shall be like a fruitful vine
    in the recesses of your home;
your children like olive plants
    around your table.—R̸.

Behold, thus is the man blessed
    who fears the LORD.
The LORD bless you from Zion:
    may you see the prosperity of Jerusalem
    all the days of your life.—R̸. ↓

SECOND READING Col 3:12-21 or 3:12-17

[Plan for Family Life]

Paul describes the life a Christian embraces through baptism.

[If the "Shorter Form" is used, the indented text in brackets is omitted.]

A reading from the Letter of Saint Paul to the Colossians

BROTHERS and sisters: Put on, as God's chosen ones, holy and beloved, heartfelt compassion, kindness, humility, gentleness, and patience, bearing with one another and forgiving one another, if one has a grievance against another; as the Lord has forgiven you, so must you also do. And over all these put on love, that is, the bond of perfection. And let the peace of Christ control your hearts, the peace into which you were also called in one body. And be thankful. Let the word of Christ dwell in you richly, as in all wisdom you teach and admonish one another, singing psalms, hymns, and spiritual songs with gratitude in your hearts to God. And whatever you do, in word or in deed, do everything in the name of the Lord Jesus, giving thanks to God the Father through him.

[Wives, be subordinate to your husbands, as is proper in the Lord. Husbands, love your wives, and avoid any bitterness toward them. Children, obey your parents in everything, for this is pleasing to the Lord. Fathers, do not provoke your children, so they may not become discouraged.]

The word of the Lord. ℟. **Thanks be to God.** ↓

ALLELUIA Col 3:15a, 16a   [Peace of Christ]

℟. **Alleluia, alleluia.**
Let the peace of Christ control your hearts;
let the word of Christ dwell in you richly.
℟. **Alleluia, alleluia.**

"He was named Jesus . . ."

JANUARY 1, 2021

SOLEMNITY OF MARY, THE HOLY MOTHER OF GOD

ENTRANCE ANT.   [Hail, Holy Mother]
Hail, Holy Mother, who gave birth to the King who
rules heaven and earth for ever.   → No. 2, p. 10

OR Cf. Is 9:1, 5; Lk 1:33   [Wondrous God]

Today a light will shine upon us, for the Lord is born for us; and he will be called Wondrous God, Prince of peace, Father of future ages: and his reign will be without end.   → No. 2, p. 10

COLLECT   [Mary's Intercession]

O God, who through the fruitful virginity of Blessed
    Mary
bestowed on the human race
the grace of eternal salvation,
grant, we pray,
that we may experience the intercession of her,
through whom we were found worthy
to receive the author of life,
our Lord Jesus Christ, your Son.
Who lives and reigns with you in the unity of the Holy
    Spirit,
one God, for ever and ever. ℟. **Amen.** ↓

FIRST READING Nm 6:22-27   [The Aaronic Blessing]

   **God speaks to Moses instructing him to have Aaron and
   the Israelites pray that he may answer their prayers with
   blessings.**

          A reading from the Book of Numbers

THE LORD said to Moses: "Speak to Aaron and his
   sons and tell them: This is how you shall bless the
Israelites. Say to them:

   The LORD bless you and keep you!
   The LORD let his face shine upon you, and be gra-
      cious to you!
   The LORD look upon you kindly and give you peace!

So shall they invoke my name upon the Israelites and
I will bless them."—The word of the Lord. ℟. **Thanks
be to God.** ↓

RESPONSORIAL PSALM Ps 67   [God Bless Us]

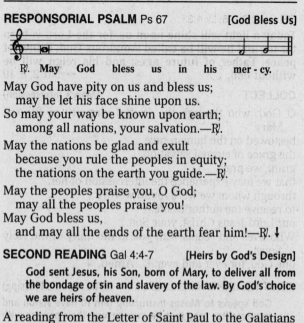

℟. **May God bless us in his mer - cy.**

May God have pity on us and bless us;
   may he let his face shine upon us.
So may your way be known upon earth;
   among all nations, your salvation.—℟.

May the nations be glad and exult
   because you rule the peoples in equity;
   the nations on the earth you guide.—℟.

May the peoples praise you, O God;
   may all the peoples praise you!
May God bless us,
   and may all the ends of the earth fear him!—℟. ↓

SECOND READING Gal 4:4-7   [Heirs by God's Design]

**God sent Jesus, his Son, born of Mary, to deliver all from
the bondage of sin and slavery of the law. By God's choice
we are heirs of heaven.**

A reading from the Letter of Saint Paul to the Galatians

BROTHERS and sisters: When the fullness of time
had come, God sent his Son, born of a woman, born
under the law, to ransom those under the law, so that we
might receive adoption as sons. As proof that you are
sons, God sent the Spirit of his Son into our hearts, crying out, "Abba, Father!" So you are no longer a slave but
a son, and if a son then also an heir, through God.—The
word of the Lord. ℟. **Thanks be to God.** ↓

ALLELUIA Heb 1:1-2   [God Speaks]

℟. **Alleluia, alleluia.**
In the past God spoke to our ancestors through the
   prophets;

in these last days, he has spoken to us through the Son.
℟. **Alleluia, alleluia.** ↓

GOSPEL Lk 2:16-21   [The Name of Jesus]

When the shepherds came to Bethlehem, they began to
understand the message of the angels. Mary prayed about
this great event. Jesus received his name according to the
Jewish ritual of circumcision.

℣. The Lord be with you. ℟. **And with your spirit.**
✝ A reading from the holy Gospel according to Luke.
℟. **Glory to you, O Lord.**

THE shepherds went in haste to Bethlehem and found
Mary and Joseph, and the infant lying in the manger.
When they saw this, they made known the message that
had been told them about this child. All who heard it
were amazed by what had been told them by the shepherds. And Mary kept all these things, reflecting on them
in her heart. Then the shepherds returned, glorifying and
praising God for all they had heard and seen, just as it
had been told to them.

When eight days were completed for his circumcision,
he was named Jesus, the name given him by the angel
before he was conceived in the womb.—The Gospel of
the Lord. ℟. **Praise to you, Lord Jesus Christ.**

→ No. 15, p. 18

PRAYER OVER THE OFFERINGS   [Rejoice in Grace]

O God, who in your kindness begin all good things
and bring them to fulfillment,
grant to us, who find joy in the Solemnity of the holy
   Mother of God,
that, just as we glory in the beginnings of your grace,
so one day we may rejoice in its completion.
Through Christ our Lord.
℟. **Amen.** ↓

PREFACE (P 56)   [Mary, Virgin and Mother]

℣. The Lord be with you. ℟. **And with your spirit.**

℣. Lift up your hearts. ℟. **We lift them up to the Lord.**

℣. Let us give thanks to the Lord our God. ℟. **It is right and just.**

It is truly right and just, our duty and our salvation,
always and everywhere to give you thanks,
Lord, holy Father, almighty and eternal God,
and to praise, bless, and glorify your name
on the Solemnity of the Motherhood
of the Blessed ever-Virgin Mary.

For by the overshadowing of the Holy Spirit
she conceived your Only Begotten Son,
and without losing the glory of virginity,
brought forth into the world the eternal Light,
Jesus Christ our Lord.

Through him the Angels praise your majesty,
Dominions adore and Powers tremble before you.
Heaven and the Virtues of heaven and the blessed
   Seraphim
worship together with exultation.
May our voices, we pray, join with theirs
in humble praise, as we acclaim: → No. 23, p. 23

When the Roman Canon is used, the proper form of the
Communicantes *(In communion with those) is said.*

COMMUNION ANT. Heb 13:8   [Jesus Forever]

Jesus Christ is the same yesterday, today, and for ever. ↓

PRAYER AFTER COMMUNION   [Mother of the Church]

We have received this heavenly Sacrament with joy,
   O Lord:
grant, we pray,
that it may lead us to eternal life,
for we rejoice to proclaim the blessed ever-Virgin Mary

Mother of your Son and Mother of the Church.
Through Christ our Lord.
R̹. **Amen.**   → No. 30, p. 77

Optional Solemn Blessings, p. 97, and Prayers over the People, p. 105

"They prostrated themselves and did him homage."

JANUARY 3

THE EPIPHANY OF THE LORD
AT THE VIGIL MASS (January 2)
Solemnity

ENTRANCE ANT. Cf. Bar 5:5   [Arise, Jerusalem]
**Arise, Jerusalem, and look to the East and see your
children gathered from the rising to the setting of the
sun.**   → No. 2, p. 10

COLLECT   [Splendor of God's Majesty]
May the splendor of your majesty, O Lord, we pray,
shed its light upon our hearts,
that we may pass through the shadows of this world
and reach the brightness of our eternal home.
Through our Lord Jesus Christ, your Son,

who lives and reigns with you in the unity of the Holy
   Spirit,
one God, for ever and ever.
℟. **Amen.** ↓

FIRST READING Is 60:1-6   [Glory of God's Church]

**Jerusalem is favored by the Lord. Kings and peoples will
come before you. The riches of the earth will be placed at
the gates of Jerusalem.**

A reading from the Book of the Prophet Isaiah

RISE up in splendor, Jerusalem! Your light has
   come,
   the glory of the Lord shines upon you.
See, darkness covers the earth,
   and thick clouds cover the peoples;
but upon you the LORD shines,
   and over you appears his glory.
Nations shall walk by your light,
   and kings by your shining radiance.
Raise your eyes and look about;
   they all gather and come to you:
your sons come from afar,
   and your daughters in the arms of their nurses.

Then you shall be radiant at what you see,
   your heart shall throb and overflow,
for the riches of the sea shall be emptied out before
      you,
   the wealth of nations shall be brought to you.
Caravans of camels shall fill you,
   dromedaries from Midian and Ephah;
all from Sheba shall come
   bearing gold and frankincense,
      and proclaiming the praises of the LORD.
The word of the Lord. ℟. **Thanks be to God.** ↓

RESPONSORIAL PSALM Ps 72   [The Messiah-King]

℞. Lord, every nation on earth will adore you.

O God, with your judgment endow the king,
    and with your justice, the king's son;
he shall govern your people with justice
    and your afflicted ones with judgment.—℞.

Justice shall flower in his days,
    and profound peace, till the moon be no more.
May he rule from sea to sea,
    and from the River to the ends of the earth.—℞.

The kings of Tarshish and the Isles shall offer gifts;
    the kings of Arabia and Seba shall bring tribute.
All kings shall pay him homage,
    all nations shall serve him.—℞.

For he shall rescue the poor man when he cries out,
    and the afflicted when he has no one to help him.
He shall have pity for the lowly and the poor;
    the lives of the poor he shall save.—℞. ↓

SECOND READING Eph 3:2-3a, 5-6   [Good News for All]

Paul admits that God has revealed the divine plan of salvation to him. Not only the Jews, but also the whole Gentile world, will share in the Good News.

A reading from the Letter of Saint Paul to the Ephesians

BROTHERS and sisters: You have heard of the stewardship of God's grace that was given to me for your benefit, namely, that the mystery was made known to me by revelation. It was not made known to people in other generations as it has now been revealed to his holy apostles and prophets by the Spirit: that the Gentiles are coheirs, members of the same body, and copartners in the promise in Christ Jesus through the gospel.—The word of the Lord. ℟. **Thanks be to God.** ↓

ALLELUIA Mt 2:2   [Leading Star]

℟. **Alleluia, alleluia.**
We saw his star at its rising
and have come to do him homage.
℟. **Alleluia, alleluia.** ↓

GOSPEL Mt 2:1-12   [Magi with Gifts]

King Herod, being jealous of his earthly crown, was threatened by the coming of another king. The astrologers from the east followed the star to Bethlehem from which a ruler was to come.

℣. The Lord be with you. ℟. **And with your spirit.**
✠ A reading from the holy Gospel according to Matthew. ℟. **Glory to you, O Lord.**

WHEN Jesus was born in Bethlehem of Judea, in the days of King Herod, behold, magi from the east arrived in Jerusalem, saying, "Where is the newborn king of the Jews? We saw his star at its rising and have come to do him homage." When King Herod heard this, he was greatly troubled, and all Jerusalem with him. Assembling all the chief priests and the scribes of the people, he inquired of them where the Christ was to be born. They said to him, "In Bethlehem of Judea, for thus it has been written through the prophet:

And you, Bethlehem, land of Judah,
*   are by no means least among the rulers of Judah;*
since from you shall come a ruler,
*   who is to shepherd my people Israel."*

Then Herod called the magi secretly and ascertained from them the time of the star's appearance. He sent them to Bethlehem and said, "Go and search diligently for the child. When you have found him, bring me word, that I too may go and do him homage." After their audience with the king they set out. And behold, the star that they had seen at its rising preceded them, until it came and stopped over the place where the child was. They were overjoyed at seeing the star, and on entering the house they saw the child with Mary his mother. They prostrated themselves and did him homage. Then they opened their treasures and offered him gifts of gold, frankincense, and myrrh. And having been warned in a dream not to return to Herod, they departed for their country by another way.—The Gospel of the Lord. ℟. **Praise to you, Lord Jesus Christ.**   ➜ No. 15, p. 18

PRAYER OVER THE OFFERINGS   [Render Praise]

Accept we pray, O Lord, our offerings,
in honor of the appearing of your Only Begotten Son
and the first fruits of the nations,
that to you praise may be rendered
and eternal salvation be ours.
Through Christ our Lord. ℟. **Amen.** ↓

PREFACE (P 6)   [Jesus Revealed to All]

℣. The Lord be with you. ℟. **And with your spirit.**
℣. Lift up your hearts. ℟. **We lift them up to the Lord.**
℣. Let us give thanks to the Lord our God. ℟. **It is right and just.**

It is truly right and just, our duty and our salvation,
always and everywhere to give you thanks,
Lord, holy Father, almighty and eternal God.

For today you have revealed the mystery
of our salvation in Christ
as a light for the nations,

and, when he appeared in our mortal nature,
you made us new by the glory of his immortal nature.

And so, with Angels and Archangels,
with Thrones and Dominions,
and with all the hosts and Powers of heaven,
we sing the hymn of your glory,
as without end we acclaim: ➔ No. 23, p. 23

COMMUNION ANT. Cf. Rev 21:23   [Walking by God's Light]
**The brightness of God illumined the holy city Jeru-
salem, and the nations will walk by its light.** ↓

PRAYER AFTER COMMUNION   [True Treasure]

Renewed by sacred nourishment,
we implore your mercy, O Lord,
that the star of your justice
may shine always bright in our minds
and that our true treasure may ever consist in our
    confession of you.
Through Christ our Lord.
R̸. **Amen.**   ➔ No. 30, p. 77

Optional Solemn Blessings, p. 97, and Prayers over the People, p. 105

AT THE MASS DURING THE DAY

ENTRANCE ANT. Cf. Mal 3:1; 1 Chr 29:12 [Lord and Ruler]

Behold, the Lord, the Mighty One, has come; and king-ship is in his grasp, and power and dominion.

→ No. 2, p. 10

COLLECT [Behold Glory]

O God, who on this day
revealed your Only Begotten Son to the nations
by the guidance of a star,
grant in your mercy
that we, who know you already by faith,
may be brought to behold the beauty of your sublime
    glory.
Through our Lord Jesus Christ, your Son,
who lives and reigns with you in the unity of the Holy
    Spirit,
one God, for ever and ever.
℟. **Amen.** ↓

The readings for this Mass can be found beginning on p. 164.

PRAYER OVER THE OFFERINGS [Offering of Jesus]

Look with favor, Lord, we pray,
on these gifts of your Church,
in which are offered now not gold or frankincense or
    myrrh,
but he who by them is proclaimed,
sacrificed and received, Jesus Christ.
Who lives and reigns for ever and ever.
℟. **Amen.** → Pref. P 6, p. 167

When the Roman Canon is used, the proper form of the
Communicantes *(In communion with those) is said.*

COMMUNION ANT. Cf. Mt 2:2   [Adore the Lord]

We have seen his star in the East, and have come with gifts to adore the Lord. ↓

PRAYER AFTER COMMUNION   [Heavenly Light]

Go before us with heavenly light, O Lord,
always and everywhere,
that we may perceive with clear sight
and revere with true affection
the mystery in which you have willed us to participate.
Through Christ our Lord.
℟. **Amen.**

→ No. 30, p. 77

Optional Solemn Blessings, p. 97, and Prayers over the People, p. 105

"You are my beloved Son; with you I am well pleased."

JANUARY 10

THE BAPTISM OF THE LORD

Feast

ENTRANCE ANT. Cf. Mt 3:16-17   [Beloved Son]

After the Lord was baptized, the heavens were opened, and the Spirit descended upon him like a

dove, and the voice of the Father thundered: This is my
beloved Son, with whom I am well pleased.

→ No. 2, p. 10

COLLECT   [Children by Adoption]

Almighty ever-living God,
who, when Christ had been baptized in the River
    Jordan
and as the Holy Spirit descended upon him,
solemnly declared him your beloved Son,
grant that your children by adoption,
reborn of water and the Holy Spirit,
may always be well pleasing to you.
Through our Lord Jesus Christ, your Son,
who lives and reigns with you in the unity of the Holy
    Spirit,
one God, for ever and ever. ℟. **Amen.** ↓

OR   [God Became Man]

O God, whose Only Begotten Son
has appeared in our very flesh,
grant, we pray, that we may be inwardly transformed
through him whom we recognize as outwardly like
    ourselves.
Who lives and reigns with you in the unity of the Holy
    Spirit,
one God, for ever and ever.
  ℟. **Amen.** ↓

The following readings (except the Gospel) are optional. In
their place, the readings for Year A, pp. 177-178, may be used.

FIRST READING Is 55:1-11   [Called through Baptism]
    The "water" stands for Baptism but also for the word of
    God. Both will give us strength to keep moving, especial-
    ly if we make use of daily Bible readings.

    A reading from the Book of the Prophet Isaiah

THUS says the Lord:
  All you who are thirsty,
    come to the water!
You who have no money,
    come, receive grain and eat;
come, without paying and without cost,
    drink wine and milk!
Why spend your money for what is not bread,
    your wages for what fails to satisfy?
Heed me, and you shall eat well,
    you shall delight in rich fare.
Come to me heedfully,
    listen, that you may have life.
I will renew with you the everlasting covenant,
    the benefits assured to David.
As I made him a witness to the peoples,
    a leader and commander of nations,
so shall you summon a nation you knew not,
    and nations that knew you not shall run to you,
because of the Lord, your God,
    the Holy One of Israel, who has glorified you.

Seek the Lord while he may be found,
    call him while he is near.
Let the scoundrel forsake his way,
    and the wicked man his thoughts;
let him turn to the Lord for mercy;
    to our God, who is generous in forgiving.
For my thoughts are not your thoughts,
    nor are your ways my ways, says the Lord.
As high as the heavens are above the earth
    so high are my ways above your ways
    and my thoughts above your thoughts.

For just as from the heavens
    the rain and snow come down

and do not return there
    till they have watered the earth,
    making it fertile and fruitful,
giving seed to the one who sows
    and bread to the one who eats,
so shall my word be
    that goes forth from my mouth;
my word shall not return to me void,
    but shall do my will,
    achieving the end for which I sent it.
The word of the Lord. ℟. **Thanks be to God.** ↓

RESPONSORIAL PSALM Is 12   [Sing for Joy]

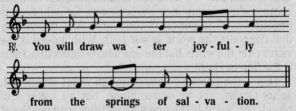

℟.   You will draw wa - ter   joy - ful - ly
     from   the   springs   of sal - va - tion.

God indeed is my savior;
    I am confident and unafraid.
My strength and my courage is the LORD,
    and he has been my savior.
With joy you will draw water
    at the fountain of salvation.—℟.

Give thanks to the LORD, acclaim his name;
    among the nations make known his deeds,
    proclaim how exalted is his name.—℟.

Sing praise to the LORD for his glorious achievement;
    let this be known throughout all the earth.
Shout with exultation, O city of Zion,
    for great in your midst
    is the Holy One of Israel!—℟. ↓

SECOND READING 1 Jn 5:1-9   [Born of God]

At baptism, we had the love of God placed in us as in a seed, and it bore fruit both vertically and horizontally toward God and neighbor. If we practice our faith by keeping the commandments, we end up victors over the world.

A reading from the first Letter of Saint John

BELOVED: Everyone who believes that Jesus is the Christ is begotten by God, and everyone who loves the Father loves also the one begotten by him. In this way we know that we love the children of God when we love God and obey his commandments. For the love of God is this, that we keep his commandments. And his commandments are not burdensome, for whoever is begotten by God conquers the world. And the victory that conquers the world is our faith. Who indeed is the victor over the world but the one who believes that Jesus is the Son of God?

This is the one who came through water and blood, Jesus Christ, not by water alone, but by water and blood. The Spirit is the one who testifies, and the Spirit is truth. So there are three that testify, the Spirit, the water, and the blood, and the three are of one accord. If we accept human testimony, the testimony of God is surely greater. Now the testimony of God is this, that he has testified on behalf of his Son.—The word of the Lord. ℟. **Thanks be to God.** ↓

ALLELUIA Cf. Jn 1:29   [The Lamb of God]

℟. **Alleluia, alleluia.**

John saw Jesus approaching him, and said:

Behold the Lamb of God who takes away the sin of the world.

℟. **Alleluia, alleluia.** ↓

GOSPEL Mk 1:7-11   [Beloved Son]

The Spirit of God is seen coming upon Christ. The words of Isaiah are beginning to be fulfilled.

℣. The Lord be with you. ℟. **And with your spirit.**

✛ A reading from the holy Gospel according to Mark.
℟. **Glory to you, O Lord.**

T HIS is what John the Baptist proclaimed: "One
   mightier than I is coming after me. I am not worthy
to stoop and loosen the thongs of his sandals. I have
baptized you with water; he will baptize you with the
Holy Spirit."

It happened in those days that Jesus came from
Nazareth of Galilee and was baptized in the Jordan by
John. On coming up out of the water he saw the
heavens being torn open and the Spirit, like a dove,
descending upon him. And a voice came from the
heavens, "You are my beloved Son; with you I am well
pleased."—The Gospel of the Lord. ℟. **Praise to you,
Lord Jesus Christ.**   → No. 15, p. 18

PRAYER OVER THE OFFERINGS   [Christ's Revelation]

Accept, O Lord, the offerings
we have brought to honor the revealing of your beloved
    Son,
so that the oblation of your faithful
may be transformed into the sacrifice of him
who willed in his compassion
to wash away the sins of the world.
Who lives and reigns for ever and ever. ℟. **Amen.** ↓

PREFACE (P 7)   [A New Baptism]

℣. The Lord be with you. ℟. **And with your spirit.**
℣. Lift up your hearts. ℟. **We lift them up to the
Lord.** ℣. Let us give thanks to the Lord our God. ℟. **It
is right and just.**

It is truly right and just, our duty and our salvation,
always and everywhere to give you thanks,
Lord, holy Father, almighty and eternal God.

For in the waters of the Jordan
you revealed with signs and wonders a new Baptism,
so that through the voice that came down from heaven
we might come to believe in your Word dwelling among
us,
and by the Spirit's descending in the likeness of a dove
we might know that Christ your Servant
has been anointed with the oil of gladness
and sent to bring the good news to the poor.

And so, with the Powers of heaven,
we worship you constantly on earth,
and before your majesty
without end we acclaim: → No. 23, p. 23

COMMUNION ANT. Jn 1:32, 34   [Witness to God's Son]

**Behold the One of whom John said: I have seen and
testified that this is the Son of God.** ↓

PRAYER AFTER COMMUNION   [Children in Truth]

Nourished with these sacred gifts,
we humbly entreat your mercy, O Lord,
that, faithfully listening to your Only Begotten Son,
we may be your children in name and in truth.
Through Christ our Lord.
℟. **Amen.**   → No. 30, p. 77

Optional Solemn Blessings, p. 97, and Prayers over the People, p. 105

———————

*The following readings from Year A may be used in place of
the optional ones given on pp. 171-174.*

FIRST READING Is 42:1-4, 6-7   [Works of the Messiah]

The prophet Isaiah sees the spirit upon the Lord's servant who will proclaim the "good news" to the poor, freedom to prisoners and joy to those in sorrow.

A reading from the Book of the Prophet Isaiah

THUS says the LORD:
Here is my servant whom I uphold,
    my chosen one with whom I am pleased,
upon whom I have put my spirit;
    he shall bring forth justice to the nations,
not crying out, not shouting,
    not making his voice heard in the street.
A bruised reed he shall not break,
    and a smoldering wick he shall not quench,
until he establishes justice on the earth;
    the coastlands will wait for his teaching.

I, the LORD, have called you for the victory of justice,
    I have grasped you by the hand;
I formed you, and set you
    as a covenant of the people,
    a light for the nations,
to open the eyes of the blind,
    to bring out prisoners from confinement,
    and from the dungeon, those who live in darkness.

The word of the Lord. ℟. **Thanks be to God.** ↓

RESPONSORIAL PSALM Ps 29   [Peace for God's People]

℟. The   Lord   will   bless   his   peo - ple with peace.

Give to the LORD, you sons of God,
    give to the LORD glory and praise,
give to the LORD the glory due his name;
    adore the LORD in holy attire.—℟.

The voice of the LORD is over the waters,
 the LORD, over vast waters.
The voice of the LORD is mighty;
 the voice of the LORD is majestic.

℟. **The Lord will bless his people with peace.**

The God of glory thunders,
 and in his temple all say, "Glory!"
The LORD is enthroned above the flood;
 the LORD is enthroned as king forever.—℟. ↓

SECOND READING Acts 10:34-38   [Anointed to Do Good]

God anointed Jesus the Savior with the Holy Spirit and power. Jesus is the Lord of all, and he brought healing to all who were in the grip of the devil.

A reading from the Acts of the Apostles

PETER proceeded to speak to those gathered in the house of Cornelius, saying: "In truth, I see that God shows no partiality. Rather, in every nation whoever fears him and acts uprightly is acceptable to him. You know the word that he sent to the Israelites as he proclaimed peace through Jesus Christ, who is Lord of all, what has happened all over Judea, beginning in Galilee after the baptism that John preached, how God anointed Jesus of Nazareth with the Holy Spirit and power. He went about doing good and healing all those oppressed by the devil, for God was with him."—The word of the Lord. ℟. **Thanks be to God.** ↓

ALLELUIA Cf. Mk 9:7   [Hear Him]

℟. **Alleluia, alleluia.**
The heavens were opened and the voice of the Father
 thundered:
This is my beloved Son, listen to him.
℟. **Alleluia, alleluia.**

"Behold, the Lamb of God."

JANUARY 17

2nd SUNDAY IN ORDINARY TIME

ENTRANCE ANT. Ps 66 (65):4   **[Proclaim His Glory]**

All the earth shall bow down before you, O God, and shall sing to you, shall sing to your name, O Most High!   → No. 2, p. 10

COLLECT   **[Peace on Our Times]**

Almighty ever-living God,
who govern all things,
both in heaven and on earth,
mercifully hear the pleading of your people
and bestow your peace on our times.
Through our Lord Jesus Christ, your Son,
who lives and reigns with you in the unity of the Holy
   Spirit,
one God, for ever and ever.
℟. **Amen.** ↓

FIRST READING 1 Sm 3:3b-10, 19   **[Answering God's Call]**
   The Lord called Samuel, but he did not recognize him.
   Samuel receives advice from Eli, who is already a prophet

for the Lord. Following instructions from Eli, Samuel listens to the Lord.

A reading from the first Book of Samuel

SAMUEL was sleeping in the temple of the LORD where the ark of God was. The LORD called to Samuel, who answered, "Here I am." Samuel ran to Eli and said, "Here I am. You called me." "I did not call you," Eli said. "Go back to sleep." So he went back to sleep. Again the LORD called Samuel, who rose and went to Eli. "Here I am," he said. "You called me." But Eli answered, "I did not call you, my son. Go back to sleep."

At that time Samuel was not familiar with the LORD, because the LORD had not revealed anything to him as yet. The LORD called Samuel again, for the third time. Getting up and going to Eli, he said, "Here I am. You called me." Then Eli understood that the LORD was calling the youth. So he said to Samuel, "Go to sleep, and if you are called, reply, 'Speak, LORD, for your servant is listening.'" When Samuel went to sleep in his place, the LORD came and revealed his presence, calling out as before, "Samuel, Samuel!" Samuel answered, "Speak, for your servant is listening."

Samuel grew up, and the LORD was with him, not permitting any word of his to be without effect.—The word of the Lord. ℟. **Thanks be to God.** ↓

RESPONSORIAL PSALM Ps 40   [Doing God's Will]

℟. Here am I, Lord; I come to do your will.

I have waited, waited for the LORD,
    and he stooped toward me and heard my cry.
And he put a new song into my mouth,
    a hymn to our God.—℟.

Sacrifice or offering you wished not,
 but ears open to obedience you gave me.
Holocausts or sin-offerings you sought not;
 then said I, "Behold I come."—℞.

"In the written scroll it is prescribed for me,
to do your will, O my God, is my delight,
 and your law is within my heart!"—℞.

I announced your justice in the vast assembly;
 I did not restrain my lips, as you, O LORD, know.
 —℞. ↓

SECOND READING 1 Cor 6:13c-15a, 17-20 [The Spirit in Us]

The body is made for the Lord. With the price of the Cross, Jesus redeemed all humanity. The Holy Spirit dwells within each person.

A reading from the first Letter of Saint Paul
to the Corinthians

BROTHERS and sisters: The body is not for immorality, but for the Lord, and the Lord is for the body;
God raised the Lord and will also raise us by his power.
 Do you not know that your bodies are members of
Christ? But whoever is joined to the Lord becomes one
Spirit with him. Avoid immorality. Every other sin a
person commits is outside the body, but the immoral
person sins against his own body. Do you not know
that your body is a temple of the Holy Spirit within
you, whom you have from God, and that you are not
your own? For you have been purchased at a price.
Therefore glorify God in your body.—The word of the
Lord. ℞. **Thanks be to God.** ↓

ALLELUIA Jn 1:41, 17b   [The Messiah]

℞. **Alleluia, alleluia.**
We have found the Messiah:
Jesus Christ, who brings us truth and grace.
℞. **Alleluia, alleluia.** ↓

In place of the Alleluia given for each Sunday in Ordinary Time, another may be selected.

GOSPEL Jn 1:35-42   [Encountering Christ]

It was John the Baptist's purpose to point out Jesus, the Messiah. Andrew and his companion followed Jesus. Andrew summons Peter. Jesus identifies Peter and gives him a new name.

℣. The Lord be with you. ℟. **And with your spirit.**
✚ A reading from the holy Gospel according to John.
℟. **Glory to you, O Lord.**

JOHN was standing with two of his disciples, and as he watched Jesus walk by, he said, "Behold, the Lamb of God." The two disciples heard what he said and followed Jesus. Jesus turned and saw them following him and said to them, "What are you looking for?" They said to him, "Rabbi"—which translated means Teacher—, "where are you staying?" He said to them, "Come, and you will see." So they went and saw where Jesus was staying, and they stayed with him that day. It was about four in the afternoon. Andrew, the brother of Simon Peter, was one of the two who heard John and followed Jesus. He first found his own brother Simon and told him, "We have found the Messiah"— which is translated Christ. Then he brought him to Jesus. Jesus looked at him and said, "You are Simon the son of John; you will be called Cephas"—which is translated Peter.—The Gospel of the Lord. ℟. **Praise to you, Lord Jesus Christ.**   → No. 15, p. 18

PRAYER OVER THE OFFERINGS   [Work of Redemption]

Grant us, O Lord, we pray,
that we may participate worthily in these mysteries,
for whenever the memorial of this sacrifice is celebrated
the work of our redemption is accomplished.
Through Christ our Lord.
℟. **Amen.**   → No. 21, p. 22 (Pref. P 29-36)

COMMUNION ANT. Cf. Ps 23 (22):5   [Thirst Quenched]

You have prepared a table before me, and how precious is the chalice that quenches my thirst. ↓

OR 1 Jn 4:16   [God's Love]

We have come to know and to believe in the love that God has for us. ↓

PRAYER AFTER COMMUNION   [One in Heart]

Pour on us, O Lord, the Spirit of your love,
and in your kindness
make those you have nourished
by this one heavenly Bread
one in mind and heart.
Through Christ our Lord.
℟. **Amen.**   → No. 30, p. 77

Optional Solemn Blessings, p. 97, and Prayers over the People, p. 105

"Come after me, and I will make you fishers of men."

JANUARY 24

3rd SUNDAY IN ORDINARY TIME

ENTRANCE ANT. Cf. Ps 96 (95):1, 6   [Sing to the Lord]

O sing a new song to the Lord; sing to the Lord, all the earth. In his presence are majesty and splendor, strength and honor in his holy place.   → No. 2, p. 10

COLLECT   [Abound in Good Works]

Almighty ever-living God,
direct our actions according to your good pleasure,
that in the name of your beloved Son
we may abound in good works.
Through our Lord Jesus Christ, your Son,
who lives and reigns with you in the unity of the Holy
  Spirit,
one God, for ever and ever.
℟. **Amen.** ↓

FIRST READING Jon 3:1-5, 10   [God's Mercy for All]

The mercy of God is shown to the people of Nineveh. He sends Jonah to Nineveh to preach penance for sin. The king proclaims a universal fast to appease the Lord.

184

A reading from the Book of the Prophet Jonah

THE word of the LORD came to Jonah, saying: "Set out for the great city of Nineveh, and announce to it the message that I will tell you." So Jonah made ready and went to Nineveh, according to the LORD's bidding. Now Nineveh was an enormously large city; it took three days to go through it. Jonah began his journey through the city, and had gone but a single day's walk announcing, "Forty days more and Nineveh shall be destroyed," when the people of Nineveh believed God; they proclaimed a fast and all of them, great and small, put on sackcloth.

When God saw by their actions how they turned from their evil way, he repented of the evil that he had threatened to do to them; he did not carry it out.—The word of the Lord. ℞. **Thanks be to God.** ↓

RESPONSORIAL PSALM Ps 25   [God's Ways]

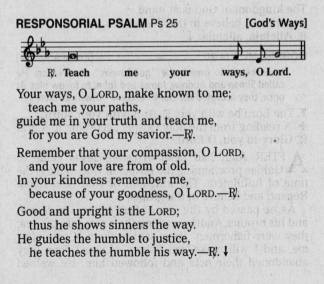

℞. Teach   me   your   ways, O Lord.

Your ways, O LORD, make known to me;
    teach me your paths,
guide me in your truth and teach me,
    for you are God my savior.—℞.

Remember that your compassion, O LORD,
    and your love are from of old.
In your kindness remember me,
    because of your goodness, O LORD.—℞.

Good and upright is the LORD;
    thus he shows sinners the way.
He guides the humble to justice,
    he teaches the humble his way.—℞. ↓

SECOND READING 1 Cor 7:29-31   [Shortness of Time]

Paul warns the Corinthians of the shortness of time in this world. All must conduct themselves worthily in the eyes of God and be detached from this world's pleasure.

A reading from the first Letter of Saint Paul
to the Corinthians

I TELL you, brothers and sisters, the time is running out. From now on, let those having wives act as not having them, those weeping as not weeping, those rejoicing as not rejoicing, those buying as not owning, those using the world as not using it fully. For the world in its present form is passing away.—The word of the Lord. ℟. **Thanks be to God.** ↓

ALLELUIA Mk 1:15   [Repent and Believe]

℟. **Alleluia, alleluia.**
The kingdom of God is at hand.
Repent and believe in the Gospel.
℟. **Alleluia, alleluia.** ↓

GOSPEL Mk 1:14-20   [Come After Me]

Jesus began to preach the "good news" of salvation. He called Simon and Andrew, James and John, to follow him. At once, they accepted the call to become "fishers of men."

℣. The Lord be with you. ℟. **And with your spirit.**
✠ A reading from the holy Gospel according to Mark.
℟. **Glory to you, O Lord.**

A FTER John had been arrested, Jesus came to Galilee proclaiming the gospel of God: "This is the time of fulfillment. The kingdom of God is at hand. Repent, and believe in the gospel."

As he passed by the Sea of Galilee, he saw Simon and his brother Andrew casting their nets into the sea; they were fishermen. Jesus said to them, "Come after me, and I will make you fishers of men." Then they abandoned their nets and followed him. He walked

along a little farther and saw James, the son of
Zebedee, and his brother John. They too were in a boat
mending their nets. Then he called them. So they left
their father Zebedee in the boat along with the hired
men and followed him.—The Gospel of the Lord. ℟.
Praise to you, Lord Jesus Christ.   → No. 15, p. 18

PRAYER OVER THE OFFERINGS   [Offerings for Salvation]

Accept our offerings, O Lord, we pray,
and in sanctifying them
grant that they may profit us for salvation.
Through Christ our Lord.
℟. **Amen.**   → No. 21, p. 22 (Pref. P 29-36)

COMMUNION ANT. Cf. Ps 34 (33):6   [Radiance]
**Look toward the Lord and be radiant; let your faces
not be abashed. ↓**

OR Jn 8:12   [Light of Life]
**I am the light of the world, says the Lord; whoever fol-
lows me will not walk in darkness, but will have the
light of life. ↓**

PRAYER AFTER COMMUNION   [New Life]

Grant, we pray, almighty God,
that, receiving the grace
by which you bring us to new life,
we may always glory in your gift.
Through Christ our Lord.
℟. **Amen.**   → No. 30, p. 77

Optional Solemn Blessings, p. 97, and Prayers over the People, p. 105

"He commands . . . unclean spirits and they obey him."

JANUARY 31

4th SUNDAY IN ORDINARY TIME

ENTRANCE ANT. Ps 106 (105):47   **[Save Us]**

Save us, O Lord our God! And gather us from the
nations, to give thanks to your holy name, and make
it our glory to praise you.   ➙ No. 2, p. 10

COLLECT   **[Christian Love]**

Grant us, Lord our God,
that we may honor you with all our mind,
and love everyone in truth of heart.
Through our Lord Jesus Christ, your Son,
who lives and reigns with you in the unity of the Holy
    Spirit,
one God, for ever and ever.
℟. **Amen.** ↓

FIRST READING Dt 18:15-20   **[The Prophet]**

The Israelites ask the Lord for a prophet. The Lord promises to select a prophet from among them. He then shall
speak for the Lord. Anyone who refuses to listen shall
answer to the Lord. A prophet who speaks falsely will die.

A reading from the Book of Deuteronomy

188

MOSES spoke to the people, saying: "A prophet like me will the LORD, your God, raise up for you from among your own kin; to him you shall listen. This is exactly what you requested of the LORD, your God, at Horeb on the day of the assembly, when you said, 'Let us not again hear the voice of the LORD, our God, nor see this great fire any more, lest we die.' And the LORD said to me, 'This was well said. I will raise up for them a prophet like you from among their kin, and will put my words into his mouth; he shall tell them all that I command him. Whoever will not listen to my words which he speaks in my name, I myself will make him answer for it. But if a prophet presumes to speak in my name an oracle that I have not commanded him to speak, or speaks in the name of other gods, he shall die.' "—The word of the Lord. ℟. **Thanks be to God.** ↓

RESPONSORIAL PSALM Ps 95   [Open Hearts]

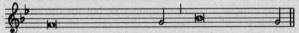

℟. If today you hear his voice, harden not your hearts.

Come, let us sing joyfully to the LORD;
    let us acclaim the rock of our salvation.
Let us come into his presence with thanksgiving;
    let us joyfully sing psalms to him.—℟.

Come, let us bow down in worship;
    let us kneel before the LORD who made us.
For he is our God,
    and we are the people he shepherds, the flock he
    guides.—℟.

Oh, that today you would hear his voice:
    "Harden not your hearts as at Meribah,
    as in the day of Massah in the desert,
where your fathers tempted me;
    they tested me though they had seen my works."—℟. ↓

SECOND READING 1 Cor 7:32-35   [Living for the Lord]

Paul speaks about the value of a celibate life. One who is unmarried is busy for the Lord. One who is married must be concerned for spouse and family. Paul is anxious to promote what helps a Christian live entirely for the Lord.

A reading from the first Letter of Saint Paul
to the Corinthians

BROTHERS and sisters: I should like you to be free of anxieties. An unmarried man is anxious about the things of the Lord, how he may please the Lord. But a married man is anxious about the things of the world, how he may please his wife, and he is divided. An unmarried woman or a virgin is anxious about the things of the Lord, so that she may be holy in both body and spirit. A married woman, on the other hand, is anxious about the things of the world, how she may please her husband. I am telling you this for your own benefit, not to impose a restraint upon you, but for the sake of propriety and adherence to the Lord without distraction.—The word of the Lord. ℟. **Thanks be to God.** ↓

ALLELUIA Mt 4:16   [A Great Light]

℟. **Alleluia, alleluia.**
The people who sit in darkness have seen a great light; on those dwelling in a land overshadowed by death, light has arisen.
℟. **Alleluia, alleluia.** ↓

GOSPEL Mk 1:21-28   [A New Teaching]

Jesus teaches in the synagogue with outstanding authority. In a possessed man, an unclean spirit shrieks out identifying Jesus. Jesus commands the unclean spirit to leave the man. The people are amazed.

℣. The Lord be with you. ℟. **And with your spirit.**
✛ A reading from the holy Gospel according to Mark.
℟. **Glory to you, O Lord.**

T HEN they came to Capernaum, and on the sabbath
Jesus entered the synagogue and taught. The people
were astonished at his teaching, for he taught them as
one having authority and not as the scribes. In their synagogue was a man with an unclean spirit; he cried out,
"What have you to do with us, Jesus of Nazareth? Have
you come to destroy us? I know who you are—the Holy
One of God!" Jesus rebuked him and said, "Quiet! Come
out of him!" The unclean spirit convulsed him and with a
loud cry came out of him. All were amazed and asked
one another, "What is this? A new teaching with authority. He commands even the unclean spirits and they obey
him." His fame spread everywhere throughout the whole
region of Galilee.—The Gospel of the Lord. ℟. **Praise to
you, Lord Jesus Christ.**   ➥ No. 15, p. 18

PRAYER OVER THE OFFERINGS [Sacrament of Redemption]

O Lord, we bring to your altar
these offerings of our service:
be pleased to receive them, we pray,
and transform them
into the Sacrament of our redemption.
Through Christ our Lord.
℟. **Amen.**   ➥ No. 21, p. 22 (Pref. P 29-36)

COMMUNION ANT. Cf. Ps 31 (30):17-18   [Save Me]

Let your face shine on your servant. Save me in your
merciful love. O Lord, let me never be put to shame,
for I call on you. ↓

OR Mt 5:3-4   [Poor in Spirit]

Blessed are the poor in spirit, for theirs is the
Kingdom of Heaven. Blessed are the meek, for they
shall possess the land. ↓

PRAYER AFTER COMMUNION   [True Faith]

Nourished by these redeeming gifts,
we pray, O Lord,

that through this help to eternal salvation
true faith may ever increase.
Through Christ our Lord.
℟. **Amen.**

→ No. 30, p. 77

Optional Solemn Blessings, p. 97, and Prayers over the People, p. 105

"[Jesus] helped her . . . [and] the fever left her."

FEBRUARY 7

5th SUNDAY IN ORDINARY TIME

ENTRANCE ANT. Ps 95 (94):6-7 [Adoration]
O come, let us worship God and bow low before the
God who made us, for he is the Lord our God.

→ No. 2, p. 10

COLLECT [God's Protection]
Keep your family safe, O Lord, with unfailing care,
that, relying solely on the hope of heavenly grace,
they may be defended always by your protection.
Through our Lord Jesus Christ, your Son,
who lives and reigns with you in the unity of the Holy
  Spirit,

one God, for ever and ever.

℟. **Amen.** ↓

FIRST READING Jb 7:1-4, 6-7   [Life Is Fleeting]

> Job describes our life on earth. The days of our life come
> to a swift end. However, we are heartened by the fuller
> revelation of an eternal life hereafter, which Christ brought
> to us and about which Job did not have a clear idea.

A reading from the Book of Job

JOB spoke, saying:
Is not man's life on earth a drudgery?
    Are not his days those of a hireling?
He is a slave who longs for the shade,
    a hireling who waits for his wages.
So I have been assigned months of misery,
    and troubled nights have been allotted to me.
If in bed I say, "When shall I arise?"
    then the night drags on;
    I am filled with restlessness until the dawn.
My days are swifter than a weaver's shuttle;
    they come to an end without hope.
Remember that my life is like the wind;
    I shall not see happiness again.
The word of the Lord. ℟. **Thanks be to God.** ↓

RESPONSORIAL PSALM Ps 147 [Healer of Brokenhearted]

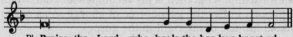

℟. **Praise the Lord, who heals the bro-ken-heart-ed.**
Or: ℟. **Alleluia.**

Praise the LORD, for he is good;
    sing praise to our God, for he is gracious;
    it is fitting to praise him.
The LORD rebuilds Jerusalem;
    the dispersed of Israel he gathers.

℟. **Praise the Lord, who heals the brokenhearted.**

Or: ℟. **Alleluia.**

He heals the brokenhearted
    and binds up their wounds.
He tells the number of the stars;
    he calls each by name.—℟.

Great is our LORD and mighty in power;
    to his wisdom there is no limit.
The LORD sustains the lowly;
    the wicked he casts to the ground.—℟. ↓

SECOND READING 1 Cor 9:16-19, 22-23 [All Things to All]

Paul writes that he must preach the gospel. Although he
has no obligation to any person, he has tried to become
one with his hearers to convince them of the saving message of the gospel.

A reading from the first Letter of Saint Paul
to the Corinthians

BROTHERS and sisters: If I preach the gospel, this
is no reason for me to boast, for an obligation has
been imposed on me, and woe to me if I do not preach
it! If I do so willingly, I have a recompense, but if
unwillingly, then I have been entrusted with a
stewardship. What then is my recompense? That, when
I preach, I offer the gospel free of charge so as not to
make full use of my right in the gospel.

    Although I am free in regard to all, I have made
myself a slave to all so as to win over as many as possible. To the weak I became weak, to win over the weak.
I have become all things to all, to save at least some. All
this I do for the sake of the gospel, so that I too may
have a share in it.—The word of the Lord. ℟. **Thanks be
to God.** ↓

ALLELUIA Mt 8:17   [Look to Christ]

℟. **Alleluia, alleluia.**
Christ took away our infirmities
and bore our diseases.
℟. **Alleluia, alleluia.** ↓

GOSPEL Mk 1:29-39   [Jesus the Healer]

Jesus visits the home of Simon and Andrew. He cures
Simon's mother-in-law. Jesus also expels many demons
and then goes off to pray alone. When found by Simon,
Jesus goes in the villages to preach the good news.

℣. The Lord be with you. ℟. **And with your spirit.**
✚ A reading from the holy Gospel according to Mark.
℟. **Glory to you, O Lord.**

ON leaving the synagogue Jesus entered the house
of Simon and Andrew with James and John.
Simon's mother-in-law lay sick with a fever. They
immediately told him about her. He approached,
grasped her hand, and helped her up. Then the fever
left her and she waited on them.

When it was evening, after sunset, they brought to
him all who were ill or possessed by demons. The
whole town was gathered at the door. He cured many
who were sick with various diseases, and he drove out
many demons, not permitting them to speak because
they knew him.

Rising very early before dawn, he left and went off to
a deserted place, where he prayed. Simon and those who
were with him pursued him and on finding him said,
"Everyone is looking for you." He told them, "Let us go on
to the nearby villages that I may preach there also. For
this purpose have I come." So he went into their syna-
gogues, preaching and driving out demons throughout
the whole of Galilee.—The Gospel of the Lord. ℟. **Praise
to you, Lord Jesus Christ.**   → No. 15, p. 18

PRAYER OVER THE OFFERINGS   [Eternal Life]

O Lord our God,
who once established these created things
to sustain us in our frailty,
grant, we pray,
that they may become for us now
the Sacrament of eternal life.
Through Christ our Lord.
℞. Amen.   → No. 21, p. 22 (Pref. P 29-36)

COMMUNION ANT. Cf. Ps 107 (106):8-9   [The Lord's Mercy]

Let them thank the Lord for his mercy, his wonders
for the children of men, for he satisfies the thirsty
soul, and the hungry he fills with good things. ↓

OR Mt 5:5-6   [Those Who Mourn]

Blessed are those who mourn, for they shall be consoled. Blessed are those who hunger and thirst for
righteousness, for they shall have their fill. ↓

PRAYER AFTER COMMUNION   [Salvation and Joy]

O God, who have willed that we be partakers
in the one Bread and the one Chalice,
grant us, we pray, so to live
that, made one in Christ,
we may joyfully bear fruit
for the salvation of the world.
Through Christ our Lord.
℞. Amen.   → No. 30, p. 77

Optional Solemn Blessings, p. 97, and Prayers over the People, p. 105

————————

"[Jesus] stretched out his hand, touched him, and said, . . . 'Be made clean.' "

FEBRUARY 14

6th SUNDAY IN ORDINARY TIME

ENTRANCE ANT. Cf. Ps 31 (30):3-4   [Protector]

Be my protector, O God, a mighty stronghold to save me. For you are my rock, my stronghold! Lead me, guide me, for the sake of your name.   → No. 2, p. 10

COLLECT   [Fashioned by God's Grace]

O God, who teach us that you abide
in hearts that are just and true,
grant that we may be so fashioned by your grace
as to become a dwelling pleasing to you.
Through our Lord Jesus Christ, your Son,
who lives and reigns with you in the unity of the Holy
  Spirit,
one God, for ever and ever.
℟. **Amen.** ↓

FIRST READING Lv 13:1-2, 44-46   [Law of Leprosy]
The Lord instructs Moses and Aaron on the legal prescriptions that are to be followed by those who have leprosy.

197

A reading from the Book of Leviticus

THE LORD said to Moses and Aaron, "If someone has on his skin a scab or pustule or blotch which appears to be the sore of leprosy, he shall be brought to Aaron, the priest, or to one of the priests among his descendants. If the man is leprous and unclean, the priest shall declare him unclean by reason of the sore on his head.

"The one who bears the sore of leprosy shall keep his garments rent and his head bare, and shall muffle his beard; he shall cry out, 'Unclean, unclean!' As long as the sore is on him he shall declare himself unclean, since he is in fact unclean. He shall dwell apart, making his abode outside the camp."—The word of the Lord. ℟. **Thanks be to God.** ↓

RESPONSORIAL PSALM Ps 32   [Turning to God]

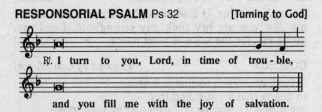

℟. I turn to you, Lord, in time of trou-ble,

and you fill me with the joy of salvation.

Blessed is he whose fault is taken away,
  whose sin is covered.
Blessed the man to whom the LORD imputes not guilt,
  in whose spirit there is no guile.—℟.

Then I acknowledged my sin to you,
  my guilt I covered not.
I said, "I confess my faults to the LORD,"
  and you took away the guilt of my sin.—℟.

Be glad in the LORD and rejoice, you just;
  exult, all you upright of heart.—℟. ↓

SECOND READING 1 Cor 10:31—11:1 [All for God's Glory]

Paul directs that whatever is done should be for the glory
of God. Since he is acting in imitation of Christ, the people should follow his example.

A reading from the first Letter of Saint Paul
to the Corinthians

BROTHERS and sisters: Whether you eat or drink,
or whatever you do, do everything for the glory of
God. Avoid giving offense, whether to the Jews or
Greeks or the church of God, just as I try to please
everyone in every way, not seeking my own benefit but
that of the many, that they may be saved. Be imitators
of me, as I am of Christ.—The word of the Lord. ℟.
Thanks be to God. ↓

ALLELUIA Lk 7:16   [God's Prophet]

℟. **Alleluia, alleluia.**
A great prophet has arisen in our midst,
God has visited his people.
℟. **Alleluia, alleluia.** ↓

GOSPEL Mk 1:40-45   [Gratitude]

Upon request, Jesus cured a leper, reminding him to follow
the directions of the Mosaic law and to tell no one. Since
the cured leper spread the news of his cure, Jesus could no
longer openly enter a town.

℣. The Lord be with you. ℟. **And with your spirit.**
✛ A reading from the holy Gospel according to Mark.
℟. **Glory to you, O Lord.**

A LEPER came to Jesus and kneeling down begged
him and said, "If you wish, you can make me clean."
Moved with pity, he stretched out his hand, touched him,
and said to him, "I do will it. Be made clean." The leprosy
left him immediately, and he was made clean. Then,
warning him sternly, he dismissed him at once.

He said to him, "See that you tell no one anything, but go, show yourself to the priest and offer for your cleansing what Moses prescribed; that will be proof for them."

The man went away and began to publicize the whole matter. He spread the report abroad so that it was impossible for Jesus to enter a town openly. He remained outside in deserted places, and people kept coming to him from everywhere.—The Gospel of the Lord. ℟. **Praise to you, Lord Jesus Christ.**   → No. 15, p. 18

PRAYER OVER THE OFFERINGS   [Renewal]

May this oblation, O Lord, we pray,
cleanse and renew us
and may it become for those who do your will
the source of eternal reward.
Through Christ our Lord.
℟. **Amen.**   → No. 21, p. 22 (Pref. P 29-36)

COMMUNION ANT. Cf. Ps 78 (77):29-30   [God's Food]
They ate and had their fill, and what they craved the Lord gave them; they were not disappointed in what they craved. ↓

OR Jn 3:16   [God's Love]
God so loved the world that he gave his Only Begotten Son, so that all who believe in him may not perish, but may have eternal life. ↓

PRAYER AFTER COMMUNION   [Heavenly Delights]

Having fed upon these heavenly delights,
we pray, O Lord,
that we may always long
for that food by which we truly live.
Through Christ our Lord.
℟. **Amen.**   → No. 30, p. 77

Optional Solemn Blessings, p. 97, and Prayers over the People, p. 105

Jesus was "tempted by Satan."

FEBRUARY 21

1st SUNDAY OF LENT

ENTRANCE ANT. Cf. Ps 91 (90):15-16   [Length of Days]
When he calls on me, I will answer him; I will deliver
him and give him glory, I will grant him length of days.

➔ No. 2, p. 10 (Omit Gloria)

COLLECT   [Grow in Understanding]
Grant, almighty God,
through the yearly observances of holy Lent,
that we may grow in understanding
of the riches hidden in Christ
and by worthy conduct pursue their effects.
Through our Lord Jesus Christ, your Son,
who lives and reigns with you in the unity of the Holy
   Spirit,
one God, for ever and ever.
℟. **Amen.** ↓

FIRST READING Gn 9:8-15   **[Sign of the Covenant]**

God promises Noah that the world will never again be destroyed by a flood. God gives a sign of his covenant—his rainbow among the clouds.

A reading from the Book of Genesis

GOD said to Noah and to his sons with him: "See, I am now establishing my covenant with you and your descendants after you and with every living creature that was with you: all the birds, and the various tame and wild animals that were with you and came out of the ark. I will establish my covenant with you, that never again shall all bodily creatures be destroyed by the waters of a flood; there shall not be another flood to devastate the earth." God added: "This is the sign that I am giving for all ages to come, of the covenant between me and you and every living creature with you: I set my bow in the clouds to serve as a sign of the covenant between me and the earth. When I bring clouds over the earth, and the bow appears in the clouds, I will recall the covenant I have made between me and you and all living beings, so that the waters shall never again become a flood to destroy all mortal beings."—The word of the Lord. ℟. **Thanks be to God.** ↓

RESPONSORIAL PSALM Ps 25   **[Keeping God's Covenant]**

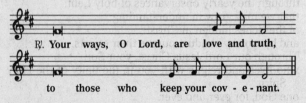

℟. Your ways, O Lord, are love and truth, to those who keep your cov - e - nant.

Your ways, O LORD, make known to me;
   teach me your paths.

Guide me in your truth and teach me,
  for you are God my savior.—R⫽.

Remember that your compassion, O LORD,
  and your love are from of old.
In your kindness remember me,
  because of your goodness, O LORD.—R⫽.

Good and upright is the LORD;
  thus he shows sinners the way.
He guides the humble to justice,
  and he teaches the humble his way.—R⫽. ↓

SECOND READING 1 Pt 3:18-22   [Power of the Resurrection]
  Christ died once for sin. Because of sin, God destroyed the earth by water. Now Christians are saved by the water of baptism. It becomes the pledge of resurrection.

  A reading from the first Letter of Saint Peter

B ELOVED: Christ suffered for sins once, the righteous for the sake of the unrighteous, that he might lead you to God. Put to death in the flesh, he was brought to life in the Spirit. In it he also went to preach to the spirits in prison, who had once been disobedient while God patiently waited in the days of Noah during the building of the ark, in which a few persons, eight in all, were saved through water. This prefigured baptism, which saves you now. It is not a removal of dirt from the body but an appeal to God for a clear conscience, through the resurrection of Jesus Christ, who has gone into heaven and is at the right hand of God, with angels, authorities, and powers subject to him.—The word of the Lord. R⫽. **Thanks be to God.** ↓

VERSE BEFORE THE GOSPEL Mt 4:4b   [God's Living Word]
R⫽. **Praise to you, Lord Jesus Christ, King of endless glory!***

_____
* See p. 16 for other Gospel Acclamations.

One does not live on bread alone,
but on every word that comes forth from the mouth of
   God.

℞. **Praise to you, Lord Jesus Christ, King of endless
glory!** ↓

GOSPEL Mk 1:12-15   [Time of Fulfillment]

**Jesus prayed in the desert for forty days. After John's
arrest, Jesus came forth, announcing the time of fulfillment. It is the time to believe and reform.**

℣. The Lord be with you. ℞. **And with your spirit.**
✜ A reading from the holy Gospel according to Mark.
℞. **Glory to you, O Lord.**

THE Spirit drove Jesus out into the desert, and he
   remained in the desert for forty days, tempted by
Satan. He was among wild beasts, and the angels ministered to him.

   After John had been arrested, Jesus came to Galilee
proclaiming the gospel of God: "This is the time of fulfillment. The kingdom of God is at hand. Repent, and
believe in the gospel."—The Gospel of the Lord. ℞.
Praise to you, Lord Jesus Christ.   → No. 15, p. 18

PRAYER OVER THE OFFERINGS   [Sacred Time]

Give us the right dispositions, O Lord, we pray,
to make these offerings,
for with them we celebrate the beginning
of this venerable and sacred time.
Through Christ our Lord. ℞. **Amen.** ↓

PREFACE (P 12)   [Christ's Abstinence]

℣. The Lord be with you. ℞. **And with your spirit.**
℣. Lift up your hearts. ℞. **We lift them up to the
Lord.** ℣. Let us give thanks to the Lord our God. ℞. **It
is right and just.**

It is truly right and just, our duty and our salvation,
always and everywhere to give you thanks,
Lord, holy Father, almighty and eternal God,
through Christ our Lord.

By abstaining forty long days from earthly food,
he consecrated through his fast
the pattern of our Lenten observance
and, by overturning all the snares of the ancient serpent,
taught us to cast out the leaven of malice,
so that, celebrating worthily the Paschal Mystery,
we might pass over at last to the eternal paschal feast.

And so, with the company of Angels and Saints,
we sing the hymn of your praise,
as without end we acclaim: ➔ No. 23, p. 23

COMMUNION ANT. Mt 4:4   **[Life-Giving Word]**

**One does not live by bread alone, but by every word
that comes forth from the mouth of God.** ↓

OR Cf. Ps 91 (90):4   **[Refuge in God]**

**The Lord will conceal you with his pinions, and under
his wings you will trust.** ↓

PRAYER AFTER COMMUNION   **[Heavenly Bread]**

Renewed now with heavenly bread,
by which faith is nourished, hope increased,
and charity strengthened,
we pray, O Lord,
that we may learn to hunger for Christ,
the true and living Bread,
and strive to live by every word
which proceeds from your mouth.
Through Christ our Lord.
℟. **Amen.** ↓

*The Deacon or, in his absence, the Priest himself, says the
invitation:* Bow down for the blessing.

PRAYER OVER THE PEOPLE   [Bountiful Blessing]

May bountiful blessing, O Lord, we pray,
come down upon your people,
that hope may grow in tribulation,
virtue be strengthened in temptation,
and eternal redemption be assured.
Through Christ our Lord.
℟. **Amen.**

→ No. 32, p. 77

*"Elijah appeared to them along with Moses,
and they were conversing with Jesus."*

FEBRUARY 28

2nd SUNDAY OF LENT

ENTRANCE ANT. Cf. Ps 27 (26):8-9   [God's Face]

**Of you my heart has spoken: Seek his face. It is your
face, O Lord, that I seek; hide not your face from me.**

→ No. 2, p. 10 (Omit Gloria)

OR Cf. Ps 25 (24):6, 2, 22   [God's Merciful Love]

**Remember your compassion, O Lord, and your merci-
ful love, for they are from of old. Let not our enemies**

exult over us. Redeem us, O God of Israel, from all our distress.   ➔ No. 2, p. 10 (Omit Gloria)

COLLECT   [Nourish Us]

O God, who have commanded us
to listen to your beloved Son,
be pleased, we pray,
to nourish us inwardly by your word,
that, with spiritual sight made pure,
we may rejoice to behold your glory.
Through our Lord Jesus Christ, your Son,
who lives and reigns with you in the unity of the Holy
    Spirit,
one God, for ever and ever.
℟. **Amen.** ↓

FIRST READING Gn 22:1-2, 9a, 10-13, 15-18
                                        [Testing of Abraham]

Abraham and his son, Isaac, prefigure God, the Father, and Jesus, his divine Son. God tests Abraham's faith and because of it, God promises abundant blessings on the family of Abraham and all his descendants.

A reading from the Book of Genesis

GOD put Abraham to the test. He called to him, "Abraham!" "Here I am!" he replied. Then God said: "Take your son Isaac, your only one, whom you love, and go to the land of Moriah. There you shall offer him up as a holocaust on a height that I will point out to you."

When they came to the place of which God had told him, Abraham built an altar there and arranged the wood on it. Then he reached out and took the knife to slaughter his son. But the LORD's messenger called to him from heaven, "Abraham, Abraham!" "Here I am!" he answered. "Do not lay your hand on the boy," said the messenger. "Do not do the least thing to him. I know now how devoted you are to God, since you did not withhold from me your own beloved son." As Abraham looked about, he spied a ram caught by its horns in the thicket. So he went and took the ram and offered it up as a holocaust in place of his son.

Again the LORD's messenger called to Abraham from heaven and said: "I swear by myself, declares the LORD, that because you acted as you did in not withholding from me your beloved son, I will bless you abundantly and make your descendants as countless as the stars of the sky and the sands of the seashore; your descendants shall take possession of the gates of their enemies, and in your descendants all the nations of the earth shall find blessing—all this because you obeyed my command."—The word of the Lord. ℟. **Thanks be to God.** ↓

RESPONSORIAL PSALM Ps 116　　　[Walking with God]

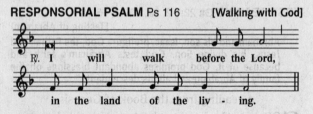

℟. I will walk before the Lord, in the land of the liv - ing.

I believed, even when I said,
　"I am greatly afflicted."
Precious in the eyes of the LORD
　is the death of his faithful ones.—℟.

O LORD, I am your servant;
　I am your servant, the son of your handmaid;
　you have loosed my bonds.
To you will I offer sacrifice of thanksgiving,
　and I will call upon the name of the LORD.—℟.

My vows to the LORD I will pay
　in the presence of all his people,

in the courts of the house of the LORD,
in your midst, O Jerusalem.—℟. ↓

SECOND READING Rom 8:31b-34   [God Is for Us]

God sent his Son into the world to die for us. Who is then
going to judge God's chosen ones? Is this not the right of
Jesus, who loves those for whom he gave his life?

A reading from the Letter of Saint Paul to the Romans

BROTHERS and sisters: If God is for us, who can be
against us? He who did not spare his own Son but
handed him over for us all, how will he not also give us
everything else along with him?

Who will bring a charge against God's chosen ones?
It is God who acquits us. Who will condemn? Christ
Jesus it is who died—or, rather, was raised—who also
is at the right hand of God, who indeed intercedes for
us.—The word of the Lord. ℟. **Thanks be to God.** ↓

VERSE BEFORE THE GOSPEL Cf. Mt 17:5   [Beloved Son]
℟. **Praise and honor to you, Lord Jesus Christ!***
From the shining cloud the Father's voice is heard:
This is my beloved Son, listen to him.
℟. **Praise and honor to you, Lord Jesus Christ!** ↓

GOSPEL Mk 9:2-10   [Jesus Transfigured]

Jesus becomes transfigured before Peter, James and John.
God spoke, "This is my Son, my beloved. Listen to him."
Jesus asked his disciples to keep this a strict secret until he
would be raised from the dead.

℣. The Lord be with you. ℟. **And with your spirit.**
✜ A reading from the holy Gospel according to Mark.
℟. **Glory to you, O Lord.**

JESUS took Peter, James, and John and led them up
a high mountain apart by themselves. And he was
transfigured before them, and his clothes became daz-

---

* See p. 16 for other Gospel Acclamations.

zling white, such as no fuller on earth could bleach them. Then Elijah appeared to them along with Moses, and they were conversing with Jesus. Then Peter said to Jesus in reply, "Rabbi, it is good that we are here! Let us make three tents: one for you, one for Moses, and one for Elijah." He hardly knew what to say, they were so terrified. Then a cloud came, casting a shadow over them; from the cloud came a voice, "This is my beloved Son. Listen to him." Suddenly, looking around, they no longer saw anyone but Jesus alone with them.

As they were coming down from the mountain, he charged them not to relate what they had seen to anyone, except when the Son of Man had risen from the dead. So they kept the matter to themselves, questioning what rising from the dead meant.—The Gospel of the Lord. ℞. **Praise to you, Lord Jesus Christ.**

→ No. 15, p. 18

PRAYER OVER THE OFFERINGS   [Cleanse Our Faults]

May this sacrifice, O Lord, we pray,
cleanse us of our faults
and sanctify your faithful in body and mind
for the celebration of the paschal festivities.
Through Christ our Lord.
℞. **Amen.** ↓

PREFACE (P 13)   [Jesus in Glory]

℣. The Lord be with you. ℞. **And with your spirit.**
℣. Lift up your hearts. ℞. **We lift them up to the Lord.** ℣. Let us give thanks to the Lord our God. ℞. **It is right and just.**

It is truly right and just, our duty and our salvation,
always and everywhere to give you thanks,
Lord, holy Father, almighty and eternal God,
through Christ our Lord.

For after he had told the disciples of his coming Death,
on the holy mountain he manifested to them his glory,
to show, even by the testimony of the law and the
  prophets,
that the Passion leads to the glory of the Resurrection.

And so, with the Powers of heaven,
we worship you constantly on earth,
and before your majesty
without end we acclaim: → No. 23, p. 23

COMMUNION ANT. Mt 17:5   [Son of God]
**This is my beloved Son, with whom I am well pleased;
listen to him.** ↓

PRAYER AFTER COMMUNION   [Things of Heaven]
As we receive these glorious mysteries,
we make thanksgiving to you, O Lord,
for allowing us while still on earth
to be partakers even now of the things of heaven.
Through Christ our Lord.
℟. **Amen.** ↓

*The Deacon or, in his absence, the Priest himself, says the
invitation:* Bow down for the blessing.

PRAYER OVER THE PEOPLE   [Faithful to the Gospel]
Bless your faithful, we pray, O Lord,
with a blessing that endures for ever,
and keep them faithful
to the Gospel of your Only Begotten Son,
so that they may always desire and at last attain
that glory whose beauty he showed in his own Body,
to the amazement of his Apostles.
Through Christ our Lord.
℟. **Amen.**   → No. 32, p. 77

"Stop making my Father's house a marketplace."

MARCH 7
3rd SUNDAY OF LENT

On this Sunday is celebrated the First Scrutiny in preparation for the Baptism of the catechumens who are to be admitted to the Sacraments of Christian Initiation at the Easter Vigil. The Ritual Mass for the First Scrutiny is found on p. 218.

ENTRANCE ANT. Cf. Ps 25 (24):15-16   [Eyes on God]

My eyes are always on the Lord, for he rescues my feet from the snare. Turn to me and have mercy on me, for I am alone and poor. → No. 2, p. 10 (Omit Gloria)

OR Ez 36:23-26   [A New Spirit]

When I prove my holiness among you, I will gather you from all the foreign lands; and I will pour clean water upon you and cleanse you from all your impurities, and I will give you a new spirit, says the Lord.

→ No. 2, p. 10 (Omit Gloria)

COLLECT   [Fasting, Prayer, Almsgiving]

O God, author of every mercy and of all goodness,
who in fasting, prayer and almsgiving
have shown us a remedy for sin,

212

look graciously on this confession of our lowliness,
that we, who are bowed down by our conscience,
may always be lifted up by your mercy.
Through our Lord Jesus Christ, your Son,
who lives and reigns with you in the unity of the Holy
    Spirit,
one God, for ever and ever.
℟. Amen. ↓

FIRST READING Ex 20:1-17 or 20:1-3, 7-8, 12-17

[Ten Commandments]

**God speaks to his people and gives them a code of life to
follow—the Commandments. The first three describe how
he is to be worshiped and the remaining rules outline how
the people are to respect and live with one another.**

*[If the "Shorter Form" is used, the indented text in brackets is
omitted.]*

A reading from the Book of Exodus

IN those days, God delivered all these commandments: "I, the LORD, am your God, who brought you
out of the land of Egypt, that place of slavery. You shall
not have other gods besides me.

[You shall not carve idols for yourselves in the
shape of anything in the sky above or on the earth
below or in the waters beneath the earth; you
shall not bow down before them or worship them.
For I, the LORD, your God, am a jealous God,
inflicting punishment for their fathers' wickedness on the children of those who hate me, down
to the third and fourth generation; but bestowing
mercy down to the thousandth generation, on the
children of those who love me and keep my commandments.]

"You shall not take the name of the LORD, your God,
in vain. For the LORD will not leave unpunished him
who takes his name in vain.

"Remember to keep holy the sabbath day.

[Six days you may labor and do all your work, but the seventh day is the sabbath of the L ord , your God. No work may be done then either by you, or your son or daughter, or your male or female slave, or your beast, or by the alien who lives with you. In six days the L ord made the heavens and the earth, the sea and all that is in them; but on the seventh day he rested. That is why the L ord has blessed the sabbath day and made it holy.]

"Honor your father and your mother, that you may have a long life in the land which the L ord , your God, is giving you.

You shall not kill.

You shall not commit adultery.

You shall not steal.

You shall not bear false witness against your neighbor.

You shall not covet your neighbor's house. You shall not covet your neighbor's wife, nor his male or female slave, nor his ox or ass, nor anything else that belongs to him."—The word of the Lord. ℟. **Thanks be to God.** ↓

RESPONSORIAL PSALM Ps 19   [Words of Life]

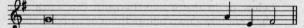

℟. **Lord, you have the words of ever - last - ing life.**

The law of the L ord is perfect,
   refreshing the soul;
the decree of the L ord is trustworthy,
   giving wisdom to the simple.—℟.

The precepts of the L ord are right,
   rejoicing the heart;
the command of the L ord is clear,
   enlightening the eye.—℟.

The fear of the LORD is pure,
   enduring forever;
the ordinances of the LORD are true,
   all of them just.—℞.

They are more precious than gold,
   than a heap of purest gold;
sweeter also than syrup
   or honey from the comb.—℞. ↓

SECOND READING 1 Cor 1:22-25   [Christ, the Power of God]

   Paul admits that the preaching of Christ crucified is regarded as absurd by some. Still, for those who have faith, Christ is the power and wisdom of God.

A reading from the first Letter of Saint Paul
to the Corinthians

BROTHERS and sisters: Jews demand signs and Greeks look for wisdom, but we proclaim Christ crucified, a stumbling block to Jews and foolishness to Gentiles, but to those who are called, Jews and Greeks alike, Christ the power of God and the wisdom of God. For the foolishness of God is wiser than human wisdom, and the weakness of God is, stronger than human strength.—The word of the Lord. ℞. **Thanks be to God.** ↓

VERSE BEFORE THE GOSPEL Jn 3:16   [God's Love]

℞. **Glory and praise to you, Lord Jesus Christ!***
God so loved the world that he gave his only Son,
so that everyone who believes in him might have
   eternal life.
℞. **Glory and praise to you, Lord Jesus Christ!** ↓

GOSPEL Jn 2:13-25   [Prediction of the Resurrection]

   Jesus becomes angry when the temple, which is to be a house of prayer, is turned into a place of business. He drives the merchants out.

* See p. 16 for other Gospel Acclamations.

℣. The Lord be with you. ℟. **And with your spirit.**

✝ A reading from the holy Gospel according to John.
℟. **Glory to you, O Lord.**

SINCE the Passover of the Jews was near, Jesus went up to Jerusalem. He found in the temple area those who sold oxen, sheep, and doves, as well as the money changers seated there. He made a whip out of cords and drove them all out of the temple area, with the sheep and oxen, and spilled the coins of the money changers and overturned their tables, and to those who sold doves he said, "Take these out of here, and stop making my Father's house a marketplace." His disciples recalled the words of Scripture, *Zeal for your house will consume me.* At this the Jews answered and said to him, "What sign can you show us for doing this?" Jesus answered and said to them, "Destroy this temple and in three days I will raise it up." The Jews said, "This temple has been under construction for forty-six years, and you will raise it up in three days?" But he was speaking about the temple of his body. Therefore, when he was raised from the dead, his disciples remembered that he had said this, and they came to believe the Scripture and the word Jesus had spoken.

While he was in Jerusalem for the feast of Passover, many began to believe in his name when they saw the signs he was doing. But Jesus would not trust himself to them because he knew them all, and did not need anyone to testify about human nature. He himself understood it well.—The Gospel of the Lord. ℟. **Praise to you, Lord Jesus Christ.**   → No. 15, p. 18

Or the Gospel (Jn 4:5-42) from Year A may be said, p. 220.

PRAYER OVER THE OFFERINGS   [Pardon]

Be pleased, O Lord, with these sacrificial offerings,
and grant that we who beseech pardon for our own sins,

may take care to forgive our neighbor.
Through Christ our Lord.
R̸. **Amen.**   → No. 21, p. 22 (Pref. P 8-9)

*When the Gospel of the Samaritan Woman is read, see
p. 223 for Preface (P 14).*

COMMUNION ANT. Ps 84 (83):4-5   [God's House]
**The sparrow finds a home, and the swallow a nest for
her young: by your altars, O Lord of hosts, my King
and my God. Blessed are they who dwell in your
house, for ever singing your praise.** ↓

When the Gospel of the Samaritan Woman is read:

COMMUNION ANT. Jn 4:13-14   [Water of Eternal Life]
**For anyone who drinks it, says the Lord, the water I
shall give will become in him a spring welling up to
eternal life.** ↓

PRAYER AFTER COMMUNION   [Nourishment from Heaven]

As we receive the pledge
of things yet hidden in heaven
and are nourished while still on earth
with the Bread that comes from on high,
we humbly entreat you, O Lord,
that what is being brought about in us in mystery
may come to true completion.
Through Christ our Lord. R̸. **Amen.** ↓

*The Deacon or, in his absence, the Priest himself, says the
invitation:* Bow down for the blessing.

PRAYER OVER THE PEOPLE   [Love of God and Neighbor]

Direct, O Lord, we pray, the hearts of your faithful,
and in your kindness grant your servants this grace:
that, abiding in the love of you and their neighbor,
they may fulfill the whole of your commands.
Through Christ our Lord.
R̸. **Amen.**   → No. 32, p. 77

MASS FOR THE FIRST SCRUTINY

This Mass is celebrated when the First Scrutiny takes place during the Rite of Christian Initiation of Adults, usually on the 3rd Sunday of Lent.

ENTRANCE ANT. Ez 36:23-26   **[A New Spirit]**

When I prove my holiness among you, I will gather you from all the foreign lands and I will pour clean water upon you and cleanse you from all your impurities, and I will give you a new spirit, says the Lord.

     ➜ No. 2, p. 10 (Omit Gloria)

OR Cf. Is 55:1   **[Drink Joyfully]**

Come to the waters, you who are thirsty, says the Lord; you who have no money, come and drink joyfully.

     ➜ No. 2, p. 10 (Omit Gloria)

COLLECT   **[Fashioned Anew]**

Grant, we pray, O Lord,
that these chosen ones may come worthily and wisely
to the confession of your praise,
so that in accordance with that first dignity
which they lost by original sin
they may be fashioned anew through your glory.
Through our Lord Jesus Christ, your Son,
who lives and reigns with you in the unity of the Holy Spirit,
one God, for ever and ever. ℞. **Amen.** ↓

FIRST READING Ex 17:3-7   **[Water from Rock]**

The Israelites murmured against God in their thirst. God directs Moses to strike a rock with his staff, and water issues forth.

A reading from the Book of Exodus

IN those days, in their thirst for water, the people grumbled against Moses, saying, "Why did you ever make us leave Egypt? Was it just to have us die here of thirst with our children and our livestock?" So Moses cried out to the LORD, "What shall I do with this people? A little more and they will stone me!" The LORD answered Moses, "Go over there in front of the people, along with some of the elders of Israel, holding in your hand, as you go, the staff with which you struck the river. I will be standing there in front of you on the rock in Horeb. Strike the rock, and the water will flow from it for the people to drink." This Moses did, in the presence of the elders of Israel. The place was called Massah and Meribah, because the Israelites quarreled there and tested the LORD, saying, "Is the LORD in our midst or not?"— The word of the Lord. ℟. **Thanks be to God.** ↓

RESPONSORIAL PSALM Ps 95   [The Lord Our Rock]

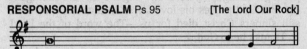

℟. If today you hear his voice, harden not your hearts.

Come, let us sing joyfully to the LORD;
    let us acclaim the Rock of our salvation.
Let us come into his presence with thanksgiving;
    let us joyfully sing psalms to him.—℟.

Come, let us bow down in worship;
    let us kneel before the LORD who made us.
For he is our God,
    and we are the people he shepherds, the flock he
    guides.—℟.

Oh, that today you would hear his voice:
    "Harden not your hearts as at Meribah,
    as in the day of Massah in the desert,
where your fathers tempted me;
    they tested me though they had seen my works."—℟. ↓

SECOND READING Rom 5:1-2, 5-8   [God's Love for Us]
    Through Jesus we have received the grace of faith. The love of
    God has been poured upon us. Jesus laid down his life for us
    while we were still sinners.

A reading from the Letter of Saint Paul to the Romans

BROTHERS and sisters: Since we have been justified by
faith, we have peace with God through our Lord Jesus

Christ, through whom we have gained access by faith to this grace in which we stand, and we boast in hope of the glory of God.

And hope does not disappoint, because the love of God has been poured out into our hearts through the Holy Spirit who has been given to us. For Christ, while we were still helpless, died at the appointed time for the ungodly. Indeed, only with difficulty does one die for a just person, though perhaps for a good person one might even find courage to die. But God proves his love for us in that while we were still sinners Christ died for us.—The word of the Lord. ℟. **Thanks be to God.** ↓

VERSE BEFORE THE GOSPEL Cf. Jn 4:42, 15   [Living Water]

℟. **Glory and praise to you, Lord Jesus Christ!***
Lord, you are truly the Savior of the world;
give me living water, that I may never thirst again.
℟. **Glory and praise to you, Lord Jesus Christ!** ↓

GOSPEL Jn 4:5-42 or 4:5-15, 19b-26, 39a, 40-42   [Samaritan Woman]

Jesus speaks to the Samaritan woman at the well. He searches her soul, and she recognizes him as a prophet. Jesus speaks of the water of eternal life. He also notes the fields are ready for harvest.

[If the "Shorter Form" is used, the indented text in brackets is omitted.]

℣. The Lord be with you. ℟. **And with your spirit.**
✛ A reading from the holy Gospel according to John.
℟. **Glory to you, O Lord.**

J ESUS came to a town of Samaria called Sychar, near the plot of land that Jacob had given to his son Joseph. Jacob's well was there. Jesus, tired from his journey, sat down there at the well. It was about noon.

---

* *See p. 16 for other Gospel Acclamations.*

A woman of Samaria came to draw water. Jesus said to her, "Give me a drink." His disciples had gone into the town to buy food. The Samaritan woman said to him, "How can you, a Jew, ask me, a Samaritan woman, for a drink?"—For Jews use nothing in common with Samaritans.—Jesus answered and said to her, "If you knew the gift of God and who is saying to you, 'Give me a drink,' you would have asked him and he would have given you living water." The woman said to him, "Sir, you do not even have a bucket and the cistern is deep; where then can you get this living water? Are you greater than our father Jacob, who gave us this cistern and drank from it himself with his children and his flocks?" Jesus answered and said to her, "Everyone who drinks this water will be thirsty again; but whoever drinks the water I shall give will never thirst; the water I shall give will become in him a spring of water welling up to eternal life." The woman said to him, "Sir, give me this water, so that I may not be thirsty or have to keep coming here to draw water."

[Jesus said to her, "Go call your husband and come back." The woman answered and said to him, "I do not have a husband." Jesus answered her, "You are right in saying, 'I do not have a husband.' For you have had five husbands, and the one you have now is not your husband. What you have said is true."]

[The woman said to him, "Sir,] I can see that you are a prophet. Our ancestors worshiped on this mountain; but you people say that the place to worship is in Jerusalem." Jesus said to her, "Believe me, woman, the hour is coming when you will worship the Father neither on this mountain nor in Jerusalem. You people worship what you do not understand; we worship what we understand, because salvation is from the Jews. But the hour is coming, and is now here, when true worshipers will worship the Father in Spirit and truth; and indeed the Father seeks such people to worship him. God is Spirit, and those who worship him must worship in Spirit and truth." The woman said to him,

"I know that the Messiah is coming, the one called the Christ; when he comes, he will tell us everything." Jesus said to her, "I am he, the one (who is) [in Shorter Form] speaking with you."

[At that moment his disciples returned, and were amazed that he was talking with a woman, but still no one said, "What are you looking for?" or "Why are you talking with her?" The woman left her water jar and went into the town and said to the people, "Come see a man who told me everything I have done. Could he possibly be the Christ?" They went out of the town and came to him. Meanwhile, the disciples urged him, "Rabbi, eat." But he said to them, "I have food to eat of which you do not know." So the disciples said to one another, "Could someone have brought him something to eat?" Jesus said to them, "My food is to do the will of the one who sent me and to finish his work. Do you not say, 'In four months the harvest will be here'? I tell you, look up and see the fields ripe for the harvest. The reaper is already receiving payment and gathering crops for eternal life, so that the sower and reaper can rejoice together. For here the saying is verified that 'One sows and another reaps.' I sent you to reap what you have not worked for; others have done the work, and you are sharing the fruits of their work."]

Many of the Samaritans of that town began to believe in him [because of the word of the woman who testified, "He told me everything I have done."] When the Samaritans came to him, they invited him to stay with them; and he stayed there two days. Many more began to believe in him because of his word, and they said to the woman, "We no longer believe because of your word; for we have heard for ourselves, and we know that this is truly the savior of the world."—The Gospel of the Lord. ℟. **Praise to you, Lord Jesus Christ.**   → No. 15, p. 18

PRAYER OVER THE OFFERINGS   [Merciful Grace]

May your merciful grace prepare your servants, O Lord,
for the worthy celebration of these mysteries
and lead them to it by a devout way of life.
Through Christ our Lord.
℞. Amen. ↓

PREFACE (P 14)   [Gift of Faith]

℣. The Lord be with you. ℞. **And with your spirit.**
℣. Lift up your hearts. ℞. **We lift them up to the Lord.**
℣. Let us give thanks to the Lord our God. ℞. **It is right and just.**

It is truly right and just, our duty and our salvation,
always and everywhere to give you thanks,
Lord, holy Father, almighty and eternal God,
through Christ our Lord.

For when he asked the Samaritan woman for water to drink,
he had already created the gift of faith within her
and so ardently did he thirst for her faith,
that he kindled in her the fire of divine love.

And so we, too, give you thanks
and with the Angels
praise your mighty deeds, as we acclaim: → No. 23, p. 23

When the Roman Canon is used, in the section Memento,
Domine *(Remember, Lord, your servants) there is a commemoration of the godparents, and the proper form of the*
Hanc igitur *(Therefore, Lord, we pray), is said.*

Remember, Lord, your servants
who are to present your chosen ones
for the holy grace of your Baptism,

Here the names of the godparents are read out.

and all gathered here,
whose faith and devotion are known to you . . . (p. 24)

Therefore, Lord, we pray:
graciously accept this oblation
which we make to you for your servants,
whom you have been pleased
to enroll, choose and call for eternal life
and for the blessed gift of your grace.
(Through Christ our Lord. Amen.)

The rest follows the Roman Canon, pp. 25-29.

When Eucharistic Prayer II is used, after the words and all
the clergy, *the following is added:*

Remember also, Lord, your servants
who are to present these chosen ones
at the font of rebirth.

When Eucharistic Prayer III is used, after the words the
entire people you have gained for your own, *the following
is added:*

Assist your servants with your grace,
O Lord, we pray,
that they may lead these chosen ones by word and example
to new life in Christ, our Lord.

COMMUNION ANT. Jn 4:13-14   [Water of Eternal Life]

**For anyone who drinks it, says the Lord, the water I shall
give will become in him a spring welling up to eternal
life.** ↓

PRAYER AFTER COMMUNION   [God's Protection]

Give help, O Lord, we pray,
by the grace of your redemption
and be pleased to protect and prepare
those you are to initiate
through the Sacraments of eternal life.
Through Christ our Lord.
℟. **Amen.**   → No. 30, p. 77

Optional Solemn Blessings, p. 97, and Prayers over the People, p. 105

*"The light came into the world,
but people preferred darkness to light."*

MARCH 14

4th SUNDAY OF LENT

*On this Sunday is celebrated the Second Scrutiny in prepa-
ration for the Baptism of the catechumens who are to be
admitted to the Sacraments of Christian Initiation at the
Easter Vigil. The Ritual Mass for the Second Scrutiny is
found on p. 230.*

ENTRANCE ANT. Cf. Is 66:10-11   [Rejoice]
**Rejoice, Jerusalem, and all who love her. Be joyful, all
who were in mourning; exult and be satisfied at her
consoling breast.**   → No. 2, p. 10 (Omit Gloria)

COLLECT   [Devotion and Faith]
O God, who through your Word
reconcile the human race to yourself in a wonderful way,
grant, we pray,
that with prompt devotion and eager faith
the Christian people may hasten
toward the solemn celebrations to come.
Through our Lord Jesus Christ, your Son,

who lives and reigns with you in the unity of the Holy
  Spirit,
one God, for ever and ever. ℟. **Amen.** ↓

FIRST READING 2 Chr 36:14-16, 19-23

[Punishment for Infidelity]

**The Israelites were repeatedly unfaithful to God. They
ignored the prophets sent to them. God allowed them to fall
to the Chaldeans. Jeremiah had foretold this punishment.**

A reading from the second Book of Chronicles

IN those days, all the princes of Judah, the priests, and
the people added infidelity to infidelity, practicing all
the abominations of the nations and polluting the LORD's
temple which he had consecrated in Jerusalem.

Early and often did the LORD, the God of their fathers,
send his messengers to them, for he had compassion on
his people and his dwelling place. But they mocked the
messengers of God, despised his warnings, and scoffed at
his prophets, until the anger of the LORD against his people was so inflamed that there was no remedy. Their enemies burnt the house of God, tore down the walls of
Jerusalem, set all its palaces afire, and destroyed all its
precious objects. Those who escaped the sword were carried captive to Babylon, where they became servants of
the king of the Chaldeans and his sons until the kingdom
of the Persians came to power. All this was to fulfill the
word of the LORD spoken by Jeremiah: "Until the land has
retrieved its lost sabbaths, during all the time it lies waste
it shall have rest while seventy years are fulfilled."

In the first year of Cyrus, king of Persia, in order to fulfill the word of the LORD spoken by Jeremiah, the LORD
inspired King Cyrus of Persia to issue this proclamation
throughout his kingdom, both by word of mouth and in
writing: "Thus says Cyrus, king of Persia: All the kingdoms of the earth the LORD, the God of heaven, has given
to me, and he has also charged me to build him a house

in Jerusalem, which is in Judah. Whoever, therefore, among you belongs to any part of his people, let him go up, and may his God be with him!"—The word of the Lord. ℟. **Thanks be to God.** ↓

RESPONSORIAL PSALM Ps 137   [Remembrance of Zion]

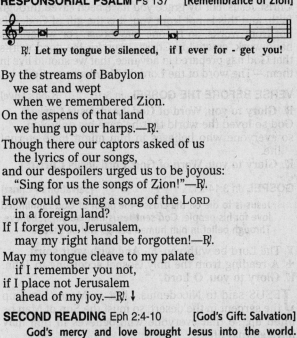

℟. Let my tongue be silenced,   if I ever for - get you!

By the streams of Babylon
   we sat and wept
   when we remembered Zion.
On the aspens of that land
   we hung up our harps.—℟.

Though there our captors asked of us
   the lyrics of our songs,
and our despoilers urged us to be joyous:
   "Sing for us the songs of Zion!"—℟.

How could we sing a song of the LORD
   in a foreign land?
If I forget you, Jerusalem,
   may my right hand be forgotten!—℟.

May my tongue cleave to my palate
   if I remember you not,
if I place not Jerusalem
   ahead of my joy.—℟. ↓

SECOND READING Eph 2:4-10   [God's Gift: Salvation]
   God's mercy and love brought Jesus into the world.
   Salvation is God's gift; it is not the work of human beings.
   Jesus leads all to perform good works.

A reading from the Letter of Saint Paul
to the Ephesians

BROTHERS and sisters: God, who is rich in mercy, because of the great love he had for us, even when we were dead in our transgressions, brought us to life with Christ—by grace you have been saved—, raised us up with him, and seated us with him in the heavens in Christ Jesus, that in the ages to come he might show the immeasurable riches of his grace in his kindness to us in Christ Jesus. For by grace you have been saved through faith, and this is not from you; it is the gift of God; it is not from works, so no one may boast. For we are his handiwork, created in Christ Jesus for the good works that God has prepared in advance, that we should live in them.—The word of the Lord. ℟. **Thanks be to God.** ↓

VERSE BEFORE THE GOSPEL Jn 3:16   [God's Love]

℟. **Glory to you, Word of God, Lord Jesus Christ!***
God so loved the world that he gave his only Son,
so everyone who believes in him might have eternal
    life.
℟. **Glory to you, Word of God, Lord Jesus Christ!** ↓

GOSPEL Jn 3:14-21   [Salvation in Christ]

Jesus is to die on the cross—the proof of God's unlimited love for his people. God sent Jesus that we might believe. Through belief in him human beings will be saved.

℣. The Lord be with you. ℟. **And with your spirit.**
✚ A reading from the holy Gospel according to John.
℟. **Glory to you, O Lord.**

JESUS said to Nicodemus: "Just as Moses lifted up the serpent in the desert, so must the Son of Man be lifted up, so that everyone who believes in him may have eternal life."

For God so loved the world that he gave his only Son, so that everyone who believes in him might not perish but might have eternal life. For God did not send his Son into the world to condemn the world, but that the world might be saved through him. Whoever

---

* *See p. 16 for other Gospel Acclamations.*

believes in him will not be condemned, but whoever does not believe has already been condemned, because he has not believed in the name of the only Son of God. And this is the verdict, that the light came into the world, but people preferred darkness to light, because their works were evil. For everyone who does wicked things hates the light and does not come toward the light, so that his works might not be exposed. But whoever lives the truth comes to the light, so that his works may be clearly seen as done in God.—The Gospel of the Lord. ℟. **Praise to you, Lord Jesus Christ.**   → No. 15, p. 18

Or the Gospel (Jn 9:1-41) from Year A may be said, p. 233.

PRAYER OVER THE OFFERINGS   [Eternal Remedy]

We place before you with joy these offerings,
which bring eternal remedy, O Lord,
praying that we may both faithfully revere them
and present them to you, as is fitting,
for the salvation of all the world.
Through Christ our Lord.
℟. **Amen.**   → No. 21, p. 22 (Pref. P 8-9)

When the Gospel of the Man Born Blind is read, see p. 236 for Preface (P 15).

COMMUNION ANT. Cf. Ps 122 (121):3-4   [Praise]

Jerusalem is built as a city bonded as one together. It is there that the tribes go up, the tribes of the Lord, to praise the name of the Lord. ↓

When the Gospel of the Man Born Blind is read:

COMMUNION ANT. Cf. Jn 9:11, 38   [Spiritual Sight]

The Lord anointed my eyes: I went, I washed, I saw and I believed in God. ↓

PRAYER AFTER COMMUNION   [Illuminate Our Hearts]

O God, who enlighten everyone who comes into this
    world,
illuminate our hearts, we pray,
with the splendor of your grace,
that we may always ponder
what is worthy and pleasing to your majesty
and love you in all sincerity.
Through Christ our Lord.
℟. **Amen.** ↓

*The Deacon or, in his absence, the Priest himself, says the
invitation:* Bow down for the blessing.

PRAYER OVER THE PEOPLE   [Life-Giving Light]

Look upon those who call to you, O Lord,
and sustain the weak;
give life by your unfailing light
to those who walk in the shadow of death,
and bring those rescued by your mercy from every evil
to reach the highest good.
Through Christ our Lord.
℟. **Amen.**   → No. 32, p. 77

MASS FOR THE SECOND SCRUTINY

*This Mass is celebrated when the Second Scrutiny takes place
during the Rite of Christian Initiation of Adults, usually on
the 4th Sunday of Lent.*

ENTRANCE ANT. Cf. Ps 25 (24):15-16   [Have Mercy]

**My eyes are always on the Lord, for he rescues my feet
from the snare. Turn to me and have mercy on me, for I
am alone and poor.** → No. 2, p. 10 (Omit Gloria)

COLLECT   [Spiritual Joy]

Almighty ever-living God,
give to your Church an increase in spiritual joy,
so that those once born of earth
may be reborn as citizens of heaven.
Through our Lord Jesus Christ, your Son,
who lives and reigns with you in the unity of the Holy Spirit,
one God, for ever and ever. ℟. **Amen.** ↓

FIRST READING 1 Sm 16:1b, 6-7, 10-13a   [The Lord's Anointed]

God directs Samuel to anoint David king. God looks into the heart
of each person.

A reading from the first Book of Samuel

THE LORD said to Samuel: "Fill your horn with oil, and be
on your way. I am sending you to Jesse of Bethlehem, for
I have chosen my king from among his sons."

As Jesse and his sons came to the sacrifice, Samuel
looked at Eliab and thought, "Surely the LORD's anointed is
here before him." But the LORD said to Samuel: "Do not judge
from his appearance or from his lofty stature, because I have
rejected him. Not as man sees does God see, because man
sees the appearance but the LORD looks into the heart." In
the same way Jesse presented seven sons before Samuel, but
Samuel said to Jesse, "The LORD has not chosen any one of
these." Then Samuel asked Jesse, "Are these all the sons you
have?" Jesse replied, "There is still the youngest, who is tend-
ing the sheep." Samuel said to Jesse, "Send for him; we will
not begin the sacrificial banquet until he arrives here." Jesse
sent and had the young man brought to them. He was ruddy,
a youth handsome to behold and making a splendid appearance. The LORD said, "There—anoint him, for this is the one!"
Then Samuel, with the horn of oil in hand, anointed him in
the presence of his brothers; and from that day on, the spirit of the LORD rushed upon David.—The word of the Lord.
℟. **Thanks be to God.** ↓

RESPONSORIAL PSALM Ps 23   [The Lord's Protection]

℞. **The Lord is my shep-herd, there is noth-ing I shall want.**

The LORD is my shepherd, I shall not want.
    In verdant pastures he gives me repose;
beside restful waters he leads me;
    he refreshes my soul.—℞.

He guides me in right paths
    for his name's sake.
Even though I walk in the dark valley
    I fear no evil; for you are at my side
with your rod and your staff
    that give me courage.—℞.

You spread the table before me
    in the sight of my foes;
you anoint my head with oil;
    my cup overflows.—℞.

Only goodness and kindness follow me
    all the days of my life;
and I shall dwell in the house of the LORD
    for years to come.—℞. ↓

SECOND READING Eph 5:8-14   [Children of Light]

We are to walk in the light which shows goodness, justice, and truth. Christ gives this light whereby we live.

A reading from the Letter of Saint Paul to the Ephesians

BROTHERS and sisters: You were once darkness, but
now you are light in the Lord. Live as children of light,
for light produces every kind of goodness and righteousness and truth. Try to learn what is pleasing to the Lord.
Take no part in the fruitless works of darkness; rather
expose them, for it is shameful even to mention the things
done by them in secret; but everything exposed by the

light becomes visible, for everything that becomes visible
is light. Therefore, it says:

"Awake, O sleeper,
and arise from the dead,
and Christ will give you light."

The word of the Lord. ℟. **Thanks be to God.** ↓

VERSE BEFORE THE GOSPEL Jn 8:12   [Light of Life]

℟. **Glory to you, Word of God, Lord Jesus Christ!***
I am the light of the world, says the Lord;
whoever follows me will have the light of life.
℟. **Glory to you, Word of God, Lord Jesus Christ!** ↓

GOSPEL Jn 9:1-41 or 9:1, 6-9, 13-17, 34-38   [Cure of Blind Man]

Jesus is the light. He cures a man born blind by bringing him
to see. Jesus identifies himself as the Son of Man.

*[If the "Shorter Form" is used, the indented text in brackets is
omitted.]*

℣. The Lord be with you. ℟. **And with your spirit.**
✤ A reading from the holy Gospel according to John.
℟. **Glory to you, O Lord.**

AS Jesus passed by he saw a man blind from birth.
[His disciples asked him, "Rabbi, who sinned, this
man or his parents, that he was born blind?" Jesus
answered, "Neither he nor his parents sinned; it is so
that the works of God might be made visible through
him. We have to do the works of the one who sent me
while it is day. Night is coming when no one can
work. While I am in the world, I am the light of the
world." When he had said this,]
he spat on the ground and made clay with the saliva, and
smeared the clay on his eyes, and said to him, "Go wash in
the Pool of Siloam"—which means Sent—. So he went
and washed, and came back able to see.

His neighbors and those who had seen him earlier as a
beggar said, "Isn't this the one who used to sit and beg?"

---

* *See p. 16 for other Gospel Acclamations.*

Some said, "It is," but others said, "No, he just looks like him." He said, "I am."

[So they said to him, "How were your eyes opened?" He replied, "The man called Jesus made clay and anointed my eyes and told me, 'Go to Siloam and wash.' So I went there and washed and was able to see." And they said to him, "Where is he?" He said, "I don't know."]

They brought the one who was once blind to the Pharisees. Now Jesus had made clay and opened his eyes on a sabbath. So then the Pharisees also asked him how he was able to see. He said to them, "He put clay on my eyes, and I washed, and now I can see." So some of the Pharisees said, "This man is not from God, because he does not keep the sabbath." But others said, "How can a sinful man do such signs?" And there was a division among them. So they said to the blind man again, "What do you have to say about him, since he opened your eyes?" He said, "He is a prophet."

[Now the Jews did not believe that he had been blind and gained his sight until they summoned the parents of the one who had gained his sight. They asked them, "Is this your son, who you say was born blind? How does he now see?" His parents answered and said, "We know that this is our son and that he was born blind. We do not know how he sees now, nor do we know who opened his eyes. Ask him, he is of age; he can speak for himself." His parents said this because they were afraid of the Jews, for the Jews had already agreed that if anyone acknowledged him as the Christ, he would be expelled from the synagogue. For this reason his parents said, "He is of age; question him."

So a second time they called the man who had been blind and said to him, "Give God the praise! We know that this man is a sinner." He replied, "If he is a sinner, I do not know. One thing I do know is that I was blind and now I see." So they said to him, "What did he do to you? How did he open your eyes?" He answered them, "I told you already and you did not listen. Why do you want to hear it again? Do you want to become his disciples, too?" They ridiculed him and said, "You are that man's disciple; we are disciples of Moses! We know that God spoke to Moses, but we do not know where this one is from." The man answered and said to them, "This is what is so amazing, that you do not know where he is from, yet he opened my eyes. We know that God does not listen to sinners, but if one is devout and does his will, he listens to him. It is unheard of that anyone ever opened the eyes of a person born blind. If this man were not from God, he would not be able to do anything."]

They answered and said to him, "You were born totally in sin, and are you trying to teach us?" Then they threw him out.

When Jesus heard that they had thrown him out, he found him and said, "Do you believe in the Son of Man?" He answered and said, "Who is he, sir, that I may believe in him?" Jesus said to him, "You have seen him, and the one speaking with you is he." He said, "I do believe, Lord," and he worshiped him.

[Then Jesus said, "I came into this world for judgment, so that those who do not see might see, and those who do see might become blind."

Some of the Pharisees who were with him heard this and said to him, "Surely we are not also blind, are we?" Jesus said to them, "If you were blind, you would have no sin; but now you are saying, 'We see,' so your sin remains."]

The Gospel of the Lord. ℟. **Praise to you, Lord Jesus Christ.**   → No. 15, p. 18

PRAYER OVER THE OFFERINGS   [Eternal Remedy]

We place before you with joy these offerings,
which bring eternal remedy, O Lord,
praying that we may both faithfully revere them
and present them to you, as is fitting,
for those who seek salvation.
Through Christ our Lord. ℟. **Amen.** ↓

PREFACE (P 15)   [From Darkness to Radiance]

℣. The Lord be with you. ℟. **And with your spirit.**
℣. Lift up your hearts. ℟. **We lift them up to the Lord.**
℣. Let us give thanks to the Lord our God. ℟. **It is right and just.**

It is truly right and just, our duty and our salvation,
always and everywhere to give you thanks,
Lord, holy Father, almighty and eternal God,
through Christ our Lord.

By the mystery of the Incarnation,
he has led the human race that walked in darkness
into the radiance of the faith
and has brought those born in slavery to ancient sin
through the waters of regeneration
to make them your adopted children.

Therefore, all creatures of heaven and earth
sing a new song in adoration,
and we, with all the host of Angels,
cry out, and without end acclaim: → No. 23, p. 23

*The commemoration of the godparents in the Eucharistic
Prayers takes place as above (pp. 223, 224) and, if the Roman
Canon is used, the proper form of the* Hanc igitur *(Therefore,
Lord, we pray) is said, as in the First Scrutiny (p. 224). The rest
follows the Roman Canon, pp. 25-29.*

COMMUNION ANT. Cf. Jn 9:11, 38   [Spiritual Sight]

**The Lord anointed my eyes: I went, I washed, I saw and I
believed in God.** ↓

PRAYER AFTER COMMUNION   [God's Kindness]

Sustain your family always in your kindness,
O Lord, we pray,
correct them, set them in order,
graciously protect them under your rule,
and in your unfailing goodness

direct them along the way of salvation.
Through Christ our Lord.
℟. **Amen.**   → No. 30, p. 77

Optional Solemn Blessings, p. 97, and Prayers over the People, p. 105

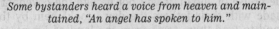

*Some bystanders heard a voice from heaven and main-
tained, "An angel has spoken to him."*

MARCH 21

5th SUNDAY OF LENT

*On this Sunday is celebrated the Third Scrutiny in prep-
aration for the Baptism of the catechumens who are to be
admitted to the Sacraments of Christian Initiation at the
Easter Vigil. The Ritual Mass for the Third Scrutiny is found
on p. 242.*

ENTRANCE ANT. Cf. Ps 43 (42):1-2   **[Rescue Me]**

**Give me justice, O God, and plead my cause against a
nation that is faithless. From the deceitful and cun-
ning rescue me, for you, O God, are my strength.**
→ No. 2, p. 10 (Omit Gloria)

COLLECT   **[Walk in Charity]**

By your help, we beseech you, Lord our God,
may we walk eagerly in that same charity

with which, out of love for the world,
your Son handed himself over to death.
Through our Lord Jesus Christ, your Son,
who lives and reigns with you in the unity of the Holy
  Spirit,
one God, for ever and ever.
℟. **Amen.** ↓

FIRST READING Jer 31:31-34   [A New Covenant]

The Lord promises a new covenant wherein his law will be
written in the hearts of his people. They will recognize
God as their Lord and he will forgive their sins.

A reading from the Book of the Prophet Jeremiah

THE days are coming, says the LORD, when I will
make a new covenant with the house of Israel and
the house of Judah. It will not be like the covenant I
made with their fathers the day I took them by the
hand to lead them forth from the land of Egypt; for
they broke my covenant, and I had to show myself
their master, says the LORD. But this is the covenant
that I will make with the house of Israel after those
days, says the LORD. I will place my law within them,
and write it upon their hearts; I will be their God, and
they shall be my people. No longer will they have need
to teach their friends and relatives how to know the
LORD. All, from least to greatest, shall know me, says
the LORD, for I will forgive their evildoing and remember their sin no more.—The word of the Lord. ℟.
Thanks be to God. ↓

RESPONSORIAL PSALM Ps 51   [A Clean Heart]

℟. Create   a   clean   heart in me, O God.

Have mercy on me, O God, in your goodness;
   in the greatness of your compassion wipe out my
      offense.
Thoroughly wash me from my guilt
   and of my sin cleanse me.—R̷.

A clean heart create for me, O God,
   and a steadfast spirit renew within me.
Cast me not out from your presence,
   and your Holy Spirit take not from me.—R̷.

Give me back the joy of your salvation,
   and a willing spirit sustain in me.
I will teach transgressors your ways,
   and sinners shall return to you.—R̷. ↓

SECOND READING Heb 5:7-9   [Christ's Obedience]
**We recall how Jesus prayed to his Father. Through obedi-
ence to suffering, Jesus became perfect and is the source
of salvation for all who obey him.**

A reading from the Letter to the Hebrews

IN the days when Christ Jesus was in the flesh, he offered prayers and supplications with loud cries and
tears to the one who was able to save him from death,
and he was heard because of his reverence. Son
though he was, he learned obedience from what he
suffered; and when he was made perfect, he became
the source of eternal salvation for all who obey him.—
The word of the Lord. R̷. **Thanks be to God.** ↓

VERSE BEFORE THE GOSPEL Jn 12:26   [Follow Me]
R̷. **Praise and honor to you, Lord Jesus Christ!***
Whoever serves me must follow me, says the Lord;
and where I am, there also will my servant be.
R̷. **Praise and honor to you, Lord Jesus Christ!** ↓

* See p. 16 for other Gospel Acclamations.

GOSPEL Jn 12:20-33   [Christ Draws All]

Jesus predicts his glorification. It comes by dying like the grain of wheat. Those who love their life inordinately will lose it. The Father from heaven answers Jesus.

℣. The Lord be with you. ℟. **And with your spirit.**

✛ A reading from the holy Gospel according to John. ℟. **Glory to you, O Lord.**

SOME Greeks who had come to worship at the Passover Feast came to Philip, who was from Bethsaida in Galilee, and asked him, "Sir, we would like to see Jesus." Philip went and told Andrew; then Andrew and Philip went and told Jesus. Jesus answered them, "The hour has come for the Son of Man to be glorified. Amen, amen, I say to you, unless a grain of wheat falls to the ground and dies, it remains just a grain of wheat; but if it dies, it produces much fruit. Whoever loves his life loses it, and whoever hates his life in this world will preserve it for eternal life. Whoever serves me must follow me, and where I am, there also will my servant be. The Father will honor whoever serves me.

"I am troubled now. Yet what should I say? 'Father, save me from this hour'? But it was for this purpose that I came to this hour. Father, glorify your name." Then a voice came from heaven, "I have glorified it and will glorify it again." The crowd there heard it and said it was thunder; but others said, "An angel has spoken to him." Jesus answered and said, "This voice did not come for my sake but for yours. Now is the time of judgment on this world; now the ruler of this world will be driven out. And when I am lifted up from the earth, I will draw everyone to myself." He said this indicating the kind of death he would die.— The Gospel of the Lord. ℟. **Praise to you, Lord Jesus Christ.**   ➔ No. 15, p. 18

Or the Gospel (Jn 11:1-45) from Year A may be said, p. 244.

PRAYER OVER THE OFFERINGS   [Hear Us]

Hear us, almighty God,
and, having instilled in your servants
the teachings of the Christian faith,
graciously purify them
by the working of this sacrifice.
Through Christ our Lord.
℟. **Amen.**   → No. 21, p. 22 (Pref. P 8-9)

When the Gospel of Lazarus is read, see p. 247 for Preface (P 16).

COMMUNION ANT. Jn 12:24   [Life Through Death]

**Amen, Amen I say to you: Unless a grain of wheat falls
to the ground and dies, it remains a single grain. But if
it dies, it bears much fruit.** ↓

When the Gospel of Lazarus is read:

COMMUNION ANT. Cf. Jn 11:26   [Eternal Life]

**Everyone who lives and believes in me will not die for
ever, says the Lord.** ↓

PRAYER AFTER COMMUNION   [Union with Jesus]

We pray, almighty God,
that we may always be counted among the members of
    Christ,
in whose Body and Blood we have communion.
Who lives and reigns for ever and ever.
℟. **Amen.** ↓

*The Deacon or, in his absence, the Priest himself, says the
invitation:* Bow down for the blessing.

PRAYER OVER THE PEOPLE   [Gift of Mercy]

Bless, O Lord, your people,
who long for the gift of your mercy,
and grant that what, at your prompting, they desire

they may receive by your generous gift.
Through Christ our Lord.
℟. **Amen.**   → No. 32, p. 77

MASS FOR THE THIRD SCRUTINY

*This Mass is celebrated when the Third Scrutiny takes place
during the Rite of Christian Initiation of Adults, usually on
the 5th Sunday of Lent.*

ENTRANCE ANT. Cf. Ps 18 (17):5-7   [The Lord Hears Me]

**The waves of death rose about me; the pains of the nether-
world surrounded me. In my anguish I called to the Lord;
and from his holy temple he heard my voice.**

→ No. 2, p. 10 (Omit Gloria)

COLLECT   [Members of the Church]
Grant, O Lord, to these chosen ones
that, instructed in the holy mysteries,
they may receive new life at the font of Baptism
and be numbered among the members of your Church.
Through our Lord Jesus Christ, your Son,
who lives and reigns with you in the unity of the Holy Spirit,
one God, for ever and ever. ℟. **Amen.** ↓

FIRST READING Ez 37:12-14   [The Lord's Promise]

**The Lord promises to bring his people back to their home-
land. He will be with them and they will know him.**

A reading from the Book of the Prophet Ezekiel

THUS says the Lord God: O my people, I will open your
graves and have you rise from them, and bring you back
to the land of Israel. Then you shall know that I am the Lord,
when I open your graves and have you rise from them, O my

people! I will put my spirit in you that you may live, and I will settle you upon your land; thus you shall know that I am the LORD. I have promised, and I will do it, says the LORD.—The word of the Lord. ℟. **Thanks be to God.** ↓

RESPONSORIAL PSALM Ps 130   [Mercy and Redemption]

℟. **With the Lord there is mer-cy and fullness of redemption.**

Out of the depths I cry to you, O LORD;
    LORD, hear my voice!
Let your ears be attentive
    to my voice in supplication.—℟.

If you, O LORD, mark iniquities,
    LORD, who can stand?
But with you is forgiveness,
    that you may be revered.—℟.

I trust in the LORD;
    my soul trusts in his word.
More than sentinels wait for the dawn,
    let Israel wait for the LORD.—℟.

For with the LORD is kindness
    and with him is plenteous redemption;
and he will redeem Israel
    from all their iniquities.—℟. ↓

SECOND READING Rom 8:8-11   [Indwelling of Christ's Spirit]

The followers of Jesus live in the Spirit of God. The same Spirit who brought Jesus back to life will bring mortal bodies to life since God's Spirit dwells in them.

A reading from the Letter of Saint Paul to the Romans

BROTHERS and sisters: Those who are in the flesh cannot please God. But you are not in the flesh; on the contrary, you are in the spirit, if only the Spirit of God dwells in you. Whoever does not have the Spirit of Christ does not belong to him. But if Christ is in you, although the body is dead because of sin, the spirit is alive because of righteousness. If the Spirit of the one who raised Jesus from the dead dwells in you, the one who raised Christ from the dead will give life to your mortal bodies also, through his Spirit dwelling in you.—The word of the Lord. ℟. **Thanks be to God.** ↓

VERSE BEFORE THE GOSPEL Jn 11:25a, 26   [Resurrection]

℟. **Praise and honor to you, Lord Jesus Christ!***
I am the resurrection and the life, says the Lord;
whoever believes in me, even if he dies, will never die.
℟. **Praise and honor to you, Lord Jesus Christ!** ↓

GOSPEL Jn 11:1-45 or 11:3-7, 17, 20-27, 33b-45   [Lazarus]

Lazarus, the brother of Martha and Mary, died and was buried. When Jesus came, he assured them that he was the resurrection and the life. Jesus gave life back to Lazarus.

[If the "Shorter Form" is used, the indented text in brackets is omitted.]

℣. The Lord be with you. ℟. **And with your spirit.**
✠ A reading from the holy Gospel according to John.
℟. **Glory to you, O Lord.**

[NOW a man was ill, Lazarus from Bethany, the village of Mary and her sister Martha. Mary was the one who had anointed the Lord with perfumed oil and dried his feet with her hair; it was her brother Lazarus who was ill.]
[So] the sisters [*only in Shorter Form:* of Lazarus] sent word to Jesus, saying, "Master, the one you love is ill." When Jesus heard this he said, "This illness is not to end in death, but is for the glory of God, that the Son of God may be glorified through it." Now Jesus loved Martha and her sister and Lazarus. So when he heard that he was ill, he remained for two days in the place where he was. Then after this he said to his disciples, "Let us go back to Judea."

* *See p. 16 for other Gospel Acclamations.*

[The disciples said to him, "Rabbi, the Jews were just trying to stone you, and you want to go back there?" Jesus answered, "Are there not twelve hours in a day? If one walks during the day, he does not stumble, because he sees the light of this world. But if one walks at night, he stumbles, because the light is not in him." He said this, and then told them, "Our friend Lazarus is asleep, but I am going to awaken him." So the disciples said to him, "Master, if he is asleep, he will be saved." But Jesus was talking about his death, while they thought that he meant ordinary sleep. So then Jesus said to them clearly, "Lazarus has died. And I am glad for you that I was not there, that you may believe. Let us go to him." So Thomas, called Didymus, said to his fellow disciples, "Let us also go to die with him."]

When Jesus arrived, he found that Lazarus had already been in the tomb for four days.

[Now Bethany was near Jerusalem, only about two miles away. And many of the Jews had come to Martha and Mary to comfort them about their brother.]

When Martha heard that Jesus was coming, she went to meet him; but Mary sat at home. Martha said to Jesus, "Lord, if you had been here, my brother would not have died. But even now I know that whatever you ask of God, God will give you." Jesus said to her, "Your brother will rise." Martha said to him, "I know he will rise, in the resurrection on the last day." Jesus told her, "I am the resurrection and the life; whoever believes in me, even if he dies, will live, and everyone who lives and believes in me will never die. Do you believe this?" She said to him, "Yes, Lord. I have come to believe that you are the Christ, the Son of God, the one who is coming into the world."

[When she had said this, she went and called her sister Mary secretly, saying, "The teacher is here and is asking for you." As soon as she heard this, she rose quickly and went to him. For Jesus had not yet come into the village, but was still where Martha had met him. So when the Jews who were with her in the house comforting her saw Mary get up quickly and go out, they followed her, presuming that she was going to the tomb to weep there. When Mary came to where Jesus was and saw him, she fell at his feet and said to him, "Lord, if you had been here, my brother would not have died." When Jesus saw her weeping and the Jews who had come with her weeping,]

he became perturbed and deeply troubled, and said, "Where have you laid him?" They said to him, "Sir, come and see." And Jesus wept. So the Jews said, "See how he loved him." But some of them said, "Could not the one who opened the eyes of the blind man have done something so that this man would not have died?"

So Jesus, perturbed again, came to the tomb. It was a cave, and a stone lay across it. Jesus said, "Take away the stone." Martha, the dead man's sister, said to him, "Lord, by now there will be a stench; he has been dead for four days." Jesus said to her, "Did I not tell you that if you believe you will see the glory of God?" So they took away the stone. And Jesus raised his eyes and said, "Father, I thank you for hearing me. I know that you always hear me; but because of the crowd here I have said this, that they may believe that you sent me." And when he had said this, he cried out in a loud voice, "Lazarus, come out!" The dead man came out, tied hand and foot with burial bands, and his face was wrapped in a cloth. So Jesus said to them, "Untie him and let him go."

Now many of the Jews who had come to Mary and seen what he had done began to believe in him.—The Gospel of the Lord. ℟. **Praise to you, Lord Jesus Christ.**

➙ No. 15, p. 18

PRAYER OVER THE OFFERINGS   [Hear Us]
Hear us, almighty God,
and, having instilled in your servants
the first fruits of the Christian faith,
graciously purify them by the working of this sacrifice.

Through Christ our Lord.
℟. **Amen.** ↓

PREFACE (P 16)   [Christ Raised Lazarus]

℣. The Lord be with you. ℟. **And with your spirit.**
℣. Lift up your hearts. ℟. **We lift them up to the Lord.**
℣. Let us give thanks to the Lord our God. ℟. **It is right and just.**

It is truly right and just, our duty and our salvation,
always and everywhere to give you thanks,
Lord, holy Father, almighty and eternal God,
through Christ our Lord.

For as true man he wept for Lazarus his friend
and as eternal God raised him from the tomb,
just as, taking pity on the human race,
he leads us by sacred mysteries to new life.

Through him the host of Angels adores your majesty
and rejoices in your presence for ever.
May our voices, we pray, join with theirs
in one chorus of exultant praise, as we acclaim:

→ No. 23, p. 23

The commemoration of the godparents in the Eucharistic Prayers takes place as above (pp. 223, 224) and, if the Roman Canon is used, the proper form of the Hanc igitur *(Therefore, Lord, we pray) is said, as in the First Scrutiny (p. 224). The rest follows the Roman Canon, pp. 25-29.*

COMMUNION ANT. Cf. Jn 11:26   [Obtain Grace]

Everyone who lives and believes in me will not die for ever, says the Lord. ↓

PRAYER AFTER COMMUNION   [God's Children]

May your people be at one, O Lord, we pray,
and in wholehearted submission to you
may they obtain this grace:
that, safe from all distress,

they may readily live out their joy at being saved
and remember in loving prayer those to be reborn.
Through Christ our Lord.

℟. **Amen.**   → No. 30, p. 77

Optional Solemn Blessings, p. 97, and Prayers over the People, p. 105

*"Blessed are you, who have come
in your abundant mercy!"*

MARCH 28

PALM SUNDAY OF THE PASSION
OF THE LORD

*On this day the Church recalls the entrance of Christ the
Lord into Jerusalem to accomplish his Paschal Mystery.
Accordingly, the memorial of this entrance of the Lord takes
place at all Masses, by means of the Procession or the Solemn
Entrance before the principal Mass or the Simple Entrance
before other Masses. The Solemn Entrance, but not the
Procession, may be repeated before other Masses that are
usually celebrated with a large gathering of people.*

*It is desirable that, where neither the Procession nor the
Solemn Entrance can take place, there be a sacred celebration
of the Word of God on the messianic entrance and on the
Passion of the Lord, either on Saturday evening or on Sunday
at a convenient time.*

The Commemoration of the Lord's Entrance
into Jerusalem

FIRST FORM: THE PROCESSION

At an appropriate hour, a gathering takes place at a smaller church or other suitable place other than inside the church to which the procession will go. The faithful hold branches in their hands.

Meanwhile, the following antiphon or another appropriate chant is sung.

ANTIPHON Mt 21:9   [Hosanna]

Hosanna to the Son of David;
blessed is he who comes
in the name of the Lord,
the King of Israel.
Hosanna in the highest.

After this, the Priest and people sign themselves, while the Priest says: In the name of the Father, and of the Son, and of the Holy Spirit. *Then he greets the people in the usual way. A brief address is given, in which the faithful are invited to participate actively and consciously in the celebration of this day, in these or similar words:*

Dear brethren (brothers and sisters),
since the beginning of Lent until now
we have prepared our hearts by penance and charitable
    works.
Today we gather together to herald with the whole
    Church
the beginning of the celebration
of our Lord's Paschal Mystery,
that is to say, of his Passion and Resurrection.
For it was to accomplish this mystery
that he entered his own city of Jerusalem.
Therefore, with all faith and devotion,
let us commemorate
the Lord's entry into the city for our salvation,
following in his footsteps,

so that, being made by his grace partakers of the Cross,
we may have a share also in his Resurrection and in his
   life.

After the address, the Priest says one of the following prayers
with hands extended.

PRAYER   [Following Christ]

Let us pray.
Almighty ever-living God,
sanctify ✠ these branches with your blessing,
that we, who follow Christ the King in exultation,
may reach the eternal Jerusalem through him.
Who lives and reigns for ever and ever. ℟. **Amen.** ↓

OR   [Christ in Triumph]

Increase the faith of those who place their hope in you,
   O God,
and graciously hear the prayers of those who call on you,
that we, who today hold high these branches
to hail Christ in his triumph,
may bear fruit for you by good works accomplished in
   him.
Who lives and reigns for ever and ever.
℟. **Amen.** ↓

The Priest sprinkles the branches with holy water without
saying anything.

Then a Deacon or, if there is no Deacon, a Priest, proclaims
in the usual way the Gospel concerning the Lord's entrance
according to one of the four Gospels.

GOSPEL Mk 11:1-10   [Jesus' Triumphal Entry]

   In triumphant glory Jesus comes into Jerusalem. The people spread their cloaks on the ground for him, wave olive
   branches and sing in his honor.

℣. The Lord be with you. ℟. **And with your spirit.**
✠ A reading from the holy Gospel according to Mark.
℟. **Glory to you, O Lord.**

WHEN Jesus and his disciples drew near to Jerusalem, to Bethphage and Bethany at the Mount of Olives, he sent two of his disciples and said to them, "Go into the village opposite you, and immediately on entering it, you will find a colt tethered on which no one has ever sat. Untie it and bring it here. If anyone should say to you, 'Why are you doing this?' reply, 'The Master has need of it and will send it back here at once.' " So they went off and found a colt tethered at a gate outside on the street, and they untied it. Some of the bystanders said to them, "What are you doing, untying the colt?" They answered them just as Jesus had told them to, and they permitted them to do it. So they brought the colt to Jesus and put their cloaks over it. And he sat on it. Many people spread their cloaks on the road, and others spread leafy branches that they had cut from the fields. Those preceding him as well as those following kept crying out:

"Hosanna!
   Blessed is he who comes in the name of the Lord!
   Blessed is the kingdom of our father David that is
      to come!
Hosanna in the highest!"

The Gospel of the Lord. ℟. **Praise to you, Lord Jesus Christ.**

OR

GOSPEL Jn 12:12-16   [Blessed Is Israel's King]

(See commentary in preceding Gospel.)

℣. The Lord be with you. ℟. **And with your spirit.**
✤ A reading from the holy Gospel according to John.
℟. **Glory to you, O Lord.**

WHEN the great crowd that had come to the feast heard that Jesus was coming to Jerusalem, they took palm branches and went out to meet him, and cried out:

"Hosanna!
Blessed is he who comes in the name of the Lord,
    the king of Israel."
Jesus found an ass and sat upon it, as is written:
    Fear no more, O daughter Zion;
    see, your king comes, seated upon an ass's colt.
His disciples did not understand this at first, but when
Jesus had been glorified they remembered that these
things were written about him and that they had done
this for him.—The Gospel of the Lord. ℟. **Praise to you,
Lord Jesus Christ.**

*After the Gospel, a brief homily may be given. Then, to begin
the Procession, an invitation may be given by a Priest or a
Deacon or a lay minister, in these or similar words:*

Dear brethren (brothers and sisters),
like the crowds who acclaimed Jesus in Jerusalem,
let us go forth in peace.

OR

Let us go forth in peace.
℟. **In the name of Christ. Amen.**

*The Procession to the church where Mass will be celebrated
then sets off in the usual way. If incense is used, the thurifer
goes first, carrying a thurible with burning incense, then an
acolyte or another minister, carrying a cross decorated with
palm branches according to local custom, between two ministers with lighted candles. Then follow the Deacon carrying
the Book of the Gospels, the Priest with the ministers, and,
after them, all the faithful carrying branches.*

*As the Procession moves forward, the following or other suit-
able chants in honor of Christ the King are sung by the choir
and people.*

ANTIPHON 1   [Hosanna]
**The children of the Hebrews, carrying olive branches,
went to meet the Lord, crying out and saying:
Hosanna in the highest.**

If appropriate, this antiphon is repeated between the strophes (verses) of the following Psalm.

PSALM 24 (23)   [The King of Glory]

The LORD's is the earth and its fullness,
the world, and those who dwell in it.
It is he who set it on the seas;
on the rivers he made it firm. *(The antiphon is repeated.)*

Who shall climb the mountain of the LORD?
Who shall stand in his holy place?
The clean of hands and pure of heart,
whose soul is not set on vain things,
who has not sworn deceitful words.

(The antiphon is repeated.)

Blessings from the LORD shall he receive,
and right reward from the God who saves him.
Such are the people who seek him,
who seek the face of the God of Jacob.

(The antiphon is repeated.)

O gates, lift high your heads;
grow higher, ancient doors.
Let him enter, the king of glory!

(The antiphon is repeated.)

Who is this king of glory?
The LORD, the mighty, the valiant;
the LORD, the valiant in war. *(The antiphon is repeated.)*

O gates, lift high your heads;
grow higher, ancient doors.
Let him enter, the king of glory!

(The antiphon is repeated.)

Who is this king of glory?
He, the LORD of hosts,
he is the king of glory. *(The antiphon is repeated.)*

ANTIPHON 2   [Hosanna]

The children of the Hebrews spread their garments on
     the road,
crying out and saying: Hosanna to the Son of David;
blesssed is he who comes in the name of the Lord.

*If appropriate, this antiphon is repeated between the
strophes (verses) of the following Psalm.*

PSALM 47 (46)   **[The Great King]**

**All peoples, clap your hands.
Cry to God with shouts of joy!
For the LORD, the Most High, is awesome,
the great king over all the earth.** *(The antiphon is repeated.)*

**He humbles peoples under us
and nations under our feet.
Our heritage he chose for us,
the pride of Jacob whom he loves.**

(The antiphon is repeated.)

**God goes up with shouts of joy.
The LORD goes up with trumpet blast.
Sing praise for God; sing praise!
Sing praise to our king; sing praise!**

(The antiphon is repeated.)

**God is king of all the earth.
Sing praise with all your skill.
God reigns over the nations.
God sits upon his holy throne.**   *(The antiphon is repeated.)*

**The princes of the peoples are assembled
with the people of the God of Abraham.
The rulers of the earth belong to God,
who is greatly exalted.**   *(The antiphon is repeated.)*

Hymn to Christ the King

Chorus:
**Glory and honor and praise be to you, Christ, King and
    Redeemer,
to whom young children cried out loving Hosannas with
    joy.**

All repeat: **Glory and honor . . .**

Chorus:
**Israel's King are you, King David's magnificent off-
    spring;**

you are the ruler who come blest in the name of the
　Lord.

All repeat: **Glory and honor ...**

Chorus:
Heavenly hosts on high unite in singing your praises;
men and women on earth and all creation join in.

All repeat: **Glory and honor ...**

Chorus:
Bearing branches of palm, Hebrews came crowding to
　greet you;
see how with prayers and hymns we come to pay you
　our vows.

All repeat: **Glory and honor ...**

Chorus:
They offered gifts of praise to you, so near to your
　Passion;
see how we sing this song now to you reigning on high.

All repeat: **Glory and honor ...**

Chorus:
Those you were pleased to accept; now accept our gifts
　of devotion,
good and merciful King, lover of all that is good.

All repeat: **Glory and honor ...**

As the procession enters the church, there is sung the follow-
ing responsory or another chant, which should speak of the
Lord's entrance.

RESPONSORY　　　　　　　　　　　　　　　　[Hosanna]
R̷. **As the Lord entered the holy city, the children of**
the Hebrews proclaimed the resurrection of life.
Waving their branches of palm, they cried: Hosanna in
the Highest.

V̷. **When the people had heard that Jesus was coming to**
Jerusalem, they went out to meet him. Waving their
branches of palms, they cried: Hosanna in the Highest.

When the Priest arrives at the altar, he venerates it and, if appropriate, incenses it. Then he goes to the chair, where he puts aside the cope, if he has worn one, and puts on the chasuble. Omitting the other Introductory Rites of the Mass and, if appropriate, the Kyrie (Lord, have mercy), *he says the Collect of the Mass, and then continues the Mass in the usual way.*

SECOND FORM: THE SOLEMN ENTRANCE

When a procession outside the church cannot take place, the entrance of the Lord is celebrated inside the church by means of a Solemn Entrance before the principal Mass.

Holding branches in their hands, the faithful gather either outside, in front of the church door, or inside the church itself. The Priest and ministers and a representative group of the faithful go to a suitable place in the church outside the sanctuary, where at least the greater part of the faithful can see the rite.

While the Priest approaches the appointed place, the antiphon Hosanna *or another appropriate chant is sung. Then the blessing of branches and the proclamation of the Gospel of the Lord's entrance into Jerusalem take place as above (pp. 250-252). After the Gospel, the Priest processes solemnly with the ministers and the representative group of the faithful through the church to the sanctuary, while the responsory* As the Lord entered *(p. 255, bottom) or another appropriate chant is sung.*

Arriving at the altar, the Priest venerates it. He then goes to the chair and, omitting the Introductory Rites of the Mass and, if appropriate, the Kyrie (Lord, have mercy), *he says the Collect of the Mass, and then continues the Mass in the usual way.*

THIRD FORM: THE SIMPLE ENTRANCE

At all other Masses of this Sunday at which the Solemn Entrance is not held, the memorial of the Lord's entrance into Jerusalem takes place by means of a Simple Entrance.

While the Priest proceeds to the altar, the Entrance Antiphon with its Psalm (p. 257) or another chant on the same theme is sung. Arriving at the altar, the Priest venerates it and goes to the chair. After the Sign of the Cross, he greets the people and continues the Mass in the usual way.

At other Masses, in which singing at the entrance cannot take place, the Priest, as soon as he has arrived at the altar and venerated it, greets the people, reads the Entrance Antiphon, and continues the Mass in the usual way.

ENTRANCE ANT. Cf. Jn 12:1, 12-13; Ps 24 (23): 9-10
[Hosanna in the Highest]

Six days before the Passover, when the Lord came into the city of Jerusalem, the children ran to meet him; in their hands they carried palm branches and with a loud voice cried out: Hosanna in the highest! Blessed are you, who have come in your abundant mercy!

O gates, lift high your heads; grow higher, ancient doors. Let him enter, the king of glory! Who is this king of glory? He, the Lord of hosts, he is the king of glory. Hosanna in the highest! Blessed are you, who have come in your abundant mercy!

AT THE MASS

After the Procession or Solemn Entrance the Priest begins the Mass with the Collect.

COLLECT   [Patient Suffering]

Almighty ever-living God,
who as an example of humility for the human race to
    follow
caused our Savior to take flesh and submit to the Cross,
graciously grant that we may heed his lesson of patient
    suffering
and so merit a share in his Resurrection.
Who lives and reigns with you in the unity of the Holy
    Spirit,
one God, for ever and ever.
℟. **Amen.** ↓

FIRST READING Is 50:4-7   **[Christ's Suffering]**

The servant was persecuted and struck by his own people; he was spit upon and beaten. He proclaims the true faith and suffers to atone for the sins of his people. Here we see a foreshadowing of the true servant of God.

A reading from the Book of the Prophet Isaiah

THE Lord GOD has given me
    a well-trained tongue,
that I might know how to speak to the weary
    a word that will rouse them.
Morning after morning
    he opens my ear that I may hear;
and I have not rebelled,
    have not turned back.
I gave my back to those who beat me,
    my cheeks to those who plucked my beard;
my face I did not shield
    from buffets and spitting.

The Lord GOD is my help,
    therefore I am not disgraced;
I have set my face like flint,
    knowing that I shall not be put to shame.
The word of the Lord. ℟. **Thanks be to God.** ↓

RESPONSORIAL PSALM Ps 22   **[Christ's Abandonment]**

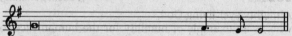

   ℟. **My God, my God, why have you a - ban - doned me?**

All who see me scoff at me;
   they mock me with parted lips, they wag their heads:
"He relied on the LORD; let him deliver him,
   let him rescue him, if he loves him."—℟.

Indeed, many dogs surround me,
   a pack of evildoers closes in upon me;
they have pierced my hands and my feet;
   I can count all my bones.—℟.

They divide my garments among them,
  and for my vesture they cast lots.
But you, O LORD, be not far from me;
  O my help, hasten to aid me.—℟.

I will proclaim your name to my brethren;
  in the midst of the assembly I will praise you:
"You who fear the LORD, praise him;
  all you descendants of Jacob, give glory to him;
  revere him, all you descendants of Israel!"—℟. ↓

SECOND READING Phil 2:6-11   [Humility]

**Paul urges us to humility by which we are made like to
Christ, our Lord, who, putting off the majesty of his divinity, became man and humbled himself in obedience to the
ignominious death of the cross.**

A reading from the Letter of Saint Paul
to the Philippians

CHRIST Jesus, though he was in the form of God,
  did not regard equality with God
    something to be grasped.
Rather, he emptied himself,
    taking the form of a slave,
    coming in human likeness;
    and found human in appearance,
    he humbled himself,
    becoming obedient to the point of death,
    even death on a cross.
Because of this, God greatly exalted him
    and bestowed on him the name
    which is above every name,
    that at the name of Jesus
    every knee should bend,
    of those in heaven and on the earth and under the
      earth,
    and every tongue confess that

Jesus Christ is Lord,
　　to the glory of God the Father.
The word of the Lord. ℟. **Thanks be to God.** ↓

VERSE BEFORE THE GOSPEL Phil 2:8-9 [Obedient to Death]

℟. **Praise to you, Lord Jesus Christ, King of endless
　　glory!***
Christ became obedient to the point of death,
even death on a cross.
Because of this, God greatly exalted him
and bestowed on him the name which is above every
　　name.
℟. **Praise to you, Lord Jesus Christ, King of endless
　　glory!** ↓

GOSPEL Mk 14:1—15:47 or 15:1-39　　　[Christ's Passion]

**Mark recounts the events that led up to the betrayal of
Jesus and his final condemnation—his death on the cross.
At the Last Supper, Jesus institutes the Holy Eucharist.**

*When the Shorter Form is read, the Passion begins at no. 8
below and ends after no. 13, pp. 266-268.*

*The fourteen subheadings introduced into the reading enable
those who so desire to meditate on this text while making the
Stations of the Cross.*

*The Passion may be read by lay readers, with the part of
Christ, if possible, read by a Priest. The Narrator is noted by
N, the words of Jesus by a ✠ and the words of others by V
(Voice) and C (Crowd). The part of the Crowd (C) printed in
boldface type may be recited by the people.*

*We participate in the passion narrative in several ways: by
reading it and reflecting on it during the week ahead; by listening with faith as it is proclaimed; by respectful posture
during the narrative; by reverent silence after the passage
about Christ's death. We do not hold the palms during the
reading on Palm Sunday.*

---

* *See p. 16 for other Gospel Acclamations.*

The message of the liturgy in proclaiming the passion narratives in full is to enable the assembly to see vividly the love of Christ for each person, despite their sins, a love that even death could not vanquish. The crimes during the Passion of Christ cannot be attributed indiscriminately to all Jews of that time, nor to Jews today. The Jewish people should not be referred to as though rejected or cursed, as if this view followed Scripture. The Church ever keeps in mind that Jesus, his mother Mary, and the Apostles were Jewish. As the Church has always held, Christ freely suffered his Passion and Death because of the sins of all, that all might be saved.

N. **T**HE Passion of our Lord Jesus Christ according to Mark.

1. PLOT AGAINST JESUS AND SUPPER AT BETHANY

N. **T**HE Passover and the Feast of Unleavened Bread were to take place in two days' time. So the chief priests and the scribes were seeking a way to arrest him by treachery and put him to death. They said, **C. "Not during the festival, for fear that there may be a riot among the people."**

N. When he was in Bethany reclining at table in the house of Simon the leper, a woman came with an alabaster jar of perfumed oil, costly genuine spikenard. She broke the alabaster jar and poured it on his head. There were some who were indignant. **C. "Why has there been this waste of perfumed oil? It could have been sold for more than three hundred days' wages and the money given to the poor."N.** They were infuriated with her. Jesus said, ✝ "Let her alone. Why do you make trouble for her? She has done a good thing for me. The poor you will always have with you, and whenever you wish you can do good to them, but you will not always have me. She has done what she could. She has anticipated anointing my body for burial. Amen, I say to you, wherever the gospel is proclaimed to the whole world, what she has done will be told in memory of her."

2. THE TREASON OF JUDAS

N. **T**HEN Judas Iscariot, one of the Twelve, went off to the chief priests to hand him over to them. When they heard him they were pleased and promised to pay him money. Then he looked for an opportunity to hand him over.

3. THE LAST SUPPER

N. **O**N the first day of the Feast of Unleavened Bread, when they sacrificed the Passover lamb, his disciples said to him, **C.** **"Where do you want us to go and prepare for you to eat the Passover?"** **N.** He sent two of his disciples and said to them, ✢ "Go into the city and a man will meet you, carrying a jar of water. Follow him. Wherever he enters, say to the master of the house, 'The Teacher says, "Where is my guest room where I may eat the Passover with my disciples?" ' Then he will show you a large upper room furnished and ready. Make the preparations for us there." **N.** The disciples then went off, entered the city, and found it just as he had told them; and they prepared the Passover.

When it was evening, he came with the Twelve. And as they reclined at table and were eating, Jesus said, ✢ "Amen, I say to you, one of you will betray me, one who is eating with me." **N.** They began to be distressed and to say to him, one by one, **V.** "Surely it is not I?" **N.** He said to them, ✢ "One of the Twelve, the one who dips with me into the dish. For the Son of Man indeed goes, as it is written of him, but woe to that man by whom the Son of Man is betrayed. It would be better for that man if he had never been born."

N. While they were eating, he took bread, said the blessing, broke it, and gave it to them, and said,

✠ "Take it; this is my body." **N.** Then he took a cup, gave thanks, and gave it to them, and they all drank from it. He said to them, ✠ "This is my blood of the covenant, which will be shed for many. Amen, I say to you, I shall not drink again the fruit of the vine until the day when I drink it new in the kingdom of God." **N.** Then, after singing a hymn, they went out to the Mount of Olives.

N. Then Jesus said to them, ✠ "All of you will have your faith shaken, for it is written:

I will strike the shepherd,
and the sheep will be dispersed.

But after I have been raised up, I shall go before you to Galilee." **N.** Peter said to him, **V.** "Even though all should have their faith shaken, mine will not be." **N.** Then Jesus said to him, ✠ "Amen, I say to you, this very night before the cock crows twice you will deny me three times." **N.** But he vehemently replied, **V.** "Even though I should have to die with you, I will not deny you." **N.** And they all spoke similarly.

4. THE PRAYER IN GETHSEMANE

N. **T**HEN they came to a place named Gethsemane, and he said to his disciples, ✠ "Sit here while I pray." **N.** He took with him Peter, James, and John, and began to be troubled and distressed. Then he said to them, ✠ "My soul is sorrowful even to death. Remain here and keep watch." **N.** He advanced a little and fell to the ground and prayed that if it were possible the hour might pass by him; he said, ✠ "Abba, Father, all things are possible to you. Take this cup away from me, but not what I will but what you will." **N.** When he returned he found them asleep. He said to Peter, ✠ "Simon, are you asleep? Could you not keep watch for one hour? Watch and pray that you may not undergo the test. The spirit is willing but the flesh is weak." **N.** Withdrawing again, he prayed, saying the same thing. Then he returned once more and found them asleep, for they could not keep their eyes open and did not know what to answer him. He returned a third time and said to them, ✝ "Are you still sleeping and taking your rest? It is enough. The hour has come. Behold, the Son of Man is to be handed over to sinners. Get up, let us go. See, my betrayer is at hand."

5. THE ARREST OF JESUS

N. **T**HEN, while he was still speaking, Judas, one of the Twelve, arrived, accompanied by a crowd with swords and clubs who had come from the chief priests, the scribes, and the elders. His betrayer had arranged a signal with them, saying, **V.** "The man I shall kiss is the one; arrest him and lead him away securely." **N.** He came and immediately went over to him and said, **V.** "Rabbi." **N.** And he kissed him. At this they laid hands on him and arrested him. One of the bystanders drew his sword, struck the high priest's servant, and cut off his ear. Jesus said to them in reply, ✝ "Have you come out as against a robber, with swords and clubs, to seize me? Day after day I was with you teaching in the temple area, yet you did not arrest me; but that the Scriptures may be fulfilled." **N.** And they all left him and fled. Now a young man followed him wearing nothing but a linen cloth about his body. They seized him, but he left the cloth behind and ran off naked.

6. JESUS BEFORE CAIAPHAS

N. **T**HEY led Jesus away to the high priest, and all the chief priests and the elders and the scribes came together. Peter followed him at a distance into the high priest's courtyard and was seated with the guards, warming himself at the fire. The chief priests and the entire Sanhedrin kept trying to obtain testimony against Jesus in order to put him to death, but they found none. Many gave false witness against him, but their testimony did not agree. Some took the stand and testified falsely against him, alleging, **C.** **"We heard him say, 'I will destroy this temple made with hands and within three days I will build another not made with hands.'"** **N.** Even so their testimony did not agree. The high priest rose before the assembly and questioned Jesus, saying, **V.** "Have you no answer? What are these men testifying against you?" **N.** But he was silent and answered nothing. Again the high priest asked him and said to him, **V.** "Are you the Christ, the son of the Blessed One?" **N.** Then Jesus answered, ✝ "I am;

and 'you will see the Son of Man
   seated at the right hand of the Power
   and coming with the clouds of heaven.'"

N. At that the high priest tore his garments and said, **V.** "What further need have we of witnesses? You have heard the blasphemy. What do you think?" **N.** They all condemned him as deserving to die. Some began to spit on him. They blindfolded him and struck him and said to him, **C.** "Prophesy!" **N.** And the guards greeted him with blows.

7. PETER'S DENIAL

N. WHILE Peter was below in the courtyard, one of the high priest's maids came along. Seeing Peter warming himself, she looked intently at him and said, **C.** **"You too were with the Nazarene, Jesus."** **N.** But he denied it saying, **V.** "I neither know nor understand what you are talking about." **N.** So he went out into the outer court. Then the cock crowed. The maid saw him and began again to say to the bystanders, **C.** **"This man is one of them."** **N.** Once again he denied it. A little later the bystanders said to Peter once more, **C.** **"Surely you are one of them; for you too are a**

Galilean." **N.** He began to curse and to swear, **V.** "I do not know this man about whom you are talking." **N.** And immediately a cock crowed a second time. Then Peter remembered the word that Jesus had said to him, "Before the cock crows twice you will deny me three times." He broke down and wept.

[Beginning of Shorter Form]

8. JESUS BEFORE PILATE

N. **A**S soon as morning came, the chief priests with the elders and the scribes, that is, the whole Sanhedrin, held a council. They bound Jesus, led him away, and handed him over to Pilate. Pilate questioned him, **V.** "Are you the king of the Jews?" **N.** He said to him in reply, ✝ "You say so." **N.** The chief priests accused him of many things. Again Pilate questioned him, **V.** "Have you no answer? See how many things they accuse you of." **N.** Jesus gave him no further answer, so that Pilate was amazed.

9. BARABBAS

N. **N**OW on the occasion of the feast he used to release to them one prisoner whom they requested. A man called Barabbas was then in prison along with the rebels who had committed murder in a rebellion. The crowd came forward and began to ask him to do for them as he was accustomed. Pilate answered, **V.** "Do you want me to release to you the king of the Jews?" **N.** For he knew that it was out of envy that the chief priests had handed him over. But the chief priests stirred up the crowd to have him release Barabbas for them instead. Pilate again said to them in reply, **V.** "Then what do you want me to do with the man you call the king of the Jews?" **N.** They shouted again, **C. "Crucify him." N.** Pilate said to them, **V.** "Why? What evil has he done?" **N.** They only shouted the louder, **C. "Crucify him." N.** So Pilate, wishing to satisfy the crowd, released Barabbas to them and, after he had Jesus scourged, handed him over to be crucified.

10. THE CROWNING WITH THORNS

N. THE soldiers led him away inside the palace, that is, the praetorium, and assembled the whole cohort. They clothed him in purple and, weaving a crown of thorns, placed it on him. They began to salute him with, **C. "Hail, King of the Jews!" N.** and kept striking his head with a reed and spitting upon him. They knelt before him in homage. And when they had mocked him, they stripped him of the purple cloak, dressed him in his own clothes, and led him out to crucify him.

11. THE CRUCIFIXION

N. THEY pressed into service a passer-by, Simon, a Cyrenian, who was coming in from the country, the father of Alexander and Rufus, to carry his cross.

They brought him to the place of Golgotha—which is translated Place of the Skull—. They gave him wine drugged with myrrh, but he did not take it. Then they crucified him and divided his garments by casting lots for them to see what each should take. It was nine o'clock in the morning when they crucified him. The inscription of the charge against him read, "The King of the Jews." With him they crucified two revolutionaries, one on his right and one on his left. *[12. ON CALVARY]* **N.** Those passing by reviled him, shaking their heads and saying, **C. "Aha! You who would destroy the temple and rebuild it in three days, save yourself by coming down from the cross." N.** Likewise the chief priests, with the scribes, mocked him among themselves and said, **C. "He saved others; he cannot save himself. Let the Christ, the King of Israel, come down now from the cross that we may see and believe."** N. Those who were crucified with him also kept abusing him.

13. THE DEATH OF JESUS

N. **A**T noon darkness came over the whole land until three in the afternoon. And at three o'clock Jesus cried out in a loud voice, ✝ *"Eloi, Eloi, lema sabachthani?"* N. which is translated, ✝ "My God, my God, why have you forsaken me?" N. Some of the bystanders who heard it said, **C. "Look, he is calling Elijah."** N. One of them ran, soaked a sponge with wine, put it on a reed and gave it to him to drink, saying, **V. "Wait, let us see if Elijah comes to take him down."** N. Jesus gave a loud cry and breathed his last.

Here all kneel and pause for a short time.

The veil of the sanctuary was torn in two from top to bottom. When the centurion who stood facing him saw how he breathed his last he said, **V. "Truly this man was the Son of God!"** *[End of Shorter Form] [14. THE BURIAL]* N. There were also women looking on from a distance. Among them were Mary Magdalene, Mary the mother of the younger James and of Joses, and Salome. These women had followed him when he was in Galilee and ministered to him. There were also many other women who had come up with him to Jerusalem.

When it was already evening, since it was the day of preparation, the day before the sabbath, Joseph of Arimathea, a distinguished member of the council, who was himself awaiting the kingdom of God, came and courageously went to Pilate and asked for the body of Jesus. Pilate was amazed that he was already dead. He summoned the centurion and asked him if Jesus had already died. And when he learned of it from the centurion, he gave the body to Joseph. Having bought a linen cloth, he took him down, wrapped him in the linen cloth, and laid him in a tomb that had been hewn out of the rock. Then he rolled a stone against the entrance to the tomb. Mary Magdalene and Mary the mother of Joses watched where he was laid.—The Gospel of the Lord. ℟. **Praise to you, Lord Jesus Christ.**   → No. 15, p. 18

After the narrative of the Passion, a brief homily should take place, if appropriate. A period of silence may also be observed.

PRAYER OVER THE OFFERINGS   [Reconciled with God]

Through the Passion of your Only Begotten Son, O Lord,
may our reconciliation with you be near at hand,
so that, though we do not merit it by our own deeds,
yet by this sacrifice made once for all,
we may feel already the effects of your mercy.
Through Christ our Lord. ℟. **Amen.** ↓

PREFACE (P 19)   [Purchased Our Justification]

℣. The Lord be with you. ℟. **And with your spirit.**
℣. Lift up your hearts. ℟. **We lift them up to the Lord.** ℣. Let us give thanks to the Lord our God. ℟. **It is right and just.**

It is truly right and just, our duty and our salvation,
always and everywhere to give you thanks,
Lord, holy Father, almighty and eternal God,
through Christ our Lord.

For, though innocent, he suffered willingly for sinners
and accepted unjust condemnation to save the guilty.

His Death has washed away our sins,
and his Resurrection has purchased our justification.

And so, with all the Angels,
we praise you, as in joyful celebration we acclaim:

→ No. 23, p. 23

COMMUNION ANT. Mt 26:42   [God's Will]
Father, if this chalice cannot pass without my drinking it, your will be done. ↓

PRAYER AFTER COMMUNION   [Nourishing Gifts]

Nourished with these sacred gifts,
we humbly beseech you, O Lord,
that, just as through the death of your Son
you have brought us to hope for what we believe,
so by his Resurrection
you may lead us to where you call.
Through Christ our Lord.
℟. **Amen.** ↓

The Deacon or, in his absence, the Priest himself, says the invitation: Bow down for the blessing.

PRAYER OVER THE PEOPLE   [God's Family]

Look, we pray, O Lord, on this your family,
for whom our Lord Jesus Christ
did not hesitate to be delivered into the hands of the
    wicked
and submit to the agony of the Cross.
Who lives and reigns for ever and ever.
℟. **Amen.**

→ No. 32, p. 77

"The Spirit of the Lord is upon me."

APRIL 1

THURSDAY OF HOLY WEEK
[HOLY THURSDAY]

THE CHRISM MASS

This Mass, which the Bishop concelebrates with his presbyterate, should be, as it were, a manifestation of the Priests' communion with their Bishop. Accordingly it is desirable that all the Priests participate in it, insofar as is possible, and during it receive Communion even under both kinds. To signify the unity of the presbyterate of the diocese, the Priests who concelebrate with the Bishop should be from different regions of the diocese.

In accord with traditional practice, the blessing of the Oil of the Sick takes place before the end of the Eucharistic Prayer, but the blessing of the Oil of Catechumens and the consecration of the Chrism take place after Communion. Nevertheless, for pastoral reasons, it is permitted for the entire rite of blessing to take place after the Liturgy of the Word.

ENTRANCE ANT. Rev 1:6   [Kingdom of Priests]
Jesus Christ has made us into a kingdom, priests for his God and Father. To him be glory and power for ever and ever. Amen.   ➙ No. 2, p. 10

271

The Gloria *is said.*

COLLECT [Faithful Witnesses]

O God, who anointed your Only Begotten Son with the
    Holy Spirit
and made him Christ and Lord,
graciously grant
that, being made sharers in his consecration,
we may bear witness to your Redemption in the world.
Through our Lord Jesus Christ, your Son,
who lives and reigns with you in the unity of the Holy
    Spirit,
one God, for ever and ever.
℟. **Amen.** ↓

FIRST READING Is 61:1-3ab, 6a, 8b-9 [The Lord's Anointed]

**The prophet, anointed by God to bring the Good News to
the poor, proclaims a message filled with hope. It is one
that replaces mourning with gladness.**

A reading from the Book of the Prophet Isaiah

THE Spirit of the Lord GOD is upon me,
    because the LORD has anointed me;
He has sent me to bring glad tidings to the lowly,
    to heal the brokenhearted,
To proclaim liberty to the captives
    and release to the prisoners,
To announce a year of favor from the LORD
    and a day of vindication by our God,
    to comfort all who mourn;
To place on those who mourn in Zion
    a diadem instead of ashes,
To give them oil of gladness in place of mourning,
    a glorious mantle instead of a listless spirit.

You yourselves shall be named priests of the LORD,
    ministers of our God you shall be called.

I will give them their recompense faithfully,
  a lasting covenant I will make with them.
Their descendants shall be renowned among the
    nations,
  and their offspring among the peoples;
All who see them shall acknowledge them
  as a race the LORD has blessed.

The word of the Lord. ℟. **Thanks be to God.** ↓

RESPONSORIAL PSALM Ps 89   [God the Savior]

℟. For ev - er I   will sing the good-ness of the Lord.

"I have found David, my servant;
  with my holy oil I have anointed him,
that my hand may be always with him,
  and that my arm may make him strong."—℟.

"My faithfulness and my kindness shall be with him,
  and through my name shall his horn be exalted.
He shall say of me, 'You are my father,
  my God, the Rock my savior.' "—℟. ↓

SECOND READING Rv 1:5-8   [The Alpha and the Omega]

**God says, "I am the Alpha and the Omega, the one who is
and who was and who is to come, the Almighty!" All shall
see God as he comes amid the clouds.**

A reading from the Book of Revelation

[G RACE to you and peace] from Jesus Christ, who is
the faithful witness, the firstborn of the dead and
ruler of the kings of earth. To him who loves us and has
freed us from our sins by his Blood, who has made us into
a Kingdom, priests for his God and Father, to him be
glory and power forever and ever! Amen.
  Behold, he is coming amid the clouds,
    and every eye will see him,
    even of those who pierced him.

All the peoples of the earth will lament him.
   Yes. Amen.
"I am the Alpha and the Omega," says the Lord God,
"the one who is and who was and who is to come, the
Almighty!"—The word of the Lord. ℟. **Thanks be to
God.** ↓

VERSE BEFORE THE GOSPEL Is 61:1(cited in Lk 4:18)

[Glad Tidings]

℟. **Glory to you, Word of God, Lord Jesus Christ!***
The Spirit of the LORD is upon me
for he sent me to bring glad tidings to the poor.
℟. **Glory to you, Word of God, Lord Jesus Christ!** ↓

GOSPEL Lk 4:16-21   [Christ the Messiah]

Jesus reads in the synagogue at Nazareth the words of Isaiah
quoted in the first reading. Jesus is the Anointed One. He
tells the people that today Isaiah's prophecy is fulfilled.

℣. The Lord be with you. ℟. **And with your spirit.**
✛ A reading from the holy Gospel according to Luke.
℟. **Glory to you, O Lord.**

JESUS came to Nazareth, where he had grown up,
and went according to his custom into the synagogue on the sabbath day. He stood up to read and
was handed a scroll of the prophet Isaiah. He unrolled
the scroll and found the passage where it was written:
   The Spirit of the Lord is upon me,
   because he has anointed me
      to bring glad tidings to the poor.
   He has sent me to proclaim liberty to captives
      and recovery of sight to the blind,
         to let the oppressed go free,
   and to proclaim a year acceptable to the Lord.
Rolling up the scroll, he handed it back to the atten-
dant and sat down, and the eyes of all in the syna-

* See p. 16 for other Gospel Acclamations.

gogue looked intently at him. He said to them, "Today this Scripture passage is fulfilled in your hearing."— The Gospel of the Lord. ℟. **Praise to you, Lord Jesus Christ.** ↓

After the reading of the Gospel, the Bishop preaches the Homily in which, taking his starting point from the text of the readings proclaimed in the Liturgy of the Word, he speaks to the people and to his Priests about priestly anointing, urging the Priests to be faithful in their office and calling on them to renew publicly their priestly promises.

Renewal of Priestly Promises

After the Homily, the Bishop speaks with the Priests in these or similar words.

Beloved sons,
on the anniversary of that day
when Christ our Lord conferred his priesthood
on his Apostles and on us,
are you resolved to renew,
in the presence of your Bishop and God's holy people,
the promises you once made?
Priests: I am.

Bishop:
Are you resolved to be more united with the Lord Jesus
and more closely conformed to him,
denying yourselves and confirming those promises
about sacred duties towards Christ's Church
which, prompted by love of him,
you willingly and joyfully pledged
on the day of your priestly ordination?
Priests: I am.

Bishop:
Are you resolved to be faithful stewards of the mysteries
    of God
in the Holy Eucharist and the other liturgical rites
and to discharge faithfully the sacred office of teaching,

following Christ the Head and Shepherd,
not seeking any gain,
but moved only by zeal for souls?
Priests: I am.

Then, turned towards the people, the Bishop continues:

As for you, dearest sons and daughters,
pray for your Priests,
that the Lord may pour out his gifts abundantly upon them,
and keep them faithful as ministers of Christ, the High Priest,
so that they may lead you to him,
who is the source of salvation.
People: Christ, hear us. Christ, graciously hear us.

Bishop:
And pray also for me,
that I may be faithful to the apostolic office
entrusted to me in my lowliness
and that in your midst I may be made day by day
a living and more perfect image of Christ,
the Priest, the Good Shepherd,
the Teacher and the Servant of all.
People: Christ, hear us. Christ, graciously hear us.

Bishop:
May the Lord keep us all in his charity
and lead all of us,
shepherds and flock,
to eternal life.
All: Amen.

The Creed is not said.   → No. 17, p. 20

PRAYER OVER THE OFFERINGS   [New Life]

May the power of this sacrifice, O Lord, we pray,
mercifully wipe away what is old in us
and increase in us grace of salvation and newness of life.

Through Christ our Lord.
℟. **Amen.** ↓

PREFACE (P 20)   [Continuation of Christ's Priesthood]

℣. The Lord be with you. ℟. **And with your spirit.**
℣. Lift up your hearts. ℟. **We lift them up to the Lord.** ℣. Let us give thanks to the Lord our God. ℟. **It is right and just.**

It is truly right and just, our duty and our salvation,
always and everywhere to give you thanks,
Lord, holy Father, almighty and eternal God.

For by the anointing of the Holy Spirit
you made your Only Begotten Son
High Priest of the new and eternal covenant,
and by your wondrous design were pleased to decree
that his one Priesthood should continue in the Church.

For Christ not only adorns with a royal priesthood
the people he has made his own,
but with a brother's kindness he also chooses men
to become sharers in his sacred ministry
through the laying on of hands.

They are to renew in his name
the sacrifice of human redemption,
to set before your children the paschal banquet,
to lead your holy people in charity,
to nourish them with the word
and strengthen them with the Sacraments.

As they give up their lives for you
and for the salvation of their brothers and sisters,
they strive to be conformed to the image of Christ
    himself
and offer you a constant witness of faith and love.

And so, Lord, with all the Angels and Saints,
we, too, give you thanks, as in exultation we acclaim:

→ No. 23, p. 23

COMMUNION ANT. Ps 89 (88):2   [The Lord's Fidelity]

I will sing for ever of your mercies, O Lord; through all ages my mouth will proclaim your fidelity. ↓

PRAYER AFTER COMMUNION   [Renewed in Christ]

We beseech you, almighty God,
that those you renew by your Sacraments
may merit to become the pleasing fragrance of Christ.
Who lives and reigns for ever and ever.
℟. **Amen.**   → No. 30, p. 77

Optional Solemn Blessings, p. 97, and Prayers over the People, p. 105

"Do this in remembrance of me."

APRIL 1

THE SACRED PASCHAL TRIDUUM
THURSDAY OF THE LORD'S SUPPER
[HOLY THURSDAY]

AT THE EVENING MASS

The Evening Mass of the Lord's Supper commemorates the institution of the Holy Eucharist and the sacrament of Holy Orders. It was at this Mass that Jesus changed bread and wine into his Body and Blood. He then directed his disciples to carry out this same ritual: "Do this in remembrance of me."

ENTRANCE ANT. Cf. Gal 6:14   [Glory in the Cross]
We should glory in the Cross of our Lord Jesus Christ,
in whom is our salvation, life and resurrection,
through whom we are saved and delivered.

→ No. 2, p. 10

The Gloria in excelsis *(Glory to God in the highest) is
said. While the hymn is being sung, bells are rung, and when
it is finished, they remain silent until the* Gloria in excelsis
*of the Easter Vigil, unless, if appropriate, the Diocesan
Bishop has decided otherwise. Likewise, during this same
period, the organ and other musical instruments may be used
only so as to support the singing.*

COLLECT   [Fullness of Charity]
O God, who have called us to participate
in this most sacred Supper,
in which your Only Begotten Son,
when about to hand himself over to death,
entrusted to the Church a sacrifice new for all eternity,
the banquet of his love,
grant, we pray,
that we may draw from so great a mystery,
the fullness of charity and of life.
Through our Lord Jesus Christ, your Son,
who lives and reigns with you in the unity of the Holy
    Spirit,
one God, for ever and ever.
℟. **Amen.** ↓

FIRST READING Ex 12:1-8, 11-14   [The First Passover]
For the protection of the Jewish people, strict religious and
dietary instructions are given to Moses by God. The law of
the Passover meal requires that the doorposts and lintels
of each house be marked with the blood of the sacrificial
animal so that the Lord can "go through Egypt striking
down every firstborn of the land, both man and beast."

A reading from the Book of Exodus

THE LORD said to Moses and Aaron in the land of Egypt, "This month shall stand at the head of your calendar; you shall reckon it the first month of the year. Tell the whole community of Israel: On the tenth of this month every one of your families must procure for itself a lamb, one apiece for each household. If a family is too small for a whole lamb, it shall join the nearest household in procuring one and shall share in the lamb in proportion to the number of persons who partake of it. The lamb must be a year-old male and without blemish. You may take it from either the sheep or the goats. You shall keep it until the fourteenth day of this month, and then, with the whole assembly of Israel present, it shall be slaughtered during the evening twilight. They shall take some of its blood and apply it to the two doorposts and the lintel of every house in which they partake of the lamb. That same night they shall eat its roasted flesh with unleavened bread and bitter herbs.

"This is how you are to eat it: with your loins girt, sandals on your feet and your staff in hand, you shall eat like those who are in flight. It is the Passover of the LORD. For on this same night I will go through Egypt, striking down every firstborn of the land, both man and beast, and executing judgment on all the gods of Egypt—I, the LORD! But the blood will mark the houses where you are. Seeing the blood, I will pass over you; thus, when I strike the land of Egypt, no destructive blow will come upon you.

"This day shall be a memorial feast for you, which all your generations shall celebrate with pilgrimage to the LORD, as a perpetual institution."—The word of the Lord. ℞. **Thanks be to God.** ↓

RESPONSORIAL PSALM Ps 116　　　[Thanksgiving]

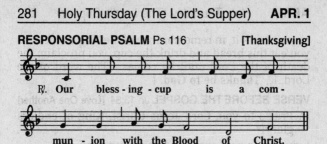

℟. Our bless-ing-cup is a com-mun-ion with the Blood of Christ.

How shall I make a return to the LORD
　for all the good he has done for me?
The cup of salvation I will take up,
　and I will call upon the name of the LORD.—℟.

Precious in the eyes of the LORD
　is the death of his faithful ones.
I am your servant, the son of your handmaid;
　you have loosed my bonds.—℟.

To you will I offer sacrifice of thanksgiving,
　and I will call upon the name of the LORD.
My vows to the LORD I will pay
　in the presence of all his people.—℟. ↓

SECOND READING 1 Cor 11:23-26　　[The Lord's Supper]

**Paul recounts the events of the Last Supper which were
handed down to him. The changing of bread and wine into
the Body and Blood of the Lord proclaimed again his
death. It was to be a sacrificial meal.**

A reading from the first Letter of Saint Paul
to the Corinthians

BROTHERS and sisters: I received from the Lord
what I also handed on to you, that the Lord Jesus,
on the night he was handed over, took bread, and, after
he had given thanks, broke it and said, "This is my
body that is for you. Do this in remembrance of me." In
the same way also the cup, after supper, saying, "This
cup is the new covenant in my blood. Do this, as often

as you drink it, in remembrance of me." For as often as you eat this bread and drink the cup, you proclaim the death of the Lord until he comes.—The word of the Lord. ℟. **Thanks be to God.** ↓

VERSE BEFORE THE GOSPEL Jn 13:34 [Love One Another]

℟. **Praise to you, Lord Jesus Christ, King of endless glory!***

I give you a new commandment, says the Lord:
love one another as I have loved you.
℟. **Praise to you, Lord Jesus Christ, King of endless glory!** ↓

GOSPEL Jn 13:1-15   [Love and Service]

Jesus washes the feet of his disciples to prove to them his sincere love and great humility which they should imitate. He teaches them that, although free from sin and not unworthy to receive his most holy body and blood, they should be purified of all evil inclinations.

℣. The Lord be with you. ℟. **And with your spirit.**
✝ A reading from the holy Gospel according to John.
℟. **Glory to you, O Lord.**

BEFORE the feast of Passover, Jesus knew that his hour had come to pass from this world to the Father. He loved his own in the world and he loved them to the end. The devil had already induced Judas, son of Simon the Iscariot, to hand him over. So, during supper, fully aware that the Father had put everything into his power and that he had come from God and was returning to God, he rose from supper and took off his outer garments. He took a towel and tied it around his waist. Then he poured water into a basin and began to wash the disciples' feet and dry them with the towel around his waist. He came to Simon Peter, who said to him, "Master, are you going to wash my feet?" Jesus

* See p. 16 for other Gospel Acclamations.

answered and said to him, "What I am doing, you do not understand now, but you will understand later." Peter said to him, "You will never wash my feet." Jesus answered him, "Unless I wash you, you will have no inheritance with me." Simon Peter said to him, "Master, then not only my feet, but my hands and head as well." Jesus said to him, "Whoever has bathed has no need except to have his feet washed, for he is clean all over; so you are clean, but not all." For he knew who would betray him; for this reason, he said, "Not all of you are clean."

So when he had washed their feet and put his garments back on and reclined at table again, he said to them, "Do you realize what I have done for you? You call me 'teacher' and 'master,' and rightly so, for indeed I am. If I, therefore, the master and teacher, have washed your feet, you ought to wash one another's feet. I have given you a model to follow, so that as I have done for you, you should also do."—The Gospel of the Lord. ℟. **Praise to you, Lord Jesus Christ.** ↓

After the proclamation of the Gospel, the Priest gives a homily in which light is shed on the principal mysteries that are commemorated in this Mass, namely, the institution of the Holy Eucharist and of the priestly Order, and the commandment of the Lord concerning fraternal charity.

The Washing of Feet

After the Homily, where a pastoral reason suggests it, the Washing of Feet follows.

Those who are chosen from among the people of God are led by the ministers to seats prepared in a suitable place. Then the Priest (removing his chasuble if necessary) goes to each one, and, with the help of the ministers, pours water over each one's feet and then dries them.

Meanwhile some of the following antiphons or other appropriate chants are sung.

ANTIPHON 1 Cf. Jn 13:4, 5, 15   [Jesus' Example]

After the Lord had risen from supper,
he poured water into a basin
and began to wash the feet of his disciples:
he left them this example.

ANTIPHON 2 Cf. Jn 13:12, 13, 15   [Do Likewise]

The Lord Jesus, after eating supper with his disciples,
washed their feet and said to them:
Do you know what I, your Lord and Master, have done
    for you?
I have given you an example, that you should do like-
    wise.

ANTIPHON 3 Jn 13:6, 7, 8   [Peter's Understanding]

Lord, are you to wash my feet? Jesus said to him in
    answer:
If I do not wash your feet, you will have no share with
    me.

℣. So he came to Simon Peter and Peter said to him:
—Lord.

℣. What I am doing, you do not know for now,
but later you will come to know.
—Lord.

ANTIPHON 4 Cf. Jn 13:14   [Service]

If I, your Lord and Master, have washed your feet,
how much more should you wash each other's feet?

ANTIPHON 5 Jn 13:35   [Identified by Love]

This is how all will know that you are my disciples:
if you have love for one another.

℣. Jesus said to his disciples:
—This is how.

ANTIPHON 6 Jn 13:34   [New Commandment]

I give you a new commandment,
that you love one another
as I have loved you, says the Lord.

ANTIPHON 7 1 Cor 13:13   [Greatest Is Charity]

Let faith, hope and charity, these three, remain among
** you,**
but the greatest of these is charity.

℣. **Now faith, hope and charity, these three, remain;**
but the greatest of these is charity.
—Let.

After the Washing of Feet, the Priest washes and dries his
hands, puts the chasuble back on, and returns to the chair,
and from there he directs the Universal Prayer.

The Creed is not said.

The Liturgy of the Eucharist

At the beginning of the Liturgy of the Eucharist, there may
be a procession of the faithful in which gifts for the poor may
be presented with the bread and wine.

Meanwhile the following, or another appropriate chant, is
sung.

[Christ's Love]

Ant. **Where true charity is dwelling, God is present there.**

℣. **By the love of Christ we have been brought to-**
**   gether:**
℣. **let us find in him our gladness and our pleasure;**
℣. **may we love him and revere him, God the living,**
℣. **and in love respect each other with sincere hearts.**

Ant. **Where true charity is dwelling, God is present there.**

℣. **So when we as one are gathered all together,**
℣. **let us strive to keep our minds free of division;**

℣. may there be an end to malice, strife and quarrels,
℣. and let Christ our God be dwelling here among us.

Ant. **Where true charity is dwelling, God is present there.**

℣. **May your face thus be our vision, bright in glory,**
℣. **Christ our God, with all the blessed Saints in heaven:**
℣. **such delight is pure and faultless, joy unbounded,**
℣. **which endures through countless ages world without end. Amen.**   ➙ No. 17, p. 20

PRAYER OVER THE OFFERINGS   [Work of Redemption]

Grant us, O Lord, we pray,
that we may participate worthily in these mysteries,
for whenever the memorial of this sacrifice is celebrated
the work of our redemption is accomplished.
Through Christ our Lord.
℟. **Amen.**   ➙ No. 21, p. 22 (Pref. P 47)

*When the Roman Canon is used, this special form of it is said,
with proper formulas for the* Communicantes (In communion with those), Hanc igitur (Therefore, Lord, we pray),
and Qui pridie (On the day before he was to suffer).

To you, therefore, most merciful Father,
we make humble prayer and petition
through Jesus Christ, your Son, our Lord:
that you accept
and bless ✠ these gifts, these offerings,
these holy and unblemished sacrifices,
which we offer you firstly
for your holy catholic Church.
Be pleased to grant her peace,
to guard, unite and govern her
throughout the whole world,
together with your servant N. our Pope

and N. our Bishop,
and all those who, holding to the truth,
hand on the catholic and apostolic faith.

Remember, Lord, your servants N. and N.
and all gathered here,
whose faith and devotion are known to you.
For them we offer you this sacrifice of praise
or they offer it for themselves
and all who are dear to them:
for the redemption of their souls,
in hope of health and well-being,
and paying their homage to you,
the eternal God, living and true.

Celebrating the most sacred day
on which our Lord Jesus Christ
was handed over for our sake,
and in communion with those whose memory we
    venerate,
especially the glorious ever-Virgin Mary,
Mother of our God and Lord, Jesus Christ,
and † blessed Joseph, her Spouse,
your blessed Apostles and Martyrs
Peter and Paul, Andrew,
(James, John,
Thomas, James, Philip,
Bartholomew, Matthew, Simon and Jude;
Linus, Cletus, Clement, Sixtus,
Cornelius, Cyprian,
Lawrence, Chrysogonus,
John and Paul,
Cosmas and Damian)
and all your Saints;
we ask that through their merits and prayers,
in all things we may be defended
by your protecting help.
(Through Christ our Lord. Amen.)

Therefore, Lord, we pray:
graciously accept this oblation of our service,
that of your whole family,
which we make to you
as we observe the day
on which our Lord Jesus Christ
handed on the mysteries of his Body and Blood
for his disciples to celebrate;
order our days in your peace,
and command that we be delivered from eternal
    damnation
and counted among the flock of those you have chosen.
(Through Christ our Lord. Amen.)

Be pleased, O God, we pray,
to bless, acknowledge,
and approve this offering in every respect;
make it spiritual and acceptable,
so that it may become for us
the Body and Blood of your most beloved Son,
our Lord Jesus Christ.

On the day before he was to suffer
for our salvation and the salvation of all,
that is today,
he took bread in his holy and venerable hands,
and with eyes raised to heaven
to you, O God, his almighty Father,
giving you thanks, he said the blessing,
broke the bread
and gave it to his disciples, saying:

Take this, all of you, and eat of it,
for this is my Body,
which will be given up for you.

In a similar way, when supper was ended,
he took this precious chalice
in his holy and venerable hands,

and once more giving you thanks, he said the blessing
and gave the chalice to his disciples, saying:

Take this, all of you, and drink from it,
for this is the chalice of my Blood,
the Blood of the new and eternal covenant,
which will be poured out for you and for many
for the forgiveness of sins.

Do this in memory of me.

The rest follows the Roman Canon, pp. 26-29.

COMMUNION ANT. 1 Cor 11:24-25   [In Memory of Christ]
**This is the Body that will be given up for you; this is
the Chalice of the new covenant in my Blood, says the
Lord; do this, whenever you receive it, in memory of
me. ↓**

*After the distribution of Communion, a ciborium with hosts
for Communion on the following day is left on the altar. The
Priest, standing at the chair, says the Prayer after Communion.*

PRAYER AFTER COMMUNION   [Renewed]
Grant, almighty God,
that, just as we are renewed
by the Supper of your Son in this present age,
so we may enjoy his banquet for all eternity.
Who lives and reigns for ever and ever.
℞. **Amen.**

The Transfer of the Most Blessed Sacrament

*After the Prayer after Communion, the Priest puts incense in
the thurible while standing, blesses it and then, kneeling,
incenses the Blessed Sacrament three times. Then, having
put on a white humeral veil, he rises, takes the ciborium, and
covers it with the ends of the veil.*

A procession is formed in which the Blessed Sacrament, accompanied by torches and incense, is carried through the church to a place of repose prepared in a part of the church or in a chapel suitably decorated. A lay minister with a cross, standing between two other ministers with lighted candles leads off. Others carrying lighted candles follow. Before the Priest carrying the Blessed Sacrament comes the thurifer with a smoking thurible. Meanwhile, the hymn Pange, lingua *(exclusive of the last two stanzas) or another eucharistic chant is sung.*

PANGE LINGUA   [Adoring the Lord]

Sing my tongue, the Savior's glory,
Of his flesh the mystery sing;
Of his blood all price exceeding,
Shed by our immortal king,
Destined for the world's redemption,
From a noble womb to spring.

Of a pure and spotless Virgin
Born for us on earth below,
He, as man with man conversing,
Stayed the seeds of truth to sow;
Then he closed in solemn order
Wondrously his life of woe.

On the night of that Last Supper,
Seated with his chosen band,
He, the paschal victim eating,
First fulfills the law's command;
Then as food to all his brethren
Gives himself with his own hand.

Word made Flesh, the bread of nature,
By his word to flesh he turns;
Wine into his blood he changes:
What though sense no change discerns,
Only be the heart in earnest,
Faith her lesson quickly learns.

When the procession reaches the place of repose, the Priest, with the help of the Deacon if necessary, places the ciborium in the tabernacle, the door of which remains open. Then he puts incense in the thurible and, kneeling, incenses the Blessed Sacrament, while Tantum ergo Sacramentum *or*

*another eucharistic chant is sung. Then the Deacon or the
Priest himself places the Sacrament in the tabernacle and
closes the door.*

**Down in adoration falling,
Lo! the sacred host we
hail,
Lo! o'er ancient forms
departing
Newer rites of grace pre-
vail;
Faith for all defects supplying,
Where the feeble senses
fail.**

**To the everlasting Father,
And the Son who reigns on
high
With the Holy Spirit pro-
ceeding
Forth from each eternally,
Be salvation, honor, bless-
ing,
Might and endless majesty.
Amen.**

*After a period of adoration in silence, the Priest and minis-
ters genuflect and return to the sacristy.*

*At an appropriate time, the altar is stripped and, if possible,
the crosses are removed from the church. It is expedient that
any crosses which remain in the church be veiled.*

*The faithful are invited to continue adoration before the
Blessed Sacrament for a suitable length of time during the
night, according to local circumstances, but after midnight
the adoration should take place without solemnity.*

"And bowing his head, [Jesus] handed over the spirit."

APRIL 2

FRIDAY OF THE PASSION OF THE LORD [GOOD FRIDAY]

THE CELEBRATION OF THE PASSION OF THE LORD

The liturgy of Good Friday recalls graphically the passion and death of Jesus. The reading of the Passion describes the suffering and death of Jesus. Today we show great reverence for the crucifix, the sign of our redemption.

On this and the following day, by a most ancient tradition, the Church does not celebrate the Sacraments at all, except for Penance and the Anointing of the Sick. On the afternoon of this day, about three o'clock (unless a later hour is chosen for a pastoral reason), there takes place the celebration of the Lord's Passion.

The Priest and the Deacon, if a Deacon is present, wearing red vestments as for Mass, go to the altar in silence and, after making a reverence to the altar, prostrate themselves or, if appropriate, kneel and pray in silence for a while. All others kneel. Then the Priest, with the ministers, goes to the chair where, facing the people, who are standing, he says, with hands extended, one of the following prayers, omitting the invitation Let us pray.

292

PRAYER　　　　　　　　　　　　[Sanctify Your Servants]

Remember your mercies, O Lord,
and with your eternal protection sanctify your servants,
for whom Christ your Son,
by the shedding of his Blood,
established the Paschal Mystery.
Who lives and reigns for ever and ever. ℟. **Amen.** ↓

OR　　　　　　　　　　　　　　　　[Image of Christ]

O God, who by the Passion of Christ your Son, our Lord,
abolished the death inherited from ancient sin
by every succeeding generation,
grant that just as, being conformed to him,
we have borne by the law of nature
the image of the man of earth,
so by the sanctification of grace
we may bear the image of the Man of heaven.
Through Christ our Lord. ℟. **Amen.** ↓

FIRST PART: THE LITURGY OF THE WORD

FIRST READING Is 52:13—53:12　　[Suffering and Glory]

The suffering Servant shall be raised up and exalted. The Servant remains one with all people in sorrow and yet distinct from each of them in innocence of life and total service to God. The doctrine of expiatory suffering finds supreme expression in these words.

A reading from the Book of the Prophet Isaiah

SEE, my servant shall prosper,
he shall be raised high and greatly exalted.
Even as many were amazed at him—
　　so marred was his look beyond human semblance
　　and his appearance beyond that of the sons of
　　　　man—
so shall he startle many nations,
　　because of him kings shall stand speechless;
for those who have not been told shall see,
　　those who have not heard shall ponder it.

Who would believe what we have heard?
  To whom has the arm of the LORD been revealed?
He grew up like a sapling before him,
  like a shoot from the parched earth;
there was in him no stately bearing to make us look
    at him,
  nor appearance that would attract us to him.
He was spurned and avoided by people,
  a man of suffering, accustomed to infirmity,
one of those from whom people hide their faces,
  spurned, and we held him in no esteem.

Yet it was our infirmities that he bore,
  our sufferings that he endured,
while we thought of him as stricken,
  as one smitten by God and afflicted.
But he was pierced for our offenses,
  crushed for our sins;
upon him was the chastisement that makes us whole,
  by his stripes we were healed.
We had all gone astray like sheep,
  each following his own way;
but the LORD laid upon him
  the guilt of us all.

Though he was harshly treated, he submitted
    and opened not his mouth;
like a lamb led to the slaughter
  or a sheep before the shearers,
  he was silent and opened not his mouth.
Oppressed and condemned, he was taken away,
    and who would have thought any more of his
    destiny?
When he was cut off from the land of the living,
  and smitten for the sin of his people,
a grave was assigned him among the wicked
  and a burial place with evildoers,
though he had done no wrong
  nor spoken any falsehood.

But the LORD was pleased
  to crush him in infirmity.

If he gives his life as an offering for sin,
  he shall see his descendants in a long life,
    and the will of the LORD shall be accomplished
      through him.

Because of his affliction
  he shall see the light in fullness of days;
through his suffering, my servant shall justify many,
  and their guilt he shall bear.

Therefore I will give him his portion among the great,
  and he shall divide the spoils with the mighty,
because he surrendered himself to death
  and was counted among the wicked;
and he shall take away the sins of many,
  and win pardon for their offenses.

The word of the Lord. ℟. **Thanks be to God.** ↓

RESPONSORIAL PSALM Ps 31   [Trust in God]

℟. Fa - ther, in - to your hands I com - mend my spir - it.

In you, O LORD, I take refuge;
  let me never be put to shame.
In your justice rescue me.
Into your hands I commend my spirit;
  you will redeem me, O LORD, O faithful God.—℟.

For all my foes I am an object of reproach,
  a laughingstock to my neighbors, and a dread to my
    friends;
  they who see me abroad flee from me.
I am forgotten like the unremembered dead;
  I am like a dish that is broken.—℟.

But my trust is in you, O LORD;
  I say, "You are my God."
In your hands is my destiny; rescue me
  from the clutches of my enemies and my persecutors.

℟. **Father, into your hands I commend my spirit.**

Let your face shine upon your servant;
  save me in your kindness.
Take courage and be stouthearted,
  all you who hope in the LORD.—℟. ↓

SECOND READING Heb 4:14-16; 5:7-9   [Access to Christ]

The theme of the compassionate high priest appears again in this passage. In him the Christian can approach God confidently and without fear. Christ learned obedience from his sufferings whereby he became the source of eternal life for all.

A reading from the Letter to the Hebrews

BROTHERS and sisters: Since we have a great high priest who has passed through the heavens, Jesus, the Son of God, let us hold fast to our confession. For we do not have a high priest who is unable to sympathize with our weaknesses, but one who has similarly been tested in every way, yet without sin. So let us confidently approach the throne of grace to receive mercy and to find grace for timely help.

In the days when Christ was in the flesh, he offered prayers and supplications with loud cries and tears to the one who was able to save him from death, and he was heard because of his reverence. Son though he was, he learned obedience from what he suffered; and when he was made perfect, he became the source of eternal salvation for all who obey him.—The word of the Lord. ℟. **Thanks be to God.** ↓

VERSE BEFORE THE GOSPEL Phil 2:8-9   [Obedient for Us]

℟. **Praise and honor to you, Lord Jesus Christ!***
Christ became obedient to the point of death,
even death on a cross.
Because of this, God greatly exalted him
and bestowed on him the name which is above every
    other name.
℟. **Praise and honor to you, Lord Jesus Christ!**

GOSPEL Jn 18:1—19:42   [Christ's Passion]

Finally the Passion is read in the same way as on the preced-ing Sunday. The narrator is noted by N, the words of Jesus by a ✠ and the words of others by V (Voice) and C (Crowd). The parts of the Crowd (C) printed in boldface type may be recit-ed by the people.

It is important for us to understand the meaning of Christ's sufferings today. See the note on p. 261.

The beginning scene is Christ's agony in the garden. Our Lord knows what is to happen. The Scriptures recount the betrayal, the trial, the condemnation, and the crucifixion of Jesus.

N. THE Passion of our Lord Jesus Christ according
    to John

1. JESUS IS ARRESTED

N. JESUS went out with his disciples across the
    Kidron valley to where there was a garden, into
which he and his disciples entered. Judas his betrayer
also knew the place, because Jesus had often met
there with his disciples. So Judas got a band of soldiers and guards from the chief priests and the
Pharisees and went there with lanterns, torches, and
weapons. Jesus, knowing everything that was going to
happen to him, went out and said to them, ✠ "Whom
are you looking for?" N. They answered him, C. "Jesus
the Nazorean." N. He said to them, ✠ "I AM." N. Judas

---
* See p. 16 for other Gospel Acclamations.

his betrayer was also with them. When he said to them, "I AM," they turned away and fell to the ground. So he again asked them, ✠ "Whom are you looking for?" **N.** They said, **C. "Jesus the Nazorean." N.** Jesus answered, ✠ "I told you that I AM. So if you are looking for me, let these men go." **N.** This was to fulfill what he had said, "I have not lost any of those you gave me." Then Simon Peter, who had a sword, drew it, struck the high priest's slave, and cut off his right ear. The slave's name was Malchus. Jesus said to Peter, ✠ "Put your sword into its scabbard. Shall I not drink the cup that the Father gave me?"

N. So the band of soldiers, the tribune, and the Jewish guards seized Jesus, bound him, and brought him to Annas first. He was the father-in-law of Caiaphas, who was high priest that year. It was Caiaphas who had counseled the Jews that it was better that one man should die rather than the people.

2. PETER'S FIRST DENIAL

N. SIMON Peter and another disciple followed Jesus. Now the other disciple was known to the high priest, and he entered the courtyard of the high priest with Jesus. But Peter stood at the gate outside. So the other disciple, the acquaintance of the high priest, went out and spoke to the gatekeeper and brought Peter in. Then the maid who was the gatekeeper said to Peter, **C. "You are not one of this man's disciples, are you?" N.** He said, **V.** "I am not." **N.** Now the slaves and the guards were standing around a charcoal fire that they had made, because it was cold, and were warming themselves. Peter was also standing there keeping warm.

3. THE INQUIRY BEFORE ANNAS

N. THE high priest questioned Jesus about his disciples and about his doctrine. Jesus answered him, ✚ "I have spoken publicly to the world. I have always taught in a synagogue or in the temple area where all the Jews gather, and in secret I have said nothing. Why ask me? Ask those who heard me what I said to them. They know what I said." N. When he had said this, one of the temple guards standing there struck Jesus and said, V. "Is this the way you answer the high priest?" N. Jesus answered him, ✚ "If I have spoken wrongly, testify to the wrong; but if I have spoken rightly, why do you strike me?" N. Then Annas sent him bound to Caiaphas the high priest.

4. THE FURTHER DENIALS

N. **N**OW Simon Peter was standing there keeping warm. And they said to him, C. **"You are not one of his disciples, are you?"** N. He denied it and said, V. "I am not." N. One of the slaves of the high priest, a relative of the one whose ear Peter had cut off, said, C. **"Didn't I see you in the garden with him?"** N. Again Peter denied it. And immediately the cock crowed.

5. JESUS BROUGHT BEFORE PILATE

N. **T**HEN they brought Jesus from Caiaphas to the praetorium. It was morning. And they themselves did not enter the praetorium, in order not to be defiled so that they could eat the Passover. So Pilate came out to them and said, V. "What charge do you bring against this man?" N. They answered and said to him, C. **"If he were not a criminal, we would not have handed him over to you."** N. At this, Pilate said to them, V. "Take him yourselves, and judge him according to your law." N. The Jews answered him, C. **"We do not have the right to execute anyone,"** N. in order that the word of Jesus might be fulfilled that he said indicating the kind of death he would die.

6. JESUS QUESTIONED BY PILATE

N. So Pilate went back into the praetorium and summoned Jesus and said to him, **V.** "Are you the King of the Jews?" **N.** Jesus answered, ✠ "Do you say this on your own or have others told you about me?" **N.** Pilate answered, **V.** "I am not a Jew, am I? Your own nation and the chief priests handed you over to me. What have you done?" **N.** Jesus answered, ✠ "My kingdom does not belong to this world. If my kingdom did belong to this world, my attendants would be fighting to keep me from being handed over to the Jews. But as it is, my kingdom is not here." **N.** So Pilate said to him, **V.** "Then you are a king?" **N.** Jesus answered, ✠ "You say I am a king. For this I was born and for this I came into the world, to testify to the truth. Everyone who belongs to the truth listens to my voice." **N.** Pilate said to him, **V.** "What is truth?"

7. BARABBAS CHOSEN OVER JESUS

N. WHEN he had said this, he again went out to the Jews and said to them, **V.** "I find no guilt in him. But you have a custom that I release one prisoner to you at Passover. Do you want me to release to you the King of the Jews?" **N.** They cried out again, **C.** "Not this one but Barabbas!" **N.** Now Barabbas was a revolutionary.

8. JESUS IS SCOURGED

N. THEN Pilate took Jesus and had him scourged. And the soldiers wove a crown out of thorns and placed it on his head, and clothed him in a purple cloak, and they came to him and said, **C.** "Hail, King of the Jews!" **N.** And they struck him repeatedly.

[9. JESUS IS PRESENTED TO THE CROWD]

N. Once more Pilate went out and said to them, **V.** "Look, I am bringing him out to you, so that you may know that I find no guilt in him." **N.** So Jesus came out, wearing the crown of thorns and the purple cloak. And Pilate said to them, **V.** "Behold, the man!" **N.** When the chief priests and the guards saw him they cried out, **C.** "**Crucify him, crucify him!**" **N.** Pilate said to them, **V.** "Take him yourselves and crucify him. I find no guilt in him." **N.** The Jews answered, **C.** "**We have a law, and according to that law he ought to die, because he made himself the Son of God.**"

[*10. JESUS AGAIN QUESTIONED BY PILATE*]

N. Now when Pilate heard this statement, he became even more afraid, and went back into the praetorium and said to Jesus, **V.** "Where are you from?" **N.** Jesus did not answer him. So Pilate said to him, **V.** "Do you not speak to me? Do you not know that I have power to release you and I have power to crucify you?" **N.** Jesus answered him, ✠ "You would have no power over me if it had not been given to you from above. For this reason the one who handed me over to you has the greater sin."

[*11. JESUS SENTENCED TO BE CRUCIFIED*]

N. Consequently, Pilate tried to release him; but the Jews cried out, **C.** "**If you release him, you are not a Friend of Caesar. Everyone who makes himself a king opposes Caesar.**"

   N. When Pilate heard these words he brought Jesus out and seated him on the judge's bench in the place called Stone Pavement, in Hebrew, Gabbatha. It was preparation day for Passover, and it was about noon. And he said to the Jews, **V.** "Behold, your king!" **N.** They cried out, **C.** "**Take him away, take him away! Crucify him!**" **N.** Pilate said to them, **V.** "Shall I crucify your king?" **N.** The chief priests answered, **C.** "**We have no king but Caesar.**" **N.** Then he handed him over to them to be crucified.

12. CRUCIFIXION AND DEATH

N. **S**O they took Jesus, and, carrying the cross himself, he went out to what is called the Place of the Skull, in Hebrew, Golgotha. There they crucified him, and with him two others, one on either side, with Jesus in the middle. Pilate also had an inscription written and put on the cross. It read, "Jesus the Nazorean, the King of the Jews." Now many of the Jews read this inscription, because the place where Jesus was crucified was near the city; and it was written in Hebrew, Latin, and Greek. So the chief priests of the Jews said to Pilate, **C.** **"Do not write 'The King of the Jews,' but that he said, 'I am the King of the Jews.' "** **N.** Pilate answered, **V.** "What I have written, I have written."

N. When the soldiers had crucified Jesus, they took his clothes and divided them into four shares, a share for each soldier. They also took his tunic, but the tunic was seamless, woven in one piece from the top down. So they said to one another, **C.** **"Let's not tear it, but cast lots for it to see whose it will be, "** **N.** in order that the passage of Scripture might be fulfilled that says:

They divided my garments among them,
and for my vesture they cast lots.

This is what the soldiers did. Standing by the cross of Jesus were his mother and his mother's sister, Mary the wife of Clopas, and Mary of Magdala. When Jesus saw his mother and the disciple there whom he loved he said to his mother, ✠ "Woman, behold, your son." **N.** Then he said to the disciple, ✠ "Behold, your mother." **N.** And from that hour the disciple took her into his home.

After this, aware that everything was now finished, in order that the Scripture might be fulfilled, Jesus said, ✠ "I thirst." **N.** There was a vessel filled with common wine. So they put a sponge soaked in wine on a sprig of hyssop and put it up to his mouth. When Jesus had taken the wine, he said, ✠ "It is finished." **N.** And bowing his head, he handed over the spirit.

Here all kneel and pause for a short time.

13. THE BLOOD AND WATER

N. **N**OW since it was preparation day, in order that the bodies might not remain on the cross on the sabbath, for the sabbath day of that week was a solemn one, the Jews asked Pilate that their legs be broken and that they be taken down. So the soldiers came and broke the legs of the first and then of the other one who was crucified with Jesus. But when they came to Jesus and saw that he was already dead, they did not break his legs, but one soldier thrust his lance into his side, and immediately blood and water flowed out. An eyewitness has testified, and his testimony is true; he knows that he is speaking the truth, so that you also may come to believe. For this happened so that the Scripture passage might be fulfilled:

Not a bone of it will be broken.

And again another passage says:

They will look upon him whom they have pierced.

14. BURIAL OF JESUS

N. **A**FTER this, Joseph of Arimathea, secretly a disciple of Jesus for fear of the Jews, asked Pilate if he could remove the body of Jesus. And Pilate permitted it. So he came and took his body. Nicodemus, the one who had first come to him at night, also came bringing a mixture of myrrh and aloes weighing about one hundred pounds. They took the body of Jesus and bound it with burial cloths along with the spices, according to the Jewish burial custom. Now in the place where he had been crucified there was a garden, and in the garden a new tomb, in which no one had yet been buried. So they laid Jesus there because of the Jewish preparation day; for the tomb was close by.— The Gospel of the Lord. ℞. **Praise to you, Lord Jesus Christ.**

THE SOLEMN INTERCESSIONS

The Liturgy of the Word concludes with the Solemn Intercessions, which take place in this way: the Deacon, if a Deacon is present, or if he is not, a lay minister, stands at the ambo, and sings or says the invitation in which the intention is expressed. Then all pray in silence for a while, and afterwards the Priest, standing at the chair or, if appropriate, at the altar, with hands extended, sings or says the prayer.

The faithful may remain either kneeling or standing throughout the entire period of the prayers.

Before the Priest's prayer, in accord with tradition, it is permissible to use the Deacon's invitations Let us kneel—Let us stand, *with all kneeling for silent prayer.*

I. For Holy Church

Let us pray, dearly beloved, for the holy Church of God,
that our God and Lord be pleased to give her peace,
to guard her and to unite her throughout the whole
    world
and grant that, leading our life in tranquility and quiet,
we may glorify God the Father almighty.

Prayer in silence. Then the Priest says:

Almighty ever-living God,
who in Christ revealed your glory to all the nations,
watch over the works of your mercy,
that your Church, spread throughout all the world,
may persevere with steadfast faith in confessing your
    name.
Through Christ our Lord. ℟. **Amen.** ↓

II. For the Pope

Let us pray also for our most Holy Father Pope *N.*,
that our God and Lord,
who chose him for the Order of Bishops,

may keep him safe and unharmed for the Lord's holy
   Church,
to govern the holy People of God.

Prayer in silence. Then the Priest says:

Almighty ever-living God,
by whose decree all things are founded,
look with favor on our prayers
and in your kindness protect the Pope chosen for us,
that, under him, the Christian people,
governed by you their maker,
may grow in merit by reason of their faith.
Through Christ our Lord. ℟. **Amen.** ↓

III. For all orders and degrees of the faithful

Let us pray also for our Bishop N.,
for all Bishops, Priests, and Deacons of the Church
and for the whole of the faithful people.

Prayer in silence. Then the Priest says:

Almighty ever-living God,
by whose Spirit the whole body of the Church
is sanctified and governed,
hear our humble prayer for your ministers,
that, by the gift of your grace,
all may serve you faithfully.
Through Christ our Lord. ℟. **Amen.** ↓

IV. For catechumens

Let us pray also for (our) catechumens,
that our God and Lord
may open wide the ears of their inmost hearts
and unlock the gates of his mercy,
that, having received forgiveness of all their sins
through the waters of rebirth,
they, too, may be one with Christ Jesus our Lord.

Prayer in silence. Then the Priest says:

Almighty ever-living God,
who make your Church ever fruitful with new offspring,
increase the faith and understanding of (our)
    catechumens,
that, reborn in the font of Baptism,
they may be added to the number of your adopted
    children.
Through Christ our Lord. ℟. **Amen.** ↓

V. For the unity of Christians

Let us pray also for all our brothers and sisters who
    believe in Christ,
that our God and Lord may be pleased,
as they live the truth,
to gather them together and keep them in his one
    Church.

Prayer in silence. Then the Priest says:

Almighty ever-living God,
who gather what is scattered
and keep together what you have gathered,
look kindly on the flock of your Son,
that those whom one Baptism has consecrated
may be joined together by integrity of faith
and united in the bond of charity.
Through Christ our Lord. ℟. **Amen.** ↓

VI. For the Jewish people

Let us pray also for the Jewish people,
to whom the Lord our God spoke first,
that he may grant them to advance in love of his name
and in faithfulness to his covenant.

Prayer in silence. Then the Priest says:

Almighty ever-living God,
who bestowed your promises on Abraham and his
    descendants,

graciously hear the prayers of your Church,
that the people you first made your own
may attain the fullness of redemption.
Through Christ our Lord. ℟. **Amen.** ↓

VII. For those who do not believe in Christ

Let us pray also for those who do not believe in Christ,
that, enlightened by the Holy Spirit,
they, too, may enter on the way of salvation.

Prayer in silence. Then the Priest says:

Almighty ever-living God,
grant to those who do not confess Christ
that, by walking before you with a sincere heart,
they may find the truth
and that we ourselves, being constant in mutual love
and striving to understand more fully the mystery of
    your life,
may be made more perfect witnesses to your love in the
    world.
Through Christ our Lord.
℟. **Amen.** ↓

VIII. For those who do not believe in God

Let us pray also for those who do not acknowledge God,
that, following what is right in sincerity of heart,
they may find the way to God himself.

Prayer in silence. Then the Priest says:

Almighty ever-living God,
who created all people
to seek you always by desiring you
and, by finding you, come to rest,
grant, we pray,
that, despite every harmful obstacle,
all may recognize the signs of your fatherly love
and the witness of the good works

done by those who believe in you,
and so in gladness confess you,
the one true God and Father of our human race.
Through Christ our Lord. ℟. **Amen.** ↓

IX. For those in public office

Let us pray also for those in public office,
that our God and Lord
may direct their minds and hearts according to his will
for the true peace and freedom of all.

Prayer in silence. Then the Priest says:

Almighty ever-living God,
in whose hand lies every human heart
and the rights of peoples,
look with favor, we pray,
on those who govern with authority over us,
that throughout the whole world,
the prosperity of peoples,
the assurance of peace,
and freedom of religion
may through your gift be made secure.
Through Christ our Lord. ℟. **Amen.** ↓

X. For those in tribulation

Let us pray, dearly beloved,
to God the Father almighty,
that he may cleanse the world of all errors,
banish disease, drive out hunger,
unlock prisons, loosen fetters,
granting to travelers safety, to pilgrims return,
health to the sick, and salvation to the dying.

Prayer in silence. Then the Priest says:

Almighty ever-living God,
comfort of mourners, strength of all who toil,
may the prayers of those who cry out in any tribulation

come before you,
that all may rejoice,
because in their hour of need
your mercy was at hand.
Through Christ our Lord. ℟. **Amen.** ↓

SECOND PART: THE ADORATION OF THE HOLY CROSS

*After the Solemn Intercessions, the solemn Adoration of the
Holy Cross takes place. Of the two forms of the showing of
the Cross presented here, the more appropriate one, according to pastoral needs, should be chosen.*

The Showing of the Holy Cross: First Form

*The Deacon accompanied by ministers, or another suitable
minister, goes to the sacristy, from which, in procession,
accompanied by two ministers with lighted candles, he carries the Cross, covered with a violet veil, through the church
to the middle of the sanctuary.*

*The Priest, standing before the altar and facing the people,
receives the Cross, uncovers a little of its upper part and elevates it while beginning the* Ecce lignum Crucis (Behold
the wood of the Cross). *He is assisted in singing by the
Deacon or, if need be, by the choir. All respond,* Come, let us
adore. *At the end of the singing, all kneel and for a brief
moment adore in silence, while the Priest stands and holds
the Cross raised.*

℣. Behold the wood of the Cross,
on which hung the salvation of the world.
℟. **Come, let us adore.**

*Then the Priest uncovers the right arm of the Cross and
again, raising up the Cross, begins,* Behold the wood of the
Cross *and everything takes place as above.*

*Finally, he uncovers the Cross entirely and, raising it up, he
begins the invitation* Behold the wood of the Cross *a third
time and everything takes place like the first time.*

The Showing of the Holy Cross: Second Form

*The Priest or the Deacon accompanied by ministers, or another suit-
able minister, goes to the door of the church, where he receives the*

unveiled Cross, and the ministers take lighted candles; then the procession sets off through the church to the sanctuary. Near the door, in the middle of the church and before the entrance of the sanctuary, the one who carries the Cross elevates it, singing, Behold the wood of the Cross, *to which all respond,* Come, let us adore. *After each response all kneel and for a brief moment adore in silence, as above.*

The Adoration of the Holy Cross

Then, accompanied by two ministers with lighted candles, the Priest or the Deacon carries the Cross to the entrance of the sanctuary or to another suitable place and there puts it down or hands it over to the ministers to hold. Candles are placed on the right and left sides of the Cross.

For the Adoration of the Cross, first the Priest Celebrant alone approaches, with the chasuble and his shoes removed, if appropriate. Then the clergy, the lay ministers, and the faithful approach, moving as if in procession, and showing reverence to the Cross by a simple genuflection or by some other sign appropriate to the usage of the region, for example, by kissing the Cross.

Only one Cross should be offered for adoration. If, because of the large number of people, it is not possible for all to approach individually, the Priest, after some of the clergy and faithful have adored, takes the Cross and, standing in the middle before the altar, invites the people in a few words to adore the Holy Cross and afterwards holds the Cross elevated higher for a brief time, for the faithful to adore it in silence.

While the adoration of the Holy Cross is taking place, the antiphon Crucem tuam adoramus *(We adore your Cross, O Lord), the Reproaches, the hymn* Crux fidelis *(Faithful Cross) or other suitable chants are sung, during which all who have already adored the Cross remain seated.*

Chants to Be Sung during the Adoration of the Holy Cross

ANTIPHON   [Holy Cross]

**We adore your Cross, O Lord,
we praise and glorify your holy Resurrection,**

for behold, because of the wood of a tree
joy has come to the whole world.

May God have mercy on us and bless us;
may he let his face shed its light upon us
and have mercy on us.   Cf. Ps 67 (66):2

And the antiphon is repeated: **We adore . . .**

THE REPROACHES

Parts assigned to one of the two choirs separately are indicated by the numbers 1 (first choir) and 2 (second choir); parts sung by both choirs together are marked: 1 and 2. Some of the verses may also be sung by two cantors.

I

1 and 2: **My people, what have I done to you?**
Or how have I grieved you? Answer me!

1: **Because I led you out of the land of Egypt,**
you have prepared a Cross for your Savior.

1: **Hagios o Theos,**
2: **Holy is God,**
1: **Hagios Ischyros,**
2: **Holy and Mighty,**
1: **Hagios Athanatos, eleison himas.**
2: **Holy and Immortal One, have mercy on us.**

1 and 2: **Because I led you out through the desert forty**
years
and fed you with manna and brought you into
a land of plenty,
you have prepared a Cross for your Savior.

1: **Hagios o Theos,**
2: **Holy is God,**
1: **Hagios Ischyros,**
2: **Holy and Mighty,**
1: **Hagios Athanatos, eleison himas.**
2: **Holy and Immortal One, have mercy on us.**

1 and 2: **What more should I have done for you and
have not done?**

**Indeed, I planted you as my most beautiful chosen
vine**

and you have turned very bitter for me,

for in my thirst you gave me vinegar to drink

and with a lance you pierced your Savior's side.

1: **Hagios o Theos,**

2: **Holy is God,**

1: **Hagios Ischyros,**

2: **Holy and Mighty,**

1: **Hagios Athanatos, eleison himas.**

2: **Holy and Immortal One, have mercy on us.**

II

Cantors:

**I scourged Egypt for your sake with its firstborn sons,
and you scourged me and handed me over.**

1 and 2 repeat:

My people, what have I done to you?

Or how have I grieved you? Answer me!

Cantors:

**I led you out from Egypt as Pharaoh lay sunk in the
Red Sea,**

and you handed me over to the chief priests.

1 and 2 repeat:

My people . . .

Cantors:

I opened up the sea before you,

and you opened my side with a lance.

1 and 2 repeat:

My people . . .

Cantors:

**I went before you in a pillar of cloud,
and you led me into Pilate's palace.**

1 and 2 repeat:

My people . . .

Cantors:

**I fed you with manna in the desert,
and on me you rained blows and lashes.**

1 and 2 repeat:

My people . . .

Cantors:

**I gave you saving water from the rock to drink,
and for drink you gave me gall and vinegar.**

1 and 2 repeat:

My people . . .

Cantors:

**I struck down for you the kings of the Canaanites,
and you struck my head with a reed.**

1 and 2 repeat:

My people . . .

Cantors:

**I put in your hand a royal scepter,
and you put on my head a crown of thorns.**

1 and 2 repeat:

My people . . .

Cantors:

**I exalted you with great power,
and you hung me on the scaffold of the Cross.**

1 and 2 repeat:

My people . . .

HYMN   [Faithful Cross]

All:

Faithful Cross the Saints rely on,
Noble tree beyond compare!
Never was there such a scion,
Never leaf or flower so rare.
Sweet the timber, sweet the iron,
Sweet the burden that they bear!

Cantors:

Sing, my tongue, in exultation
Of our banner and device!
Make a solemn proclamation
Of a triumph and its price:
How the Savior of creation
Conquered by his sacrifice!

All:

Faithful Cross the Saints rely on,
Noble tree beyond compare!
Never was there such a scion,
Never leaf or flower so rare.

Cantors:

For, when Adam first offended,
Eating that forbidden fruit,
Not all hopes of glory ended
With the serpent at the root:
Broken nature would be mended
By a second tree and shoot.

All:

Sweet the timber, sweet the iron,
Sweet the burden that they bear!

Cantors:

Thus the tempter was outwitted
By a wisdom deeper still:
Remedy and ailment fitted,
Means to cure and means to kill;

That the world might be acquitted,
Christ would do his Father's will.

All:

Faithful Cross the Saints rely on,
Noble tree beyond compare!
Never was there such a scion,
Never leaf or flower so rare.

Cantors:

So the Father, out of pity
For our self-inflicted doom,
Sent him from the heavenly city
When the holy time had come:
He, the Son and the Almighty,
Took our flesh in Mary's womb.

All:

Sweet the timber, sweet the iron,
Sweet the burden that they bear!

Cantors:

Hear a tiny baby crying,
Founder of the seas and strands;
See his virgin Mother tying
Cloth around his feet and hands;
Find him in a manger lying
Tightly wrapped in swaddling-
    bands!

All:

Faithful Cross the Saints rely on,
Noble tree beyond compare!
Never was there such a scion,
Never leaf or flower so rare.

Cantors:

So he came, the long-expected,
Not in glory, not to reign;
Only born to be rejected,

Choosing hunger, toil and pain,
Till the scaffold was erected
And the Paschal Lamb was slain.

All:

Sweet the timber, sweet the iron,
Sweet the burden that they bear!

Cantors:

No disgrace was too abhorrent:
Nailed and mocked and parched
    he died;
Blood and water, double war-
    rant,
Issue from his wounded side,
Washing in a mighty torrent
Earth and stars and oceantide.

All:

Faithful Cross the Saints rely on,
Noble tree beyond compare!
Never was there such a scion,
Never leaf or flower so rare.

Cantors:

Lofty timber, smooth your
    roughness,
Flex your boughs for blossom-
    ing;
Let your fibers lose their tough-
    ness,
Gently let your tendrils cling;

Lay aside your native gruffness,
Clasp the body of your King!

All:

Sweet the timber, sweet the iron,
Sweet the burden that they bear!

Cantors:

Noblest tree of all created,
Richly jeweled and embossed:
Post by Lamb's blood conse-
    crated;
Spar that saves the tempest-
    tossed;
Scaffold-beam which, elevated,
Carries what the world has cost!

All:

Faithful Cross the Saints rely on,
Noble tree beyond compare!
Never was there such a scion,
Never leaf or flower so rare.

*The following conclusion is
never to be omitted:*

All:

Wisdom, power, and adoration
To the blessed Trinity
For redemption and salvation
Through the Paschal Mystery,
Now, in every generation,
And for all eternity. Amen.

*In accordance with local circumstances or popular traditions
and if it is pastorally appropriate, the* Stabat Mater *may be
sung, as found in the* Graduale Romanum, *or another suitable
chant in memory of the compassion of the Blessed Virgin Mary.*

*When the adoration has been concluded, the Cross is carried
by the Deacon or a minister to its place at the altar. Lighted
candles are placed around or on the altar or near the Cross.*

THIRD PART: HOLY COMMUNION

A cloth is spread on the altar, and a corporal and the Missal put in place. Meanwhile the Deacon or, if there is no Deacon, the Priest himself, putting on a humeral veil, brings the Blessed Sacrament back from the place of repose to the altar by a shorter route, while all stand in silence. Two ministers with lighted candles accompany the Blessed Sacrament and place their candlesticks around or upon the altar.

When the Deacon, if a Deacon is present, has placed the Blessed Sacrament upon the altar and uncovered the ciborium, the Priest goes to the altar and genuflects.

Then the Priest, with hands joined, says aloud:

At the Savior's command
and formed by divine teaching,
we dare to say:

The Priest, with hands extended says, and all present continue:

Our Father . . .

With hands extended, the Priest continues alone:

Deliver us, Lord, we pray, from every evil,
graciously grant peace in our days,
that, by the help of your mercy,
we may be always free from sin
and safe from all distress,
as we await the blessed hope
and the coming of our Savior, Jesus Christ.

The people conclude the prayer, acclaiming:

**For the kingdom,
the power and the glory are yours
now and for ever.**

Then the Priest, with hands joined, says quietly:

May the receiving of your Body and Blood,
Lord Jesus Christ,
not bring me to judgment and condemnation,

but through your loving mercy
be for me protection in mind and body
and a healing remedy.

The Priest then genuflects, takes a particle, and, holding it slightly raised over the ciborium, while facing the people, says aloud:

Behold the Lamb of God,
behold him who takes away the sins of the world.
Blessed are those called to the supper of the Lamb.

And together with the people he adds once:

**Lord, I am not worthy
that you should enter under my roof,
but only say the word
and my soul shall be healed.**

And facing the altar, he reverently consumes the Body of Christ, saying quietly: May the Body of Christ keep me safe for eternal life.

He then proceeds to distribute Communion to the faithful. During Communion, Psalm 22 (21) or another appropriate chant may be sung.

When the distribution of Communion has been completed, the ciborium is taken by the Deacon or another suitable minister to a place prepared outside the church or, if circumstances so require, it is placed in the tabernacle.

Then the Priest says: Let us pray, *and, after a period of sacred silence, if circumstances so suggest, has been observed, he says the Prayer after Communion.*

Almighty ever-living God,   **[Devoted to God]**
who have restored us to life
by the blessed Death and Resurrection of your Christ,
preserve in us the work of your mercy,
that, by partaking of this mystery,
we may have a life unceasingly devoted to you.
Through Christ our Lord.
℞. **Amen.** ↓

For the Dismissal the Deacon or, if there is no Deacon, the Priest himself, may say the invitation Bow down for the blessing.

Then the Priest, standing facing the people and extending his hands over them, says this:

PRAYER OVER THE PEOPLE   [Redemption Secured]

May abundant blessing, O Lord, we pray,
descend upon your people,
who have honored the Death of your Son
in the hope of their resurrection:
may pardon come,
comfort be given,
holy faith increase,
and everlasting redemption be made secure.
Through Christ our Lord.
℟. **Amen.** ↓

And all, after genuflecting to the Cross, depart in silence.

After the celebration, the altar is stripped, but the Cross remains on the altar with two or four candlesticks.

APRIL 3

HOLY SATURDAY

On Holy Saturday the Church waits at the Lord's tomb in prayer and fasting, meditating on his Passion and Death and on his Descent into Hell, and awaiting his Resurrection.

The Church abstains from the Sacrifice of the Mass, with the sacred table left bare, until after the solemn Vigil, that is, the anticipation by night of the Resurrection, when the time comes for paschal joys, the abundance of which overflows to occupy fifty days.

"He is not here, for he has been raised."

APRIL 3

THE EASTER VIGIL
IN THE HOLY NIGHT

*By most ancient tradition, this is the night of keeping vigil
for the Lord (Ex 12:42), in which, following the Gospel admonition (Lk 12:35-37), the faithful, carrying lighted lamps in
their hands, should be like those looking for the Lord when
he returns, so that at his coming he may find them awake and
have them sit at his table.*

*Of this night's Vigil, which is the greatest and most noble of
all solemnities, there is to be only one celebration in each
church. It is arranged, moreover, in such a way that after the
Lucernarium and Easter Proclamation (which constitutes
the first part of this Vigil), Holy Church meditates on the
wonders the Lord God has done for his people from the beginning, trusting in his word and promise (the second part, that
is, the Liturgy of the Word) until, as day approaches, with
new members reborn in Baptism (the third part), the Church
is called to the table the Lord has prepared for his people, the
memorial of his Death and Resurrection until he comes again
(the fourth part).*

*Candles should be prepared for all who participate in the
Vigil. The lights of the church are extinguished.*

FIRST PART:
THE SOLEMN BEGINNING OF THE VIGIL
OR LUCERNARIUM

The Blessing of the Fire and Preparation of the Candle

A blazing fire is prepared in a suitable place outside the church. When the people are gathered there, the Priest approaches with the ministers, one of whom carries the paschal candle. The processional cross and candles are not carried.

Where, however, a fire cannot be lit outside the church, the rite is carried out as below, p. 322.

The Priest and faithful sign themselves while the Priest says:
In the name of the Father, and of the Son, and of the Holy Spirit, *and then he greets the assembled people in the usual way and briefly instructs them about the night vigil in these or similar words:*

[Keeping the Lord's Paschal Solemnity]
Dear brethren (brothers and sisters),
on this most sacred night,
in which our Lord Jesus Christ
passed over from death to life,
the Church calls upon her sons and daughters,
scattered throughout the world,
to come together to watch and pray.
If we keep the memorial
of the Lord's paschal solemnity in this way,
listening to his word and celebrating his mysteries,
then we shall have the sure hope
of sharing his triumph over death
and living with him in God.

Then the Priest blesses the fire, saying with hands extended:

Let us pray.   **[Fire of God's Glory]**

O God, who through your Son
bestowed upon the faithful the fire of your glory,
sanctify ✤ this new fire, we pray,

and grant that,
by these paschal celebrations,
we may be so inflamed with heavenly desires,
that with minds made pure
we may attain festivities of unending splendor.
Through Christ our Lord. ℟. **Amen.** ↓

*After the blessing of the new fire, one of the ministers brings
the paschal candle to the Priest, who cuts a cross into the
candle with a stylus. Then he makes the Greek letter Alpha
above the cross, the letter Omega below, and the four numer-
als of the current year between the arms of the cross, saying
meanwhile:*

1. Christ yesterday and today *(as he cuts a vertical
   line);*
2. the Beginning and the End *(he cuts a horizontal
   line);*
3. the Alpha *(he cuts the letter Alpha above the vertical line);*
4. and the Omega *(he cuts the letter Omega below
   the vertical line).*
5. All time belongs to him *(he cuts the first numeral of
   the current year in the upper left corner of the
   cross);*
6. and all the ages *(he cuts the second numeral of the
   current year in the upper right corner of the cross).*
7. To him be glory and power *(he cuts the
   third numeral of the current year in the
   lower left corner of the cross);*
8. through every age and for ever. Amen *(he
   cuts the fourth numeral of the current year
   in the lower right corner of the cross).*

```
      A
   2  |  0
   ───┼───
   2  |  1
      Ω
```

*When the cutting of the cross and of the other signs has been
completed, the Priest may insert five grains of incense into
the candle in the form of a cross, meanwhile saying:*

1. By his holy   1
2. and glorious wounds,   4 2 5
3. may Christ the Lord   3
4. guard us
5. and protect us. Amen.

Where, because of difficulties that may occur, a fire is not lit, the blessing of fire is adapted to the circumstances. When the people are gathered in the church as on other occasions, the Priest comes to the door of the church, along with the ministers carrying the paschal candle. The people, insofar as is possible, turn to face the Priest.

The greeting and address take place as above, p. 320; then the fire is blessed and the candle is prepared, as above, pp. 320-321.

The Priest lights the paschal candle from the new fire, saying:

May the light of Christ rising in glory
dispel the darkness of our hearts and minds.

Procession

When the candle has been lit, one of the ministers takes burning coals from the fire and places them in the thurible, and the Priest puts incense into it in the usual way. The Deacon or, if there is no Deacon, another suitable minister, takes the paschal candle and a procession forms. The thurifer with the smoking thurible precedes the Deacon or other minister who carries the paschal candle. After them follows the Priest with the ministers and the people, all holding in their hands unlit candles.

At the door of the church the Deacon, standing and raising up the candle, sings:

The Light of Christ.

And all reply:

Thanks be to God.

The Priest lights his candle from the flame of the paschal candle.

Then the Deacon moves forward to the middle of the church and, standing and raising up the candle, sings a second time:

The Light of Christ.

And all reply:

Thanks be to God.

All light their candles from the flame of the paschal candle and continue in procession.

When the Deacon arrives before the altar, he stands facing the people, raises up the candle and sings a third time:

The Light of Christ.

And all reply:

Thanks be to God.

Then the Deacon places the paschal candle on a large candlestand prepared next to the ambo or in the middle of the sanctuary.

And lights are lit throughout the church, except for the altar candles.

The Easter Proclamation (Exsultet)

Arriving at the altar, the Priest goes to his chair, gives his candle to a minister, puts incense into the thurible and blesses the incense as at the Gospel at Mass. The Deacon goes to the Priest and saying, Your blessing, Father, *asks for and receives a blessing from the Priest, who says in a low voice:*

May the Lord be in your heart and on your lips,
that you may proclaim his paschal praise worthily and
    well,
in the name of the Father and of the Son, ✝ and of the
    Holy Spirit.

The Deacon replies: Amen. ↓

This blessing is omitted if the Proclamation is made by someone who is not a Deacon.

The Deacon, after incensing the book and the candle, proclaims the Easter Proclamation (Exsultet) at the ambo or at a lectern, with all standing and holding lighted candles in their hands.

The Easter Proclamation may be made, in the absence of a Deacon, by the Priest himself or by another concelebrating Priest. If, however, because of necessity, a lay cantor sings the Proclamation, the words Therefore, dearest friends *up to the end of the invitation are omitted, along with the greeting* The Lord be with you.

[When the Shorter Form is used, omit the italicized parts.]

Exult, let them exult, the hosts of heaven,
exult, let Angel ministers of God exult,
let the trumpet of salvation
sound aloud our mighty King's triumph!
Be glad, let earth be glad, as glory floods her,
ablaze with light from her eternal King,
let all corners of the earth be glad,
knowing an end to gloom and darkness.
Rejoice, let Mother Church also rejoice,
arrayed with the lightning of his glory,
let this holy building shake with joy,
filled with the mighty voices of the peoples.
(Therefore, dearest friends,
standing in the awesome glory of this holy light,
invoke with me, I ask you,
the mercy of God almighty,
that he, who has been pleased to number me,
though unworthy, among the Levites,
may pour into me his light unshadowed,
that I may sing this candle's perfect praises).

(℣. The Lord be with you. ℟. **And with your spirit.**)
℣. Lift up your hearts. ℟. **We lift them up to the Lord.** ℣. Let us give thanks to the Lord our God. ℟. **It is right and just.**

It is truly right and just,
with ardent love of mind and heart
and with devoted service of our voice,
to acclaim our God invisible, the almighty Father,
and Jesus Christ, our Lord, his Son, his Only Begotten.

Who for our sake paid Adam's debt to the eternal Father,
and, pouring out his own dear Blood,
wiped clean the record of our ancient sinfulness.

These then are the feasts of Passover,
in which is slain the Lamb, the one true Lamb,
whose Blood anoints the doorposts of believers.

This is the night,
when once you led our forebears, Israel's children,
from slavery in Egypt
and made them pass dry-shod through the Red Sea.

This is the night
that with a pillar of fire
banished the darkness of sin.

This is the night
that even now, throughout the world,
sets Christian believers apart from worldly vices
and from the gloom of sin,
leading them to grace
and joining them to his holy ones.

This is the night,
when Christ broke the prison-bars of death
and rose victorious from the underworld.

Our birth would have been no gain,
had we not been redeemed.
O wonder of your humble care for us!
O love, O charity beyond all telling,
to ransom a slave you gave away your Son!

O truly necessary sin of Adam,
destroyed completely by the Death of Christ!

O happy fault
that earned so great, so glorious a Redeemer!

O truly blessed night,
worthy alone to know the time and hour
when Christ rose from the underworld!

This is the night
of which it is written:
The night shall be as bright as day,
dazzling is the night for me,
and full of gladness.

The sanctifying power of this night
dispels wickedness, washes faults away,
restores innocence to the fallen, and joy to mourners,
drives out hatred, fosters concord, and brings down the
*   mighty.*

On this, your night of grace, O holy Father,
accept this candle, a solemn offering,
the work of bees and of your servants' hands,
an evening sacrifice of praise,
this gift from your most holy Church.

But now we know the praises of this pillar,
which glowing fire ignites for God's honor,
a fire into many flames divided,
yet never dimmed by sharing of its light,
for it is fed by melting wax,
drawn out by mother bees
to build a torch so precious.

O truly blessed night,
when things of heaven are wed to those of earth,
and divine to the human.

Shorter Form only:
On this, your night of grace, O holy Father,
accept this candle, a solemn offering,
the work of bees and of your servants' hands,
an evening sacrifice of praise,
this gift from your most holy Church.

Therefore, O Lord,
we pray you that this candle,

hallowed to the honor of your name,
may persevere undimmed,
to overcome the darkness of this night.
Receive it as a pleasing fragrance,
and let it mingle with the lights of heaven.
May this flame be found still burning
by the Morning Star:
the one Morning Star who never sets,
Christ your Son,
who, coming back from death's domain,
has shed his peaceful light on humanity,
and lives and reigns for ever and ever.
℞. **Amen.** ↓

SECOND PART:
THE LITURGY OF THE WORD

*In this Vigil, the mother of all Vigils, nine readings are provid-
ed, namely seven from the Old Testament and two from the
New (the Epistle and Gospel), all of which should be read
whenever this can be done, so that the character of the Vigil,
which demands an extended period of time, may be preserved.*

*Nevertheless, where more serious pastoral circumstances
demand it, the number of readings from the Old Testament
may be reduced, always bearing in mind that the reading of
the Word of God is a fundamental part of this Easter Vigil. At
least three readings should be read from the Old Testament,
both from the Law and from the Prophets, and their respec-
tive Responsorial Psalms should be sung. Never, moreover,
should the reading of chapter 14 of Exodus with its canticle
be omitted.*

*After setting aside their candles, all sit. Before the readings
begin, the Priest instructs the people in these or similar words:*

[Listen with Quiet Hearts]

Dear brethren (brothers and sisters),
now that we have begun our solemn Vigil,
let us listen with quiet hearts to the Word of God.

Let us meditate on how God in times past saved his
   people
and in these, the last days, has sent us his Son as our
   Redeemer.
Let us pray that our God may complete this paschal
   work of salvation
by the fullness of redemption.

*Then the readings follow. A reader goes to the ambo and pro-
claims the reading. Afterwards a psalmist or a cantor sings or
says the Psalm with the people making the response. Then all
rise, the Priest says,* Let us pray *and, after all have prayed
for a while in silence, he says the prayer corresponding to the
reading. In place of the Responsorial Psalm a period of
sacred silence may be observed, in which case the pause after*
Let us pray *is omitted.*

FIRST READING Gn 1:1—2:2 or 1:1, 26-31a [God Our Creator]
**God created the world and all that is in it. He saw that it
was good. This reading from the first book of the Bible
shows that God loved all that he made.**

*[If the "Shorter Form" is used, the indented text in brackets is
omitted.]*

A reading from the Book of Genesis

IN the beginning, when God created the heavens and
the earth,
[the earth was a formless wasteland, and darkness
covered the abyss, while a mighty wind swept
over the waters.

Then God said, "Let there be light," and there
was light. God saw how good the light was. God
then separated the light from the darkness. God
called the light "day," and the darkness he called
"night." Thus evening came, and morning followed—the first day.

Then God said, "Let there be a dome in the
middle of the waters, to separate one body of
water from the other." And so it happened: God

made the dome, and it separated the water above the dome from the water below it. God called the dome "the sky." Evening came, and morning followed—the second day.

Then God said, "Let the water under the sky be gathered into a single basin, so that the dry land may appear." And so it happened: the water under the sky was gathered into its basin, and the dry land appeared. God called the dry land "the earth," and the basin of the water he called "the sea." God saw how good it was. Then God said, "Let the earth bring forth vegetation: every kind of plant that bears seed and every kind of fruit tree on earth that bears fruit with its seed in it." And so it happened: the earth brought forth every kind of plant that bears seed and every kind of fruit tree on earth that bears fruit with its seed in it. God saw how good it was. Evening came, and morning followed—the third day.

Then God said: "Let there be lights in the dome of the sky, to separate day from night. Let them mark the fixed times, the days and the years, and serve as luminaries in the dome of the sky, to shed light upon the earth." And so it happened: God made the two great lights, the greater one to govern the day, and the lesser one to govern the night; and he made the stars. God set them in the dome of the sky, to shed light upon the earth, to govern the day and the night, and to separate the light from the darkness. God saw how good it was. Evening came, and morning followed—the fourth day.

Then God said, "Let the water teem with an abundance of living creatures, and on the earth let birds fly beneath the dome of the sky." And so it happened: God created the great sea monsters and all kinds of swimming creatures with which the water teems, and all kinds of winged birds. God saw how good it was, and God blessed them, saying, "Be fertile, multiply, and fill the water of the seas; and let the birds multiply on the earth." Evening came, and morning followed—the fifth day.

Then God said, "Let the earth bring forth all kinds of living creatures: cattle, creeping things, and wild animals of all kinds." And so it happened: God made all kinds of wild animals, all kinds of cattle, and all kinds of creeping things of the earth. God saw how good it was. Then]

God said: "Let us make man in our image, after our likeness. Let them have dominion over the fish of the sea, the birds of the air, and the cattle, and over all the wild animals and all the creatures that crawl on the ground."

God created man in his image;
   in the divine image he created him;
   male and female he created them.

God blessed them, saying: "Be fertile and multiply; fill the earth and subdue it. Have dominion over the fish of the sea, the birds of the air, and all the living things that move on the earth." God also said: "See, I give you every seed-bearing plant all over the earth and every tree that has seed-bearing fruit on it to be your food; and to all the animals of the land, all the birds of the air, and all the living creatures that crawl on the ground, I give all the green plants for food." And so it happened. God looked at everything he had made, and he found it very good.

[Evening came, and morning followed—the sixth day.

Thus the heavens and the earth and all their array were completed. Since on the seventh day God was finished with the work he had been doing, he rested on the seventh day from all the work he had undertaken.]

The word of the Lord. ℟. **Thanks be to God.** ↓

RESPONSORIAL PSALM Ps 104   [Come, Holy Spirit]

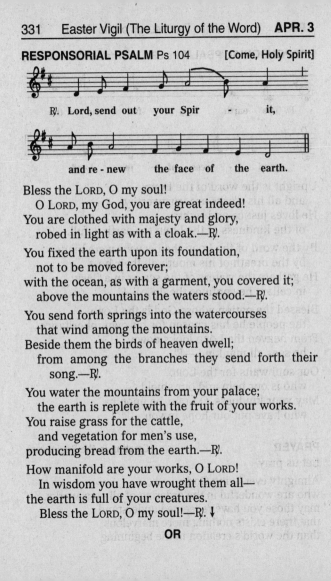

℟. Lord, send out your Spir - it,
and re - new the face of the earth.

Bless the LORD, O my soul!
    O LORD, my God, you are great indeed!
You are clothed with majesty and glory,
    robed in light as with a cloak.—℟.

You fixed the earth upon its foundation,
    not to be moved forever;
with the ocean, as with a garment, you covered it;
    above the mountains the waters stood.—℟.

You send forth springs into the watercourses
    that wind among the mountains.
Beside them the birds of heaven dwell;
    from among the branches they send forth their
      song.—℟.

You water the mountains from your palace;
    the earth is replete with the fruit of your works.
You raise grass for the cattle,
    and vegetation for men's use,
producing bread from the earth.—℟.

How manifold are your works, O LORD!
    In wisdom you have wrought them all—
the earth is full of your creatures.
    Bless the LORD, O my soul!—℟. ↓

OR

RESPONSORIAL PSALM Ps 33 [The Lord's Goodness]

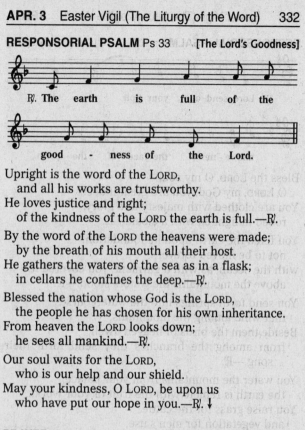

℟. The earth is full of the good - ness of the Lord.

Upright is the word of the LORD,
 and all his works are trustworthy.
He loves justice and right;
 of the kindness of the LORD the earth is full.—℟.

By the word of the LORD the heavens were made;
 by the breath of his mouth all their host.
He gathers the waters of the sea as in a flask;
 in cellars he confines the deep.—℟.

Blessed the nation whose God is the LORD,
 the people he has chosen for his own inheritance.
From heaven the LORD looks down;
 he sees all mankind.—℟.

Our soul waits for the LORD,
 who is our help and our shield.
May your kindness, O LORD, be upon us
 who have put our hope in you.—℟. ↓

PRAYER [Creation in the Beginning]

Let us pray.

Almighty ever-living God,
who are wonderful in the ordering of all your works,
may those you have redeemed understand
that there exists nothing more marvelous
than the world's creation in the beginning

except that, at the end of the ages,
Christ our Passover has been sacrificed.
Who lives and reigns for ever and ever. ℟. **Amen.** ↓

OR

PRAYER (On the creation of man)   [Eternal Joys]

O God, who wonderfully created human nature
and still more wonderfully redeemed it,
grant us, we pray,
to set our minds against the enticements of sin,
that we may merit to attain eternal joys.
Through Christ our Lord. ℟. **Amen.** ↓

SECOND READING Gn 22:1-18 or 22:1-2, 9a, 10-13, 15-18
                                                      [Obedience to God]

**Abraham is obedient to the will of God. Because God asks
him, without hesitation he prepares to sacrifice his son
Isaac. In the new order, God sends his Son to redeem man
by his death on the cross.**

*[If the "Shorter Form" is used, the indented text in brackets is
omitted.]*

A reading from the Book of Genesis

GOD put Abraham to the test. He called to him,
"Abraham!" "Here I am," he replied. Then God
said: "Take your son Isaac, your only one, whom you
love, and go to the land of Moriah. There you shall
offer him up as a holocaust on a height that I will point
out to you."

   [Early the next morning Abraham saddled his
   donkey, took with him his son Isaac, and two of
   his servants as well, and with the wood that he
   had cut for the holocaust, set out for the place of
   which God had told him.

   On the third day Abraham got sight of the
   place from afar. Then he said to his servants: "Both
   of you stay here with the donkey, while the boy

and I go on over yonder. We will worship and then come back to you." Thereupon Abraham took the wood for the holocaust and laid it on his son Isaac's shoulders, while he himself carried the fire and the knife. As the two walked on together, Isaac spoke to his father Abraham. "Father!" Isaac said. "Yes, son," he replied. Isaac continued, "Here are the fire and the wood, but where is the sheep for the holocaust?" "Son," Abraham answered, "God himself will provide the sheep for the holocaust." Then the two continued going forward.]

When they came to the place of which God had told him, Abraham built an altar there and arranged the wood on it.

[Next he tied up his son Isaac, and put him on top of the wood on the altar.]

Then he reached out and took the knife to slaughter his son. But the LORD's messenger called to him from heaven, "Abraham, Abraham!" "Here I am," he answered. "Do not lay your hand on the boy," said the messenger. "Do not do the least thing to him. I know now how devoted you are to God, since you did not withhold from me your own beloved son." As Abraham looked about, he spied a ram caught by its horns in the thicket. So he went and took the ram and offered it up as a holocaust in place of his son.

[Abraham named the site Yahweh-yireh; hence people now say, "On the mountain the LORD will see."]

Again the LORD's messenger called to Abraham from heaven and said: "I swear by myself, declares the LORD, that because you acted as you did in not withholding from me your beloved son, I will bless you abundantly and make your descendants as countless as the stars of the sky and the sands of the seashore; your descendants shall take possession of the gates of their enemies, and in your descendants all the nations of the earth shall find blessing—all this because you obeyed my command."—The word of the Lord. ℟. **Thanks be to God.** ↓

RESPONSORIAL PSALM Ps 16   [God Our Hope]

℟. You are my in-her-i-tance, O Lord.

O LORD, my allotted portion and my cup,
    you it is who hold fast my lot.
I set the LORD ever before me;
    with him at my right I shall not be disturbed.—℟.

Therefore my heart is glad and my soul rejoices,
    my body, too, abides in confidence;
because you will not abandon my soul to the nether-
    world,
    nor will you suffer your faithful one to undergo cor-
    ruption.—℟.

You will show me the path to life,
    fullness of joys in your presence,
    the delights at your right hand forever.—℟. ↓

PRAYER   [Entering into Grace]

Let us pray.

O God, supreme Father of the faithful,
who increase the children of your promise
by pouring out the grace of adoption
throughout the whole world
and who through the Paschal Mystery
make your servant Abraham father of nations,
as once you swore,
grant, we pray,
that your peoples may enter worthily
into the grace to which you call them.

Through Christ our Lord.
℞. **Amen.** ↓

THIRD READING Ex 14:15—15:1   **[Exodus]**

Moses leads the Israelites out of Egypt. He opens a path of
escape through the Red Sea. God protects his people.
Through the waters of baptism, human beings are freed
from sin.

A reading from the Book of Exodus

THE LORD said to Moses, "Why are you crying out to
me? Tell the Israelites to go forward. And you, lift
up your staff and, with hand outstretched over the sea,
split the sea in two, that the Israelites may pass
through it on dry land. But I will make the Egyptians
so obstinate that they will go in after them. Then I will
receive glory through Pharaoh and all his army, his
chariots and charioteers. The Egyptians shall know
that I am the LORD, when I receive glory through
Pharaoh and his chariots and charioteers."

The angel of God, who had been leading Israel's
camp, now moved and went around behind them. The
column of cloud also, leaving the front, took up its
place behind them, so that it came between the camp
of the Egyptians and that of Israel. But the cloud now
became dark, and thus the night passed without the
rival camps coming any closer together all night long.
Then Moses stretched out his hand over the sea, and
the LORD swept the sea with a strong east wind
throughout the night and so turned it into dry land.
When the water was thus divided, the Israelites
marched into the midst of the sea on dry land, with the
water like a wall to their right and to their left.

The Egyptians followed in pursuit; all Pharaoh's
horses and chariots and charioteers went after them
right into the midst of the sea. In the night watch just
before dawn the LORD cast through the column of the

fiery cloud upon the Egyptian force a glance that threw it into a panic; and he so clogged their chariot wheels that they could hardly drive. With that the Egyptians sounded the retreat before Israel, because the LORD was fighting for them against the Egyptians.

Then the LORD told Moses, "Stretch out your hand over the sea, that the water may flow back upon the Egyptians, upon their chariots and their charioteers." So Moses stretched out his hand over the sea, and at dawn the sea flowed back to its normal depth. The Egyptians were fleeing head on toward the sea, when the LORD hurled them into its midst. As the water flowed back, it covered the chariots and the charioteers of Pharaoh's whole army which had followed the Israelites into the sea. Not a single one of them escaped. But the Israelites had marched on dry land through the midst of the sea, with the water like a wall to their right and to their left. Thus the LORD saved Israel on that day from the power of the Egyptians. When Israel saw the Egyptians lying dead on the seashore and beheld the great power that the LORD had shown against the Egyptians, they feared the LORD and believed in him and in his servant Moses.

Then Moses and the Israelites sang this song to the LORD:

I will sing to the LORD, for he is gloriously triumphant;

horse and chariot he has cast into the sea.

The word of the Lord. ℞. **Thanks be to God.** ↓

RESPONSORIAL PSALM Ex 15   [God the Savior]

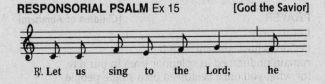

℞. Let   us   sing   to   the   Lord;   he

has cov-ered him-self in glo - ry.

I will sing to the LORD, for he is gloriously triumphant;
  horse and chariot he has cast into the sea.
My strength and my courage is the LORD,
  and he has been my savior.
He is my God, I praise him;
  the God of my father, I extol him.

℟. **Let us sing to the Lord; he has covered himself in glory.**

The LORD is a warrior,
  LORD is his name!
Pharaoh's chariots and army he hurled into the sea;
  the elite of his officers were submerged into the Red
  Sea.—℟.

The flood waters covered them,
  they sank into the depths like a stone.
Your right hand, O LORD, magnificent in power,
  your right hand, O LORD, has shattered the enemy.
  —℟.

You brought in the people you redeemed
  and planted them on the mountain of your inheritance—
the place where you made your seat, O LORD,
  the sanctuary, O LORD, which your hands established.
The LORD shall reign forever and ever.—℟. ↓

PRAYER [Children of Abraham]

Let us pray.

O God, whose ancient wonders
remain undimmed in splendor even in our day,
for what you once bestowed on a single people,

freeing them from Pharaoh's persecution
by the power of your right hand,
now you bring about as the salvation of the nations
through the waters of rebirth,
grant, we pray, that the whole world
may become children of Abraham
and inherit the dignity of Israel's birthright.
Through Christ our Lord. ℟. **Amen.** ↓

OR

PRAYER   [Reborn]

O God, who by the light of the New Testament
have unlocked the meaning
of wonders worked in former times,
so that the Red Sea prefigures the sacred font
and the nation delivered from slavery
foreshadows the Christian people,
grant, we pray, that all nations,
obtaining the privilege of Israel by merit of faith,
may be reborn by partaking of your Spirit.
Through Christ our Lord. ℟. **Amen.** ↓

FOURTH READING Is 54:5-14   [God's Love]

> For a time, God hid from his people, but his love for them
> is everlasting. He takes pity on them and promises them
> prosperity.

A reading from the Book of the Prophet Isaiah

THE One who has become your husband is your
    Maker;
    his name is the LORD of hosts;
your redeemer is the Holy One of Israel,
    called God of all the earth.
The LORD calls you back,
    like a wife forsaken and grieved in spirit,
    a wife married in youth and then cast off,
    says your God.

For a brief moment I abandoned you,
  but with great tenderness I will take you back.
In an outburst of wrath, for a moment
  I hid my face from you;
but with enduring love I take pity on you,
  says the LORD, your redeemer.
This is for me like the days of Noah,
  when I swore that the waters of Noah
  should never again deluge the earth;
so I have sworn not to be angry with you,
  or to rebuke you.
Though the mountains leave their place
  and the hills be shaken,
my love shall never leave you
  nor my covenant of peace be shaken,
  says the LORD, who has mercy on you.
O afflicted one, storm-battered and unconsoled,
  I lay your pavements in carnelians,
  and your foundations in sapphires;
I will make your battlements of rubies,
  your gates of carbuncles,
  and all your walls of precious stones.
All your children shall be taught by the LORD,
  and great shall be the peace of your children.
In justice shall you be established,
  far from the fear of oppression,
  where destruction cannot come near you.
The word of the Lord. ℟. **Thanks be to God.** ↓

RESPONSORIAL PSALM Ps 30   [God Our Help]

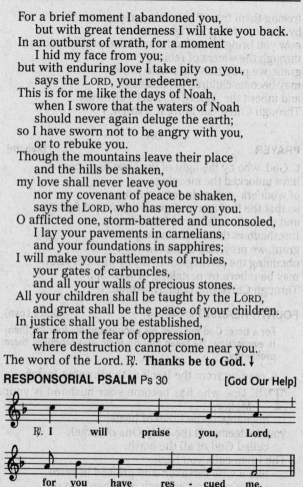

℟. I will praise you, Lord,
for you have res - cued me.

I will extol you, O LORD, for you drew me clear
    and did not let my enemies rejoice over me.
O LORD, you brought me up from the netherworld;
    you preserved me from among those going down
       into the pit.—R̶.

Sing praise to the LORD, you his faithful ones,
    and give thanks to his holy name.
For his anger lasts but a moment;
    a lifetime, his good will.
At nightfall, weeping enters in,
    but with the dawn, rejoicing.—R̶.

Hear, O LORD, and have pity on me;
    O LORD, be my helper.
You changed my mourning into dancing;
    O LORD, my God, forever will I give you thanks.
    —R̶. ↓

PRAYER   [Fulfillment of God's Promise]
Let us pray.
Almighty ever-living God,
surpass, for the honor of your name,
what you pledged to the Patriarchs by reason of their
    faith,
and through sacred adoption increase the children of
    your promise,
so that what the Saints of old never doubted would come
    to pass
your Church may now see in great part fulfilled.
Through Christ our Lord. R̶. **Amen.** ↓

*Alternatively, other prayers may be used from among those
which follow the readings that have been omitted.*

FIFTH READING Is 55:1-11   [God of Forgiveness]

> God is a loving Father and he calls his people back. He promises an everlasting covenant with them. God is merciful, generous, and forgiving.

A reading from the Book of the Prophet Isaiah

THUS says the LORD:
    All you who are thirsty,
        come to the water!
You who have no money,
        come, receive grain and eat;
come, without paying and without cost,
        drink wine and milk!
Why spend your money for what is not bread;
        your wages for what fails to satisfy?
Heed me, and you shall eat well,
        you shall delight in rich fare.
Come to me heedfully,
        listen, that you may have life.
I will renew with you the everlasting covenant,
        the benefits assured to David.
As I made him a witness to the peoples,
        a leader and commander of nations,
so shall you summon a nation you knew not,
        and nations that knew you not shall run to you,
because of the LORD, your God,
        the Holy One of Israel, who has glorified you.

Seek the LORD while he may be found,
        call him while he is near.
Let the scoundrel forsake his way,
        and the wicked man his thoughts;
let him turn to the LORD for mercy;
        to our God, who is generous in forgiving.
For my thoughts are not your thoughts,
        nor are your ways my ways, says the LORD.

As high as the heavens are above the earth,
　　so high are my ways above your ways,
　　and my thoughts above your thoughts.

For just as from the heavens
　　the rain and snow come down
and do not return there
　　till they have watered the earth,
　　making it fertile and fruitful,
giving seed to the one who sows
　　and bread to the one who eats,
so shall my word be
　　that goes forth from my mouth;
my word shall not return to me void,
　　but shall do my will,
　　achieving the end for which I sent it.
The word of the Lord. ℟. **Thanks be to God.** ↓

RESPONSORIAL PSALM Is 12　[Make Known God's Deeds]

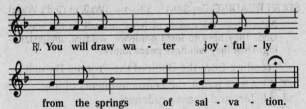

℟. You will draw water joyfully
from the springs of salvation.

God indeed is my savior;
　　I am confident and unafraid.
My strength and my courage is the LORD,
　　and he has been my savior.
With joy you will draw water
　　at the fountain of salvation.—℟.

Give thanks to the LORD, acclaim his name;
　　among the nations make known his deeds,
　　proclaim how exalted is his name.—℟.

Sing praise to the LORD for his glorious achievement;
   let this be known throughout all the earth.
Shout with exultation, O city of Zion,
   for great in your midst
   is the Holy One of Israel!

℟. **You will draw water joyfully from the springs of salvation.** ↓

PRAYER   [Progress in Virtue]

Let us pray.

Almighty ever-living God,
sole hope of the world,
who by the preaching of your Prophets
unveiled the mysteries of this present age,
graciously increase the longing of your people,
for only at the prompting of your grace
do the faithful progress in any kind of virtue.
Through Christ our Lord. ℟. **Amen.** ↓

SIXTH READING Bar 3:9-15, 32—4:4 [Walk in God's Ways]

> Baruch tells the people of Israel to walk in the ways of
> God. They have to learn prudence, wisdom, understand-
> ing. Then they will have peace forever.

A reading from the Book of the Prophet Baruch

HEAR, O Israel, the commandments of life:
   listen, and know prudence!
How is it, Israel,
   that you are in the land of your foes,
   grown old in a foreign land,
defiled with the dead,
   accounted with those destined for the netherworld?
You have forsaken the fountain of wisdom!
   Had you walked in the way of God,
   you would have dwelt in enduring peace.
Learn where prudence is,
   where strength, where understanding;

that you may know also
    where are length of days, and life,
    where light of the eyes, and peace.
Who has found the place of wisdom,
    who has entered into her treasuries?

The One who knows all things knows her;
    he has probed her by his knowledge—
the One who established the earth for all time,
    and filled it with four-footed beasts;
he who dismisses the light, and it departs,
    calls it, and it obeys him trembling;
before whom the stars at their posts
    shine and rejoice;
when he calls them, they answer,"Here we are!"
    shining with joy for their Maker.
Such is our God;
    no other is to be compared to him:
he has traced out all the way of understanding,
    and has given her to Jacob, his servant,
    to Israel, his beloved son.

Since then she has appeared on earth,
    and moved among people.
She is the book of the precepts of God,
    the law that endures forever;
all who cling to her will live,
    but those will die who forsake her.
Turn, O Jacob, and receive her:
    walk by her light toward splendor.
Give not your glory to another,
    your privileges to an alien race.
Blessed are we, O Israel;
    for what pleases God is known to us!
The word of the Lord. ℟. **Thanks be to God.** ↓

RESPONSORIAL PSALM Ps 19 [Words of Eternal Life]

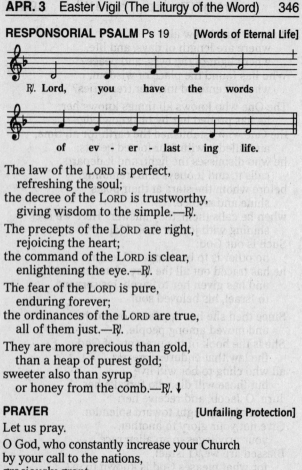

℟. Lord, you have the words of ev-er-last-ing life.

The law of the LORD is perfect,
refreshing the soul;
the decree of the LORD is trustworthy,
giving wisdom to the simple.—℟.

The precepts of the LORD are right,
rejoicing the heart;
the command of the LORD is clear,
enlightening the eye.—℟.

The fear of the LORD is pure,
enduring forever;
the ordinances of the LORD are true,
all of them just.—℟.

They are more precious than gold,
than a heap of purest gold;
sweeter also than syrup
or honey from the comb.—℟. ↓

PRAYER [Unfailing Protection]

Let us pray.

O God, who constantly increase your Church
by your call to the nations,
graciously grant
to those you wash clean in the waters of Baptism
the assurance of your unfailing protection.
Through Christ our Lord. ℟. **Amen.** ↓

SEVENTH READING Ez 36:16-17a, 18-28   [God's People]

Ezekiel, as God's prophet, speaks for God who is to keep his name holy among his people. All shall know the holiness of God. He will cleanse his people from idol worship and make them his own again. This promise is again fulfilled in baptism in the restored order of redemption.

A reading from the Book of the Prophet Ezekiel

THE word of the LORD came to me, saying: Son of man, when the house of Israel lived in their land, they defiled it by their conduct and deeds. Therefore I poured out my fury upon them because of the blood that they poured out on the ground, and because they defiled it with idols. I scattered them among the nations, dispersing them over foreign lands; according to their conduct and deeds I judged them. But when they came among the nations wherever they came, they served to profane my holy name, because it was said of them: "These are the people of the LORD, yet they had to leave their land." So I have relented because of my holy name which the house of Israel profaned among the nations where they came. Therefore say to the house of Israel: Thus says the Lord GOD: Not for your sakes do I act, house of Israel, but for the sake of my holy name, which you profaned among the nations to which you came. I will prove the holiness of my great name, profaned among the nations, in whose midst you have profaned it. Thus the nations shall know that I am the LORD, says the Lord GOD, when in their sight I prove my holiness through you. For I will take you away from among the nations, gather you from all the foreign lands, and bring you back to your own land. I will sprinkle clean water upon you to cleanse you from all your impurities, and from all your idols I will cleanse you. I will give you a new heart and place a new spirit within you, taking from your bodies your stony hearts and giving you natural hearts. I will put my spirit within you and make you live by my statutes, careful to observe my decrees. You shall live in the land I gave your fathers; you shall be my people, and I will be your God.—The word of the Lord. ℟. **Thanks be to God.** ↓

When Baptism is celebrated, Responsorial Psalm 42 is used; when Baptism is not celebrated, Is 12 or Ps 51 is used.

RESPONSORIAL PSALM Ps 42   [Longing for God]

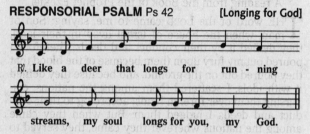

℟. Like a deer that longs for running streams, my soul longs for you, my God.

Athirst is my soul for God, the living God.
    When shall I go and behold the face of God?—℟.

I went with the throng
    and led them in procession to the house of God,
amid loud cries of joy and thanksgiving,
    with the multitude keeping festival.—℟.

Send forth your light and your fidelity;
    they shall lead me on
and bring me to your holy mountain,
    to your dwelling-place.—℟.

Then will I go into the altar of God,
    the God of my gladness and joy;
then will I give you thanks upon the harp,
    O God, my God!—℟. ↓

OR

When Baptism is not celebrated, the Responsorial Psalm after the Fifth Reading (Is 12:2-3, 4bcd, 5-6) as above, p. 343, may be used; or the following:

RESPONSORIAL PSALM Ps 51   [A Clean Heart]

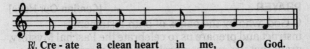

R̸. Cre-ate   a clean heart   in   me,   O   God.

A clean heart create for me, O God,
 and a steadfast spirit renew within me.
Cast me not out from your presence,
 and your Holy Spirit take not from me.—R̸.

Give me back the joy of your salvation,
 and a willing spirit sustain in me.
I will teach transgressors your ways,
 and sinners shall return to you.—R̸.

For you are not pleased with sacrifices;
 should I offer a holocaust, you would not accept it.
My sacrifice, O God, is a contrite spirit;
 a heart contrite and humbled, O God, you will not
 spurn.—R̸. ↓

PRAYER   [Human Salvation]
Let us pray.

O God of unchanging power and eternal light,
look with favor on the wondrous mystery of the whole
 Church
and serenely accomplish the work of human salvation,
which you planned from all eternity;
may the whole world know and see
that what was cast down is raised up,
what had become old is made new,
and all things are restored to integrity through Christ,
just as by him they came into being.
Who lives and reigns for ever and ever.
R̸. **Amen.** ↓

OR

PRAYER   [Confirm Our Hope]

O God, who by the pages of both Testaments
instruct and prepare us to celebrate the Paschal Mystery,
grant that we may comprehend your mercy,
so that the gifts we receive from you this night
may confirm our hope of the gifts to come.
Through Christ our Lord. ℟. **Amen.** ↓

*After the last reading from the Old Testament with its
Responsorial Psalm and its prayer, the altar candles are lit,
and the Priest intones the hymn* Gloria in excelsis Deo
*(Glory to God in the highest), which is taken up by all,
while bells are rung, according to local custom.*

COLLECT   [Renewed in Body and Mind]

Let us pray.

O God, who make this most sacred night radiant
with the glory of the Lord's Resurrection,
stir up in your Church a spirit of adoption,
so that, renewed in body and mind,
we may render you undivided service.
Through our Lord Jesus Christ, your Son,
who lives and reigns with you in the unity of the Holy
    Spirit,
one God, for ever and ever. ℟. **Amen.** ↓

Then the reader proclaims the reading from the Apostle.

EPISTLE Rom 6:3-11   [Alive in Christ]

> By Baptism the Christian is not merely identified with the
> dying Christ, who has won a victory over sin, but is intro-
> duced into the very act by which Christ died to sin.

A reading from the Letter of Saint Paul to the Romans

BROTHERS and sisters: Are you unaware that we
who were baptized into Christ Jesus were baptized
into his death? We were indeed buried with him
through baptism into death, so that, just as Christ was

raised from the dead by the glory of the Father, we too might live in newness of life.

For if we have grown into union with him through a death like his, we shall also be united with him in the resurrection. We know that our old self was crucified with him, so that our sinful body might be done away with, that we might no longer be in slavery to sin. For a dead person has been absolved from sin. If, then, we have died with Christ, we believe that we shall also live with him. We know that Christ, raised from the dead, dies no more; death no longer has power over him. As to his death, he died to sin once and for all; as to his life, he lives for God. Consequently, you too must think of yourselves as being dead to sin and living for God in Christ Jesus.—The word of the Lord. ℟. **Thanks be to God.** ↓

After the Epistle has been read, all rise, then the Priest solemnly intones the Alleluia *three times, raising his voice by a step each time, with all repeating it. If necessary, the psalmist intones the* Alleluia.

RESPONSORIAL PSALM Ps 118   [God's Mercy]

℟. **Al -le -lu -ia.   Al -   le -lu - ia.   Al -   le -lu - ia.**

Give thanks to the Lᴏʀᴅ, for he is good,
    for his mercy endures forever.
Let the house of Israel say,
    "His mercy endures forever."—℟.

The right hand of the Lᴏʀᴅ has struck with power;
    the right hand of the Lᴏʀᴅ is exalted.
I shall not die, but live,
    and declare the works of the Lᴏʀᴅ.—℟.

The stone which the builders rejected
    has become the cornerstone.

By the LORD has this been done;
  it is wonderful in our eyes.

℟. **Alleluia. Alleluia. Alleluia.** ↓

The Priest, in the usual way, puts incense in the thurible and blesses the Deacon. At the Gospel lights are not carried, but only incense.

GOSPEL Mk 16:1-7   [The Resurrection]

Jesus has risen; he is not here. The cross has yielded to the empty tomb. Although Peter is singled out, the Easter message is first announced to the faithful, devoted women who followed Jesus.

℣. The Lord be with you. ℟. **And with your spirit.**
✠ A reading from the holy Gospel according to Mark.
℟. **Glory to you, O Lord.**

WHEN the sabbath was over, Mary Magdalene, Mary, the mother of James, and Salome brought spices so that they might go and anoint him. Very early when the sun had risen, on the first day of the week, they came to the tomb. They were saying to one another, "Who will roll back the stone for us from the entrance of the tomb?" When they looked up, they saw that the stone had been rolled back; it was very large. On entering the tomb they saw a young man sitting on the right side, clothed in a white robe, and they were utterly amazed. He said to them, "Do not be amazed! You seek Jesus of Nazareth, the crucified. He has been raised; he is not here. Behold the place where they laid him. But go and tell his disciples and Peter, 'He is going before you to Galilee; there you will see him, as he told you.' "—The Gospel of the Lord. ℟. **Praise to you, Lord Jesus Christ.**

After the Gospel, the Homily, even if brief, is not to be omitted.
Then the Celebration of the Sacraments of Initiation begins.

THIRD PART:
CELEBRATION OF THE SACRAMENTS OF INITIATION

The following is adapted from the Rite of Christian Initiation of Adults.

Celebration of Baptism

PRESENTATION OF THE CANDIDATES

An assisting Deacon or other minister calls the candidates for Baptism forward and their godparents present them. The Invitation to Prayer and the Litany of the Saints follow.

INVITATION TO PRAYER   [Supportive Prayer]

The Priest addresses the following or a similar invitation for the assembly to join in prayer for the candidates for Baptism.

Dearly beloved,
with one heart and one soul, let us by our prayers
come to the aid of these our brothers and sisters in their
    blessed hope,
so that, as they approach the font of rebirth,
the almighty Father may bestow on them
all his merciful help.

LITANY OF THE SAINTS   [Petitioning the Saints]

The singing of the Litany of the Saints is led by cantors and may include, at the proper place, names of other saints (for example, the titular of the church, the patron saints of the place or of those to be baptized) or petitions suitable to the occasion.

Lord, have mercy.
Lord, have mercy.

Christ, have mercy.
Christ, have mercy.

Lord, have mercy.
Lord, have mercy.

Holy Mary, Mother of God,
    pray for us.
Saint Michael, **pray for us.**
Holy Angels of God, **pray for us.**

Saint John the Baptist, **pray for us.**

Saint Joseph, **pray for us.**

Saint Peter and Saint Paul, **pray for us.**

Saint Andrew, **pray for us.**

Saint John, **pray for us.**

Saint Mary Magdalene, **pray for us.**

Saint Stephen, **pray for us.**

Saint Ignatius of Antioch, **pray for us.**

Saint Lawrence, **pray for us.**

Saint Perpetua and Saint Felicity, **pray for us.**

Saint Agnes, **pray for us.**

Saint Gregory, **pray for us.**

Saint Augustine, **pray for us.**

Saint Athanasius, **pray for us.**

Saint Basil, **pray for us.**

Saint Martin, **pray for us.**

Saint Benedict, **pray for us.**

Saint Francis and Saint Dominic, **pray for us.**

Saint Francis Xavier, **pray for us.**

Saint John Vianney, **pray for us.**

Saint Catherine of Siena, **pray for us.**

Saint Teresa of Jesus, **pray for us.**

All holy men and women, Saints of God, **pray for us.**

Lord, be merciful, **Lord, deliver us, we pray.**

From all evil, **Lord, deliver us, we pray.**

From every sin, **Lord, deliver us, we pray.**

From everlasting death, **Lord, deliver us, we pray.**

By your Incarnation, **Lord, deliver us, we pray.**

By your Death and Resurrection, **Lord, deliver us, we pray.**

By the outpouring of the Holy Spirit, **Lord, deliver us, we pray.**

Be merciful to us sinners, **Lord, we ask you, hear our prayer.**

Bring these chosen ones to new birth through the grace of Baptism, **Lord, we ask you, hear our prayer.**

Jesus, Son of the living God, **Lord, we ask you, hear our prayer.**

Christ, hear us.

Christ, hear us.

Christ, graciously hear us.

Christ, graciously hear us.

BLESSING OF BAPTISMAL WATER   [Grace-Filled Water]

The Priest then blesses the baptismal water, saying the following prayer with hands extended:

O God, who by invisible power
accomplish a wondrous effect
through sacramental signs
and who in many ways have prepared water, your
   creation,
to show forth the grace of Baptism;

O God, whose Spirit
in the first moments of the world's creation
hovered over the waters,
so that the very substance of water
would even then take to itself the power to sanctify;

O God, who by the outpouring of the flood
foreshadowed regeneration,
so that from the mystery of one and the same element of
   water
would come an end to vice and a beginning of virtue;

O God, who caused the children of Abraham
to pass dry-shod through the Red Sea,
so that the chosen people,
set free from slavery to Pharaoh,
would prefigure the people of the baptized;

O God, whose Son,
baptized by John in the waters of the Jordan,
was anointed with the Holy Spirit,
and, as he hung upon the Cross,
gave forth water from his side along with blood,
and after his Resurrection, commanded his disciples:
"Go forth, teach all nations, baptizing them
in the name of the Father and of the Son and of the Holy
   Spirit,"
look now, we pray, upon the face of your Church
and graciously unseal for her the fountain of Baptism.

May this water receive by the Holy Spirit
the grace of your Only Begotten Son,
so that human nature, created in your image
and washed clean through the Sacrament of Baptism
from all the squalor of the life of old,
may be found worthy to rise to the life of newborn
   children
through water and the Holy Spirit.

*And, if appropriate, lowering the paschal candle into the
water either once or three times, he continues:*

May the power of the Holy Spirit,
O Lord, we pray,
come down through your Son
into the fullness of this font,

and, holding the candle in the water, he continues:

so that all who have been buried with Christ
by Baptism into death
may rise again to life with him.
Who lives and reigns with you in the unity of the Holy
   Spirit,
one God, for ever and ever. ℟. **Amen.**

*Then the candle is lifted out of the water, as the people
acclaim:*

**Springs of water, bless the Lord;
praise and exalt him above all for ever.**

THE BLESSING OF WATER

*If no one present is to be baptized and the font is not to be
blessed, the Priest introduces the faithful to the blessing of
water, saying:*

Dear brothers and sisters,
let us humbly beseech the Lord our God
to bless this water he has created,
which will be sprinkled upon us
as a memorial of our Baptism.

May he graciously renew us,
that we may remain faithful to the Spirit
whom we have received.

And after a brief pause in silence, he proclaims the following prayer, with hands extended:

Lord our God,
in your mercy be present to your people
who keep vigil on this most sacred night,
and, for us who recall the wondrous work of our creation
and the still greater work of our redemption,
graciously bless this water.
For you created water to make the fields fruitful
and to refresh and cleanse our bodies.
You also made water the instrument of your mercy:
for through water you freed your people from slavery
and quenched their thirst in the desert;
through water the Prophets proclaimed the new
    covenant
you were to enter upon with the human race;
and last of all,
through water, which Christ made holy in the Jordan,
you have renewed our corrupted nature
in the bath of regeneration.

Therefore, may this water be for us
a memorial of the Baptism we have received,
and grant that we may share
in the gladness of our brothers and sisters,
who at Easter have received their Baptism.
Through Christ our Lord.
℟. **Amen.**

RENUNCIATION OF SIN AND PROFESSION OF FAITH
[Witnessing to Our Faith]

If there are baptismal candidates, the Priest, in a series of questions to which the candidates reply, **I do**, *asks the candidates to renounce sin and profess their faith.*

BAPTISM   [Children of God]

*The Priest baptizes each candidate either by immersion or by
the pouring of water.*

N., I baptize you in the name of the Father, and of the
Son, and of the Holy Spirit.

EXPLANATORY RITES

*The celebration of Baptism continues with the explanatory
rites, after which the celebration of Confirmation normally
follows.*

ANOINTING AFTER BAPTISM   [Chrism of Salvation]

*If the Confirmation of those baptized is separated from their
Baptism, the Priest anoints them with chrism immediately
after Baptism.*

The God of power and Father of our Lord Jesus Christ
has freed you from sin
and brought you to new life
through water and the Holy Spirit.

He now anoints you with the chrism of salvation,
so that, united with his people,
you may remain for ever a member of Christ
who is Priest, Prophet, and King.

Newly baptized: **Amen.**

*In silence each of the newly baptized is anointed with chrism
on the crown of the head.*

CLOTHING WITH A BAPTISMAL GARMENT
[Clothed in Christ]

*The garment used in this Rite may be white or of a color that
conforms to local custom. If circumstances suggest, this Rite
may be omitted.*

N. and N., you have become a new creation
and have clothed yourselves in Christ.

Receive this baptismal garment
and bring it unstained to the judgment seat of our Lord
    Jesus Christ,
so that you may have everlasting life.

Newly baptized: **Amen.**

PRESENTATION OF A LIGHTED CANDLE [Light of Christ]

*The Priest takes the Easter candle in his hands or touches it,
saying:*

Godparents, please come forward to give to the newly
baptized the light of Christ.

*A godparent of each of the newly baptized goes to the Priest,
lights a candle from the Easter candle, then presents it to the
newly baptized.*

You have been enlightened by Christ.
Walk always as children of the light
and keep the flame of faith alive in your hearts.
When the Lord comes, may you go out to meet him
with all the saints in the heavenly kingdom.

Newly baptized: **Amen.**

The Renewal of Baptismal Promises

INVITATION   [Call to Renewal]

*After the celebration of Baptism, the Priest addresses the com-
munity, in order to invite those present to the renewal of their
baptismal promises; the candidates for reception into full communion join the rest of the community in this renunciation of
sin and profession of faith. All stand and hold lighted candles.*

The Priest addresses the faithful in these or similar words.

Dear brethren (brothers and sisters), through the
    Paschal Mystery
we have been buried with Christ in Baptism,
so that we may walk with him in newness of life.
And so, now that our Lenten observance is concluded,
let us renew the promises of Holy Baptism,

by which we once renounced Satan and his works
and promised to serve God in the holy catholic Church.
And so I ask you:

A   [Reject Evil]

Priest: Do you renounce Satan?
All: **I do.**

Priest: And all his works?
All: **I do.**

Priest: And all his empty show?
All: **I do.**

B

Priest: Do you renounce sin,
   so as to live in the freedom of the children of God?
All: **I do.**

Priest: Do you renounce the lure of evil,
   so that sin may have no mastery over you?
All: **I do.**

Priest: Do you renounce Satan,
   the author and prince of sin?
All: **I do.**

PROFESSION OF FAITH   [I Believe]

Then the Priest continues:

Priest: Do you believe in God,
         the Father almighty,
         Creator of heaven and earth?
All: **I do.**

Priest: Do you believe in Jesus Christ, his only Son, our
         Lord,
         who was born of the Virgin Mary,
         suffered death and was buried,
         rose again from the dead
         and is seated at the right hand of the Father?
All: **I do.**

Priest: Do you believe in the Holy Spirit,
the holy catholic Church,
the communion of saints,
the forgiveness of sins,
the resurrection of the body,
and life everlasting?

All: **I do.**

And the Priest concludes:

And may almighty God, the Father of our Lord Jesus
Christ,
who has given us new birth by water and the Holy Spirit
and bestowed on us forgiveness of our sins,
keep us by his grace,
in Christ Jesus our Lord,
for eternal life.

All: **Amen.**

SPRINKLING WITH BAPTISMAL WATER   [Water of Life]

*The Priest sprinkles all the people with the blessed baptismal
water, while all sing the following song or any other that is
baptismal in character.*

Antiphon

**I saw water flowing from the Temple,
from its right-hand side, alleluia;
and all to whom this water came were saved
and shall say: Alleluia, alleluia.**

Celebration of Reception

INVITATION   [Call To Come Forward]

*If Baptism has been celebrated at the font, the Priest, the
assisting ministers, and the newly baptized with their godparents proceed to the sanctuary. As they do so the assembly
may sing a suitable song.*

*Then in the following or similar words the Priest invites the
candidates for reception, along with their sponsors, to come
into the sanctuary and before the community to make a profession of faith.*

N. and N., of your own free will you have asked to be received into the full communion of the Catholic Church. You have made your decision after careful thought under the guidance of the Holy Spirit. I now invite you to come forward with your sponsors and in the presence of this community to profess the Catholic faith. In this faith you will be one with us for the first time at the eucharistic table of the Lord Jesus, the sign of the Church's unity.

PROFESSION BY THE CANDIDATES [Belief in Church]

When the candidates for reception and their sponsors have taken their places in the sanctuary, the Priest asks the candidates to make the following profession of faith. The candidates say:

I believe and profess all that the holy Catholic Church believes, teaches, and proclaims to be revealed by God.

ACT OF RECEPTION [Full Communion]

Then the candidates with their sponsors go individually to the Priest, who says to each candidate (laying his right hand on the head of any candidate who is not to receive Confirmation):

N., the Lord receives you into the Catholic Church.
His loving kindness has led you here,
so that in the unity of the Holy Spirit
you may have full communion with us
in the faith that you have professed in the presence of
his family.

Celebration of Confirmation

INVITATION [Strength in the Spirit]

The newly baptized with their godparents and, if they have not received the Sacrament of Confirmation, the newly received with their sponsors, stand before the Priest. He first speaks briefly to the newly baptized and the newly received in these or similar words.

My dear candidates for Confirmation, by your Baptism you have been born again in Christ and you have become members of Christ and of his priestly people. Now you are to share in the outpouring of the Holy Spirit among us, the Spirit sent by the Lord upon his apostles at Pentecost and given by them and their successors to the baptized.

The promised strength of the Holy Spirit, which you are to receive, will make you more like Christ and help you to be witnesses to his suffering, death, and resurrection. It will strengthen you to be active members of the Church and to build up the Body of Christ in faith and love.

My dear friends, let us pray to God our Father, that he will pour out the Holy Spirit on these candidates for Confirmation to strengthen them with his gifts and anoint them to be more like Christ, the Son of God.

All pray briefly in silence.

LAYING ON OF HANDS   [Gifts of the Spirit]

The Priest holds his hands outstretched over the entire group of those to be confirmed and says the following prayer.

Almighty God, Father of our Lord Jesus Christ,
who brought these your servants to new birth
by water and the Holy Spirit,
freeing them from sin:
send upon them, O Lord, the Holy Spirit, the Paraclete;
give them the spirit of wisdom and understanding,
the spirit of counsel and fortitude,
the spirit of knowledge and piety;

fill them with the spirit of the fear of the Lord.
Through Christ our Lord.
℟. **Amen.**

ANOINTING WITH CHRISM   [Sealed in the Spirit]

*Either or both godparents and sponsors place the right hand
on the shoulder of the candidate; and a godparent or a spon-
sor of the candidate gives the candidate's name to the minister of the sacrament. During the conferral of the sacrament
an appropriate song may be sung.*

*The minister of the sacrament dips his right thumb in the
chrism and makes the Sign of the Cross on the forehead of the
one to be confirmed as he says:*

N., be sealed with the Gift of the Holy Spirit.
Newly confirmed: **Amen.**
Minister: Peace be with you.
Newly confirmed: **And with your spirit.**

*After all have received the sacrament, the newly confirmed as
well as the godparents and sponsors are led to their places in
the assembly.*

*[Since the Profession of Faith is not said, the Universal
Prayer (no. 16, p. 19) begins immediately and for the first time
the neophytes take part in it.]*

FOURTH PART:
THE LITURGY OF THE EUCHARIST

*The Priest goes to the altar and begins the Liturgy of the
Eucharist in the usual way.*

*It is desirable that the bread and wine be brought forward by
the newly baptized or, if they are children, by their parents
or godparents.*

PRAYER OVER THE OFFERINGS   [God's Saving Work]

Accept, we ask, O Lord,
the prayers of your people

with the sacrificial offerings,
that what has begun in the paschal mysteries
may, by the working of your power,
bring us to the healing of eternity.
Through Christ our Lord.
℟. **Amen.**

→ No. 21, p. 22 (Pref. P 21: on this night above all)

*In the Eucharistic Prayer, a commemoration is made of the
baptized and their godparents in accord with the formulas
which are found in the Roman Missal and Roman Ritual for
each of the Eucharistic Prayers.*

COMMUNION ANT. 1 Cor 5:7-8   [Purity and Truth]
**Christ our Passover has been sacrificed; therefore let
us keep the feast with the unleavened bread of purity
and truth, alleluia.** ↓

Psalm 118 (117) may appropriately be sung.

PRAYER AFTER COMMUNION   [One in Mind and Heart]

Pour out on us, O Lord, the Spirit of your love,
and in your kindness make those you have nourished
by this paschal Sacrament
one in mind and heart.
Through Christ our Lord. ℟. **Amen.**

SOLEMN BLESSING   [God's Blessings]

May almighty God bless you
through today's Easter Solemnity
and, in his compassion,
defend you from every assault of sin. ℟. **Amen.**

And may he, who restores you to eternal life
in the Resurrection of his Only Begotten,
endow you with the prize of immortality. ℟. **Amen.**

Now that the days of the Lord's Passion have drawn to a
   close,
may you who celebrate the gladness of the Paschal Feast
come with Christ's help, and exulting in spirit,
to those feasts that are celebrated in eternal joy.
℞. **Amen.**

And may the blessing of almighty God,
the Father, and the Son, ✠ and the Holy Spirit,
come down on you and remain with you for ever.
℞. **Amen.** ↓

*The final blessing formula from the Rite of Baptism of Adults
or of Children may also be used, according to circumstances.*

*To dismiss the people the Deacon or, if there is no Deacon, the
Priest himself sings or says:*

Go forth, the Mass is ended, alleluia, alleluia.

Or:

Go in peace, alleluia, alleluia.

℞. **Thanks be to God, alleluia, alleluia.**

This practice is observed throughout the Octave of Easter.

"I have risen, and I am with you still."

APRIL 4

EASTER SUNDAY

ENTRANCE ANT. Cf. Ps 139 (138):18, 5-6

[Christ's Resurrection]

I have risen, and I am with you still, alleluia. You have laid your hand upon me, alleluia. Too wonderful for me, this knowledge, alleluia, alleluia. → No. 2, p. 10

OR Lk 24:34; cf. Rev 1:6 [King and Lord]

The Lord is truly risen, alleluia. To him be glory and power for all the ages of eternity, alleluia, alleluia.
→ No. 2, p. 10

COLLECT [Renewal]

O God, who on this day,
through your Only Begotten Son,
have conquered death
and unlocked for us the path to eternity,
grant, we pray, that we who keep
the solemnity of the Lord's Resurrection
may, through the renewal brought by your Spirit,
rise up in the light of life.
Through our Lord Jesus Christ, your Son,

367

who lives and reigns with you in the unity of the Holy Spirit,
one God, for ever and ever. ℟. **Amen.** ↓

FIRST READING Acts 10:34a, 37-43 [Salvation in Christ]

**In his sermon Peter sums up the "good news," the Gospel.
Salvation comes through Christ, the beloved Son of the
Father, the anointed of the Holy Spirit.**

A reading from the Acts of the Apostles

PETER proceeded to speak and said: "You know
what has happened all over Judea, beginning in
Galilee after the baptism that John preached, how God
anointed Jesus of Nazareth with the Holy Spirit and
power. He went about doing good and healing all those
oppressed by the devil, for God was with him. We are
witnesses of all that he did both in the country of the
Jews and in Jerusalem. They put him to death by hang-
ing him on a tree. This man God raised on the third day
and granted that he be visible, not to all the people, but
to us, the witnesses chosen by God in advance, who ate
and drank with him after he rose from the dead. He
commissioned us to preach to the people and testify
that he is the one appointed by God as judge of the living and the dead. To him all the prophets bear witness,
that everyone who believes in him will receive forgiveness of sins through his name."—The word of the Lord.
℟. **Thanks be to God.** ↓

RESPONSORIAL PSALM Ps 118 [The Day of the Lord]

℟. This is the day the Lord has made;
let us re - joice and be glad.

Or: ℟. **Alleluia.**

Give thanks to the LORD, for he is good,
  for his mercy endures forever.
Let the house of Israel say,
  "His mercy endures forever."—R̸.

"The right hand of the LORD has struck with power;
  the right hand of the LORD is exalted.
I shall not die, but live,
  and declare the works of the LORD."—R̸.

The stone which the builders rejected
  has become the cornerstone.
By the LORD has this been done;
  it is wonderful in our eyes.—R̸. ↓

One of the following texts may be chosen as the Second Reading.

SECOND READING Col 3:1-4   [Seek Heavenly Things]

> Look to the glory of Christ in which we share because our lives are hidden in him (through baptism) and we are destined to share in the glory.

A reading from the Letter of Saint Paul to the Colossians

BROTHERS and sisters: If then you were raised with Christ, seek what is above, where Christ is seated at the right hand of God. Think of what is above, not of what is on earth. For you have died, and your life is hidden with Christ in God. When Christ your life appears, then you too will appear with him in glory.—The word of the Lord. R̸. **Thanks be to God.** ↓

OR

SECOND READING 1 Cor 5:6b-8   [Change of Heart]

> Turn away from your old ways, from sin. Have a change of heart; be virtuous.

A reading from the first Letter of Saint Paul
to the Corinthians

BROTHERS and sisters: Do you not know that a little yeast leavens all the dough? Clear out the old yeast, so that you may become a fresh batch of dough, inasmuch as you are unleavened. For our paschal lamb, Christ, has been sacrificed. Therefore, let us celebrate the feast, not with the old yeast, the yeast of malice and wickedness, but with the unleavened bread of sincerity and truth.—The word of the Lord. ℟. **Thanks be to God.** ↓

SEQUENCE *(Victimae paschali laudes)*   [Hymn to the Victor]

Christians, to the Paschal Victim
   Offer your thankful praises!
A Lamb the sheep redeems;
   Christ, who only is sinless,
   Reconciles sinners to the Father.
Death and life have contended in that combat stupendous:
   The Prince of life, who died, reigns immortal.
Speak, Mary, declaring
   What you saw, wayfaring.
"The tomb of Christ, who is living,
   The glory of Jesus' resurrection;
Bright angels attesting,
   The shroud and napkin resting.
Yes, Christ my hope is arisen;
   To Galilee he goes before you."
Christ indeed from death is risen, our new life obtaining.
   Have mercy, victor King, ever reigning!
   Amen. Alleluia. ↓

ALLELUIA Cf. 1 Cor 5:7b-8a   [Joy in the Lord]
℟. **Alleluia, alleluia.**
Christ, our paschal lamb, has been sacrificed;
let us then feast with joy in the Lord.
℟. **Alleluia, alleluia.** ↓

(For Morning Mass)

GOSPEL Jn 20:1-9   [Renewed Faith]

Let us discover the empty tomb and ponder this mystery, and like Christ's first followers be strengthened in our faith.

℣. The Lord be with you. ℟. **And with your spirit.**

✤ A reading from the holy Gospel according to John.
℟. **Glory to you, O Lord.**

O N the first day of the week, Mary of Magdala came to the tomb early in the morning, while it was still dark, and saw the stone removed from the tomb. So she ran and went to Simon Peter and to the other disciple whom Jesus loved, and told them, "They have taken the Lord from the tomb, and we don't know where they put him." So Peter and the other disciple went out and came to the tomb. They both ran, but the other disciple ran faster than Peter and arrived at the tomb first; he bent down and saw the burial cloths there, but did not go in. When Simon Peter arrived after him, he went into the tomb and saw the burial cloths there, and the cloth that had covered his head, not with the burial cloths but rolled up in a separate place. Then the other disciple also went in, the one who had arrived at the tomb first, and he saw and believed. For they did not yet understand the Scripture that he had to rise from the dead.— The Gospel of the Lord. ℟. **Praise to you, Lord Jesus Christ.**   → No. 15, p. 18

However, in Easter Sunday Masses which are celebrated with a congregation, the rite of the renewal of baptismal promises may take place after the Homily, according to the text used at the Easter Vigil (p. 359). In that case the Creed is omitted.

OR

GOSPEL Mk 16:1-7   [The Resurrection]
See p. 352.

(For an Afternoon or Evening Mass)

GOSPEL Lk 24:13-35   [The Messiah's Need To Suffer]

Let us accept the testimony of these two witnesses that our hearts may burn with the fire of faith.

℣. The Lord be with you. ℟. **And with your spirit.**

✛ A reading from the holy Gospel according to Luke.
℟. **Glory to you, O Lord.**

THAT very day, the first day of the week, two of Jesus' disciples were going to a village seven miles from Jerusalem called Emmaus, and they were conversing about all the things that had occurred. And it happened that while they were conversing and debating, Jesus himself drew near and walked with them, but their eyes were prevented from recognizing him. He asked them, "What are you discussing as you walk along?" They stopped, looking downcast. One of them, named Cleopas, said to him in reply, "Are you the only visitor to Jerusalem who does not know of the things that have taken place there in these days?" And he replied to them, "What sort of things?" They said to him, "The things that happened to Jesus the Nazarene, who was a prophet mighty in deed and word before God and all the people, how our chief priests and rulers both handed him over to a sentence of death and crucified him. But we were hoping that he would be the one to redeem Israel; and besides all this, it is now the third day since this took place. Some women from our group, however, have astounded us: they were at the tomb early in the morning and did not find his body; they came back and reported that they had indeed seen a vision of angels who announced that he was alive. Then some of those with us went to the tomb and found things just as the women had described, but him they did not see." And he said to them, "Oh, how

foolish you are! How slow of heart to believe all that
the prophets spoke! Was is not necessary that the
Christ should suffer these things and enter into his
glory?" Then beginning with Moses and all the
prophets, he interpreted to them what referred to him
in all the Scriptures. As they approached the village to
which they were going, he gave the impression that he
was going on farther. But they urged him, "Stay with
us, for it is nearly evening and the day is almost over."
So he went in to stay with them. And it happened that,
while he was with them at table, he took bread, said
the blessing, broke it, and gave it to them. With that
their eyes were opened and they recognized him, but
he vanished from their sight. They said to each other,
"Were not our hearts burning within us while he spoke
to us on the way and opened the Scriptures to us?" So
they set out at once and returned to Jerusalem where
they found gathered together the eleven and those
with them who were saying, "The Lord has truly been
raised and has appeared to Simon!" Then the two
recounted what had taken place on the way and how
he was made known to them in the breaking of
bread.—The Gospel of the Lord. ℟. **Praise to you, Lord
Jesus Christ.**   ➜ No. 15, p. 18

*However, in Easter Sunday Masses which are celebrated with
a congregation, the rite of the renewal of baptismal promises
may take place after the Homily, according to the text used at
the Easter Vigil (p. 359). In that case the Creed is omitted.*

PRAYER OVER THE OFFERINGS [Reborn and Nourished]

Exultant with paschal gladness, O Lord,
we offer the sacrifice
by which your Church
is wondrously reborn and nourished.
Through Christ our Lord. ℟. **Amen.**

➜ No. 21, p. 22 (Pref. P 21: on this day above all)

When the Roman Canon is used, the proper forms of the Communicantes *(In communion with those) and* Hanc igitur *(Therefore, Lord, we pray) are said.*

COMMUNION ANT. 1 Cor 5:7-8   **[Purity and Truth]**

Christ our Passover has been sacrificed, alleluia; therefore let us keep the feast with the unleavened bread of purity and truth, alleluia, alleluia. ↓

PRAYER AFTER COMMUNION   [Glory of Resurrection]

Look upon your Church, O God,
with unfailing love and favor,
so that, renewed by the paschal mysteries,
she may come to the glory of the resurrection.
Through Christ our Lord.
℟. **Amen.**   → No. 30, p. 77

To impart the blessing at the end of Mass, the Priest may appropriately use the formula of Solemn Blessing for the Mass of the Easter Vigil, p. 365.

For the dismissal of the people, there is sung or said:

Go forth, the Mass is ended, alleluia, alleluia.

Or:

Go in peace, alleluia, alleluia.

℟. **Thanks be to God, alleluia, alleluia.**

"Thomas answered . . . , 'My Lord and my God!' "

APRIL 11

2nd SUNDAY OF EASTER
(or of Divine Mercy)

ENTRANCE ANT. 1 Pt 2:2   [Long for Spiritual Milk]
Like newborn infants, you must long for the pure,
spiritual milk, that in him you may grow to salvation,
alleluia.   → No. 2, p. 10

OR 4 Esdr 2:36-37   [Give Thanks]
Receive the joy of your glory, giving thanks to God,
who has called you into the heavenly Kingdom, alleluia.   → No. 2, p. 10

COLLECT   [Kindle Faith]
God of everlasting mercy,
who in the very recurrence of the paschal feast
kindle the faith of the people you have made your own,
increase, we pray, the grace you have bestowed,
that all may grasp and rightly understand
in what font they have been washed,
by whose Spirit they have been reborn,

by whose Blood they have been redeemed.
Through our Lord Jesus Christ, your Son,
who lives and reigns with you in the unity of the Holy
　　Spirit,
one God, for ever and ever. ℞. **Amen.** ↓

FIRST READING Acts 4:32-35　　[True Christian Fellowship]

**The faithful lived a common life, sharing all their goods.
The apostles worked many miracles. They prayed together
and broke bread. Daily their numbers increased.**

A reading from the Acts of the Apostles

THE community of believers was of one heart and
　　mind, and no one claimed that any of his possessions was his own, but they had everything in common. With great power the apostles bore witness to the
resurrection of the Lord Jesus, and great favor was
accorded them all. There was no needy person among
them, for those who owned property or houses would
sell them, bring the proceeds of the sale, and put them
at the feet of the apostles, and they were distributed to
each according to need.—The word of the Lord. ℞.
Thanks be to God. ↓

RESPONSORIAL PSALM Ps 118　　[The Lord's Goodness]

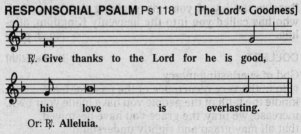

℞. **Give thanks to the Lord for he is good,
his love is everlasting.**

Or: ℞. **Alleluia.**

Let the house of Israel say,
　　"His mercy endures forever."
Let the house of Aaron say,
　　"His mercy endures forever."

Let those who fear the LORD say,
  "His mercy endures forever."—R̵.

I was hard pressed and was falling,
  but the LORD helped me.
My strength and my courage is the LORD,
  and he has been my savior.
The joyful shout of victory
  in the tents of the just:—R̵.

The stone which the builders rejected
  has become the cornerstone.
By the LORD has this been done;
  it is wonderful in our eyes.
This is the day the LORD has made;
  let us be glad and rejoice in it.—R̵. ↓

SECOND READING 1 Jn 5:1-6   **[The Power of Faith]**

A believing faith comes from God. The proof of loving God comes from observing his commandments. The Spirit, the Spirit of truth, will testify to this.

A reading from the first Letter of Saint John

BELOVED: Everyone who believes that Jesus is the Christ is begotten by God, and everyone who loves the Father loves also the one begotten by him. In this way we know that we love the children of God when we love God and obey his commandments. For the love of God is this, that we keep his commandments. And his commandments are not burdensome, for whoever is begotten by God conquers the world. And the victory that conquers the world is our faith. Who indeed is the victor over the world but the one who believes that Jesus is the Son of God?

This is the one who came through water and blood, Jesus Christ, not by water alone, but by water and blood. The Spirit is the one that testifies, and the Spirit is truth.—The word of the Lord. R̵. **Thanks be to God.** ↓

ALLELUIA Jn 20:29   **[Blind Faith]**

℟. **Alleluia, alleluia.**

You believe in me, Thomas, because you have seen me,
   says the Lord;

blessed are those who have not seen me, but still
   believe!

℟. **Alleluia, alleluia.** ↓

GOSPEL Jn 20:19-31   **[Living Faith]**

> Jesus appears to the disciples, coming through locked
> doors. He shows them his hands and side. He greets them
> in peace and gives them the power to forgive sin. A week
> later Jesus appears again and speaks directly to Thomas
> who now professes his belief.

℣. The Lord be with you. ℟. **And with your spirit.**

✜ A reading from the holy Gospel according to John.

℟. **Glory to you, O Lord.**

O N the evening of that first day of the week, when
the doors were locked, where the disciples were,
for fear of the Jews, Jesus came and stood in their
midst and said to them, "Peace be with you." When he
had said this, he showed them his hands and
his side. The disciples rejoiced when they saw the
Lord. Jesus said to them again, "Peace be with you. As
the Father has sent me, so I send you." And when he
had said this, he breathed on them and said
to them, "Receive the Holy Spirit. Whose sins you forgive are forgiven them, and whose sins you retain are
retained."

Thomas, called Didymus, one of the Twelve, was not
with them when Jesus came. So the other disciples
said to him, "We have seen the Lord." But he said to
them, "Unless I see the mark of the nails in his hands
and put my finger into the nailmarks and put my hand
into his side, I will not believe."

Now a week later his disciples were again inside and Thomas was with them. Jesus came, although the doors were locked, and stood in their midst and said, "Peace be with you." Then he said to Thomas, "Put your finger here and see my hands, and bring your hand and put it into my side, and do not be unbelieving, but believe." Thomas answered and said to him, "My Lord and my God!" Jesus said to him, "Have you come to believe because you have seen me? Blessed are those who have not seen and have believed."

Now Jesus did many other signs in the presence of his disciples that are not written in this book. But these are written that you may come to believe that Jesus is the Christ, the Son of God, and that through this belief you may have life in his name.—The Gospel of the Lord. ℟. **Praise to you, Lord Jesus Christ.**

→ No. 15, p. 18

PRAYER OVER THE OFFERINGS   [Unending Happiness]

Accept, O Lord, we pray,
the oblations of your people
(and of those you have brought to new birth),
that, renewed by confession of your name and by Baptism,
they may attain unending happiness.
Through Christ our Lord. ℟. **Amen.**

→ No. 21, p. 22 (Pref. P 21: on this day above all)

When the Roman Canon is used, the proper forms of the Communicantes *(In communion with those) and* Hanc igitur *(Therefore, Lord, we pray) are said.*

COMMUNION ANT. Cf. Jn 20:27   [Believe]
Bring your hand and feel the place of the nails, and do not be unbelieving but believing, alleluia. ↓

PRAYER AFTER COMMUNION   [Devout Reception]

Grant, we pray, almighty God,
that our reception of this paschal Sacrament
may have a continuing effect
in our minds and hearts.
Through Christ our Lord.
℟. **Amen.**   ➜ No. 30, p. 77

Optional Solemn Blessings, p. 97, and Prayers over the People, p. 105

For the dismissal of the people, there is sung or said: Go
forth, the Mass is ended alleluia, alleluia. *Or:* Go in
peace, alleluia, alleluia. *The people respond:* **Thanks be to
God, alleluia, alleluia.**

*"It is written that the Christ would suffer
and rise from the dead. . . ."*

APRIL 18

3rd SUNDAY OF EASTER

ENTRANCE ANT. Cf. Ps 66 (65):1-2   [Praise the Lord]

**Cry out with joy to God, all the earth; O sing to the
glory of his name. O render him glorious praise,
alleluia.**   ➜ No. 2, p. 10

COLLECT   [Hope of Resurrection]

May your people exult for ever, O God,
in renewed youthfulness of spirit,
so that, rejoicing now in the restored glory of our
    adoption,
we may look forward in confident hope
to the rejoicing of the day of resurrection.
Through our Lord Jesus Christ, your Son,
who lives and reigns with you in the unity of the Holy
    Spirit,
one God, for ever and ever. ℟. **Amen.** ↓

FIRST READING Acts 3:13-15, 17-19   [Culpable Ignorance]

Peter teaches how God glorified his Son, but the people
were guilty of crucifying Jesus. They acted out of ignorance, however. Now they are to reform and ask God for
forgiveness.

A reading from the Acts of the Apostles

PETER said to the people: "The God of Abraham, the
God of Isaac, and the God of Jacob, the God of our
fathers, has glorified his servant Jesus, whom you
handed over and denied in Pilate's presence when he
had decided to release him. You denied the Holy and
Righteous One and asked that a murderer be released
to you. The author of life you put to death, but God
raised him from the dead; of this we are witnesses.
Now I know, brothers, that you acted out of ignorance,
just as your leaders did; but God has thus brought to
fulfillment what he had announced beforehand
through the mouth of all the prophets, that his Christ
would suffer. Repent, therefore, and be converted, that
your sins may be wiped away."—The word of the Lord.
℟. **Thanks be to God.** ↓

RESPONSORIAL PSALM Ps 4   [Divine Security]

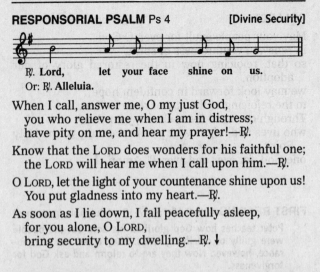

R̶). **Lord,   let your face   shine on   us.**
Or: R̶). **Alleluia.**

When I call, answer me, O my just God,
  you who relieve me when I am in distress;
  have pity on me, and hear my prayer!—R̶).

Know that the Lᴏʀᴅ does wonders for his faithful one;
  the Lᴏʀᴅ will hear me when I call upon him.—R̶).

O Lᴏʀᴅ, let the light of your countenance shine upon us!
  You put gladness into my heart.—R̶).

As soon as I lie down, I fall peacefully asleep,
  for you alone, O Lᴏʀᴅ,
  bring security to my dwelling.—R̶). ↓

SECOND READING 1 Jn 2:1-5a   [Fruitful Knowledge]

**If anyone should sin, Jesus is an offering for sin—for the
sins of the whole world. Anyone who claims to know Jesus
but disobeys the commandments is a liar.**

A reading from the first Letter of Saint John

MY children, I am writing this to you so that you
may not commit sin. But if anyone does sin, we
have an Advocate with the Father, Jesus Christ the
righteous one. He is expiation for our sins, and not for
our sins only but for those of the whole world. The way
we may be sure that we know him is to keep his
commandments. Those who say, "I know him," but do
not keep his commandments are liars, and the truth is
not in them. But whoever keeps his word, the love of
God is truly perfected in him.—The word of the Lord.
R̶). **Thanks be to God.** ↓

ALLELUIA Cf. Lk 24:32   [With Hearts Burning]

℟. **Alleluia, alleluia.**

Lord Jesus, open the Scriptures to us;
make our hearts burn while you speak to us.

℟. **Alleluia, alleluia.** ↓

GOSPEL Lk 24:35-48   [Understanding the Scriptures]

**Again Jesus appears in the midst of the disciples. He
proves he is not a ghost. He eats with them and reassures
them that all that happened was to fulfill the words of the
Scriptures.**

℣. The Lord be with you. ℟. **And with your spirit.**

✠ A reading from the holy Gospel according to Luke.

℟. **Glory to you, O Lord.**

THE two disciples recounted what had taken place
on the way, and how Jesus was made known to
them in the breaking of bread.

While they were still speaking about this, he stood
in their midst and said to them, "Peace be with you."
But they were startled and terrified and thought that
they were seeing a ghost. Then he said to them, "Why
are you troubled? And why do questions arise in your
hearts? Look at my hands and my feet, that it is I
myself. Touch me and see, because a ghost does not
have flesh and bones as you can see I have." And as he
said this, he showed them his hands and his feet. While
they were still incredulous for joy and were amazed,
he asked them, "Have you anything here to eat?" They
gave him a piece of baked fish; he took it and ate it in
front of them.

He said to them, "These are my words that I spoke to
you while I was still with you, that everything written
about me in the law of Moses and in the prophets and
psalms must be fulfilled." Then he opened their minds
to understand the Scriptures. And he said to them,
"Thus it is written that the Christ would suffer and rise

from the dead on the third day and that repentance, for
the forgiveness of sins, would be preached in his name
to all the nations, beginning from Jerusalem. You are
witnesses of these things."—The Gospel of the Lord. ℟.
Praise to you, Lord Jesus Christ.   → No. 15, p. 18

PRAYER OVER THE OFFERINGS   [Exultant Church]

Receive, O Lord, we pray,
these offerings of your exultant Church,
and, as you have given her cause for such great
    gladness,
grant also that the gifts we bring
may bear fruit in perpetual happiness.
Through Christ our Lord.
℟. **Amen.**   → No. 21, p. 22 (Pref. P 21-25)

COMMUNION ANT. Cf. Lk 24:35   [Christ's Presence]

**The disciples recognized the Lord Jesus in the break-
ing of the bread, alleluia.** ↓

OR Lk 24:46-47   [Repentance]

**The Christ had to suffer and on the third day rise from
the dead; in his name repentance and remission of
sins must be preached to all the nations, alleluia.** ↓

PRAYER AFTER COMMUNION   [The Lord's Kindness]

Look with kindness upon your people, O Lord,
and grant, we pray,
that those you were pleased to renew by eternal
    mysteries
may attain in their flesh
the incorruptible glory of the resurrection.
Through Christ our Lord.
℟. **Amen.**   → No. 30, p. 77

Optional Solemn Blessings, p. 97, and Prayers over the People, p. 105

"I am the good shepherd."

APRIL 25

4th SUNDAY OF EASTER

ENTRANCE ANT. Cf. Ps 33 (32):5-6   [God the Creator]
The merciful love of the Lord fills the earth; by the
word of the Lord the heavens were made, alleluia.

→ No. 2, p. 10

COLLECT   [Joys of Heaven]
Almighty ever-living God,
lead us to a share in the joys of heaven,
so that the humble flock may reach
where the brave Shepherd has gone before.
Who lives and reigns with you in the unity of the Holy
    Spirit,
one God, for ever and ever.
℟. **Amen.** ↓

FIRST READING Acts 4:8-12   [Salvation in Jesus]
Peter explains the cure of the cripple. It was a miracle performed in the name of Jesus, whom the people had rejected and crucified. There is no salvation except in Jesus.

A reading from the Acts of the Apostles

385

PETER, filled with the Holy Spirit, said: "Leaders of the people and elders: If we are being examined today about a good deed done to a cripple, namely, by what means he was saved, then all of you and all the people of Israel should know that it was in the name of Jesus Christ the Nazorean whom you crucified, whom God raised from the dead; in his name this man stands before you healed. He is *the stone rejected by you, the builders, which has become the cornerstone.* There is no salvation through anyone else, nor is there any other name under heaven given to the human race by which we are to be saved."—The word of the Lord. ℟. **Thanks be to God.** ↓

RESPONSORIAL PSALM Ps 118   [Refuge in God]

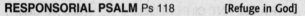

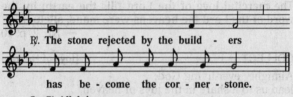

℟. The stone rejected by the build - ers has be - come the cor - ner - stone.

Or: ℟. Alleluia.

Give thanks to the Lord, for he is good,
   for his mercy endures forever.
It is better to take refuge in the Lord
   than to trust in man.
It is better to take refuge in the Lord
   than to trust in princes.—℟.

I will give thanks to you, for you have answered me
   and have been my savior.
The stone which the builders rejected
   has become the cornerstone.
By the Lord has this been done;
   it is wonderful in our eyes.—℟.

Blessed is he who comes in the name of the LORD;
  we bless you from the house of the LORD.
I will give thanks to you, for you have answered me
  and have been my savior.
Give thanks to the LORD, for he is good;
  for his kindness endures forever.—R℣. ↓

SECOND READING 1 Jn 3:1-2   [Children of God]

The Father shows his love for human beings by calling them his children. The world does not recognize the followers of Christ because it did not recognize Christ himself.

A reading from the first Letter of Saint John

BELOVED: See what love the Father has bestowed on us that we may be called the children of God. Yet so we are. The reason the world does not know us is that it did not know him. Beloved, we are God's children now; what we shall be has not yet been revealed. We do know that when it is revealed we shall be like him, for we shall see him as he is.—The word of the Lord. R℣. **Thanks be to God.** ↓

ALLELUIA Jn 10:14   [God's Sheep]

R℣. **Alleluia, alleluia.**
I am the good shepherd, says the Lord;
I know my sheep, and mine know me.
R℣. **Alleluia, alleluia.** ↓

GOSPEL Jn 10:11-18   [The Good Shepherd]

Jesus compares himself to "the good Shepherd." A shepherd cares for his sheep, lives and dies for them if necessary. There is to be one flock and one shepherd.

℣. The Lord be with you. R℣. **And with your spirit.**
✛ A reading from the holy Gospel according to John.
R℣. **Glory to you, O Lord.**

JESUS said: "I am the good shepherd. A good shepherd lays down his life for the sheep. A hired man, who is not a shepherd and whose sheep are not his own, sees a wolf coming and leaves the sheep and runs away, and the wolf catches and scatters them. This is because he works for pay and has no concern for the sheep. I am the good shepherd, and I know mine and mine know me, just as the Father knows me and I know the Father; and I will lay down my life for the sheep. I have other sheep that do not belong to this fold. These also I must lead, and they will hear my voice, and there will be one flock, one shepherd. This is why the Father loves me, because I lay down my life in order to take it up again. No one takes it from me, but I lay it down on my own. I have power to lay it down, and power to take it up again. This command I have received from my Father."—The Gospel of the Lord. ℟. **Praise to you, Lord Jesus Christ.**   → No. 15, p. 18

PRAYER OVER THE OFFERINGS   [Unending Joy]

Grant, we pray, O Lord,
that we may always find delight in these paschal mysteries,
so that the renewal constantly at work within us
may be the cause of our unending joy.
Through Christ our Lord.
℟. **Amen.**   → No. 21, p. 22 (Pref. P 21-25)

COMMUNION ANT.   [The Risen Shepherd]

The Good Shepherd has risen, who laid down his life for his sheep and willingly died for his flock, alleluia. ↓

PRAYER AFTER COMMUNION   [Kind Shepherd]

Look upon your flock, kind Shepherd,
and be pleased to settle in eternal pastures
the sheep you have redeemed
by the Precious Blood of your Son.
Who lives and reigns for ever and ever.
℟. **Amen.**   → No. 30, p. 77

Optional Solemn Blessings, p. 97, and Prayers over the People, p. 105

"I am the true vine, and my Father is the vine grower."

MAY 2

5th SUNDAY OF EASTER

ENTRANCE ANT. Cf. Ps 98 (97):1-2　　[Wonders of the Lord]

O sing a new song to the Lord, for he has worked wonders; in the sight of the nations he has shown his deliverance, alleluia.　　　　　　　→ No. 2, p. 10

COLLECT　　　　　　　　　　　　　　　[Much Fruit]

Almighty ever-living God,
constantly accomplish the Paschal Mystery within us,
that those you were pleased to make new in Holy
　Baptism
may, under your protective care, bear much fruit
and come to the joys of life eternal.
Through our Lord Jesus Christ, your Son,
who lives and reigns with you in the unity of the Holy
　Spirit,
one God, for ever and ever.
℞. **Amen.** ↓

FIRST READING Acts 9:26-31   [Paul's Conversion]

Because of Paul's earlier reputation, the Christians were fearful of him. He was then accepted and began to spread the message of the gospel.

A reading from the Acts of the Apostles

WHEN Saul arrived in Jerusalem he tried to join the disciples, but they were all afraid of him, not believing that he was a disciple. Then Barnabas took charge of him and brought him to the apostles, and he reported to them how he had seen the Lord, and that he had spoken to him, and how in Damascus he had spoken out boldly in the name of Jesus. He moved about freely with them in Jerusalem, and spoke out boldly in the name of the Lord. He also spoke and debated with the Hellenists, but they tried to kill him. And when the brothers learned of this, they took him down to Caesarea and sent him on his way to Tarsus.

The church throughout all Judea, Galilee, and Samaria was at peace. It was being built up and walked in the fear of the Lord, and with the consolation of the Holy Spirit it grew in numbers.—The word of the Lord. ℟. **Thanks be to God.** ↓

RESPONSORIAL PSALM Ps 22   [Praise God]

℟. **I will praise you, Lord, in the assembly of your people.**

Or: ℟. **Alleluia.**

I will fulfill my vows before those who fear the LORD.
    The lowly shall eat their fill;
they who seek the LORD shall praise him:
    "May your hearts live forever!"—℟.

All the ends of the earth
    shall remember and turn to the LORD;

all the families of the nations
  shall bow down before him.—℞.

To him alone shall bow down
  all who sleep in the earth;
before him shall bend
  all who go down into the dust.—℞.

And to him my soul shall live;
  my descendants shall serve him.
Let the coming generation be told of the LORD
  that they may proclaim to a people yet to be born
  the justice he has shown.—℞. ↓

SECOND READING 1 Jn 3:18-24   [Love in Action]

Christians are to love in deed and in truth. A clear conscience is proof of God's favor. To keep the commandments is to please God.

A reading from the first Letter of Saint John

CHILDREN, let us love not in word or speech but in deed and truth.
  Now this is how we shall know that we belong to the truth and reassure our hearts before him in whatever our hearts condemn, for God is greater than our hearts and knows everything. Beloved, if our hearts do not condemn us, we have confidence in God and receive from him whatever we ask, because we keep his commandments and do what pleases him. And his commandment is this: we should believe in the name of his Son, Jesus Christ, and love one another just as he commanded us. Those who keep his commandments remain in him, and he in them, and the way we know that he remains in us is from the Spirit he gave us.—The word of the Lord. ℞. **Thanks be to God.** ↓

ALLELUIA Jn 15:4a, 5b   [Indwelling]

℞. **Alleluia, alleluia.**
Remain in me as I remain in you, says the Lord.

Whoever remains in me will bear much fruit.
℟. **Alleluia, alleluia.** ↓

GOSPEL Jn 15:1-8   [Vine and the Branches]

Jesus compared himself to the vine and the branches.
Whoever is united to Jesus will do good and be rewarded.
But anyone who does not live in Jesus will wither like a
cut-off vine.

℣. The Lord be with you. ℟. **And with your spirit.**
✠ A reading from the holy Gospel according to John.
℟. **Glory to you, O Lord.**

JESUS said to his disciples: "I am the true vine, and
my Father is the vine grower. He takes away every
branch in me that does not bear fruit, and every one
that does he prunes so that it bears more fruit. You
are already pruned because of the word that I spoke
to you. Remain in me, as I remain in you. Just as a
branch cannot bear fruit on its own unless it remains
on the vine, so neither can you unless you remain in
me. I am the vine, you are the branches. Whoever
remains in me and I in him will bear much fruit,
because without me you can do nothing. Anyone who
does not remain in me will be thrown out like a
branch and wither; people will gather them and
throw them into a fire and they will be burned. If you
remain in me and my words remain in you, ask for
whatever you want and it will be done for you. By
this is my Father glorified, that you bear much fruit
and become my disciples."—The Gospel of the Lord.
℟. **Praise to you, Lord Jesus Christ.** → No. 15, p. 18

PRAYER OVER THE OFFERINGS [Guided by God's Truth]

O God, who by the wonderful exchange effected in this
     sacrifice
have made us partakers of the one supreme Godhead,
grant, we pray,

that, as we have come to know your truth,
we may make it ours by a worthy way of life.
Through Christ our Lord.
℟. **Amen.**   ➜ No. 21, p. 22 (Pref. P 21-25)

COMMUNION ANT. Cf. Jn 15:1, 5   [Union with Christ]

**I am the true vine and you are the branches, says the
Lord. Whoever remains in me, and I in him, bears fruit
in plenty, alleluia.** ↓

PRAYER AFTER COMMUNION   [New Life]

Graciously be present to your people, we pray, O Lord,
and lead those you have imbued with heavenly
   mysteries
to pass from former ways to newness of life.
Through Christ our Lord.
℟. **Amen.**   ➜ No. 30, p. 77

Optional Solemn Blessings, p. 97, and Prayers over the People, p. 105

"This I command you: love one another."

MAY 9

6th SUNDAY OF EASTER

ENTRANCE ANT. Cf. Is 48:20   [Spiritual Freedom]

Proclaim a joyful sound and let it be heard; proclaim to the ends of the earth: The Lord has freed his people, alleluia. → No. 2, p. 10

COLLECT   [Heartfelt Devotion]

Grant, almighty God,
that we may celebrate with heartfelt devotion these
   days of joy,
which we keep in honor of the risen Lord,
and that what we relive in remembrance
we may always hold to in what we do.
Through our Lord Jesus Christ, your Son,
who lives and reigns with you in the unity of the Holy
   Spirit,
one God, for ever and ever. ℟. **Amen.** ↓

FIRST READING Acts 10:25-26, 34-35, 44-48   [God Loves All]

    Peter visits Cornelius and his family. God will favor any-
    one who acts uprightly, Jews, and Gentiles alike. He gave
    orders that all who believe should be baptized.

A reading from the Acts of the Apostles

WHEN Peter entered, Cornelius met him and, falling at his feet, paid him homage. Peter, however, raised him up, saying, "Get up. I myself am also a human being."

Then Peter proceeded to speak and said, "In truth, I see that God shows no partiality. Rather, in every nation whoever fears him and acts uprightly is acceptable to him."

While Peter was still speaking these things, the Holy Spirit fell upon all who were listening to the word. The circumcised believers who had accompanied Peter were astounded that the gift of the Holy Spirit should have been poured out on the Gentiles also, for they could hear them speaking in tongues and glorifying God. Then Peter responded, "Can anyone withhold the water for baptizing these people, who have received the Holy Spirit even as we have?" He ordered them to be baptized in the name of Jesus Christ.—The word of the Lord. ℟. **Thanks be to God.** ↓

RESPONSORIAL PSALM Ps 98 [Revelation to the Nations]

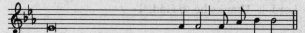

℟. **The Lord has revealed to the nations   his saving power.**
Or: ℟. **Alleluia.**

Sing to the LORD a new song,
    for he has done wondrous deeds;
his right hand has won victory for him,
    his holy arm.—℟.

The LORD has made his salvation known:
    in the sight of the nations he has revealed his justice.
He has remembered his kindness and his faithfulness
    toward the house of Israel.—℟.

All the ends of the earth have seen
   the salvation by our God.
Sing joyfully to the LORD, all you lands;
   break into song; sing praise.

℟. **The Lord has revealed to the nations his saving
   power.** ↓

Or: ℟. **Alleluia.** ↓

SECOND READING 1 Jn 4:7-10   [God Is Love]
**Christians should love one another as God himself is love.
A person without love does not know God. Love is that
God has sent his Son as an offering for sin.**

   A reading from the first Letter of Saint John

BELOVED, let us love one another, because love is
   of God; everyone who loves is begotten by God and
knows God. Whoever is without love does not know
God, for God is love. In this way the love of God was
revealed to us: God sent his only Son into the world so
that we might have life through him. In this is love: not
that we have loved God, but that he loved us and sent
his Son as expiation for our sins.—The word of the
Lord. ℟. **Thanks be to God.** ↓

ALLELUIA Jn 14:23   [Divine Love]
℟. **Alleluia, alleluia.**
Whoever loves me will keep my word, says the Lord,
and my Father will love him, and we will come to him.
℟. **Alleluia, alleluia.** ↓

GOSPEL Jn 15:9-17   [Love One Another]
**Jesus admonishes his disciples to continue the love he has
shown to them. The keeping of the commandments will
prove this. "You are to love one another. . . . It was I who
chose you."**

℣. The Lord be with you. ℟. **And with your spirit.**
✝ A reading from the holy Gospel according to John.
℟. **Glory to you, O Lord.**

JESUS said to his disciples: "As the Father loves me,
so I also love you. Remain in my love. If you keep
my commandments, you will remain in my love, just as
I have kept my Father's commandments and remain in
his love.

"I have told you this so that my joy may be in you
and your joy might be complete. This is my commandment: love one another as I love you. No one has
greater love than this, to lay down one's life for one's
friends. You are my friends if you do what I command
you. I no longer call you slaves, because a slave does
not know what his master is doing. I have called you
friends, because I have told you everything I have
heard from my Father. It was not you who chose me,
but I who chose you and appointed you to go and bear
fruit that will remain, so that whatever you ask the
Father in my name he may give you. This I command
you: love one another."—The Gospel of the Lord. ℟.
Praise to you, Lord Jesus Christ.   → No. 15, p. 18

PRAYER OVER THE OFFERINGS   [God's Mighty Love]

May our prayers rise up to you, O Lord,
together with the sacrificial offerings,
so that, purified by your graciousness,
we may be conformed to the mysteries of your mighty
    love.
Through Christ our Lord.
℟. **Amen.**   → No. 21, p. 22 (Pref. P 21-25)

COMMUNION ANT. Jn 14:15-16   [Role of the Paraclete]
**If you love me, keep my commandments, says the Lord,
and I will ask the Father and he will send you another
Paraclete, to abide with you for ever, alleluia.** ↓

PRAYER AFTER COMMUNION [Eucharistic Strength]

Almighty ever-living God,
who restore us to eternal life in the Resurrection of Christ,
increase in us, we pray, the fruits of this paschal
   Sacrament
and pour into our hearts the strength of this saving food.
Through Christ our Lord.
R̸. **Amen.**   → No. 30, p. 77

Optional Solemn Blessings, p. 97, and Prayers over the People, p. 105

*"Go into the whole world and proclaim the gospel
to every creature."*

*In those dioceses in which the Ascension is celebrated on
Sunday, the Mass of the Ascension (Vigil Mass, below, or
Mass during the Day, p. 405) is celebrated in place of the
Mass of the 7th Sunday of Easter that appears on p. 407.*

MAY 13

THE ASCENSION OF THE LORD

Solemnity

AT THE VIGIL MASS (May 12)

ENTRANCE ANT. Ps 68 (67): 33, 35   [Praise the Lord]

You kingdoms of the earth, sing to God; praise the

Lord, who ascends above the highest heavens; his majesty and might are in the skies, alleluia.

→ No. 2, p. 10

COLLECT [Jesus' Promise]

O God, whose Son today ascended to the heavens
as the Apostles looked on,
grant, we pray, that, in accordance with his promise,
we may be worthy for him to live with us always on
    earth,
and we with him in heaven.
Who lives and reigns with you in the unity of the Holy
    Spirit,
one God, for ever and ever. ℟. **Amen.** ↓

FIRST READING Acts 1:1-11 [Christ's Ascension]

Luke recounts the life, suffering and death of Jesus and
what Jesus did the forty days after his resurrection. Jesus
promises the Holy Spirit to the apostles. Jesus then
ascends into heaven while they watch.

A reading from the Acts of the Apostles

IN the first book, Theophilus, I dealt with all that
Jesus did and taught until the day he was taken up,
after giving instructions through the Holy Spirit to the
apostles whom he had chosen. He presented himself
alive to them by many proofs after he had suffered,
appearing to them during forty days and speaking about
the kingdom of God. While meeting with them, he
enjoined them not to depart from Jerusalem, but to wait
for "the promise of the Father about which you have
heard me speak; for John baptized with water, but in a
few days you will be baptized with the Holy Spirit."

When they had gathered together they asked him,
"Lord, are you at this time going to restore the kingdom to Israel?" He answered them, "It is not for you to
know the times or seasons that the Father has estab-

lished by his own authority. But you will receive power when the Holy Spirit comes upon you, and you will be my witnesses in Jerusalem, throughout Judea and Samaria, and to the ends of the earth." When he had said this, as they were looking on, he was lifted up, and a cloud took him from their sight. While they were looking intently at the sky as he was going, suddenly two men dressed in white garments stood beside them. They said, "Men of Galilee, why are you standing there looking at the sky? This Jesus who has been taken up from you into heaven will return in the same way as you have seen him going into heaven."—The word of the Lord. ℟. **Thanks be to God.** ↓

RESPONSORIAL PSALM Ps 47 [Praise to the Lord]

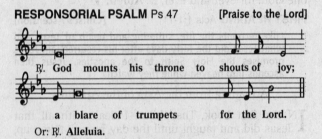

℟. God mounts his throne to shouts of joy; a blare of trumpets for the Lord.

Or: ℟. **Alleluia.**

All you peoples, clap your hands,
   shout to God with cries of gladness.
For the Lord, the Most High, the awesome,
   is the great king over all the earth.—℟.

God mounts his throne amid shouts of joy;
   the Lord, amid trumpet blasts.
Sing praise to God, sing praise;
   sing praise to our king, sing praise.—℟.

For king of all the earth is God;
   sing hymns of praise.
God reigns over the nations,
   God sits upon his holy throne.—℟. ↓

SECOND READING Eph 1:17-23   [Glorification of Jesus]

Paul writes of God the Father as the Father of glory, the one who is ready to hear our prayers and to grant wisdom and knowledge.

A reading from the Letter of Saint Paul
to the Ephesians

BROTHERS and sisters: May the God of our Lord Jesus Christ, the Father of glory, give you a Spirit of wisdom and revelation resulting in knowledge of him. May the eyes of your hearts be enlightened, that you may know what is the hope that belongs to his call, what are the riches of glory in his inheritance among the holy ones, and what is the surpassing greatness of his power for us who believe, in accord with the exercise of his great might, which he worked in Christ, raising him from the dead and seating him at his right hand in the heavens, far above every principality, authority, power, and dominion, and every name that is named not only in this age but also in the one to come. And he put all things beneath his feet and gave him as head over all things to the church, which is his body, the fullness of the one who fills all things in every way.—The word of the Lord. ℟. **Thanks be to God.** ↓

OR

SECOND READING Eph 4:1-13 or 4:1-7, 11-13   [Gifts]

Our hope is in God, our strength. With Christ our head, we his people will receive the gift of wisdom and insight.

[If the "Shorter Form" is used, the indented text in brackets is omitted.]

A reading from the Letter of Saint Paul
to the Ephesians

BROTHERS and sisters, I, a prisoner for the Lord, urge you to live in a manner worthy of the call you have received, with all humility and gentleness, with patience, bearing with one another through love, striving to preserve the unity of the spirit through the bond of peace: one body and one Spirit, as you were also called to the one hope of your call; one Lord, one faith, one baptism; one God and Father of all, who is over all and through all and in all.

But grace was given to each of us according to the measure of Christ's gift.

[Therefore, it says: *He ascended on high and took prisoners captive; he gave gifts to men.* What does "he ascended" mean except that he also descended into the lower regions of the earth? The one who descended is also the one who ascended far above all the heavens, that he might fill all things.]

And he gave some as apostles, others as prophets, others as evangelists, others as pastors and teachers, to equip the holy ones for the work of ministry, for building up the body of Christ, until we all attain to the unity of faith and knowledge of the Son of God, to mature manhood, to the extent of the full stature of Christ.— The word of the Lord. ℞. **Thanks be to God.** ↓

ALLELUIA Mt 28:19a, 20b   [Christ's Abiding Presence]

℞. **Alleluia, alleluia.**
Go and teach all nations, says the Lord;
I am with you always, until the end of the world.
℞. **Alleluia, alleluia.** ↓

GOSPEL Mk 16:15-20   [Preaching the Good News]

Jesus makes his disciples apostles to preach the good news. He promises them special signs for protection on earth and then finally Jesus is taken up into heaven.

℣. The Lord be with you. ℞. **And with your spirit.**
✛ A reading from the holy Gospel according to Mark.
℞. **Glory to you, O Lord.**

JESUS said to his disciples: "Go into the whole world and proclaim the gospel to every creature. Whoever believes and is baptized will be saved; whoever does not believe will be condemned. These signs will accompany those who believe: in my name they will drive out demons, they will speak new languages. They will pick up serpents with their hands, and if they drink any deadly thing, it will not harm them. They will lay hands on the sick, and they will recover."

So then the Lord Jesus, after he spoke to them, was taken up into heaven and took his seat at the right hand of God. But they went forth and preached everywhere, while the Lord worked with them and confirmed the word through accompanying signs.—The Gospel of the Lord. ℟. **Praise to you, Lord Jesus Christ.**

→ No. 15, p. 18

PRAYER OVER THE OFFERINGS [Obtain Mercy]

O God, whose Only Begotten Son, our High Priest,
is seated ever-living at your right hand to intercede for
us,
grant that we may approach with confidence the
throne of grace
and there obtain your mercy.
Through Christ our Lord.
℟. **Amen.** → No. 21, p. 22 (Pref. P 26-27)

When the Roman Canon is used, the proper form of the Communicantes *(In communion with those) is said.*

COMMUNION ANT. Cf. Heb 10:12

[Christ at God's Right Hand]

Christ, offering a single sacrifice for sins, is seated for ever at God's right hand, alleluia. ↓

PRAYER AFTER COMMUNION [Longing for Heaven]

May the gifts we have received from your altar, Lord,
kindle in our hearts a longing for the heavenly
homeland
and cause us to press forward, following in the
Savior's footsteps,
to the place where for our sake he entered before us.
Who lives and reigns for ever and ever.
℟. **Amen.** ➡ No. 30, p. 77

Optional Solemn Blessings, p. 97, and Prayers over the People, p. 105

AT THE MASS DURING THE DAY

ENTRANCE ANT. Acts 1:11   **[The Lord Will Return]**

Men of Galilee, why gaze in wonder at the heavens? This Jesus whom you saw ascending into heaven will return as you saw him go, alleluia.   → No. 2, p. 10

COLLECT   **[Thankful for the Ascension]**

Gladden us with holy joys, almighty God,
and make us rejoice with devout thanksgiving,
for the Ascension of Christ your Son
is our exaltation,
and, where the Head has gone before in glory,
the Body is called to follow in hope.
Through our Lord Jesus Christ, your Son,
who lives and reigns with you in the unity of the Holy
    Spirit,
one God, for ever and ever. ℟. **Amen.** ↓

OR   **[Belief in the Ascension]**

Grant, we pray, almighty God,
that we, who believe that your Only Begotten Son, our
    Redeemer,
ascended this day to the heavens,
may in spirit dwell already in heavenly realms.
Who lives and reigns with you in the unity of the Holy
    Spirit,
one God, for ever and ever. ℟. **Amen.** ↓

The readings for this Mass can be found beginning on p. 399.

PRAYER OVER THE OFFERINGS

                      [Rise to Heavenly Realms]

We offer sacrifice now in supplication, O Lord,
to honor the wondrous Ascension of your Son:
grant, we pray,
that through this most holy exchange

we, too, may rise up to the heavenly realms.
Through Christ our Lord.
℞. **Amen.**   ➜ No. 21, p. 22 (Pref. P 26-27)

When the Roman Canon is used, the proper form of the
Communicantes (In communion with those) *is said.*

COMMUNION ANT. Mt 28:20   [Christ's Presence]

**Behold, I am with you always, even to the end of the
age, alleluia.** ↓

PRAYER AFTER COMMUNION   [United with Christ]

Almighty ever-living God,
who allow those on earth to celebrate divine
   mysteries,
grant, we pray,
that Christian hope may draw us onward
to where our nature is united with you.
Through Christ our Lord.
℞. **Amen.**   ➜ No. 30, p. 77

Optional Solemn Blessings, p. 97, and Prayers over the People, p. 105

*"Holy Father, keep them in your name
that you have given me."*

*In those dioceses in which the Ascension is celebrated on
Sunday, the Mass of the Ascension (Vigil Mass, p. 398, or
Mass during the Day, p. 405) is celebrated in place of the
Mass of the 7th Sunday of Easter that appears below.*

MAY 16

7th SUNDAY OF EASTER

ENTRANCE ANT. Cf. Ps 27 (26):7-9   [Seek the Lord]

**O Lord, hear my voice, for I have called to you; of you
my heart has spoken: Seek his face; hide not your face
from me, alleluia.**   → No. 2, p. 10

COLLECT   [Experience Christ among Us]

Graciously hear our supplications, O Lord,
so that we, who believe that the Savior of the human race
is with you in your glory,
may experience, as he promised,
until the end of the world,
his abiding presence among us.
Who lives and reigns with you in the unity of the Holy
    Spirit,
one God, for ever and ever. ℟. **Amen.** ↓

FIRST READING Acts 1:15-17, 20a, 20c-26 [Choice of Matthias]

Peter discusses the question of Judas and his replacement. Two were nominated and all prayed. Then they drew lots and the choice fell to Matthias.

A reading from the Acts of the Apostles

PETER stood up in the midst of the brothers—there was a group of about one hundred and twenty persons in the one place—. He said, "My brothers, the Scripture had to be fulfilled which the Holy Spirit spoke beforehand through the mouth of David, concerning Judas, who was the guide for those who arrested Jesus. He was numbered among us and was allotted a share in this ministry.

"For it is written in the Book of Psalms:
May another take his office.

"Therefore, it is necessary that one of the men who accompanied us the whole time the Lord Jesus came and went among us, beginning from the baptism of John until the day on which he was taken up from us, become with us a witness to his resurrection." So they proposed two, Judas called Barsabbas, who was also known as Justus, and Matthias. Then they prayed, "You, Lord, who know the hearts of all, show which one of these two you have chosen to take the place in this apostolic ministry from which Judas turned away to go to his own place." Then they gave lots to them, and the lot fell upon Matthias, and he was counted with the eleven apostles.—The word of the Lord. ℟. **Thanks be to God.** ↓

RESPONSORIAL PSALM Ps 103   [Bless the Lord]

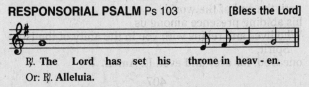

℟. **The   Lord   has   set   his   throne in heav - en.**

Or: ℟. **Alleluia.**

Bless the LORD, O my soul;
 and all my being, bless his holy name.
Bless the LORD, O my soul,
 and forget not all his benefits.—℟.
For as the heavens are high above the earth,
 so surpassing is his kindness toward those who fear
  him.
As far as the east is from the west,
 so far has he put our transgressions from us.—℟.
The LORD has established his throne in heaven,
 and his kingdom rules over all.
Bless the LORD, all you his angels,
 you mighty in strength, who do his bidding.—℟. ↓

SECOND READING 1 Jn 4:11-16 [God Dwells in Us]

Christians must have love for one another since the God of love dwells in them. When Jesus is acknowledged, God dwells in that person. God is love.

A reading from the first Letter of Saint John

B ELOVED, if God so loved us, we also must love one another. No one has ever seen God. Yet, if we love one another, God remains in us, and his love is brought to perfection in us.

This is how we know that we remain in him and he in us, that he has given us of his Spirit. Moreover, we have seen and testify that the Father sent his Son as savior of the world. Whoever acknowledges that Jesus is the Son of God, God remains in him and he in God. We have come to know and to believe in the love God has for us.

God is love, and whoever remains in love remains in God and God in him.—The word of the Lord. ℟.
Thanks be to God. ↓

ALLELUIA Cf. Jn 14:18   [Joyous Return]
℟. **Alleluia, alleluia.**
I will not leave you orphans says the Lord.

I will come back to you, and your hearts will rejoice.
℟. **Alleluia, alleluia.** ↓

GOSPEL Jn 17:11b-19   [Jesus' Prayer for Us]

Jesus prays for his followers. They have been looked after and have heard the gospel message from Jesus. He prays that his Father will continue to look after them and guard them from the evil one.

℣. The Lord be with you. ℟. **And with your spirit.**
✛ A reading from the holy Gospel according to John.
℟. **Glory to you, O Lord.**

LIFTING up his eyes to heaven, Jesus prayed, saying: "Holy Father, keep them in your name that you have given me, so that they may be one just as we are one. When I was with them I protected them in your name that you gave me, and I guarded them, and none of them was lost except the son of destruction, in order that the Scripture might be fulfilled. But now I am coming to you. I speak this in the world so that they may share my joy completely. I gave them your word, and the world hated them, because they do not belong to the world any more than I belong to the world. I do not ask that you take them out of the world but that you keep them from the evil one. They do not belong to the world any more than I belong to the world. Consecrate them in the truth. Your word is truth. As you sent me into the world, so I sent them into the world. And I consecrate myself for them, so that they also may be consecrated in truth."—The Gospel of the Lord. ℟. **Praise to you, Lord Jesus Christ.**   → No. 15, p. 18

PRAYER OVER THE OFFERINGS   [Glory of Heaven]

Accept, O Lord, the prayers of your faithful
with the sacrificial offerings,
that through these acts of devotedness
we may pass over to the glory of heaven.

Through Christ our Lord.
℟. **Amen.**   ➡ No. 21, p. 22 (Pref. P 21-25 or P 26-27)

COMMUNION ANT. Jn 17:22   [Christian Unity]
**Father, I pray that they may be one as we also are one,
alleluia.** ↓

PRAYER AFTER COMMUNION   [Grant Us Confidence]

Hear us, O God our Savior,
and grant us confidence,
that through these sacred mysteries
there will be accomplished in the body of the whole
    Church
what has already come to pass in Christ her Head.
Who lives and reigns for ever and ever.
℟. **Amen.**   ➡ No. 30, p. 77

Optional Solemn Blessings, p. 97, and Prayers over the People, p. 105

"They were all filled with the Holy Spirit."

MAY 23

PENTECOST SUNDAY

Solemnity

AT THE VIGIL MASS (Simple Form) (May 22)

ENTRANCE ANT. Rom 5:5; cf. 8:11   [Love-Imparting Spirit]

The love of God has been poured into our hearts through the Spirit of God dwelling within us, alleluia.

→ No. 2, p. 10

COLLECT   [Heavenly Grace]

Almighty ever-living God,
who willed the Paschal Mystery
to be encompassed as a sign in fifty days,
grant that from out of the scattered nations
the confusion of many tongues
may be gathered by heavenly grace
into one great confession of your name.
Through our Lord Jesus Christ, your Son,
who lives and reigns with you in the unity of the Holy
    Spirit,
one God, for ever and ever. ℟. **Amen.** ↓

412

OR [New Birth in the Spirit]

Grant, we pray, almighty God,
that the splendor of your glory
may shine forth upon us
and that, by the bright rays of the Holy Spirit,
the light of your light may confirm the hearts
of those born again by your grace.
Through our Lord Jesus Christ, your Son,
who lives and reigns with you in the unity of the Holy
    Spirit,
one God, for ever and ever. ℟. **Amen.** ↓

FIRST READING

A Gn 11:1-9 [Dangers of Human Pride]

**Those who put their trust in pride, and human ability, are
bound to fail.**

A reading from the Book of Genesis

THE whole world spoke the same language, using the
same words. While the people were migrating in the
east, they came upon a valley in the land of Shinar and
settled there. They said to one another, "Come, let us
mold bricks and harden them with fire." They used
bricks for stone, and bitumen for mortar. Then they said,
"Come, let us build ourselves a city and a tower with its
top in the sky, and so make a name for ourselves; otherwise we shall be scattered all over the earth."

The LORD came down to see the city and the tower
that the people had built. Then the LORD said: "If now,
while they are one people, all speaking the same language, they have started to do this, nothing will later
stop them from doing whatever they presume to do.
Let us then go down there and confuse their language,
so that one will not understand what another says."
Thus the LORD scattered them from there all over the
earth, and they stopped building the city. That is why it

was called Babel, because there the LORD confused the speech of all the world. It was from that place that he scattered them all over the earth.—The word of the Lord. ℟. **Thanks be to God.** ↓

OR

B Ex 19:3-8a, 16-20b   [The Lord on Mount Sinai]

The Lord God covenants with the Israelites—they are to be a holy nation, a princely Kingdom.

A reading from the Book of Exodus

MOSES went up the mountain to God. Then the LORD called to him and said, "Thus shall you say to the house of Jacob; tell the Israelites: You have seen for yourselves how I treated the Egyptians and how I bore you up on eagle wings and brought you here to myself. Therefore, if you hearken to my voice and keep my covenant, you shall be my special possession, dearer to me than all other people, though all the earth is mine. You shall be to me a kingdom of priests, a holy nation. That is what you must tell the Israelites." So Moses went and summoned the elders of the people. When he set before them all that the LORD had ordered him to tell them, the people all answered together, "Everything the LORD has said, we will do."

On the morning of the third day there were peals of thunder and lightning, and a heavy cloud over the mountain, and a very loud trumpet blast, so that all the people in the camp trembled. But Moses led the people out of the camp to meet God, and they stationed themselves at the foot of the mountain. Mount Sinai was all wrapped in smoke, for the LORD came down upon it in fire. The smoke rose from it as though from a furnace, and the whole mountain trembled violently. The trumpet blast grew louder and louder, while Moses was speaking and God answering him with thunder.

When the LORD came down to the top of Mount Sinai, he summoned Moses to the top of the mountain.—The word of the Lord. ℟. **Thanks be to God.** ↓

OR

C Ez 37:1-14   [Life-Giving Spirit]

The prophet, in a vision, sees the power of God—the band of the living and the dead, as he describes the resurrection of the dead.

A reading from the Book of the Prophet Ezekiel

THE hand of the LORD came upon me, and he led me out in the spirit of the LORD and set me in the center of the plain, which was now filled with bones. He made me walk among the bones in every direction so that I saw how many they were on the surface of the plain. How dry they were! He asked me: Son of man, can these bones come to life? I answered, "Lord GOD, you alone know that." Then he said to me: Prophesy over these bones, and say to them: Dry bones, hear the word of the LORD! Thus says the Lord GOD to these bones: See! I will bring spirit into you, that you may come to life. I will put sinews upon you, make flesh grow over you, cover you with skin, and put spirit in you so that you may come to life and know that I am the LORD. I, Ezekiel, prophesied as I had been told, and even as I was prophesying I heard a noise; it was a rattling as the bones came together, bone joining bone. I saw the sinews and the flesh come upon them, and the skin cover them, but there was no spirit in them. Then the LORD said to me: Prophesy to the spirit, prophesy, son of man, and say to the spirit: Thus says the Lord GOD: From the four winds come, O spirit, and breathe into these slain that they may come to life. I prophesied as he told me, and the spirit came into them; they came alive and stood upright, a vast army. Then he said to me: Son of man, these bones are the whole house of Israel. They have been saying, "Our bones are dried up, our hope is lost, and we are cut off." Therefore, prophesy and say to them: Thus says the Lord GOD: O my people, I will open your graves and have you rise from them, and bring you back to the land of Israel. Then you shall know that I am the LORD, when I open your graves and have you rise from them, O my people! I will put my spirit in you that you may live, and I will settle you upon your land; thus you shall know that I am the LORD. I have promised, and I will do it, says the LORD.—The word of the Lord. ℟. **Thanks be to God.** ↓

OR

D Jl 3:1-5   [Signs of the Spirit]

At the end of time, the Day of the Lord, Judgment Day, those who persevere in faith will be saved.

A reading from the Book of the Prophet Joel

THUS says the LORD:
I will pour out my spirit upon all flesh.
Your sons and daughters shall prophesy,
    your old men shall dream dreams,
    your young men shall see visions;
even upon the servants and the handmaids,
    in those days, I will pour out my spirit.
And I will work wonders in the heavens and on the
        earth,
    blood, fire, and columns of smoke;
the sun will be turned to darkness,
    and the moon to blood,
at the coming of the day of the LORD,
    the great and terrible day.
Then everyone shall be rescued
    who calls on the name of the LORD;
for on Mount Zion there shall be a remnant,
    as the LORD has said,
and in Jerusalem survivors
    whom the LORD shall call.
The word of the Lord. ℟. **Thanks be to God.** ↓

RESPONSORIAL PSALM Ps 104   [Send Out Your Spirit]

℟. Lord, send out your Spir-it,
and re-new the face of the earth.

Or: ℟. **Alleluia.**

Bless the LORD, O my soul!
  O LORD, my God, you are great indeed!
You are clothed with majesty and glory,
  robed in light as with a cloak.—℟.

How manifold are your works, O LORD!
  In wisdom you have wrought them all—
the earth is full of your creatures;
  bless the LORD, O my soul! Alleluia.—℟.

Creatures all look to you
  to give them food in due time.
When you give it to them, they gather it;
  when you open your hand, they are filled with good
    things.—℟.

If you take away their breath, they perish
  and return to their dust.
When you send forth your spirit, they are created,
  and you renew the face of the earth.—℟. ↓

SECOND READING Rom 8:22-27   [The Spirit Our Helper]
  Be patient and have hope. The Spirit intercedes for us.

A reading from the Letter of Saint Paul to the Romans

BROTHERS and sisters: We know that all creation is
  groaning in labor pains even until now; and not
only that, but we ourselves, who have the firstfruits of
the Spirit, we also groan within ourselves as we wait

for adoption, the redemption of our bodies. For in hope we were saved. Now hope that sees is not hope. For who hopes for what one sees? But if we hope for what we do not see, we wait with endurance.

In the same way, the Spirit too comes to the aid of our weakness; for we do not know how to pray as we ought, but the Spirit himself intercedes with inexpressible groanings. And the one who searches hearts knows what is the intention of the Spirit, because he intercedes for the holy ones according to God's will.— The word of the Lord. ℟. **Thanks be to God.** ↓

ALLELUIA [Fire of God's Love]

℟. **Alleluia, alleluia.**
Come, Holy Spirit, fill the hearts of the faithful
and kindle in them the fire of your love.
℟. **Alleluia, alleluia.** ↓

GOSPEL Jn 7:37-39 [Prediction of the Spirit]

The Spirit is the source of life for those who have faith and believe.

℣. The Lord be with you. ℟. **And with your spirit.**
✠ A reading from the holy Gospel according to John.
℟. **Glory to you, O Lord.**

ON the last and greatest day of the feast, Jesus stood up and exclaimed, "Let anyone who thirsts come to me and drink. As scripture says:
Rivers of living water will flow from within him who believes in me."
He said this in reference to the Spirit that those who came to believe in him were to receive. There was, of course, no Spirit yet, because Jesus had not yet been glorified.—The Gospel of the Lord. ℟. **Praise to you, Lord Jesus Christ.** → No. 15, p. 18

PRAYER OVER THE OFFERINGS [Manifestation of Salvation]

Pour out upon these gifts the blessing of your Spirit, we pray, O Lord,

so that through them your Church may be imbued
with such love
that the truth of your saving mystery
may shine forth for the whole world.
Through Christ our Lord.

℞. **Amen.**   → Pref. P 28, p. 431

When the Roman Canon is used, the proper form of the
Communicantes *(In communion with those) is said.*

COMMUNION ANT. Jn 7:37   [Thirst for the Spirit]

**On the last day of the festival, Jesus stood and cried
out: If anyone is thirsty, let him come to me and drink,
alleluia.** ↓

PRAYER AFTER COMMUNION   [Aflame with the Spirit]

May these gifts we have consumed
benefit us, O Lord,
that we may always be aflame with the same Spirit,
whom you wondrously poured out on your Apostles.
Through Christ our Lord.

℞. **Amen.**   → No. 30, p. 77

Optional Solemn Blessings, p. 97, and Prayers over the People, p. 105

(At the end of the Dismissal the people respond: **"Thanks be
to God, alleluia, alleluia."***)*

AT THE VIGIL MASS (Extended Form) (May 22)

ENTRANCE ANT. Rom 5:5; cf. 8:11   [Love-Imparting Spirit]

**The love of God has been poured into our hearts
through the Spirit of God dwelling within us, alleluia.**
→ No. 2, p. 10

Grant, we pray, almighty God,
that the splendor of your glory
may shine forth upon us
and that, by the bright rays of the Holy Spirit,

the light of your light may confirm the hearts
of those born again by your grace.
Through our Lord Jesus Christ, your Son,
who lives and reigns with you in the unity of the Holy
    Spirit,
one God, for ever and ever. ℟. **Amen.** ↓

*Then the Priest may address the people in these or similar
words:*

Dear brethren (brothers and sisters), [God's Great Deeds]
we have now begun our Pentecost Vigil,
after the example of the Apostles and disciples,
who with Mary, the Mother of Jesus, persevered in
    prayer,
awaiting the Spirit promised by the Lord;
like them, let us, too, listen with quiet hearts to the
    Word of God.
Let us meditate on how many great deeds
God in times past did for his people
and let us pray that the Holy Spirit,
whom the Father sent as the first fruits for those who
    believe,
may bring to perfection his work in the world.

FIRST READING

See p. 413, A. ↓

RESPONSORIAL PSALM Ps 33   [God's People]

℟. **Blessed the people the Lord has chosen to be his
    own.**
The LORD brings to nought the plans of nations;
    he foils the designs of peoples.
But the plan of the LORD stands forever;
    the design of his heart, through all generations.—℟.
Blessed the nation whose God is the LORD,
    the people he has chosen for his own inheritance.

From heaven the LORD looks down;
  he sees all mankind.—R̸.

From his fixed throne he beholds
  all who dwell on the earth,
He who fashioned the heart of each,
  he who knows all their works.—R̸. ↓

All rise.

PRAYER   [Church Formed as One]
Let us pray.

Grant, we pray, almighty God,
that your Church may always remain that holy people,
formed as one by the unity of Father, Son and Holy
  Spirit,
which manifests to the world
the Sacrament of your holiness and unity
and leads it to the perfection of your charity.
Through Christ our Lord.
R̸. **Amen.** ↓

SECOND READING

See p. 414, B. ↓

RESPONSORIAL PSALM Dn 3   [Praiseworthy and Exalted]

R̸. **Glory and praise for ever!**

"Blessed are you, O Lord, the God of our fathers,
  praiseworthy and exalted above all forever;
And blessed is your holy and glorious name,
  praiseworthy and exalted above all for all ages."—R̸.

"Blessed are you in the temple of your holy glory,
  praiseworthy and glorious above all forever."—R̸.

"Blessed are you on the throne of your Kingdom,
  praiseworthy and exalted above all forever."—R̸.

"Blessed are you who look into the depths
  from your throne upon the cherubim,
  praiseworthy and exalted above all forever."—R̸.

"Blessed are you in the firmament of heaven,
    praiseworthy and glorious forever."
℟. **Glory and praise for ever!** ↓

OR

Ps 19   **[The Lord's Words]**

℟. **Lord, you have the words of everlasting life.**

The law of the LORD is perfect,
    refreshing the soul;
The decree of the LORD is trustworthy,
    giving wisdom to the simple.—℟.

The precepts of the LORD are right,
    rejoicing the heart;
The command of the LORD is clear,
    enlightening the eye.—℟.

The fear of the LORD is pure,
    enduring forever;
The ordinances of the LORD are true,
    all of them just.—℟.

They are more precious than gold,
    than a heap of purest gold;
Sweeter also than syrup
    or honey from the comb.—℟.

All rise.

PRAYER   **[Fire of the Spirit]**
Let us pray.

O God, who in fire and lightning
gave the ancient Law to Moses on Mount Sinai
and on this day manifested the new covenant
in the fire of the Spirit,
grant, we pray,
that we may always be aflame with that same Spirit
whom you wondrously poured out on your Apostles,
and that the new Israel,
gathered from every people,

may receive with rejoicing
the eternal commandment of your love.
Through Christ our Lord.
℟. **Amen.** ↓

THIRD READING

See p. 415, C. ↓

RESPONSORIAL PSALM Ps 107   [God's Love]

℟. **Give thanks to the Lord; his love is everlasting.**

Or: ℟. **Alleluia.**

Let the redeemed of the LORD say,
  those whom he has redeemed from the hand of the
    foe
And gathered from the lands,
  from the east and the west, from the north and the
    south.—℟.

They went astray in the desert wilderness;
  the way to an inhabited city they did not find.
Hungry and thirsty,
  their life was wasting away within them.—℟.

They cried to the LORD in their distress;
  from their straits he rescued them.
And he led them by a direct way
  to reach an inhabited city.—℟.

Let them give thanks to the LORD for his mercy
  and his wondrous deeds to the children of men,
Because he satisfied the longing soul
  and filled the hungry soul with good things.—℟.

All rise.

PRAYER   [God Restores]
Let us pray.

Lord, God of power,
who restore what has fallen
and preserve what you have restored,

increase, we pray, the peoples
to be renewed by the sanctification of your name,
that all who are washed clean by holy Baptism
may always be directed by your prompting.
Through Christ our Lord.
℟. **Amen.** ↓

OR

O God, who have brought us to rebirth by the word of life,
pour out upon us your Holy Spirit,
that, walking in oneness of faith,
we may attain in our flesh
the incorruptible glory of the resurrection.
Through Christ our Lord.
℟. **Amen.** ↓

OR

May your people exult for ever, O God,
in renewed youthfulness of spirit,
so that, rejoicing now in the restored glory of our adoption,
we may look forward in confident hope
to the rejoicing of the day of resurrection.
Through Christ our Lord.
℟. **Amen.** ↓

FOURTH READING

See p. 416, D. ↓

RESPONSORIAL PSALM Ps 104   [Send Out Your Spirit]

See p. 417. ↓

All rise.

PRAYER   [Witnesses]
Let us pray.

Fulfill for us your gracious promise,
O Lord, we pray, so that by his coming

the Holy Spirit may make us witnesses before the world
to the Gospel of our Lord Jesus Christ.
Who lives and reigns for ever and ever.
℟. **Amen.** ↓

Then the Priest intones the hymn Gloria in excelsis Deo *(Glory to God in the highest).*

COLLECT   [Heavenly Grace]

Almighty ever-living God,
who willed the Paschal Mystery
to be encompassed as a sign in fifty days,
grant that from out of the scattered nations
the confusion of many tongues
may be gathered by heavenly grace
into one great confession of your name.
Through our Lord Jesus Christ, your Son,
who lives and reigns with you in the unity of the Holy Spirit,
one God, for ever and ever. ℟. **Amen.** ↓

EPISTLE

See p. 417, Second Reading.

The Mass continues as in the Simple Form (pp. 418-419).

AT THE MASS DURING THE DAY

ENTRANCE ANT. Wis 1:7   [The Spirit in the World]
The Spirit of the Lord has filled the whole world and that which contains all things understands what is said, alleluia.   ➜ No. 2, p. 10

OR Rom 5:5; cf. 8:11   [God's Love for Us]
The love of God has been poured into our hearts through the Spirit of God dwelling within us, alleluia.
                                        ➜ No. 2, p. 10

COLLECT   [Gifts of the Spirit]

O God, who by the mystery of today's great feast
sanctify your whole Church in every people and
    nation,
pour out, we pray, the gifts of the Holy Spirit
across the face of the earth
and, with the divine grace that was at work
when the Gospel was first proclaimed,
fill now once more the hearts of believers.
Through our Lord Jesus Christ, your Son,
who lives and reigns with you in the unity of the Holy
    Spirit,
one God, for ever and ever. ℟. **Amen.** ↓

FIRST READING Acts 2:1-11   [Coming of the Spirit]

On this day the Holy Spirit in fiery tongues descended
upon the apostles and the Mother of Jesus. Today the law
of grace and purification from sin was announced. Three
thousand were baptized.

A reading from the Acts of the Apostles

W HEN the time for Pentecost was fulfilled, they
    were all in one place together. And suddenly there
came from the sky a noise like a strong driving wind,
and it filled the entire house in which they were. Then
there appeared to them tongues as of fire, which parted
and came to rest on each of them. And they were all
filled with the Holy Spirit and began to speak in different tongues, as the Spirit enabled them to proclaim.

Now there were devout Jews from every nation
under heaven staying in Jerusalem. At this sound, they
gathered in a large crowd, but they were confused
because each one heard them speaking in his own language. They were astounded, and in amazement they
asked, "Are not all these people who are speaking
Galileans? Then how does each of us hear them in his

native language? We are Parthians, Medes, and
Elamites, inhabitants of Mesopotamia, Judea and
Cappadocia, Pontus and Asia, Phrygia and Pamphylia,
Egypt, and the districts of Libya near Cyrene, as well as
travelers from Rome, both Jews and converts to
Judaism, Cretans and Arabs, yet we hear them speak-
ing in our own tongues of the mighty acts of God."—
The word of the Lord. ℟. **Thanks be to God.** ↓

RESPONSORIAL PSALM Ps 104   [Renewal by the Spirit]

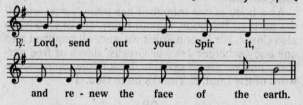

℟. Lord, send out your Spir - it,

and re - new the face of the earth.

Or: ℟. **Alleluia.**

Bless the LORD, O my soul!
  O LORD, my God, you are great indeed!
How manifold are your works, O LORD!
  the earth is full of your creatures.—℟.

May the glory of the LORD endure forever,
  may the LORD be glad in his works!
Pleasing to him be my theme;
  I will be glad in the LORD.—℟.

If you take away their breath, they perish
  and return to their dust.
When you send forth your spirit, they are created,
  and you renew the face of the earth.—℟. ↓

SECOND READING 1 Cor 12:3b-7, 12-13   [Grace of the Spirit]

No one can confess the divinity and sovereignty of Jesus
unless inspired by the Holy Spirit. Different gifts and min-
istries are given but all for the one body with Jesus.

A reading from the first Letter of Saint Paul
to the Corinthians

BROTHERS and sisters: No one can say: "Jesus is
Lord," except by the Holy Spirit.

There are different kinds of spiritual gifts but the
same Spirit; there are different forms of service but the
same Lord; there are different workings but the same
God who produces all of them in everyone. To each
individual the manifestation of the Spirit is given for
some benefit.

As a body is one though it has many parts, and all
the parts of the body, though many, are one body, so
also Christ. For in one Spirit we were all baptized into
one body, whether Jews or Greeks, slaves or free persons, and we are all given to drink of one Spirit.—The
word of the Lord. ℟. **Thanks be to God.** ↓

OR

SECOND READING Gal 5:16-25   **[Fruits of the Spirit]**

Paul's concrete advice illustrates the love which he stress-
es. "Good deeds" are not to be excluded from Christian
life. There is no law against such virtuous actions.

A reading from the Letter of Saint Paul
to the Galatians

BROTHERS and sisters, live by the Spirit and you
will certainly not gratify the desire of the flesh.
For the flesh has desires against the Spirit, and the
Spirit against the flesh; these are opposed to each
other, so that you may not do what you want. But if
you are guided by the Spirit, you are not under the
law. Now the works of the flesh are obvious: immorality, impurity, lust, idolatry, sorcery, hatreds, rivalry,
jealousy, outbursts of fury, acts of selfishness, dissen-
sions, factions, occasions of envy, drinking bouts,

orgies, and the like. I warn you, as I warned you
before, that those who do such things will not inherit
the kingdom of God. In contrast, the fruit of the Spirit
is love, joy, peace, patience, kindness, generosity,
faithfulness, gentleness, self-control. Against such
there is no law. Now those who belong to Christ Jesus
have crucified their flesh with its passions and
desires. If we live in the Spirit, let us also follow the
Spirit.—The word of the Lord. ℟. **Thanks be to God.** ↓

SEQUENCE *(Veni, Sancte Spiritus)*   [Come, Holy Spirit]

Come, Holy Spirit, come!
And from your celestial home
  Shed a ray of light divine!
Come, Father of the poor!
Come, source of all our store!
  Come, within our bosoms shine!
You, of comforters the best;
You, the soul's most welcome guest;
  Sweet refreshment here below;
In our labor, rest most sweet;
Grateful coolness in the heat;
  Solace in the midst of woe.
O most blessed Light divine,
Shine within these hearts of yours,
  And our inmost being fill!
Where you are not, we have naught,
Nothing good in deed or thought,
  Nothing free from taint of ill.
Heal our wounds, our strength renew;
On our dryness pour your dew;
  Wash the stains of guilt away:
Bend the stubborn heart and will;
Melt the frozen, warm the chill;
  Guide the steps that go astray.

On the faithful, who adore
And confess you, evermore
  In your sevenfold gift descend;
Give them virtue's sure reward;
Give them your salvation, Lord;
  Give them joys that never end. **Amen.**
  Alleluia. ↓

ALLELUIA   [Fire of God's Love]

℞. **Alleluia, alleluia.**
Come, Holy Spirit, fill the hearts of your faithful
and kindle in them the fire of your love.
℞. **Alleluia, alleluia.** ↓

GOSPEL Jn 20:19-23   [Christ Imparts the Spirit]

Jesus breathes on the disciples to indicate the conferring
of the Holy Spirit. Here we see the origin of power over
sin, the Sacrament of Penance. This shows the power of
the Holy Spirit in the hearts of human beings.

℣. The Lord be with you. ℞. **And with your spirit.**
✛ A reading from the holy Gospel according to John.
℞. **Glory to you, O Lord.**

O N the evening of that first day of the week, when
the doors were locked, where the disciples were,
for fear of the Jews, Jesus came and stood in their
midst and said to them, "Peace be with you." When he
had said this, he showed them his hands and
his side. The disciples rejoiced when they saw the
Lord. Jesus said to them again, "Peace be with you. As
the Father has sent me, so I send you." And when he
had said this, he breathed on them and said
to them, "Receive the Holy Spirit. Whose sins you forgive are forgiven them, and whose sins you retain are
retained."—The Gospel of the Lord. ℞. **Praise to you,
Lord Jesus Christ.**   → No. 15, p. 18

OR

GOSPEL Jn 15:26-27; 16:12-15   [Spirit of Truth]

Jesus indicates that the Holy Spirit will bear witness to the good news. He will guide Christians to the truth and teach about things to come.

℣. The Lord be with you. ℞. **And with your spirit.**
✢ A reading from the holy Gospel according to John.
℞. **Glory to you, O Lord.**

JESUS said to his disciples: "When the Advocate comes whom I will send you from the Father, the Spirit of truth that proceeds from the Father, he will testify to me. And you also testify, because you have been with me from the beginning.

"I have much more to tell you, but you cannot bear it now. But when he comes, the Spirit of truth, he will guide you to all truth. He will not speak on his own, but he will speak what he hears, and will declare to you the things that are coming. He will glorify me, because he will take from what is mine and declare it to you. Everything that the Father has is mine; for this reason I told you that he will take from what is mine and declare it to you."—The Gospel of the Lord. ℞. **Praise to you, Lord Jesus Christ.**   → No. 15, p. 18

PRAYER OVER THE OFFERINGS   [All Truth]

Grant, we pray, O Lord,
that, as promised by your Son,
the Holy Spirit may reveal to us more abundantly
the hidden mystery of this sacrifice
and graciously lead us into all truth.
Through Christ our Lord. ℞. **Amen.** ↓

PREFACE (P 28)   [Coming of the Spirit]

℣. The Lord be with you. ℞. **And with your spirit.**
℣. Lift up your hearts. ℞. **We lift them up to the Lord.**
℣. Let us give thanks to the Lord our God. ℞. **It is right and just.**

It is truly right and just, our duty and our salvation,
always and everywhere to give you thanks,
Lord, holy Father, almighty and eternal God.

For, bringing your Paschal Mystery to completion,
you bestowed the Holy Spirit today
on those you made your adopted children
by uniting them to your Only Begotten Son.
This same Spirit, as the Church came to birth,
opened to all peoples the knowledge of God
and brought together the many languages of the earth
in profession of the one faith.

Therefore, overcome with paschal joy,
every land, every people exults in your praise
and even the heavenly Powers, with the angelic hosts,
sing together the unending hymn of your glory,
as they acclaim: → No. 23, p. 23

When the Roman Canon is used, the proper form of the
Communicantes (In communion with those) *is said.*

COMMUNION ANT. Acts 2:4, 11   [Filled with the Spirit]
**They were all filled with the Holy Spirit and spoke of
the marvels of God, alleluia.** ↓

PRAYER AFTER COMMUNION   [Safeguard Grace]
O God, who bestow heavenly gifts upon your Church,
safeguard, we pray, the grace you have given,
that the gift of the Holy Spirit poured out upon her
may retain all its force
and that this spiritual food
may gain her abundance of eternal redemption.
Through Christ our Lord.
℟. **Amen.**   → No. 30, p. 77

Optional Solemn Blessings, p. 97, and Prayers over the People, p. 105

(At the end of the Dismissal the people respond: "**Thanks be
to God, alleluia, alleluia.**"*)*

"Blest be God the Father, and the Only Begotten Son of God, and also the Holy Spirit."

MAY 30

THE MOST HOLY TRINITY

Solemnity

ENTRANCE ANT. [Blessed Trinity]

Blest be God the Father, and the Only Begotten Son of God, and also the Holy Spirit, for he has shown us his merciful love. → No. 2, p. 10

COLLECT [Witnessing to the Trinity]

God our Father, who by sending into the world
the Word of truth and the Spirit of sanctification
made known to the human race your wondrous
    mystery,
grant us, we pray, that in professing the true faith,
we may acknowledge the Trinity of eternal glory
and adore your Unity, powerful in majesty.
Through our Lord Jesus Christ, your Son,
who lives and reigns with you in the unity of the Holy
    Spirit,
one God, for ever and ever.
℟. Amen. ↓

433

FIRST READING Dt 4:32-34, 39-40   [The One God]

Moses asks the people to reflect on what has happened and whether or not God was their sole Creator and protector. For this reason his laws and commandments must be obeyed.

A reading from the Book of Deuteronomy

MOSES said to the people: "Ask now of the days of old, before your time, ever since God created man upon the earth; ask from one end of the sky to the other: Did anything so great ever happen before? Was it ever heard of? Did a people ever hear the voice of God speaking from the midst of fire, as you did, and live? Or did any god venture to go and take a nation for himself from the midst of another nation, by testings, by signs and wonders, by war, with his strong hand and outstretched arm, and by great terrors, all of which the LORD, your God, did for you in Egypt before your very eyes? This is why you must now know, and fix in your heart, that the LORD is God in the heavens above and on earth below, and that there is no other. You must keep his statutes and commandments that I enjoin on you today, that you and your children after you may prosper, and that you may have long life on the land which the LORD, your God, is giving you forever."—The word of the Lord. ℟. **Thanks be to God.** ↓

RESPONSORIAL PSALM Ps 33   [God's People Hope in Him]

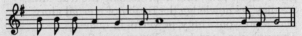

℟. **Bless-ed the peo - ple   the Lord has chosen to be his own.**

Upright is the word of the LORD,
    and all his works are trustworthy.
He loves justice and right;
    of the kindness of the LORD the earth is full.—℟.

By the word of the LORD the heavens were made;
  by the breath of his mouth all their host.
For he spoke, and it was made;
  he commanded, and it stood forth.—R̶̸.

See, the eyes of the LORD are upon those who fear him,
  upon those who hope for his kindness,
to deliver them from death
  and preserve them in spite of famine.—R̶̸.

Our soul waits for the LORD,
  who is our help and our shield.
May your kindness, O LORD, be upon us
  who have put our hope in you.—R̶̸. ↓

SECOND READING Rom 8:14-17   [Children of God]

  **The Spirit of God makes Christians adopted children of
  God. They become at the same time heirs of God with
  Christ—to suffer with him and also be glorified.**

 A reading from the Letter of Saint Paul to the Romans

BROTHERS and sisters: Those who are led by the
Spirit of God are sons of God. For you did not receive
a spirit of slavery to fall back into fear, but you received
a Spirit of adoption, through whom we cry, "Abba,
Father!" The Spirit himself bears witness with our spirit
that we are children of God, and if children, then heirs,
heirs of God and joint heirs with Christ, if only we suffer
with him so that we may also be glorified with him.—The
word of the Lord. R̶̸. **Thanks be to God.** ↓

ALLELUIA Cf. Rv 1:8   [Triune God]

R̶̸. **Alleluia, alleluia.**
Glory to the Father, the Son and the Holy Spirit:
to God who is, who was, and who is to come.
R̶̸. **Alleluia, alleluia.** ↓

GOSPEL Mt 28:16-20   [Disciples of the Trinity]

  **At Jesus' request the eleven assembled and fell down in
  homage. Jesus gives them the all pervading command to**

preach and baptize all human beings. He also promises to
be with them to the end of time.

℣. The Lord be with you. ℟. **And with your spirit.**
✠ A reading from the holy Gospel according to
Matthew. ℟. **Glory to you, O Lord.**

T HE eleven disciples went to Galilee, to the mountain to which Jesus had ordered them. When they
all saw him, they worshiped, but they doubted. Then
Jesus approached and said to them, "All power in heav-
en and on earth has been given to me. Go, therefore,
and make disciples of all nations, baptizing them in
the name of the Father, and of the Son, and of the Holy
Spirit, teaching them to observe all that I have commanded you. And behold, I am with you always, until
the end of the age."—The Gospel of the Lord. ℟. **Praise
to you, Lord Jesus Christ.**   → No. 15, p. 18

PRAYER OVER THE OFFERINGS   [Eternal Offering]

Sanctify by the invocation of your name,
we pray, O Lord our God,
this oblation of our service,
and by it make of us an eternal offering to you.
Through Christ our Lord. ℟. **Amen.** ↓

PREFACE (P 43)   [Mystery of the One Godhead]

℣. The Lord be with you. ℟. **And with your spirit.**
℣. Lift up your hearts. ℟. **We lift them up to the Lord.**
℣. Let us give thanks to the Lord our God. ℟. **It is right
and just.**

It is truly right and just, our duty and our salvation,
always and everywhere to give you thanks,
Lord, holy Father, almighty and eternal God.

For with your Only Begotten Son and the Holy Spirit
you are one God, one Lord:
not in the unity of a single person,
but in a Trinity of one substance.

For what you have revealed to us of your glory
we believe equally of your Son
and of the Holy Spirit,
so that, in the confessing of the true and eternal
    Godhead,
you might be adored in what is proper to each Person,
their unity in substance,
and their equality in majesty.

For this is praised by Angels and Archangels,
Cherubim, too, and Seraphim,
who never cease to cry out each day,
as with one voice they acclaim: → No. 23, p. 23

COMMUNION ANT. Gal 4:6   [Abba, Father]
**Since you are children of God, God has sent into your
hearts the Spirit of his Son, the Spirit who cries out:
Abba, Father.** ↓

PRAYER AFTER COMMUNION   [Eternal Trinity]

May receiving this Sacrament, O Lord our God,
bring us health of body and soul,
as we confess your eternal holy Trinity and undivided
    Unity.
Through Christ our Lord.
℟. **Amen.**   → No. 30, p. 77

Optional Solemn Blessings, p. 97, and Prayers over the People, p. 105

"This is my body. . . ."

JUNE 6

THE MOST HOLY BODY AND BLOOD OF CHRIST
(CORPUS CHRISTI)

Solemnity

ENTRANCE ANT. Cf. Ps 81 (80):17 **[Finest Wheat and Honey]**

**He fed them with the finest wheat and satisfied them
with honey from the rock.** → No. 2, p. 10

COLLECT **[Memorial of Christ's Passion]**

O God, who in this wonderful Sacrament
have left us a memorial of your Passion,
grant us, we pray,
so to revere the sacred mysteries of your Body and
    Blood
that we may always experience in ourselves
the fruits of your redemption.
Who live and reign with God the Father
in the unity of the Holy Spirit,
one God, for ever and ever. ℞. **Amen.** ↓

438

FIRST READING Ex 24:3-8   [Blood of the Covenant]

The Israelites promised to observe all the prescriptions of the Lord as related by Moses. To seal this promise Moses offered a sacrifice to the Lord and sprinkled the people with the blood offering.

A reading from the Book of Exodus

WHEN Moses came to the people and related all the words and ordinances of the LORD, they all answered with one voice, "We will do everything that the LORD has told us." Moses then wrote down all the words of the LORD and, rising early the next day, he erected at the foot of the mountain an altar and twelve pillars for the twelve tribes of Israel. Then, having sent certain young men of the Israelites to offer holocausts and sacrifice young bulls as peace offerings to the LORD, Moses took half of the blood and put it in large bowls; the other half he splashed on the altar. Taking the book of the covenant, he read it aloud to the people, who answered, "All that the LORD has said, we will heed and do." Then he took the blood and sprinkled it on the people, saying, "This is the blood of the covenant that the LORD has made with you in accordance with all these words of his."—The word of the Lord. ℟. **Thanks be to God.** ↓

RESPONSORIAL PSALM Ps 116   [The Cup of Salvation]

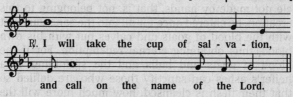

℟. I will take the cup of sal - va - tion, and call on the name of the Lord.

Or: ℟. **Alleluia.**

How shall I make a return to the LORD
  for all the good he has done for me?

The cup of salvation I will take up,
  and I will call upon the name of the LORD.

℟. **I will take the cup of salvation, and call on the name
  of the Lord.**

Or: ℟. **Alleluia.**

Precious in the eyes of the LORD
  is the death of his faithful ones.
I am your servant, the son of your handmaid;
  you have loosed my bonds.—℟.

To you will I offer sacrifice of thanksgiving,
  and I will call upon the name of the LORD.
My vows to the LORD I will pay
  in the presence of all his people.—℟. ↓

SECOND READING Heb 9:11-15   [Jesus the High Priest]

**Jesus came as high priest, not offering the blood of ani-
mals but his own blood, to achieve eternal redemption.
Jesus is mediator of the new covenant.**

A reading from the Letter to the Hebrews

BROTHERS and sisters: When Christ came as high
priest of the good things that have come to be,
passing through the greater and more perfect tabernacle not made by hands, that is, not belonging to this
creation, he entered once for all into the sanctuary, not
with the blood of goats and calves but with his own
blood, thus obtaining eternal redemption. For if the
blood of goats and bulls and the sprinkling of a
heifer's ashes can sanctify those who are defiled so
that their flesh is cleansed, how much more will the
blood of Christ, who through the eternal Spirit offered
himself unblemished to God, cleanse our consciences
from dead works to worship the living God.

For this reason he is mediator of a new covenant: since a death has taken place for deliverance from transgressions under the first covenant, those who are called may receive the promised eternal inheritance. —The word of the Lord. ℟. **Thanks be to God.** ↓

SEQUENCE *(Lauda Sion)*   [Praise of the Eucharist]

The Sequence Laud, O Zion (Lauda Sion), *or the Shorter Form beginning with the verse* Lo! the angel's food is given, *may be sung optionally before the Alleluia.*

Laud, O Zion, your salvation,
Laud with hymns of exultation,
  Christ, your king and shepherd true:

Bring him all the praise you know,
He is more than you bestow,
  Never can you reach his due.

Special theme for glad thanksgiving
Is the quick'ning and the living
  Bread today before you set:

From his hands of old partaken,
As we know, by faith unshaken,
  Where the Twelve at supper met.

Full and clear ring out your chanting,
Joy nor sweetest grace be wanting,
  From your heart let praises burst:

For today the feast is holden,
When the institution olden
  Of that supper was rehearsed.

Here the new law's new oblation,
By the new king's revelation,
  Ends the form of ancient rite:

Now the new the old effaces,
Truth away the shadow chases,
  Light dispels the gloom of night.

What he did at supper seated,
Christ ordained to be repeated,
  His memorial ne'er to cease:

And his rule for guidance taking,
Bread and wine we hallow, making
  Thus our sacrifice of peace.

This the truth each Christian learns,
Bread into his flesh he turns,
  To his precious blood the wine:

Sight has fail'd, nor thought conceives,
But a dauntless faith believes,
  Resting on a pow'r divine.

Here beneath these signs are hidden
Priceless things to sense forbidden;
  Signs, not things are all we see:

Blood is poured and flesh is broken,
Yet in either wondrous token
  Christ entire we know to be.

Whoso of this food partakes,
Does not rend the Lord nor breaks;
  Christ is whole to all that taste:

Thousands are, as one, receivers,
One, as thousands of believers,
  Eats of him who cannot waste.

Bad and good the feast are sharing,
Of what divers dooms preparing,
  Endless death, or endless life.

Life to these, to those damnation,
See how like participation
  Is with unlike issues rife.

When the sacrament is broken,
Doubt not, but believe 'tis spoken,
  That each sever'd outward token
    doth the very whole contain.

Nought the precious gift divides,
Breaking but the sign betides,
  Jesus still the same abides,
    still unbroken does remain.

The Shorter Form of the Sequence begins here.

Lo! the angel's food is given
To the pilgrim who has striven;
  See the children's bread from heaven,
    which on dogs may not be spent.

Truth the ancient types fulfilling,
Isaac bound, a victim willing,
  Paschal lamb, its lifeblood spilling,
    manna to the fathers sent.

Very bread, good shepherd, tend us,

Jesu, of your love befriend us,
  You refresh us, you defend us,
  Your eternal goodness send us
In the land of life to see.

You who all things can and know,
Who on earth such food bestow,
  Grant us with your saints, though lowest,
  Where the heav'nly feast you show,
Fellow heirs and guests to be.
  Amen. Alleluia. ↓

ALLELUIA Jn 6:51   [Living Bread]

℟. **Alleluia, alleluia.**

I am the living bread that came down from heaven,
  says the Lord;
whoever eats this bread will live forever.

℟. **Alleluia, alleluia.** ↓

GOSPEL Mk 14:12-16, 22-26   [The First Eucharist]

Jesus gave instructions for the Passover supper. At this
meal he took bread and wine and changed it into his Body
and Blood and gave this Eucharist to his disciples. They all
ate and drank at Jesus' request.

℣. The Lord be with you. ℟. **And with your spirit.**

✠ A reading from the holy Gospel according to Mark.

℟. **Glory to you, O Lord.**

ON the first day of the Feast of Unleavened Bread,
  when they sacrificed the Passover lamb, Jesus'
disciples said to him, "Where do you want us to go and
prepare for you to eat the Passover?" He sent two of his
disciples and said to them, "Go into the city and a man
will meet you, carrying a jar of water. Follow him.
Wherever he enters, say to the master of the house,
'The Teacher says, "Where is my guest room where I
may eat the Passover with my disciples?"' Then he will
show you a large upper room furnished and ready.
Make the preparations for us there." The disciples then
went off, entered the city, and found it just as he had
told them; and they prepared the Passover.

While they were eating, he took bread, said the
blessing, broke it, gave it to them, and said, "Take it;
this is my body." Then he took a cup, gave thanks, and
gave it to them, and they all drank from it. He said to
them, "This is my blood of the covenant, which will be
shed for many. Amen, I say to you, I shall not drink
again the fruit of the vine until the day when I drink it

new in the kingdom of God." Then, after singing a hymn, they went out to the Mount of Olives.—The Gospel of the Lord. ℟. **Praise to you, Lord Jesus Christ.**

➙ No. 15, p. 18

PRAYER OVER THE OFFERINGS   [Unity and Peace]

Grant your Church, O Lord, we pray,
the gifts of unity and peace,
whose signs are to be seen in mystery
in the offerings we here present.
Through Christ our Lord.
℟. **Amen.**   ➙ No. 21, p. 22 (Pref. P 47-48)

COMMUNION ANT. Jn 6:57   [Eucharistic Life]

Whoever eats my flesh and drinks my blood remains in me and I in him, says the Lord. ↓

PRAYER AFTER COMMUNION   [Divine Life]

Grant, O Lord, we pray,
that we may delight for all eternity
in that share in your divine life,
which is foreshadowed in the present age
by our reception of your precious Body and Blood.
Who live and reign for ever and ever.
℟. **Amen.**   ➙ No. 30, p. 77

Optional Solemn Blessings, p. 97, and Prayers over the People, p. 105

"The kingdom of God . . . is like a mustard seed."

JUNE 13

11th SUNDAY IN ORDINARY TIME

ENTRANCE ANT. Cf. Ps 27 (26):7, 9   [Hear My Voice]

O Lord, hear my voice, for I have called to you; be my help. Do not abandon or forsake me, O God, my Savior!   ➜ No. 2, p. 10

COLLECT   [Following God's Commands]

O God, strength of those who hope in you,
graciously hear our pleas,
and, since without you mortal frailty can do nothing,
grant us always the help of your grace,
that in following your commands
we may please you by our resolve and our deeds.
Through our Lord Jesus Christ, your Son,
who lives and reigns with you in the unity of the Holy
   Spirit,
one God, for ever and ever. ℟. **Amen.** ↓

FIRST READING Ez 17:22-24   [The Lord's Shoot]

> The restoration of Israel will be a kind of resurrection. From the modest beginnings of the Church, the Good News will be spread to all humanity.

A reading from the Book of the Prophet Ezekiel

THUS says the Lord GOD:
I, too, will take from the crest of the cedar,
    from its topmost branches tear off a tender shoot,
and plant it on a high and lofty mountain;
    on the mountain heights of Israel I will plant it.
It shall put forth branches and bear fruit,
    and become a majestic cedar.
Birds of every kind shall dwell beneath it,
    every winged thing in the shade of its boughs.
And all the trees of the field shall know
    that I, the LORD,
bring low the high tree,
    lift high the lowly tree,
wither up the green tree,
    and make the withered tree bloom.
As I, the LORD, have spoken, so will I do.
The word of the Lord. ℟. **Thanks be to God.** ↓

RESPONSORIAL PSALM Ps 92   [Rewards of the Just]

℟. **Lord, it is good to give thanks to you.**

It is good to give thanks to the LORD,
    to sing praise to your name, Most High,
to proclaim your kindness at dawn
    and your faithfulness throughout the night.—℟.

The just one shall flourish like the palm tree,
    like a cedar of Lebanon shall he grow.
They that are planted in the house of the LORD
    shall flourish in the courts of our God.—℟.

They shall bear fruit even in old age;
    vigorous and sturdy shall they be,
Declaring how just is the LORD,
    my rock, in whom there is no wrong.—℟. ↓

SECOND READING 2 Cor 5:6-10   [Trust in the Lord]

> While we wait for the Lord, we should please him in all things. Then we will be found without reproach when we appear before him in judgment.

A reading from the second Letter of Saint Paul
to the Corinthians

BROTHERS and sisters: We are always courageous, although we know that while we are at home in the body we are away from the Lord, for we walk by faith, not by sight. Yet we are courageous, and we would rather leave the body and go home to the Lord. Therefore, we aspire to please him, whether we are at home or away. For we must all appear before the judgment seat of Christ, so that each may receive recompense, according to what he did in the body, whether good or evil.—The word of the Lord. ℟. **Thanks be to God.** ↓

ALLELUIA   [God's Word]

℟. **Alleluia, alleluia.**
The seed is the word of God, Christ is the sower.
All who come to him will live for ever.
℟. **Alleluia, alleluia.** ↓

GOSPEL Mk 4:26-34   [The Kingdom of God]

> From small beginnings the Church of Christ has arisen for the salvation of all peoples. Through Christ's preaching, God the Father has revealed all that he had to say to us.

℣. The Lord be with you. ℟. **And with your spirit.**
✝ A reading from the holy Gospel according to Mark.
℟. **Glory to you, O Lord.**

JESUS said to the crowds: "This is how it is with the kingdom of God; it is as if a man were to scatter seed on the land and would sleep and rise night and day and through it all the seed would sprout and grow, he knows not how. Of its own accord the land yields fruit, first the blade, then the ear, then the full grain in the ear. And when the grain is ripe, he wields the sickle at once, for the harvest has come."

He said, "To what shall we compare the kingdom of God, or what parable can we use for it? It is like a mustard seed that, when it is sown in the ground, is the smallest of all the seeds on the earth. But once it is sown, it springs up and becomes the largest of plants and puts forth large branches, so that the birds of the sky can dwell in its shade." With many such parables he spoke the word to them as they were able to understand it. Without parables he did not speak to them, but to his own disciples he explained everything in private.—The Gospel of the Lord. ℟. **Praise to you, Lord Jesus Christ.**   → No. 15, p. 18

PRAYER OVER THE OFFERINGS   [Needs of Human Nature]

O God, who in the offerings presented here
provide for the twofold needs of human nature,
nourishing us with food
and renewing us with your Sacrament,
grant, we pray,
that the sustenance they provide
may not fail us in body or in spirit.
Through Christ our Lord.
℟. **Amen.**   → No. 21, p. 22 (Pref. P 29-36)

COMMUNION ANT. Ps 27 (26):4   [Living with the Lord]
There is one thing I ask of the Lord, only this do I seek: to live in the house of the Lord all the days of my life. ↓

OR Jn 17:11   [One with God]
Holy Father, keep in your name those you have given me, that they may be one as we are one, says the Lord. ↓

PRAYER AFTER COMMUNION   [Church Unity]

As this reception of your Holy Communion, O Lord,
foreshadows the union of the faithful in you,
so may it bring about unity in your Church.
Through Christ our Lord.
℟. **Amen.**   → No. 30, p. 77

Optional Solemn Blessings, p. 97, and Prayers over the People, p. 105

"Who then is this whom even wind and sea obey?"

JUNE 20

12th SUNDAY IN ORDINARY TIME

ENTRANCE ANT. Cf. Ps 28 (27):8-9   [Saving Refuge]

**The Lord is the strength of his people, a saving refuge
for the one he has anointed. Save your people, Lord,
and bless your heritage, and govern them for ever.**
                                              → No. 2, p. 10

COLLECT   [Foundation of God's Love]

Grant, O Lord,
that we may always revere and love your holy name,
for you never deprive of your guidance
those you set firm on the foundation of your love.

Through our Lord Jesus Christ, your Son,
who lives and reigns with you in the unity of the Holy
    Spirit,
one God, for ever and ever. ℟. **Amen.** ↓

FIRST READING Jb 38:1, 8-11   [Lord of Creation]

**God recalls for Job that he is the Lord of creation. He has
the power to do things which humans cannot explain.**

A reading from the Book of Job

T HE LORD addressed Job out of the storm and said:
    Who shut within doors the sea,
        when it burst forth from the womb;
When I made the clouds its garment
        and thick darkness its swaddling bands?
When I set limits for it
        and fastened the bar of its door,
    and said: Thus far shall you come but no farther,
        and here shall your proud waves be stilled!
The word of the Lord. ℟. **Thanks be to God.** ↓

RESPONSORIAL PSALM Ps 107 [God's Wondrous Deeds]

℟. **Give thanks to the Lord, his love is ev-er-last-ing.**

Or: **Alleluia.**

They who sailed the sea in ships,
    trading on the deep waters,
these saw the works of the LORD
    and his wonders in the abyss.—℟.

His command raised up a storm wind
    which tossed its waves on high.

They mounted up to heaven; they sank to the depths;
  their hearts melted away in their plight.—R̶/.

They cried to the LORD in their distress;
  from their straits he rescued them,
he hushed the storm to a gentle breeze,
  and the billows of the sea were stilled.—R̶/.

They rejoiced that they were calmed,
  and he brought them to their desired haven.
Let them give thanks to the LORD for his kindness
  and his wondrous deeds to the children of men.—R̶/. ↓

SECOND READING 2 Cor 5:14-17   **[A New Creation]**

**In Christ everyone is a new creation. A new world is
already born.**

A reading from the second Letter of Saint Paul
to the Corinthians

BROTHERS and sisters: The love of Christ impels
us, once we have come to the conviction that one
died for all; therefore, all have died. He indeed died for
all, so that those who live might no longer live for
themselves but for him who for their sake died and
was raised up.

  Consequently, from now on we regard no one
according to the flesh; even if we once knew Christ
according to the flesh, yet now we know him so no
longer. So whoever is in Christ is a new creation: the old
things have passed away; behold, new things have
come.—The word of the Lord. R̶/. **Thanks be to God.** ↓

ALLELUIA Lk 7:16   **[God Has Come]**

R̶/. **Alleluia, alleluia.**
A great prophet has risen in our midst.
God has visited his people.
R̶/. **Alleluia, alleluia.** ↓

GOSPEL Mk 4:35-41   [Christ Commands Creation]

Jesus is truly "God-with-us," and we should turn to him in faithful prayer.

℣. The Lord be with you. ℟. **And with your spirit.**

✣ A reading from the holy Gospel according to Mark.
℟. **Glory to you, O Lord.**

ON that day, as evening drew on, Jesus said to his disciples: "Let us cross to the other side." Leaving the crowd, they took Jesus with them in the boat just as he was. And other boats were with him. A violent squall came up and waves were breaking over the boat, so that it was already filling up. Jesus was in the stern, asleep on a cushion. They woke him and said to him, "Teacher, do you not care that we are perishing?" He woke up, rebuked the wind, and said to the sea, "Quiet! Be still!" The wind ceased and and there was a great calm. Then he asked them, "Why are you terrified? Do you not yet have faith?" They were filled with great awe and said to one another, "Who then is this whom even the wind and the sea obey?"—The Gospel of the Lord. ℟. **Praise to you, Lord Jesus Christ.**

→ No. 15, p. 18

PRAYER OVER THE OFFERINGS   [Pleasing Offering]

Receive, O Lord, the sacrifice of conciliation and praise
and grant that, cleansed by its action,
we may make offering of a heart pleasing to you.
Through Christ our Lord.
℟. **Amen.**   → No. 21, p. 22 (Pref. P 29-36)

COMMUNION ANT. Ps 145 (144):15   [Divine Food]

The eyes of all look to you, Lord, and you give them their food in due season. ↓

OR Jn 10:11, 15   [The Good Shepherd]

**I am the Good Shepherd, and I lay down my life for
my sheep, says the Lord.** ↓

PRAYER AFTER COMMUNION   [Pledge of Redemption]

Renewed and nourished
by the Sacred Body and Precious Blood of your Son,
we ask of your mercy, O Lord,
that what we celebrate with constant devotion
may be our sure pledge of redemption.
Through Christ our Lord.
℟. **Amen.**   → No. 30, p. 77

Optional Solemn Blessings, p. 97, and Prayers over the People, p. 105

"Little girl, I say to you, arise!"

JUNE 27

13th SUNDAY IN ORDINARY TIME

ENTRANCE ANT. Ps 47 (46):2   [Shouts of Joy]
**All peoples, clap your hands. Cry to God with shouts
of joy!**   → No. 2, p. 10

COLLECT   [Children of Light]

O God, who through the grace of adoption
chose us to be children of light,
grant, we pray,
that we may not be wrapped in the darkness of error
but always be seen to stand in the bright light of truth.
Through our Lord Jesus Christ, your Son,
who lives and reigns with you in the unity of the Holy
    Spirit,
one God, for ever and ever. ℟. **Amen.** ↓

FIRST READING Wis 1:13-15; 2:23-24   [Eternal Life]

**God does not rejoice in the destruction of the living.
Rather God formed human beings to be imperishable, and
if we practice justice we will live forever.**

A reading from the Book of Wisdom

GOD did not make death,
    nor does he rejoice in the destruction of the living.
For he fashioned all things that they might have being;
    and the creatures of the world are wholesome,
and there is not a destructive drug among them
    nor any domain of the netherworld on earth,
    for justice is undying.
For God formed man to be imperishable;
    the image of his own nature he made him.
But by the envy of the devil, death entered the world,
    and they who belong to his company experience it.
The word of the Lord. ℟. **Thanks be to God.** ↓

RESPONSORIAL PSALM Ps 30   [Eternal Gratitude]

℟. **I will praise you, Lord, for you have res-cued me.**

I will extol you, O LORD, for you drew me clear
    and did not let my enemies rejoice over me.

O Lᴏʀᴅ, you brought me up from the netherworld,
    you preserved me from among those going down
        into the pit.—Rʹ.

Sing praise to the Lᴏʀᴅ, you his faithful ones,
    and give thanks to his holy name.
For his anger lasts but a moment;
    a lifetime, his good will.
At nightfall, weeping enters in,
    but with the dawn, rejoicing.—Rʹ.

Hear, O Lᴏʀᴅ, and have pity on me;
    O Lᴏʀᴅ, be my helper.
You changed my mourning into dancing;
    O Lᴏʀᴅ, my God, forever will I give you thanks.—Rʹ. ↓

SECOND READING 2 Cor 8:7, 9, 13-15 [The Need for Charity]

Christians should be generous to others in imitation of the sovereign liberality of Christ who gave his life for the salvation of all.

A reading from the second Letter of Saint Paul
to the Corinthians

Bʀᴏᴛʜᴇʀs and sisters: As you excel in every respect, in faith, discourse, knowledge, all earnestness, and in the love we have for you, may you excel in this gracious act also.

For you know the gracious act of our Lord Jesus Christ, that though he was rich, for your sake he became poor, so that by his poverty you might become rich. Not that others should have relief while you are burdened, but that as a matter of equality your abundance at the present time should supply their needs, so that their abundance may also supply your needs, that there may be equality. As it is written:

Whoever had much did not have more,
    and whoever had little did not have less.

The word of the Lord. Rʹ. **Thanks be to God.** ↓

ALLELUIA Cf. 2 Tm 1:10   [Christ the Life]

℟. **Alleluia, alleluia.**
Our Savior Jesus Christ destroyed death
and brought life to light through the Gospel.
℟. **Alleluia, alleluia.** ↓

GOSPEL Mk 5:21-43 or 5:21-24, 35-43   [New Life in Christ]

Jesus overcomes the death of Jairus's daughter and the ailment of the woman with the hemorrhage. He thus prefigures his victory over the death of alienation from God. Jesus is the Prophet of the end-time who has come to bring life, in other words, to restore our relationship of love with God.

[If the Shorter Form is used, the indented text in brackets is omitted.]

℣. The Lord be with you. ℟. **And with your spirit.**
✛ A reading from the holy Gospel according to Mark.
℟. **Glory to you, O Lord.**

WHEN Jesus had crossed again in the boat to the other side, a large crowd gathered around him, and he stayed close to the sea. One of the synagogue officials, named Jairus, came forward. Seeing him he fell at his feet and pleaded earnestly with him, saying, "My daughter is at the point of death. Please, come lay your hands on her that she may get well and live." He went off with him, and a large crowd followed him and pressed upon him.

[There was a woman afflicted with hemorrhages for twelve years. She had suffered greatly at the hands of many doctors and had spent all that she had. Yet she was not helped but only grew worse. She had heard about Jesus and came up behind him in the crowd and touched his cloak. She said, "If I but touch his clothes, I shall be cured." Immediately her flow of blood dried up. She felt in her body that she was healed of her affliction. Jesus, aware at once that power had gone out from him, turned around in the crowd and asked, "Who has touched my clothes?" But his disciples said to Jesus, "You see how the crowd is pressing upon you, and yet you ask, 'Who touched me?'" And he looked around to see who had done it. The woman, realizing what had happened to her, approached in fear and trembling. She fell down before Jesus and told him the whole truth. He said to her, "Daughter, your faith has saved you. Go in peace and be cured of your affliction."]

While he was still speaking, people from the synagogue official's house arrived and said, "Your daughter has died; why trouble the teacher any longer?" Disregarding the message that was reported, Jesus said to the synagogue official, "Do not be afraid; just have faith." He did not allow anyone to accompany him inside except Peter, James, and John, the brother of James. When they arrived at the house of the synagogue official, he caught sight of a commotion, people weeping and wailing loudly. So he went in and said to them, "Why this commotion and weeping? The child is not dead but asleep." And they ridiculed him. Then he put them all out. He took along the child's father and mother and those who were with him and entered the room where the child was. He took the child by the hand and said to her, *"Talitha koum,"* which means, "Little girl, I say to you, arise!" The girl, a child of twelve, arose immediately and walked around. At that they were utterly astounded. He gave strict orders that no one should know this and said that she should be given something to eat.—The Gospel of the Lord. ℟.
Praise to you, Lord Jesus Christ.   → No. 15, p. 18

PRAYER OVER THE OFFERINGS   [Serving God]

O God, who graciously accomplish
the effects of your mysteries,
grant, we pray,
that the deeds by which we serve you
may be worthy of these sacred gifts.
Through Christ our Lord.
℟. **Amen.**   → No. 21, p. 22 (Pref. P 29-36)

COMMUNION ANT. Cf. Ps 103 (102):1   [Bless the Lord]

**Bless the Lord, O my soul, and all within me, his holy
name.** ↓

OR Jn 17:20-21   [One in God]

**O Father, I pray for them, that they may be one in us,
that the world may believe that you have sent me, says
the Lord.** ↓

PRAYER AFTER COMMUNION   [Lasting Charity]

May this divine sacrifice we have offered and received
fill us with life, O Lord, we pray,
so that, bound to you in lasting charity,
we may bear fruit that lasts for ever.
Through Christ our Lord.
℟. **Amen.**   → No. 30, p. 77

Optional Solemn Blessings, p. 97, and Prayers over the People, p. 105

"A prophet is not without honor except in his native place."

JULY 4

14th SUNDAY IN ORDINARY TIME

ENTRANCE ANT. Cf. Ps 48 (47):10-11 [God's Love and Justice]

Your merciful love, O God, we have received in the midst of your temple. Your praise, O God, like your name, reaches the ends of the earth; your right hand is filled with saving justice.　　→ No. 2, p. 10

COLLECT　　　　　　　　　　　　　　　　　[Holy Joy]

O God, who in the abasement of your Son
have raised up a fallen world,
fill your faithful with holy joy,
for on those you have rescued from slavery to sin
you bestow eternal gladness.
Through our Lord Jesus Christ, your Son,
who lives and reigns with you in the unity of the Holy
　　Spirit,
one God, for ever and ever. ℟. **Amen.** ↓

FIRST READING Ez 2:2-5　　　　　　　　　[God's Prophet]

Ezekiel is selected by God to be a prophet and messenger
to the Israelites. When resisted, Ezekiel is to say: "Thus

says the Lord GOD!" In this way they shall see that he is a prophet.

A reading from the Book of the Prophet Ezekiel

AS the LORD spoke to me, the spirit entered into me and set me on my feet, and I heard the one who was speaking say to me: Son of man, I am sending you to the Israelites, rebels who have rebelled against me; they and their ancestors have revolted against me to this very day. Hard of face and obstinate of heart are they to whom I am sending you. But you shall say to them: Thus says the Lord GOD! And whether they heed or resist—for they are a rebellious house—they shall know that a prophet has been among them.—The word of the Lord. ℟. **Thanks be to God.** ↓

RESPONSORIAL PSALM Ps 123   [Eyes on God]

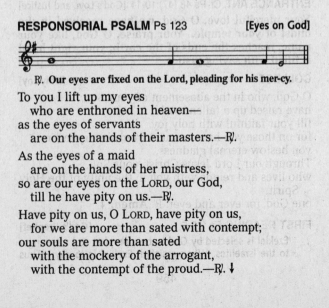

℟. **Our eyes are fixed on the Lord, pleading for his mer-cy.**

To you I lift up my eyes
   who are enthroned in heaven—
as the eyes of servants
   are on the hands of their masters.—℟.

As the eyes of a maid
   are on the hands of her mistress,
so are our eyes on the LORD, our God,
   till he have pity on us.—℟.

Have pity on us, O LORD, have pity on us,
   for we are more than sated with contempt;
our souls are more than sated
   with the mockery of the arrogant,
   with the contempt of the proud.—℟. ↓

SECOND READING 2 Cor 12:7-10   [Suffering for Christ]

Paul is given a "thorn in the flesh." He asks God for relief and God replies that his grace is sufficient.

A reading from the second Letter of Saint Paul
to the Corinthians

Brothers and sisters: That I, Paul, might not become too elated, because of the abundance of the revelations, a thorn in the flesh was given to me, an angel of Satan, to beat me, to keep me from being too elated. Three times I begged the Lord about this, that it might leave me, but he said to me, "My grace is sufficient for you, for power is made perfect in weakness." I will rather boast most gladly of my weaknesses, in order that the power of Christ may dwell with me. Therefore, I am content with weaknesses, insults, hardships, persecutions, and constraints, for the sake of Christ; for when I am weak, then I am strong.—The word of the Lord. ℟. **Thanks be to God.** ↓

ALLELUIA Cf. Lk 4:18   [God's Spirit]

℟. **Alleluia, alleluia.**
The Spirit of the Lord is upon me
for he sent me to bring glad tidings to the poor.
℟. **Alleluia, alleluia.** ↓

GOSPEL Mk 6:1-6   [Spreading the Good News]

Jesus began to teach in his home synagogue. The people, knowing Mary and Joseph, cannot understand the wisdom Jesus shows and Jesus tells them: "A prophet is not without honor except in his native place."

℣. The Lord be with you. ℟. **And with your spirit.**
✝ A reading from the holy Gospel according to Mark.
℟. **Glory to you, O Lord.**

Jesus departed from there and came to his native place, accompanied by his disciples. When the sabbath came he began to teach in the synagogue, and many who heard him were astonished. They said, "Where did this man get all this? What kind of wisdom has been given him? What mighty deeds are wrought by his hands! Is he not the carpenter, the son of Mary, and the brother of James and Joses and Judas and Simon? And are not his sisters here with us?" And they took offense at him. Jesus said to them, "A prophet is not without honor except in his native place and among his own kin and in his own house." So he was not able to perform any mighty deed there, apart from curing a few sick people by laying his hands on them. He was amazed at their lack of faith.—The Gospel of the Lord. ℞. **Praise to you, Lord Jesus Christ.**   ➜ No. 15, p. 18

PRAYER OVER THE OFFERINGS   [Purify Us]

May this oblation dedicated to your name
purify us, O Lord,
and day by day bring our conduct
closer to the life of heaven.
Through Christ our Lord.
℞. **Amen.**   ➜ No. 21, p. 22 (Pref. P 29-36)

COMMUNION ANT. Ps 34 (33):9   [The Lord's Goodness]

Taste and see that the Lord is good; blessed the man who seeks refuge in him. ↓

OR Mt 11:28   [Refuge in God]

Come to me, all who labor and are burdened, and I will refresh you, says the Lord. ↓

PRAYER AFTER COMMUNION   [Salvation and Praise]

Grant, we pray, O Lord,
that, having been replenished by such great gifts,
we may gain the prize of salvation
and never cease to praise you.

Through Christ our Lord.
R̸. **Amen.**   → No. 30, p. 77

Optional Solemn Blessings, p. 97, and Prayers over the People, p. 105

*"Jesus summoned the Twelve and began to send them out
two by two."*

JULY 11

15th SUNDAY IN ORDINARY TIME

ENTRANCE ANT. Cf. Ps 17 (16):15   [God's Face]
**As for me, in justice I shall behold your face; I shall be
filled with the vision of your glory.**   → No. 2, p. 10

COLLECT   [Right Path]
O God, who show the light of your truth
to those who go astray,
so that they may return to the right path,
give all who for the faith they profess
are accounted Christians
the grace to reject whatever is contrary to the name of
  Christ
and to strive after all that does it honor.
Through our Lord Jesus Christ, your Son,

who lives and reigns with you in the unity of the Holy
Spirit,
one God, for ever and ever. ℟. **Amen.** ↓

FIRST READING Am 7:12-15   [God Makes a Prophet]

**Amos writes how he was chosen by God to go out and
prophesy to the people of Israel.**

A reading from the Book of the Prophet Amos

AMAZIAH, priest of Bethel, said to Amos, "Off with
you, visionary, flee to the land of Judah! There
earn your bread by prophesying, but never again
prophesy in Bethel; for it is the king's sanctuary and a
royal temple." Amos answered Amaziah, "I was no
prophet, nor have I belonged to a company of prophets;
I was a shepherd and a dresser of sycamores. The Lord
took me from following the flock, and said to me, Go,
prophesy to my people Israel."—The word of the Lord.
℟. **Thanks be to God.** ↓

RESPONSORIAL PSALM Ps 85   [The Lord's Salvation]

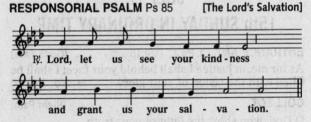

℟. **Lord, let us see your kind-ness
and grant us your sal-va-tion.**

I will hear what God proclaims;
    the Lord—for he proclaims peace.
Near indeed is his salvation to those who fear him,
    glory dwelling in our land.—℟.

Kindness and truth shall meet;
    justice and peace shall kiss.
Truth shall spring out of the earth,
    and justice shall look down from heaven.—℟.

The LORD himself will give his benefits;
  our land shall yield its increase.
Justice shall walk before him,
  and prepare the way of his steps.—R̂. ↓

SECOND READING Eph 1:3-14 or 1:3-10   [Christ's Headship]

God chose his followers to be holy, blameless, and filled with love—to be his adopted children in Jesus. In Jesus and through the seal of the Holy Spirit, full redemption shall come to humankind.

[If the "Shorter Form" is used, the indented text in brackets is omitted.]

A reading from the Letter of Saint Paul to the Ephesians

BLESSED be the God and Father of our Lord Jesus Christ, who has blessed us in Christ with every spiritual blessing in the heavens, as he chose us in him, before the foundation of the world, to be holy and without blemish before him. In love he destined us for adoption to himself through Jesus Christ, in accord with the favor of his will, for the praise of the glory of his grace that he granted us in the beloved.

In him we have redemption by his blood, the forgiveness of transgressions, in accord with the riches of his grace that he lavished upon us. In all wisdom and insight, he has made known to us the mystery of his will in accord with his favor that he set forth in him as a plan for the fullness of times, to sum up all things in Christ, in heaven and on earth.

  [In him we were also chosen, destined in accord with the purpose of the One who accomplishes all things according to the intention of his will, so that we might exist for the praise of his glory, we who first hoped in Christ. In him you also, who have heard the word of truth, the gospel of your salvation, and have believed in him, were sealed

with the promised holy Spirit, which is the first installment of our inheritance toward redemption as God's possession, to the praise of his glory.]
The word of the Lord. ℟. **Thanks be to God.** ↓

ALLELUIA Cf. Eph 1:17-18   [Our Great Hope]

℟. **Alleluia, alleluia.**
May the Father of our Lord Jesus Christ
enlighten the eyes of our hearts,
that we may know what is the hope
that belongs to our call.
℟. **Alleluia, alleluia.** ↓

GOSPEL Mk 6:7-13   [Spreading the Gospel]

Jesus sent out the Twelve, instructing them to take only a walking stick and to preach the gospel. If they were refused a listening ear, they should leave the locality. They worked many miracles.

℣. The Lord be with you. ℟. **And with your spirit.**
✛ A reading from the holy Gospel according to Mark.
℟. **Glory to you, O Lord.**

JESUS summoned the Twelve and began to send them out two by two and gave them authority over unclean spirits. He instructed them to take nothing for the journey but a walking stick—no food, no sack, no money in their belts. They were, however, to wear sandals but not a second tunic. He said to them, "Wherever you enter a house, stay there until you leave. Whatever place does not welcome you or listen to you, leave there and shake the dust off your feet in testimony against them." So they went off and preached repentance. The Twelve drove out many demons, and they anointed with oil many who were sick and cured them.—The Gospel of the Lord. ℟. **Praise to you, Lord Jesus Christ.**   → No. 15, p. 18

PRAYER OVER THE OFFERINGS   [Greater Holiness]

Look upon the offerings of the Church, O Lord,
as she makes her prayer to you,
and grant that, when consumed by those who believe,
they may bring ever greater holiness.
Through Christ our Lord.
℞. **Amen.**   ➙ No. 21, p. 22 (Pref. P 29-36)

COMMUNION ANT. Cf. Ps 84 (83):4-5   [The Lord's House]

**The sparrow finds a home, and the swallow a nest for
her young: by your altars, O Lord of hosts, my King
and my God. Blessed are they who dwell in your
house, for ever singing your praise.** ↓

OR Jn 6:57   [Remain in Jesus]

**Whoever eats my flesh and drinks my blood remains
in me and I in him, says the Lord.** ↓

PRAYER AFTER COMMUNION   [Saving Effects]

Having consumed these gifts, we pray, O Lord,
that, by our participation in this mystery,
its saving effects upon us may grow.
Through Christ our Lord.
℞. **Amen.**   ➙ No. 30, p. 77

Optional Solemn Blessings, p. 97, and Prayers over the People, p. 105

"[Jesus and the disciples] went off in the boat by themselves."

JULY 18

16th SUNDAY IN ORDINARY TIME

ENTRANCE ANT. Ps 54 (53):6, 8   [God Our Help]

See, I have God for my help. The Lord sustains my soul.
I will sacrifice to you with willing heart, and praise your
name, O Lord, for it is good.   ➔ No. 2, p. 10

COLLECT   [Keeping God's Commands]

Show favor, O Lord, to your servants
and mercifully increase the gifts of your grace,
that, made fervent in hope, faith and charity,
they may be ever watchful in keeping your commands.
Through our Lord Jesus Christ, your Son,
who lives and reigns with you in the unity of the Holy
    Spirit,
one God, for ever and ever. ℟. **Amen.** ↓

FIRST READING Jer 23:1-6   [A True Shepherd]

Woe to those who sow evil. Their evil deeds will be punished. Good shepherds will be appointed. There will come
a shoot to David in whose days Judah will be saved.

A reading from the Book of the Prophet Jeremiah

468

WOE to the shepherds who mislead and scatter the flock of my pasture, says the LORD. Therefore, thus says the LORD, the God of Israel, against the shepherds who shepherd my people: You have scattered my sheep and driven them away. You have not cared for them, but I will take care to punish your evil deeds. I myself will gather the remnant of my flock from all the lands to which I have driven them and bring them back to their meadow; there they shall increase and multiply. I will appoint shepherds for them who will shepherd them so that they need no longer fear and tremble; and none shall be missing, says the LORD.

Behold, the days are coming, says the LORD,
    when I will raise up a righteous shoot to David;
as king he shall reign and govern wisely,
    he shall do what is just and right in the land.
In his days Judah shall be saved,
    Israel shall dwell in security.
This is the name they give him:
    "The LORD our justice."
The word of the Lord. ℞. **Thanks be to God.** ↓

RESPONSORIAL PSALM Ps 23   [The Lord as Shepherd]

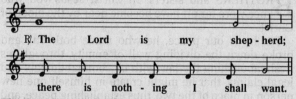

℞. The Lord is my shep - herd;
there is noth - ing I shall want.

The LORD is my shepherd; I shall not want.
    In verdant pastures he gives me repose;
beside restful waters he leads me;
    he refreshes my soul.—℞.

He guides me in right paths
    for his name's sake.

Even though I walk in the dark valley
   I fear no evil; for you are at my side
with your rod and your staff
   that give me courage.

℟. **The Lord is my shepherd; there is nothing I shall want.**

You spread the table before me
   in the sight of my foes;
you anoint my head with oil;
   my cup overflows.—℟.

Only goodness and kindness follow me
   all the days of my life;
and I shall dwell in the house of the LORD
   for years to come.—℟. ↓

SECOND READING Eph 2:13-18   [Access to the Father]
Paul tells the Ephesians that Christ has brought them together. Jesus has brought peace and reconciliation through his cross.

A reading from the Letter of Saint Paul to the
Ephesians

B ROTHERS and sisters: In Christ Jesus you who once were far off have become near by the blood of Christ.

For he is our peace, he who made both one and broke down the dividing wall of enmity, through his flesh, abolishing the law with its commandments and legal claims, that he might create in himself one new person in place of the two, thus establishing peace, and might reconcile both with God, in one body, through the cross, putting that enmity to death by it. He came and preached peace to you who were far off and peace to those who were near, for through him we both have access in one Spirit to the Father.—The word of the Lord. ℟. **Thanks be to God.** ↓

ALLELUIA Jn 10:27   [God's Sheep]

℟. **Alleluia, alleluia.**

My sheep hear my voice, says the Lord;

I know them, and they follow me.

℟. **Alleluia, alleluia.** ↓

GOSPEL Mk 6:30-34   [Jesus the Shepherd]

Jesus called the apostles aside to rest. Still the people came, so Jesus and the apostles went to a deserted place. Yet the people came.

℣. The Lord be with you. ℟. **And with your spirit.**

✛ A reading from the holy Gospel according to Mark.

℟. **Glory to you, O Lord.**

THE apostles gathered together with Jesus and reported all they had done and taught. He said to them, "Come away by yourselves to a deserted place and rest a while." People were coming and going in great numbers, and they had no opportunity even to eat. So they went off in the boat by themselves to a deserted place. People saw them leaving and many came to know about it. They hastened there on foot from all the towns and arrived at the place before them.

When he disembarked and saw the vast crowd, his heart was moved with pity for them, for they were like sheep without a shepherd; and he began to teach them many things.—The Gospel of the Lord. ℟. **Praise to you, Lord Jesus Christ.**   → No. 15, p. 18

PRAYER OVER THE OFFERINGS   [Saving Offerings]

O God, who in the one perfect sacrifice

brought to completion varied offerings of the law,

accept, we pray, this sacrifice from your faithful
    servants

and make it holy, as you blessed the gifts of Abel,

so that what each has offered to the honor of your
　majesty
may benefit the salvation of all.
Through Christ our Lord.
℟. **Amen.**   → No. 21, p. 22 (Pref. P 29-36)

COMMUNION ANT. Ps 111 (110):4-5   [Jesus Gives]

**The Lord, the gracious, the merciful, has made a
memorial of his wonders; he gives food to those who
fear him. ↓**

OR Rev 3:20   [Jesus Knocks]

**Behold, I stand at the door and knock, says the Lord.
If anyone hears my voice and opens the door to me, I
will enter his house and dine with him, and he with
me. ↓**

PRAYER AFTER COMMUNION   [New Life]

Graciously be present to your people, we pray, O Lord,
and lead those you have imbued with heavenly
　mysteries
to pass from former ways to newness of life.
Through Christ our Lord.
℟. **Amen.**   → No. 30, p. 77

Optional Solemn Blessings, p. 97, and Prayers over the People, p. 105

"Jesus took the loaves, gave thanks, and distributed them to those who were reclining."

JULY 25

17th SUNDAY IN ORDINARY TIME

ENTRANCE ANT. Cf. Ps 68 (67):6-7, 36 [God Our Strength]

God is in his holy place, God who unites those who dwell in his house; he himself gives might and strength to his people. → No. 2, p. 10

COLLECT [Enduring Things]

O God, protector of those who hope in you,
without whom nothing has firm foundation, nothing is
  holy,
bestow in abundance your mercy upon us
and grant that, with you as our ruler and guide,
we may use the good things that pass
in such a way as to hold fast even now
to those that ever endure.
Through our Lord Jesus Christ, your Son,
who lives and reigns with you in the unity of the Holy
  Spirit,
one God, for ever and ever. ℟. **Amen.** ↓

473

FIRST READING 2 Kgs 4:42-44   [Miracle of the Loaves]

> At the command from Elisha, the man of God, the barley bread was placed before the people, indicating that this comes from the Lord. Even though the number to be fed from the twenty loaves was a hundred, some was left over.

A reading from the second Book of Kings

A MAN came from Baal-shalishah bringing to Elisha, the man of God, twenty barley loaves made from the firstfruits, and fresh grain in the ear. Elisha said, "Give it to the people to eat." But his servant objected, "How can I set this before a hundred people?" Elisha insisted, "Give it to the people to eat. For thus says the LORD, 'They shall eat and there shall be some left over.' " And when they had eaten, there was some left over, as the LORD had said.—The word of the Lord.
℟. **Thanks be to God.** ↓

RESPONSORIAL PSALM Ps 145   [The Bounty of the Lord]

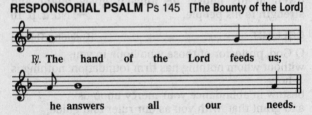

℟. The hand of the Lord feeds us; he answers all our needs.

Let all your works give you thanks, O LORD,
    and let your faithful ones bless you.
Let them discourse of the glory of your kingdom
    and speak of your might.—℟.

The eyes of all look hopefully to you,
    and you give them their food in due season;
you open your hand
    and satisfy the desire of every living thing.—℟.

The LORD is just in all his ways
  and holy in all his works.
The LORD is near to all who call upon him,
  to all who call upon him in truth.—℟. ↓

SECOND READING Eph 4:1-6   [Unity in the Spirit]

A life worthy of the Lord consists of humility, meekness, patience and bearing love for one another.

A reading from the Letter of Saint Paul to the
Ephesians

BROTHERS and sisters: I, a prisoner for the Lord, urge you to live in a manner worthy of the call you have received, with all humility and gentleness, with patience, bearing with one another through love, striving to preserve the unity of the spirit through the bond of peace: one body and one Spirit, as you were also called to the one hope of your call; one Lord, one faith, one baptism; one God and Father of all, who is over all and through all and in all.—The word of the Lord. ℟.
Thanks be to God. ↓

ALLELUIA Lk 7:16   [God's Prophet]

℟. **Alleluia, alleluia.**
A great prophet has risen in our midst.
God has visited his people.
℟. **Alleluia, alleluia.** ↓

GOSPEL Jn 6:1-15   [Multiplication of Loaves and Fish]

Jesus told the five thousand to sit down. He took the five barley loaves and a couple of dried fish, gave thanks and told the disciples to pass out the food.

℣. The Lord be with you. ℟. **And with your spirit.**
✠ A reading from the holy Gospel according to John.
℟. **Glory to you, O Lord.**

JESUS went across the Sea of Galilee. A large crowd followed him, because they saw the signs he was performing on the sick. Jesus went up on the mountain, and there he sat down with his disciples. The Jewish feast of Passover was near. When Jesus raised his eyes and saw that a large crowd was coming to him, he said to Philip, "Where can we buy enough food for them to eat?" He said this to test him, because he himself knew what he was going to do. Philip answered him, "Two hundred days' wages worth of food would not be enough for each of them to have a little." One of his disciples, Andrew, the brother of Simon Peter, said to him, "There is a boy here who has five barley loaves and two fish; but what good are these for so many?" Jesus said, "Have the people recline." Now there was a great deal of grass in that place. So the men reclined, about five thousand in number. Then Jesus took the loaves, gave thanks, and distributed them to those who were reclining, and also as much of the fish as they wanted. When they had had their fill, he said to his disciples, "Gather the fragments left over, so that nothing will be wasted." So they collected them, and filled twelve wicker baskets with fragments from the five barley loaves that had been more than they could eat. When the people saw the sign he had done, they said, "This is truly the Prophet, the one who is to come into the world." Since Jesus knew that they were going to come and carry him off to make him king, he withdrew again to the mountain alone.—The Gospel of the Lord. ℟. **Praise to you, Lord Jesus Christ.**   → No. 15, p. 18

PRAYER OVER THE OFFERINGS   [Sanctifying Mysteries]

Accept, O Lord, we pray, the offerings
which we bring from the abundance of your gifts,
that through the powerful working of your grace

these most sacred mysteries may sanctify our present
way of life
and lead us to eternal gladness.
Through Christ our Lord.
℟. **Amen.**   ➜ No. 21, p. 22 (Pref. P 29-36)

COMMUNION ANT. Ps 103 (102):2   [Bless the Lord]
**Bless the Lord, O my soul, and never forget all his
benefits.** ↓

OR Mt 5:7-8   [Blessed the Clean of Heart]
**Blessed are the merciful, for they shall receive mercy.
Blessed are the clean of heart, for they shall see God.** ↓

PRAYER AFTER COMMUNION   [Memorial of Christ]

We have consumed, O Lord, this divine Sacrament,
the perpetual memorial of the Passion of your Son;
grant, we pray, that this gift,
which he himself gave us with love beyond all telling,
may profit us for salvation.
Through Christ our Lord.
℟. **Amen.**   ➜ No. 30, p. 77

Optional Solemn Blessings, p. 97, and Prayers over the People, p. 105

"The bread of God . . . . comes down from heaven and gives life to the world."

AUGUST 1

18th SUNDAY IN ORDINARY TIME

ENTRANCE ANT. Ps 70 (69):2, 6   [God's Help]

O God, come to my assistance; O Lord, make haste to help me! You are my rescuer, my help; O Lord, do not delay.   → No. 2, p. 10

COLLECT   [God's Unceasing Kindness]

Draw near to your servants, O Lord,
and answer their prayers with unceasing kindness,
that, for those who glory in you as their Creator and
     guide,
you may restore what you have created
and keep safe what you have restored.
Through our Lord Jesus Christ, your Son,
who lives and reigns with you in the unity of the Holy
     Spirit,
one God, for ever and ever. ℟. **Amen.** ↓

FIRST READING Ex 16:2-4, 12-15   [Manna from Heaven]

The Israelites begin to grumble, and the Lord promises to rain down bread from heaven and give them quail to eat at twilight. In this they will know that the Lord is God.

A reading from the Book of Exodus

THE whole Israelite community grumbled against Moses and Aaron. The Israelites said to them, "Would that we had died at the LORD's hand in the land of Egypt, as we sat by our fleshpots and ate our fill of bread! But you had to lead us into this desert to make the whole community die of famine!"

Then the LORD said to Moses, "I will now rain down bread from heaven for you. Each day the people are to go out and gather their daily portion; thus will I test them, to see whether they follow my instructions or not.

"I have heard the grumbling of the Israelites. Tell them: In the evening twilight you shall eat flesh, and in the morning you shall have your fill of bread, so that you may know that I, the LORD, am your God."

In the evening quail came up and covered the camp. In the morning a dew lay all about the camp, and when the dew evaporated, there on the surface of the desert were fine flakes like hoarfrost on the ground. On seeing it, the Israelites asked one another, "What is this?" for they did not know what it was. But Moses told them, "This is the bread which the LORD has given you to eat."—The word of the Lord. ℟. **Thanks be to God.** ↓

RESPONSORIAL PSALM Ps 78   [Heavenly Bread]

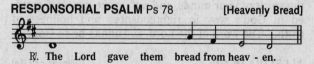

℟. The Lord gave them bread from heav - en.

What we have heard and know,
    and what our fathers have declared to us,

we will declare to the generation to come,
   the glorious deeds of the LORD and his strength
   and the wonders that he wrought.

℟. **The Lord gave them bread from heaven.**

He commanded the skies above
   and the doors of heaven he opened;
he rained manna upon them for food
   and gave them heavenly bread.—℟.

Man ate the bread of angels,
   food he sent them in abundance.
And he brought them to his holy land,
   to the mountain his right hand had won.—℟. ↓

SECOND READING Eph 4:17, 20-24   [A New Self]

**Paul tells the Ephesians that they must abandon their old
pagan ways and acquire a fresh, spiritual way of living—
to become new people created in God's image.**

A reading from the Letter of Saint Paul
to the Ephesians

BROTHERS and sisters: I declare and testify in the
Lord that you must no longer live as the Gentiles
do, in the futility of their minds; that is not how you
learned Christ, assuming that you have heard of him
and were taught in him, as truth is in Jesus, that you
should put away the old self of your former way of life,
corrupted through deceitful desires, and be renewed in
the spirit of your minds, and put on the new self, created in God's way in righteousness and holiness of
truth.—The word of the Lord. ℟. **Thanks be to God.** ↓

ALLELUIA Mt 4:4b   [Words of Life]
℟. **Alleluia, alleluia.**
One does not live on bread alone,

but on every word that comes forth from the mouth of
God.
℟. **Alleluia, alleluia.** ↓

GOSPEL Jn 6:24-35   [Christ, True Bread from Heaven]

After feeding the multitude, Jesus and his disciples went
across the lake. The people found them, and Jesus cau-
tioned them that they were looking only for signs and food
but the work of God demands faith in the One he sent.

℣. The Lord be with you. ℟. **And with your spirit.**
✚ A reading from the holy Gospel according to John.
℟. **Glory to you, O Lord.**

WHEN the crowd saw that neither Jesus nor his
disciples were there, they themselves got into
boats and came to Capernaum looking for Jesus. And
when they found him across the sea they said to him,
"Rabbi, when did you get here?" Jesus answered them
and said, "Amen, amen, I say to you, you are looking
for me not because you saw signs but because you ate
the loaves and were filled. Do not work for food that
perishes but for the food that endures for eternal life,
which the Son of Man will give you. For on him the
Father, God, has set his seal." So they said to him,
"What can we do to accomplish the works of God?"
Jesus answered and said to them, "This is the work of
God, that you believe in the one he sent." So they said
to him, "What sign can you do, that we may see and
believe in you? What can you do? Our ancestors ate
manna in the desert, as it is written:

He gave them bread from heaven to eat."
So Jesus said to them, "Amen, amen, I say to you, it was
not Moses who gave the bread from heaven; my Father
gives you the true bread from heaven. For the bread of
God is that which comes down from heaven and gives
life to the world."

So they said to him, "Sir, give us this bread always."
Jesus said to them, "I am the bread of life; whoever
comes to me will never hunger, and whoever believes
in me will never thirst."—The Gospel of the Lord. ℟.
Praise to you, Lord Jesus Christ.   → No. 15, p. 18

PRAYER OVER THE OFFERINGS   [Spiritual Sacrifice]

Graciously sanctify these gifts, O Lord, we pray,
and, accepting the oblation of this spiritual sacrifice,
make of us an eternal offering to you.
Through Christ our Lord.
℟. **Amen.**   → No. 21, p. 22 (Pref. P 29-36)

COMMUNION ANT. Wis 16:20   [Bread from Heaven]

**You have given us, O Lord, bread from heaven, endowed
with all delights and sweetness in every taste.** ↓

OR Jn 6:35   [Bread of Life]

**I am the bread of life, says the Lord; whoever comes
to me will not hunger and whoever believes in me will
not thirst.** ↓

PRAYER AFTER COMMUNION   [Heavenly Gifts]

Accompany with constant protection, O Lord,
those you renew with these heavenly gifts
and, in your never-failing care for them,
make them worthy of eternal redemption.
Through Christ our Lord.
℟. **Amen.**   → No. 30, p. 77

Optional Solemn Blessings, p. 97, and Prayers over the People, p. 105

"I am the bread of life."

AUGUST 8

19th SUNDAY IN ORDINARY TIME

ENTRANCE ANT. Cf. Ps 74 (73):20, 19, 22, 23

[Arise, O God]

Look to your covenant, O Lord, and forget not the life of your poor ones for ever. Arise, O God, and defend your cause, and forget not the cries of those who seek you. → No. 2, p. 10

COLLECT [Spirit of Adoption]

Almighty ever-living God,
whom, taught by the Holy Spirit,
we dare to call our Father,
bring, we pray, to perfection in our hearts
the spirit of adoption as your sons and daughters,
that we may merit to enter into the inheritance
which you have promised.
Through our Lord Jesus Christ, your Son,
who lives and reigns with you in the unity of the Holy
    Spirit,
one God, for ever and ever. ℟. **Amen.** ↓

FIRST READING 1 Kgs 19:4-8   [Supernatural Food]

Elijah, being discouraged, prayed for death. Twice an angel came to him and supplied him with food. Strengthened by food and the word of God, Elijah got up and continued his journey to the mountain of God, Horeb.

A reading from the first Book of Kings

ELIJAH went a day's journey into the desert, until he came to a broom tree and sat beneath it. He prayed for death, saying: "This is enough, O LORD! Take my life, for I am no better than my fathers." He lay down and fell asleep under the broom tree, but then an angel touched him and ordered him to get up and eat. Elijah looked and there at his head was a hearth cake and a jug of water. After he ate and drank, he lay down again, but the angel of the LORD came back a second time, touched him, and ordered, "Get up and eat, else the journey will be too long for you!" He got up, ate, and drank; then strengthened by that food, he walked forty days and forty nights to the mountain of God, Horeb.—The word of the Lord. ℟. **Thanks be to God.** ↓

RESPONSORIAL PSALM Ps 34   [Refuge in God]

℟. Taste and see   the goodness of   the Lord.

I will bless the LORD at all times;
    his praise shall be ever in my mouth.
Let my soul glory in the LORD;
    the lowly will hear me and be glad.—℟.

Glorify the LORD with me,
    let us together extol his name.
I sought the LORD, and he answered me
    and delivered me from all my fears.—℟.

Look to him that you may be radiant with joy,
    and your faces may not blush with shame.
When the afflicted man called out, the LORD heard,
    and from all his distress he saved him.—R̞.

The angel of the LORD encamps
    around those who fear him and delivers them.
Taste and see how good the LORD is;
    blessed the man who takes refuge in him.—R̞. ↓

SECOND READING Eph 4:30—5:2 [Imitating God's Goodness]

Paul directs the Ephesians to be kind, compassionate, and forgiving. They are to imitate God as his children and follow the way of love as Christ loved.

A reading from the Letter of Saint Paul to the Ephesians

B ROTHERS and sisters: Do not grieve the Holy Spirit of God, with which you were sealed for the day of redemption. All bitterness, fury, anger, shouting, and reviling must be removed from you, along with all malice. And be kind to one another, compassionate, forgiving one another as God has forgiven you in Christ.

So be imitators of God, as beloved children, and live in love, as Christ loved us and handed himself over for us as a sacrificial offering to God for a fragrant aroma.—The word of the Lord. R̞. **Thanks be to God.** ↓

ALLELUIA Jn 6:51   [Eternal Life]

R̞. **Alleluia, alleluia.**
I am the living bread that came down from heaven,
    says the Lord;
whoever eats this bread will live forever.
R̞. **Alleluia, alleluia.** ↓

GOSPEL Jn 6:41-51   [Jesus, the Living Bread]

The Jews question Jesus' origin, and Jesus tells them that no one can come to him unless drawn by the Father. Those who believe will have eternal life.

℣. The Lord be with you. ℟. **And with your spirit.**

✠ A reading from the holy Gospel according to John.

℟. **Glory to you, O Lord.**

THE Jews murmured about Jesus because he said, "I am the bread that came down from heaven," and they said, "Is this not Jesus, the son of Joseph? Do we not know his father and mother? Then how can he say, 'I have come down from heaven'?" Jesus answered and said to them, "Stop murmuring among yourselves. No one can come to me unless the Father who sent me draw him, and I will raise him on the last day. It is written in the prophets:

They shall all be taught by God.

Everyone who listens to my Father and learns from him comes to me. Not that anyone has seen the Father except the one who is from God; he has seen the Father. Amen, amen, I say to you, whoever believes has eternal life. I am the bread of life. Your ancestors ate the manna in the desert, but they died; this is the bread that comes down from heaven so that one may eat it and not die. I am the living bread that came down from heaven; whoever eats this bread will live forever; and the bread that I will give is my flesh for the life of the world."—The Gospel of the Lord. ℟. **Praise to you, Lord Jesus Christ.**   → No. 15, p. 18

PRAYER OVER THE OFFERINGS   [Mystery of Salvation]

Be pleased, O Lord, to accept the offerings of your Church,

for in your mercy you have given them to be offered

and by your power you transform them

into the mystery of our salvation.

Through Christ our Lord.

℟. **Amen.**   → No. 21, p. 22 (Pref. P 29-36)

COMMUNION ANT. Ps 147 (146):12, 14   [Glorify the Lord]

O Jerusalem, glorify the Lord, who gives you your fill of finest wheat. ↓

OR Cf. Jn 6:51 [The Flesh of Jesus]

The bread that I will give, says the Lord, is my flesh for the life of the world. ↓

PRAYER AFTER COMMUNION [Confirm Us in God's Truth]

May the communion in your Sacrament
that we have consumed, save us, O Lord,
and confirm us in the light of your truth.
Through Christ our Lord.
℟. **Amen.** → No. 30, p. 77

Optional Solemn Blessings, p. 97, and Prayers over the People, p. 105

"Alleluia. Mary is taken up to heaven."

AUGUST 15

THE ASSUMPTION OF THE BLESSED VIRGIN MARY

Solemnity

AT THE VIGIL MASS (August 14)

ENTRANCE ANT. [Mary Exalted]

Glorious things are spoken of you, O Mary, who today were exalted above the choirs of Angels into eternal triumph with Christ. → No. 2, p. 10

COLLECT   **[Crowned with Glory]**

O God, who, looking on the lowliness of the Blessed
   Virgin Mary,
raised her to this grace,
that your Only Begotten Son was born of her
   according to the flesh
and that she was crowned this day with surpassing
   glory,
grant through her prayers,
that, saved by the mystery of your redemption,
we may merit to be exalted by you on high.
Through our Lord Jesus Christ, your Son,
who lives and reigns with you in the unity of the Holy
   Spirit,
one God, for ever and ever. ℟. **Amen.** ↓

FIRST READING 1 Chr 15:3-4, 15-16; 16:1-2
                         [Procession of Glory]

**Under David's direction the Israelites brought the ark of
the Lord to the tent prepared for it. They showed great
respect for it. They offered holocausts and peace offerings.
This becomes a figure of Mary who bore the Son of God.**

A reading from the first Book of Chronicles

DAVID assembled all Israel in Jerusalem to bring the
ark of the LORD to the place which he had prepared
for it. David also called together the sons of Aaron and
the Levites.

The Levites bore the ark of God on their shoulders
with poles, as Moses had ordained according to the word
of the LORD.

David commanded the chiefs of the Levites to appoint
their kinsmen as chanters, to play on musical instruments, harps, lyres, and cymbals, to make a loud sound
of rejoicing.

They brought in the ark of God and set it within the
tent which David had pitched for it. Then they offered up

burnt offerings and peace offerings to God. When David had finished offering up the burnt offerings and peace offerings, he blessed the people in the name of the LORD.—The word of the Lord. ℟. **Thanks be to God.** ↓

RESPONSORIAL PSALM Ps 132   [Mary, Ark of God]

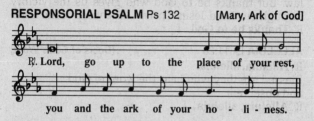

℟. Lord, go up to the place of your rest, you and the ark of your ho - li - ness.

Behold, we heard of it in Ephrathah;
  we found it in the fields of Jaar.
Let us enter into his dwelling,
  let us worship at his footstool.—℟.

May your priests be clothed with justice;
  let your faithful ones shout merrily for joy.
For the sake of David your servant,
  reject not the plea of your anointed.—℟.

For the LORD has chosen Zion;
  he prefers her for his dwelling.
"Zion is my resting place forever;
  in her will I dwell, for I prefer her."—℟. ↓

SECOND READING 1 Cor 15:54b-57   [Victory over Death]
Paul reminds the Corinthians that in life after death there is victory. Through his love for us, God has given victory over sin and death in Jesus, his Son.

A reading from the first Letter of Saint Paul
to the Corinthians

BROTHERS and sisters: When that which is mortal clothes itself with immortality, then the word that is written shall come about:

Death is swallowed up in victory.
Where, O death, is your victory?
Where, O death, is your sting?

The sting of death is sin, and the power of sin is the law. But thanks be to God who gives us the victory through our Lord Jesus Christ.—The word of the Lord. ℟. **Thanks be to God.** ↓

ALLELUIA Lk 11:28   [Doers of God's Word]
℟. **Alleluia, alleluia.**
Blessed are they who hear the word of God
and observe it.
℟. **Alleluia, alleluia.** ↓

GOSPEL Lk 11:27-28   [Keeping God's Word]

Mary's relationship as the mother of Jesus is unique in all of history. But Jesus reminds us that those who keep his word are most pleasing to God. In this Mary has set an example.

℣. The Lord be with you. ℟. **And with your spirit.**
✤ A reading from the holy Gospel according to Luke.
℟. **Glory to you, O Lord.**

WHILE Jesus was speaking, a woman from the crowd called out and said to him, "Blessed is the womb that carried you and the breasts at which you nursed." He replied, "Rather, blessed are those who hear the word of God and observe it."—The Gospel of the Lord. ℟. **Praise to you, Lord Jesus Christ.**   → No. 15, p. 18

PRAYER OVER THE OFFERINGS   [Sacrifice of Praise]

Receive, we pray, O Lord,
the sacrifice of conciliation and praise,
which we celebrate on the Assumption of the holy
    Mother of God,
that it may lead us to your pardon
and confirm us in perpetual thanksgiving.
Through Christ our Lord. ℟. **Amen.**
                    → Pref. P 59, p. 495

COMMUNION ANT. Cf. Lk 11:27   [Mary Carried Christ]

Blessed is the womb of the Virgin Mary, which bore the Son of the eternal Father. ↓

PRAYER AFTER COMMUNION   [Beseech God's Mercy]

Having partaken of this heavenly table,
we beseech your mercy, Lord our God,
that we, who honor the Assumption of the Mother of
    God,
may be freed from every threat of harm.
Through Christ our Lord.
℟. **Amen.**   → No. 30, p. 77

Optional Solemn Blessings, p. 97, and Prayers over the People, p. 105

AT THE MASS DURING THE DAY

ENTRANCE ANT. Cf. Rev 12:1   [Mary's Glory]

A great sign appeared in heaven: a woman clothed with the sun, and the moon beneath her feet, and on her head a crown of twelve stars.   → No. 2, p. 10

OR   [Joy in Heaven]

Let us all rejoice in the Lord, as we celebrate the feast day in honor of the Virgin Mary, at whose Assumption the Angels rejoice and praise the Son of God.
                                                → No. 2, p. 10

COLLECT   [Sharing Mary's Glory]

Almighty ever-living God,
who assumed the Immaculate Virgin Mary, the Mother
    of your Son,
body and soul into heavenly glory,
grant, we pray,
that, always attentive to the things that are above,

we may merit to be sharers of her glory.
Through our Lord Jesus Christ, your Son,
who lives and reigns with you in the unity of the Holy
    Spirit,
one God, for ever and ever. ℟. **Amen.** ↓

FIRST READING   Rv 11:19a; 12:1-6a, 10ab   [Mary, the Ark]

The appearance of the Ark in this time of retribution indicates that God is now accessible—no longer hidden, but
present in the midst of his people. Filled with hatred, the
devil spares no pains to destroy Christ and his Church. The
dragon seeks to destroy the celestial woman and her Son.
Its hatred is futile.

A reading from the Book of Revelation

GOD'S temple in heaven was opened, and the ark of
his covenant could be seen in the temple.

A great sign appeared in the sky, a woman clothed
with the sun, with the moon beneath her feet, and on
her head a crown of twelve stars. She was with child
and wailed aloud in pain as she labored to give birth.
Then another sign appeared in the sky; it was a huge
red dragon, with seven heads and ten horns, and on its
heads were seven diadems. Its tail swept away a third
of the stars in the sky and hurled them down to the
earth. Then the dragon stood before the woman about
to give birth, to devour her child when she gave birth.
She gave birth to a son, a male child, destined to rule all
the nations with an iron rod. Her child was caught up
to God and his throne. The woman herself fled into the
desert where she had a place prepared by God.

Then I heard a loud voice in heaven say:
    "Now have salvation and power come,
        and the Kingdom of our God
        and the authority of his Anointed One."
The word of the Lord. ℟. **Thanks be to God.** ↓

RESPONSORIAL PSALM Ps 45   [Mary the Queen]

℟. The queen stands at your right hand, ar-rayed in gold.

The queen takes her place at your right hand in gold
    of Ophir.—℟.

Hear, O daughter, and see; turn your ear,
    forget your people and your father's house.—℟.

So shall the king desire your beauty;
    for he is your lord.—℟.

They are borne in with gladness and joy;
    they enter the palace of the king.—℟. ↓

SECOND READING 1 Cor 15:20-27   [Christ the King]

**The offering of the firstfruits was the symbol of the dedication
of the entire harvest to God. So the Resurrection of Christ
involves the resurrection of all who are in him. Since his glorious Resurrection, Christ reigns in glory; he is the Lord.**

A reading from the first Letter of Saint Paul
to the Corinthians

BROTHERS and sisters: Christ has been raised from
the dead, the firstfruits of those who have fallen
asleep. For since death came through man, the resurrection of the dead came also through man. For just as in
Adam all die, so too in Christ shall all be brought to life,
but each one in proper order: Christ the firstfruits; then,
at his coming, those who belong to Christ; then comes the
end, when he hands over the Kingdom to his God and
Father, when he has destroyed every sovereignty and
every authority and power. For he must reign until he has
put all his enemies under his feet. The last enemy to be
destroyed is death, for "he subjected everything under his
feet."—The word of the Lord. ℟. **Thanks be to God.** ↓

ALLELUIA   [Mary in Heaven]

℟. **Alleluia, alleluia.**
Mary is taken up to heaven;
a chorus of angels exults.
℟. **Alleluia, alleluia.** ↓

GOSPEL Lk 1:39-56   [Blessed among Women]

Mary visits her kinswoman, Elizabeth. Mary's song of
thanksgiving, often called the "Magnificat," has been put
together from many Old Testament phrases.

℣. The Lord be with you. ℟. **And with your spirit.**
✛ A reading from the holy Gospel according to Luke.
℟. **Glory to you, O Lord.**

MARY set out and traveled to the hill country in
haste to a town of Judah, where she entered the
house of Zechariah and greeted Elizabeth. When
Elizabeth heard Mary's greeting, the infant leaped in
her womb, and Elizabeth, filled with the Holy Spirit,
cried out in a loud voice and said, "Blessed are you
among women, and blessed is the fruit of your womb.
And how does this happen to me, that the mother of my
Lord should come to me? For at the moment the sound
of your greeting reached my ears, the infant in my
womb leaped for joy. Blessed are you who believed that
what was spoken to you by the Lord would be fulfilled."
    And Mary said:
    "My soul proclaims the greatness of the Lord;
        my spirit rejoices in God my Savior
        for he has looked with favor upon his lowly servant.
    From this day all generations will call me blessed:
        the Almighty has done great things for me,
        and holy is his Name.
    He has mercy on those who fear him
        in every generation.

He has shown the strength of his arm,
    and has scattered the proud in their conceit.
He has cast down the mighty from their thrones,
    and has lifted up the lowly.
He has filled the hungry with good things,
    and the rich he has sent away empty.
He has come to the help of his servant Israel
    for he has remembered his promise of mercy,
    the promise he made to our fathers,
    to Abraham and his children for ever."

Mary remained with her about three months and then returned to her home.—The Gospel of the Lord.

℟. **Praise to you, Lord Jesus Christ.** → No. 15, p. 18

PRAYER OVER THE OFFERINGS   [Longing for God]

May this oblation, our tribute of homage,
rise up to you, O Lord,
and, through the intercession of the most Blessed
   Virgin Mary,
whom you assumed into heaven,
may our hearts, aflame with the fire of love,
constantly long for you.
Through Christ our Lord.
℟. **Amen.** ↓

PREFACE (P 59)   [Assumption—Sign of Hope]

℣. The Lord be with you. ℟. **And with your spirit.**
℣. Lift up your hearts. ℟. **We lift them up to the Lord.**
℣. Let us give thanks to the Lord our God. ℟. **It is right and just.**

It is truly right and just, our duty and our salvation,
always and everywhere to give you thanks,
Lord, holy Father, almighty and eternal God,
through Christ our Lord.

For today the Virgin Mother of God
was assumed into heaven

as the beginning and image
of your Church's coming to perfection
and a sign of sure hope and comfort to your pilgrim
    people;
rightly you would not allow her
to see the corruption of the tomb
since from her own body she marvelously brought forth
your incarnate Son, the Author of all life.

And so, in company with the choirs of Angels,
we praise you, and with joy we proclaim:

→ No. 23, p. 23

COMMUNION ANT. Lk 1:48-49   [Blessed Is Mary]

**All generations will call me blessed, for he who is
mighty has done great things for me.** ↓

PRAYER AFTER COMMUNION   [Mary's Intercession]

Having received the Sacrament of salvation,
we ask you to grant, O Lord,
that, through the intercession of the Blessed Virgin
    Mary,
whom you assumed into heaven,
we may be brought to the glory of the resurrection.
Through Christ our Lord.
℟. **Amen.**   → No. 30, p. 77

Optional Solemn Blessings, p. 97, and Prayers over the People, p. 105

"No one can come to me unless it is granted him by my Father."

AUGUST 22

21st SUNDAY IN ORDINARY TIME

ENTRANCE ANT. Cf. Ps 86 (85):1-3   **[Save Us]**

Turn your ear, O Lord, and answer me; save the servant who trusts in you, my God. Have mercy on me, O Lord, for I cry to you all the day long.   → No. 2, p. 10

COLLECT   **[One in Mind and Heart]**

O God, who cause the minds of the faithful
to unite in a single purpose,
grant your people to love what you command
and to desire what you promise,
that, amid the uncertainties of this world,
our hearts may be fixed on that place
where true gladness is found.
Through our Lord Jesus Christ, your Son,
who lives and reigns with you in the unity of the Holy
    Spirit,
one God, for ever and ever. ℞. **Amen.** ↓

FIRST READING Jos 24:1-2a, 15-17, 18b [Serving the Lord]

Joshua admonished the Israelites to decide their allegiance to God. They answered that they would serve the God of their fathers who delivered them from slavery and protected them.

A reading from the Book of Joshua

JOSHUA gathered together all the tribes of Israel at Shechem, summoning their elders, their leaders, their judges, and their officers. When they stood in ranks before God, Joshua addressed all the people: "If it does not please you to serve the LORD, decide today whom you will serve, the gods your fathers served beyond the River or the gods of the Amorites in whose country you are dwelling. As for me and my household, we will serve the LORD."

But the people answered, "Far be it from us to forsake the LORD for the service of other gods. For it was the LORD, our God, who brought us and our fathers up out of the land of Egypt, out of a state of slavery. He performed those great miracles before our very eyes and protected us along our entire journey and among all the peoples through whom we passed. Therefore we also will serve the LORD, for he is our God."—The word of the Lord. ℟. **Thanks be to God.** ↓

RESPONSORIAL PSALM Ps 34   [Refuge in God]

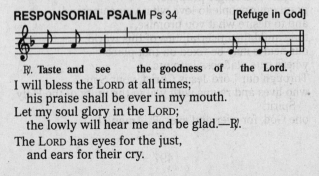

℟. **Taste and see   the goodness of   the Lord.**

I will bless the LORD at all times;
   his praise shall be ever in my mouth.
Let my soul glory in the LORD;
   the lowly will hear me and be glad.—℟.

The LORD has eyes for the just,
   and ears for their cry.

The LORD confronts the evildoers,
  to destroy remembrance of them from the earth.—℟.

When the just cry out, the LORD hears them,
  and from all their distress he rescues them.
The LORD is close to the brokenhearted;
  and those who are crushed in spirit he saves.—℟.

Many are the troubles of the just one,
  but out of them all the LORD delivers him;
he watches over all his bones;
  not one of them shall be broken.—℟. ↓

SECOND READING Eph 5:21-32 or 5:2a, 25-32

[Sacrament of Marriage]

**Paul gives specific directives to wives and husbands. Wives
are to be submissive to their husbands as the Church submits
to Christ. Husbands must love their wives as their own bodies. They are to be ever faithful to each other.**

*[If the "Shorter Form" is used, the indented text in brackets is
omitted.]*

A reading from the Letter of Saint Paul to the Ephesians

BROTHERS and sisters:
  [Be subordinate to one another out of reverence
  for Christ. Wives should be subordinate to their
  husbands as to the Lord. For the husband is head
  of his wife just as Christ is head of the church, he
  himself the savior of the body. As the church is
  subordinate to Christ, so wives should be subordinate to their husbands in everything.]
Live in love, as Christ loved us.* Husbands, love your
wives, even as Christ loved the church and handed
himself over for her to sanctify her, cleansing her by
the bath of water with the word, that he might present
to himself the church in splendor, without spot or
wrinkle or any such thing, that she might be holy and

*The words "Live . . . us" are said only in the Shorter Form.

without blemish. So also husbands should love their
wives as their own bodies. He who loves his wife loves
himself. For no one hates his own flesh but rather
nourishes and cherishes it, even as Christ does the
church, because we are members of his body.

> For this reason a man shall leave his father and his
>   mother
>   and be joined to his wife,
> and the two shall become one flesh.

This is a great mystery, but I speak in reference to
Christ and the church.—The word of the Lord. ℟.
Thanks be to God. ↓

ALLELUIA Jn 6:63c, 68c   [Living Words]

℟. **Alleluia, alleluia.**
Your words, Lord, are Spirit and life;
you have the words of everlasting life.
℟. **Alleluia, alleluia.** ↓

GOSPEL Jn 6:60-69   [Words of Life]

Jesus emphasizes that to believe in him demands faith—a
gift from his Father. Many left Jesus, but his Twelve turned
and said, "Master, to whom shall we go? You have the
words of eternal life."

℣. The Lord be with you. ℟. **And with your spirit.**
✛ A reading from the holy Gospel according to John.
℟. **Glory to you, O Lord.**

MANY of Jesus' disciples who were listening said,
"This saying is hard; who can accept it?" Since
Jesus knew that his disciples were murmuring about
this, he said to them, "Does this shock you? What if you
were to see the Son of Man ascending to where he was
before? It is the spirit that gives life, while the flesh is of

no avail. The words I have spoken to you are Spirit and life. But there are some of you who do not believe." Jesus knew from the beginning the ones who would not believe and the one who would betray him. And he said, "For this reason I have told you that no one can come to me unless it is granted him by my Father."

As a result of this, many of his disciples returned to their former way of life and no longer accompanied him. Jesus then said to the Twelve, "Do you also want to leave?" Simon Peter answered him, "Master, to whom shall we go? You have the words of eternal life. We have come to believe and are convinced that you are the Holy One of God."—The Gospel of the Lord. ℟. **Praise to you, Lord Jesus Christ.**   → No. 15, p. 18

PRAYER OVER THE OFFERINGS   [Unity and Peace]

O Lord, who gained for yourself a people by adoption through the one sacrifice offered once for all,
bestow graciously on us, we pray,
the gifts of unity and peace in your Church.
Through Christ our Lord.
℟. **Amen.**   → No. 21, p. 22 (Pref. P 29-36)

COMMUNION ANT. Cf. Ps 104 (103):13-15
[Sacred Bread and Wine]

The earth is replete with the fruits of your work, O Lord; you bring forth bread from the earth and wine to cheer the heart. ↓

OR Cf. Jn 6:54   [Eternal Life]

Whoever eats my flesh and drinks my blood has eternal life, says the Lord, and I will raise him up on the last day. ↓

PRAYER AFTER COMMUNION   [Pleasing God]

Complete within us, O Lord, we pray,
the healing work of your mercy
and graciously perfect and sustain us,
so that in all things we may please you.
Through Christ our Lord.
℟. **Amen.**   → No. 30, p. 77

Optional Solemn Blessings, p. 97, and Prayers over the People, p. 105

"Nothing that enters one from outside can defile that person."

AUGUST 29

22nd SUNDAY IN ORDINARY TIME

ENTRANCE ANT. Cf. Ps 86 (85):3, 5   [Call Upon God]
**Have mercy on me, O Lord, for I cry to you all the day
long. O Lord, you are good and forgiving, full of mercy
to all who call to you.**   → No. 2, p. 10

COLLECT   [God's Watchful Care]

God of might, giver of every good gift,
put into our hearts the love of your name,
so that, by deepening our sense of reverence,
you may nurture in us what is good
and, by your watchful care,
keep safe what you have nurtured.
Through our Lord Jesus Christ, your Son,
who lives and reigns with you in the unity of the Holy
    Spirit,
one God, for ever and ever. ℟. **Amen.** ↓

FIRST READING Dt 4:1-2, 6-8   [Observing God's Law]

Moses warns the people that they are not to add or subtract from the statutes and decrees of the Lord. God is
looking after them directly.

A reading from the Book of Deuteronomy

MOSES said to the people: "Now, Israel, hear the
    statutes and decrees which I am teaching you to
observe, that you may live, and may enter in and take
possession of the land which the LORD, the God of your
fathers, is giving you. In your observance of the commandments of the LORD, your God, which I enjoin
upon you, you shall not add to what I command you
nor subtract from it. Observe them carefully, for thus
will you give evidence of your wisdom and intelligence
to the nations, who will hear of all these statutes and
say, 'This great nation is truly a wise and intelligent
people.' For what great nation is there that has gods so
close to it as the LORD, our God, is to us whenever we
call upon him? Or what great nation has statutes and
decrees that are as just as this whole law which I am
setting before you today?"—The word of the Lord. ℟.
Thanks be to God. ↓

RESPONSORIAL PSALM Ps 15   [Practicing Justice]

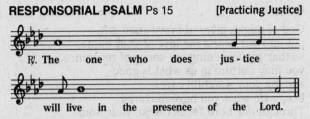

R. The one who does jus-tice will live in the presence of the Lord.

Whoever walks blamelessly and does justice;
　who thinks the truth in his heart
　and slanders not with his tongue.—R.

Who harms not his fellow man,
　nor takes up a reproach against his neighbor;
by whom the reprobate is despised,
　while he honors those who fear the LORD.—R.

Who lends not his money at usury
　and accepts no bribe against the innocent.
Whoever does these things
　shall never be disturbed.—R. ↓

SECOND READING Jas 1:17-18, 21b-22, 27
                 [Act on God's Word]
**Everything worthwhile comes from God. Christians should
welcome God's word, listen and act upon it.**

A reading from the Letter of Saint James

DEAREST brothers and sisters: All good giving and
every perfect gift is from above, coming down
from the Father of lights, with whom there is no alter-
ation or shadow caused by change. He willed to give
us birth by the word of truth that we may be a kind of
firstfruits of his creatures.

Humbly welcome the word that has been planted in
you and is able to save your souls.

Be doers of the word and not hearers only, deluding yourselves.

Religion that is pure and undefiled before God and the Father is this: to care for orphans and widows in their affliction and to keep oneself unstained by the world.— The word of the Lord. ℟. **Thanks be to God.** ↓

ALLELUIA Jas 1:18   **[Firstfruits]**

℟. **Alleluia, alleluia.**
The Father willed to give us birth by the word of truth, that we may be a kind of firstfruits of his creatures.
℟. **Alleluia, alleluia.** ↓

GOSPEL Mk 7:1-8, 14-15, 21-23 **[Sin Comes from the Heart]**
    Jesus condemned lip service. It is wicked thoughts from the heart that really make a person impure.

℣. The Lord be with you. ℟. **And with your spirit.**
✛ A reading from the holy Gospel according to Mark.
℟. **Glory to you, O Lord.**

WHEN the Pharisees with some scribes who had come from Jerusalem gathered around Jesus, they observed that some of his disciples ate their meals with unclean, that is, unwashed, hands.—For the Pharisees and, in fact, all Jews, do not eat without carefully washing their hands, keeping the tradition of the elders. And on coming from the marketplace they do not eat without purifying themselves. And there are many other things that they have traditionally observed, the purification of cups and jugs and kettles and beds.—So the Pharisees and scribes questioned him, "Why do your disciples not follow the tradition of the elders but instead eat a meal with unclean hands?" He responded, "Well did Isaiah prophesy about you hypocrites, as it is written:
    This people honors me with their lips,
        but their hearts are far from me;

in vain do they worship me,
teaching as doctrines human precepts.

You disregard God's commandment but cling to human tradition." He summoned the crowd again and said to them, "Hear me, all of you, and understand. Nothing that enters one from outside can defile that person; but the things that come out from within are what defile.

"From within people, from their hearts, come evil thoughts, unchastity, theft, murder, adultery, greed, malice, deceit, licentiousness, envy, blasphemy, arrogance, folly. All these evils come from within and they defile."—The Gospel of the Lord. ℟. **Praise to you, Lord Jesus Christ.**   ➡ No. 15, p. 18

PRAYER OVER THE OFFERINGS   [Blessing of Salvation]

May this sacred offering, O Lord,
confer on us always the blessing of salvation,
that what it celebrates in mystery
it may accomplish in power.
Through Christ our Lord.
℟. **Amen.**   ➡ No. 21, p. 22 (Pref. P 29-36)

COMMUNION ANT. Ps 31 (30):20   [God's Goodness]

How great is the goodness, Lord, that you keep for those who fear you.↓

OR Mt 5:9-10   [Blessed the Peacemakers]

Blessed are the peacemakers, for they shall be called children of God. Blessed are they who are persecuted for the sake of righteousness, for theirs is the Kingdom of Heaven. ↓

PRAYER AFTER COMMUNION   [Serving God in Neighbor]

Renewed by this bread from the heavenly table,
we beseech you, Lord,
that, being the food of charity,
it may confirm our hearts

and stir us to serve you in our neighbor.
Through Christ our Lord.
℟. **Amen.**   → No. 30, p. 77

Optional Solemn Blessings, p. 97, and Prayers over the People, p. 105

" 'Ephphatha!'—that is, 'Be opened!' "

SEPTEMBER 5

23rd SUNDAY IN ORDINARY TIME

ENTRANCE ANT. Ps 119 (118):137, 124   [Plea for Mercy]

You are just, O Lord, and your judgment is right; treat your servant in accord with your merciful love.

→ No. 2, p. 10

COLLECT   [Christian Freedom]

O God, by whom we are redeemed and receive adoption,
look graciously upon your beloved sons and daughters,
that those who believe in Christ
may receive true freedom
and an everlasting inheritance.
Through our Lord Jesus Christ, your Son,
who lives and reigns with you in the unity of the Holy
   Spirit,
one God, for ever and ever. ℟. **Amen.** ↓

FIRST READING Is 35:4-7a   [The Messiah's Coming]

Isaiah speaks of the Messiah's coming. At that time God will come to save his people and bring many blessings to them.

A reading from the Book of the Prophet Isaiah

THUS says the LORD:
Say to those whose hearts are frightened:
    Be strong, fear not!
Here is your God,
    he comes with vindication;
with divine recompense
    he comes to save you.
Then will the eyes of the blind be opened,
    the ears of the deaf be cleared;
then will the lame leap like a stag,
    then the tongue of the dumb will sing.
Streams will burst forth in the desert,
    and rivers in the steppe.
The burning sands will become pools,
    and the thirsting ground, springs of water.
The word of the Lord. ℟. **Thanks be to God.** ↓

RESPONSORIAL PSALM Ps 146   [The Lord's Saving Deeds]

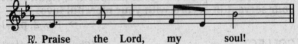

℟. **Praise   the   Lord,   my   soul!**
Or: ℟. **Alleluia.**

The God of Jacob keeps faith forever,
    secures justice for the oppressed,
    gives food to the hungry.
The LORD sets captives free.—℟.

The LORD gives sight to the blind;
    the LORD raises up those that were bowed down.
The LORD loves the just;
    the LORD protects strangers.—℟.

The fatherless and the widow the LORD sustains,
   but the way of the wicked he thwarts.
The LORD shall reign forever;
   your God, O Zion, through all generations.
   Alleluia.—R̸. ↓

SECOND READING Jas 2:1-5   [No Favoritism with God]

James warns the Christians about showing favoritism to
the rich. No one is in a position to judge. God chose those
who were poor according to worldly standards to become
rich in faith.

A reading from the Letter of Saint James

MY brothers and sisters, show no partiality as you
adhere to the faith in our glorious Lord Jesus
Christ. For if a man with gold rings and fine clothes
comes into your assembly, and a poor person in shab-
by clothes also comes in, and you pay attention to the
one wearing the fine clothes and say, "Sit here, please,"
while you say to the poor one, "Stand there," or "Sit at
my feet," have you not made distinctions among yourselves and become judges with evil designs?

   Listen, my beloved brothers and sisters. Did not God
choose those who are poor in the world to be rich in
faith and heirs of the kingdom that he promised to
those who love him?—The word of the Lord. R̸. **Thanks
be to God.** ↓

ALLELUIA Cf. Mt 4:23   [The Healer]

R̸. **Alleluia, alleluia.**
Jesus proclaimed the Gospel of the kingdom
and cured every disease among the people.
R̸. **Alleluia, alleluia.** ↓

GOSPEL Mk 7:31-37   [Cure of a Deaf-Mute]

The people brought to Jesus a deaf and dumb man to be
cured. Taking him aside, Jesus cured him, asking him to

keep this a secret. But the man proclaimed the cure all the
more. The people were amazed at this power.

℣. The Lord be with you. ℟. **And with your spirit.**
✠ A reading from the holy Gospel according to Mark.
℟. **Glory to you, O Lord.**

AGAIN Jesus left the district of Tyre and went by
way of Sidon to the Sea of Galilee, into the district
of the Decapolis. And people brought to him a deaf
man who had a speech impediment and begged him to
lay his hand on him. He took him off by himself away
from the crowd. He put his finger into the man's ears
and, spitting, touched his tongue; then he looked up to
heaven and groaned, and said to him, *"Ephphatha!"*—
that is, "Be opened!"—And immediately the man's ears
were opened, his speech impediment was removed,
and he spoke plainly. He ordered them not to tell anyone. But the more he ordered them not to, the more
they proclaimed it. They were exceedingly astonished
and they said, "He has done all things well. He makes
the deaf hear and the mute speak."—The Gospel of the
Lord. ℟. **Praise to you, Lord Jesus Christ.**

→ No. 15, p. 18

PRAYER OVER THE OFFERINGS   [True Prayer and Peace]

O God, who give us the gift of true prayer and of peace,
graciously grant that through this offering,
we may do fitting homage to your divine majesty
and, by partaking of the sacred mystery,
we may be faithfully united in mind and heart.
Through Christ our Lord.
℟. **Amen.**   → No. 21, p. 22 (Pref. P 29-36)

COMMUNION ANT. Cf. Ps 42 (41):2-3   [Yearning for God]

**Like the deer that yearns for running streams, so my
soul is yearning for you, my God; my soul is thirsting
for God, the living God.** ↓

OR Jn 8:12   [The Light of Life]

I am the light of the world, says the Lord; whoever follows me will not walk in darkness, but will have the light of life. ↓

PRAYER AFTER COMMUNION   [Word and Sacrament]

Grant that your faithful, O Lord,
whom you nourish and endow with life
through the food of your Word and heavenly
  Sacrament,
may so benefit from your beloved Son's great gifts
that we may merit an eternal share in his life.
Who lives and reigns for ever and ever.
℟. **Amen.**   → No. 30, p. 77

Optional Solemn Blessings, p. 97, and Prayers over the People, p. 105

*"Whoever wishes to come after me must deny himself,
take up his cross, and follow me."*

SEPTEMBER 12

24th SUNDAY IN ORDINARY TIME

ENTRANCE ANT. Cf. Sir 36:18   [God's Peace]

Give peace, O Lord, to those who wait for you, that
your prophets be found true. Hear the prayers of your
servant, and of your people Israel.   → No. 2, p. 10

COLLECT   [Serving God]

Look upon us, O God,
Creator and ruler of all things,
and, that we may feel the working of your mercy,
grant that we may serve you with all our heart.
Through our Lord Jesus Christ, your Son,
who lives and reigns with you in the unity of the Holy
   Spirit,
one God, for ever and ever. ℟. **Amen.** ↓

FIRST READING Is 50:5-9a   [The Lord Our Help]

Isaiah speaks of his sufferings, but God is his help and he
upholds him in misery.

A reading from the Book of the Prophet Isaiah

512

THE Lord GOD opens my ear that I may hear;
and I have not rebelled,
have not turned back.
I gave my back to those who beat me,
my cheeks to those who plucked my beard;
my face I did not shield
from buffets and spitting.

The Lord GOD is my help,
therefore I am not disgraced;
I have set my face like flint,
knowing that I shall not be put to shame.
He is near who upholds my right;
if anyone wishes to oppose me,
let us appear together.
Who disputes my right?
Let that man confront me.
See, the Lord GOD is my help;
who will prove me wrong?
The word of the Lord. ℟. **Thanks be to God.** ↓

RESPONSORIAL PSALM Ps 116   [Saved by God]

℟. I will walk be-fore the Lord,
in the land of the liv-ing.
Or: ℟. **Alleluia.**

I love the LORD because he has heard
my voice in supplication,
because he has inclined his ear to me
the day I called.—℟.

The cords of death encompassed me;
the snares of the netherworld seized upon me;
I fell into distress and sorrow,

and I called upon the name of the LORD,
"O LORD, save my life!"

℞. **I will walk before the Lord, in the land of the living.**

Or: ℞. **Alleluia.**

Gracious is the LORD and just;
yes, our God is merciful.
The LORD keeps the little ones;
I was brought low, and he saved me.—℞.

For he has freed my soul from death,
my eyes from tears, my feet from stumbling.
I shall walk before the LORD
in the land of the living.—℞. ↓

SECOND READING Jas 2:14-18   [Faith and Good Works]

Faith in words is dead; it must carry out into action. Words alone will not cover the naked nor bring food to the hungry.

A reading from the Letter of Saint James

WHAT good is it, my brothers and sisters, if someone says he has faith but does not have works? Can that faith save him? If a brother or sister has nothing to wear and has no food for the day, and one of you says to them, "Go in peace, keep warm, and eat well," but you do not give them the necessities of the body, what good is it? So also faith of itself, if it does not have works, is dead.

Indeed someone might say, "You have faith and I have works." Demonstrate your faith to me without works, and I will demonstrate my faith to you from my works.—The word of the Lord. ℞. **Thanks be to God.** ↓

ALLELUIA Gal 6:14   [The Triumphant Cross]

℞. **Alleluia, alleluia.**

May I never boast except in the cross of our Lord

through which the world has been crucified to me and
I to the world.
℟. **Alleluia, alleluia.** ↓

GOSPEL Mk 8:27-35   [Glorying In Christ's Cross]
> In answer to Jesus' question about himself, Peter acknowl-
> edges that Jesus is the Messiah. Jesus then tells of his
> future sufferings, death and resurrection. To follow him,
> we must take up our cross.

℣. The Lord be with you. ℟. **And with your spirit.**
✠ A reading from the holy Gospel according to Mark.
℟. **Glory to you, O Lord.**

JESUS and his disciples set out for the villages of
Caesarea Philippi. Along the way he asked his disciples, "Who do people say that I am?" They said in
reply, "John the Baptist, others Elijah, still others one
of the prophets." And he asked them, "But who do you
say that I am?" Peter said to him in reply, "You are the
Christ." Then he warned them not to tell anyone about
him.

He began to teach them that the Son of Man must
suffer greatly and be rejected by the elders, the chief
priests, and the scribes, and be killed, and rise after
three days. He spoke this openly. Then Peter took him
aside and began to rebuke him. At this he turned
around and, looking at his disciples, rebuked Peter and
said, "Get behind me, Satan. You are thinking not as
God does, but as human beings do."

He summoned the crowd with his disciples and said
to them, "Whoever wishes to come after me must deny
himself, take up his cross, and follow me. For whoever
wishes to save his life will lose it, but whoever loses his
life for my sake and that of the gospel will save it."—
The Gospel of the Lord. ℟. **Praise to you, Lord Jesus
Christ.**
➜ No. 15, p. 18

PRAYER OVER THE OFFERINGS   [Accept Our Offerings]

Look with favor on our supplications, O Lord,
and in your kindness accept these, your servants'
   offerings,
that what each has offered to the honor of your name
may serve the salvation of all.
Through Christ our Lord.
℟. **Amen.**   ➜ No. 21, p. 22 (Pref. P 29-36)

COMMUNION ANT. Cf. Ps 36 (35):8   [God's Mercy]

**How precious is your mercy, O God! The children of
men seek shelter in the shadow of your wings.** ↓

OR Cf. 1 Cor 10:16   [Share of Christ]

**The chalice of blessing that we bless is a communion
in the Blood of Christ; and the bread that we break is
a sharing in the Body of the Lord.** ↓

PRAYER AFTER COMMUNION   [Heavenly Gift]

May the working of this heavenly gift, O Lord, we pray,
take possession of our minds and bodies,
so that its effects, and not our own desires,
may always prevail in us.
Through Christ our Lord.
℟. **Amen.**   ➜ No. 30, p. 77

Optional Solemn Blessings, p. 97, and Prayers over the People, p. 105

"Whoever receives one child such as this in my name, receives me."

SEPTEMBER 19

25th SUNDAY IN ORDINARY TIME

ENTRANCE ANT.   [Salvation of People]

I am the salvation of the people, says the Lord. Should they cry to me in any distress, I will hear them, and I will be their Lord for ever.   → No. 2, p. 10

COLLECT   [Attaining Eternal Life]

O God, who founded all the commands of your sacred
   Law
upon love of you and of our neighbor,
grant that, by keeping your precepts,
we may merit to attain eternal life.
Through our Lord Jesus Christ, your Son,
who lives and reigns with you in the unity of the Holy
   Spirit,
one God, for ever and ever. ℟. **Amen.** ↓

FIRST READING Wis 2:12, 17-20   [The Just Are Persecuted]

The wicked detest the just one because the person of God
disturbs their conscience. They are anxious to do away

517

with the good, saying that God will care for them if they
are really his.

A reading from the Book of Wisdom

THE wicked say:
Let us beset the just one, because he is obnoxious
to us;
he sets himself against our doings,
reproaches us for transgressions of the law
and charges us with violations of our training.
Let us see whether his words be true;
let us find out what will happen to him.
For if the just one be the son of God, God will defend
him
and deliver him from the hand of his foes.
With revilement and torture let us put the just one to
the test
that we may have proof of his gentleness
and try his patience.
Let us condemn him to a shameful death;
for according to his own words, God will take care
of him.

The word of the Lord. ℟. **Thanks be to God.** ↓

RESPONSORIAL PSALM Ps 54   [God Our Helper]

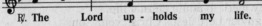

℟. The Lord up - holds my life.

O God, by your name save me,
and by your might defend my cause.
O God, hear my prayer;
hearken to the words of my mouth.—℟.

For the haughty have risen up against me,
the ruthless seek my life;
they set not God before their eyes.—℟.

Behold, God is my helper;
   the Lord sustains my life.
Freely will I offer you sacrifice;
   I will praise your name, O LORD, for its goodness.
   —R̸. ↓

SECOND READING Jas 3:16—4:3   [Avoiding Conflicts]

Wisdom begets innocence. It is peace-loving, kind, docile, impartial, and sincere. The inner cravings of human beings lead to murder, envy, and squandering.

A reading from the Letter of Saint James

BELOVED: Where jealousy and selfish ambition exist, there is disorder and every foul practice. But the wisdom from above is first of all pure, then peaceable, gentle, compliant, full of mercy and good fruits, without inconstancy or insincerity. And the fruit of righteousness is sown in peace for those who cultivate peace.

Where do the wars and where do the conflicts among you come from? Is it not from your passions that make war within your members? You covet but do not possess. You kill and envy but you cannot obtain; you fight and wage war. You do not possess because you do not ask. You ask but do not receive, because you ask wrongly, to spend it on your passions.—The word of the Lord. R̸. **Thanks be to God.** ↓

ALLELUIA Cf. 2 Thes 2:14   [Shared Glory]

R̸. **Alleluia, alleluia.**
God has called us through the Gospel
to possess the glory of our Lord Jesus Christ.
R̸. **Alleluia, alleluia.** ↓

GOSPEL Mk 9:30-37   [Service of Others]

Jesus tells his trusted disciples of his forthcoming sufferings, death and resurrection. Then he tells the Twelve about humility. To rank first, one must remain the last and be the servant of all.

℣. The Lord be with you. ℟. **And with your spirit.**
✚ A reading from the holy Gospel according to Mark.
℟. **Glory to you, O Lord.**

JESUS and his disciples left from there and began a
journey through Galilee, but he did not wish anyone
to know about it. He was teaching his disciples and
telling them, "The Son of Man is to be handed over to
men and they will kill him, and three days after his
death the Son of Man will rise." But they did not understand the saying, and they were afraid to question him.

They came to Capernaum and, once inside the
house, he began to ask them, "What were you arguing
about on the way?" But they remained silent. They had
been discussing among themselves on the way who
was the greatest. Then he sat down, called the Twelve,
and said to them, "If anyone wishes to be first, he shall
be the last of all and the servant of all." Taking a child,
he placed it in their midst, and putting his arms around
it, he said to them, "Whoever receives one child such as
this in my name, receives me; and whoever receives
me, receives not me but the One who sent me."—The
Gospel of the Lord. ℟. **Praise to you, Lord Jesus
Christ.**
→ No. 15, p. 18

PRAYER OVER THE OFFERINGS [Devotion and Faith]

Receive with favor, O Lord, we pray,
the offerings of your people,
that what they profess with devotion and faith
may be theirs through these heavenly mysteries.
Through Christ our Lord.
℟. **Amen.**
→ No. 21, p. 22 (Pref. P 29-36)

COMMUNION ANT. Ps 119 (118):4-5
[Keeping God's Statutes]
**You have laid down your precepts to be carefully kept;
may my ways be firm in keeping your statutes.** ↓

OR Jn 10:14   [The Good Shepherd]

I am the Good Shepherd, says the Lord; I know my sheep, and mine know me. ↓

PRAYER AFTER COMMUNION   [Possessing Redemption]

Graciously raise up, O Lord,
those you renew with this Sacrament,
that we may come to possess your redemption
both in mystery and in the manner of our life.
Through Christ our Lord.
℟. **Amen.**   → No. 30, p. 77

Optional Solemn Blessings, p. 97, and Prayers over the People, p. 105

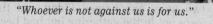

"Whoever is not against us is for us."

SEPTEMBER 26

26th SUNDAY IN ORDINARY TIME

ENTRANCE ANT. Dn 3:31, 29, 30, 43, 42   [God's Mercy]

All that you have done to us, O Lord, you have done with true judgment, for we have sinned against you and not obeyed your commandments. But give glory to your name and deal with us according to the bounty of your mercy.   → No. 2, p. 10

COLLECT   [God's Pardon]

O God, who manifest your almighty power
above all by pardoning and showing mercy,
bestow, we pray, your grace abundantly upon us
and make those hastening to attain your promises
heirs to the treasures of heaven.
Through our Lord Jesus Christ, your Son,
who lives and reigns with you in the unity of the Holy
    Spirit,
one God, for ever and ever. ℟. **Amen.** ↓

FIRST READING Nm 11:25-29   [Prophets Chosen by God]

The Lord empowered seventy elders with the gift of
prophecy. Eldad and Medad were absent but they also
received the gift. Some elders complained but Moses
replied that it would be even more wonderful if all the
people were prophets.

A reading from the Book of Numbers

THE Lord came down in the cloud and spoke to
Moses. Taking some of the spirit that was on Moses,
the Lord bestowed it on the seventy elders; and as the
spirit came to rest on them, they prophesied.

Now two men, one named Eldad and the other
Medad, were not in the gathering but had been left in
the camp. They too had been on the list, but had not
gone out to the tent; yet the spirit came to rest on them
also, and they prophesied in the camp. So, when a
young man quickly told Moses, "Eldad and Medad are
prophesying in the camp," Joshua, son of Nun, who
from his youth had been Moses' aide, said, "Moses, my
lord, stop them." But Moses answered him, "Are you
jealous for my sake? Would that all the people of the

LORD were prophets! Would that the LORD might bestow his spirit on them all!"—The word of the Lord.
℟. **Thanks be to God.** ↓

RESPONSORIAL PSALM Ps 19   [God's Law]

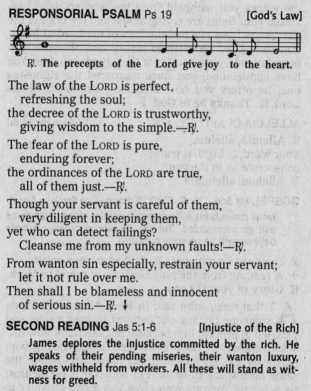

℟. **The precepts of the Lord give joy to the heart.**

The law of the LORD is perfect,
  refreshing the soul;
the decree of the LORD is trustworthy,
  giving wisdom to the simple.—℟.

The fear of the LORD is pure,
  enduring forever;
the ordinances of the LORD are true,
  all of them just.—℟.

Though your servant is careful of them,
  very diligent in keeping them,
yet who can detect failings?
  Cleanse me from my unknown faults!—℟.

From wanton sin especially, restrain your servant;
  let it not rule over me.
Then shall I be blameless and innocent
  of serious sin.—℟. ↓

SECOND READING Jas 5:1-6   [Injustice of the Rich]

James deplores the injustice committed by the rich. He speaks of their pending miseries, their wanton luxury, wages withheld from workers. All these will stand as witness for greed.

A reading from the Letter of Saint James

COME now, you rich, weep and wail over your impending miseries. Your wealth has rotted away, your clothes have become moth-eaten, your gold and silver have corroded, and that corrosion will be a testimony against you; it will devour your flesh like a fire. You have stored up treasure for the last days. Behold, the wages you withheld from the workers who harvested your fields are crying aloud; and the cries of the harvesters have reached the ears of the Lord of hosts. You have lived on earth in luxury and pleasure; you have fattened your hearts for the day of slaughter. You have condemned; you have murdered the righteous one; he offers you no resistance.—The word of the Lord. ℟. **Thanks be to God.** ↓

ALLELUIA Cf. Jn 17:17b, 17a   [Holy in the Truth]

℟. **Alleluia, alleluia.**
Your word, O Lord, is truth;
consecrate us in the truth.
℟. **Alleluia, alleluia.** ↓

GOSPEL Mk 9:38-43, 45, 47-48 [Everyone Can Proclaim Christ]

Jesus reminds his followers that nothing done in his name will go unrewarded. But anyone who deceives a simple believer will be severely punished.

℣. The Lord be with you. ℟. **And with your spirit.**
✠ A reading from the holy Gospel according to Mark.
℟. **Glory to you, O Lord.**

AT that time, John said to Jesus, "Teacher, we saw someone driving out demons in your name, and we tried to prevent him because he does not follow us." Jesus replied, "Do not prevent him. There is no one who performs a mighty deed in my name who can at the same time speak ill of me. For whoever is not against us is for us. Anyone who gives you a cup of water to drink because you belong to Christ, amen, I say to you, will surely not lose his reward.

"Whoever causes one of these little ones who believe in me to sin, it would be better for him if a great mill-

stone were put around his neck and he were thrown
into the sea. If your hand causes you to sin, cut it off. It
is better for you to enter into life maimed than with
two hands to go into Gehenna, into the unquenchable
fire. And if your foot causes you to sin, cut it off. It is
better for you to enter into life crippled than with two
feet to be thrown into Gehenna. And if your eye causes you to sin, pluck it out. Better for you to enter into
the kingdom of God with one eye than with two eyes
to be thrown into Gehenna, where 'their worm does
not die, and the fire is not quenched.' "—The Gospel of
the Lord. ℟. **Praise to you, Lord Jesus Christ.**

→ No. 15, p. 18

PRAYER OVER THE OFFERINGS   [Offering as a Blessing]

Grant us, O merciful God,
that this our offering may find acceptance with you
and that through it the wellspring of all blessing
may be laid open before us.
Through Christ our Lord.
℟. **Amen.**   → No. 21, p. 22 (Pref. P 29-36)

COMMUNION ANT. Cf. Ps 119 (118):49-50 [Words of Hope]

**Remember your word to your servant, O Lord, by
which you have given me hope. This is my comfort
when I am brought low.** ↓

OR 1 Jn 3:16   [Offering of Self]

**By this we came to know the love of God: that Christ
laid down his life for us; so we ought to lay down our
lives for one another.** ↓

PRAYER AFTER COMMUNION   [Coheirs with Christ]

May this heavenly mystery, O Lord,
restore us in mind and body,
that we may be coheirs in glory with Christ,
to whose suffering we are united

whenever we proclaim his Death.
Who lives and reigns for ever and ever.
℟. **Amen.**   → No. 30, p. 77

Optional Solemn Blessings, p. 97, and Prayers over the People, p. 105

*"A man shall leave his father and mother and be joined to
his wife, and the two shall become one flesh."*

OCTOBER 3

27th SUNDAY IN ORDINARY TIME

ENTRANCE ANT. Cf. Est 4:17   [Lord of All]
**Within your will, O Lord, all things are established,
and there is none that can resist your will. For you
have made all things, the heaven and the earth, and all
that is held within the circle of heaven; you are the
Lord of all.**   → No. 2, p. 10

COLLECT   [Mercy and Pardon]
Almighty ever-living God,
who in the abundance of your kindness
surpass the merits and the desires of those who
    entreat you,

pour out your mercy upon us
to pardon what conscience dreads
and to give what prayer does not dare to ask.
Through our Lord Jesus Christ, your Son,
who lives and reigns with you in the unity of the Holy
    Spirit,
one God, for ever and ever. ℟. **Amen.** ↓

FIRST READING Gn 2:18-24   [Man's Companion]

God, knowing that man needs companionship, created animals and birds and finally placed Adam in a deep sleep and took one of his ribs, forming a woman.

A reading from the Book of Genesis

THE LORD God said: "It is not good for the man to be alone. I will make a suitable partner for him." So the LORD God formed out of the ground various wild animals and various birds of the air, and he brought them to the man to see what he would call them; whatever the man called each of them would be its name. The man gave names to all the cattle, all the birds of the air, and all wild animals; but none proved to be the suitable partner for the man.

So the LORD God cast a deep sleep on the man, and while he was asleep, he took out one of his ribs and closed up its place with flesh. The LORD God then built up into a woman the rib that he had taken from the man. When he brought her to the man, the man said:

"This one, at last, is bone of my bones
    and flesh of my flesh;
this one shall be called 'woman,'
    for out of 'her man' this one has been taken."
That is why a man leaves his father and mother and clings to his wife, and the two of them become one flesh.—The word of the Lord. ℟. **Thanks be to God.** ↓

RESPONSORIAL PSALM Ps 128   [Fear of the Lord]

R̶). **May the Lord bless us   all the days of our lives.**

Blessed are you who fear the LORD,
  who walk in his ways!
For you shall eat the fruit of your handiwork;
  blessed shall you be, and favored.—R̶).

Your wife shall be like a fruitful vine
  in the recesses of your home;
your children like olive plants
  around your table.—R̶).

Behold, thus is the man blessed
  who fears the LORD.
The LORD bless you from Zion:
  may you see the prosperity of Jerusalem
  all the days of your life.—R̶).

May you see your children's children.
  Peace be upon Israel!—R̶). ↓

SECOND READING Heb 2:9-11   [Christ Our Brother]

To suffer, Jesus took a human body. In this way God made
our leader perfect through suffering, bringing salvation.
All who are consecrated have thereby a common Father
and become brothers and sisters.

A reading from the Letter to the Hebrews

BROTHERS and sisters: He "for a little while" was
made "lower than the angels," that by the grace of
God he might taste death for everyone.

For it was fitting that he, for whom and through
whom all things exist, in bringing many children to
glory, should make the leader to their salvation perfect
through suffering. He who consecrates and those who
are being consecrated all have one origin. Therefore,

he is not ashamed to call them "brothers."—The word of the Lord. ℞. **Thanks be to God.** ↓

ALLELUIA 1 Jn 4:12   [Love One Another]

℞. **Alleluia, alleluia.**
If we love one another, God remains in us
and his love is brought to perfection in us.
℞. **Alleluia, alleluia.** ↓

GOSPEL Mk 10:2-16 or 10:2-12   [Unity of Marriage]

The Pharisees, knowing the permission of Moses about divorce, test Jesus, but he recalls the reason for the command and reminds them of God's intention for the unity of marriage. Divorce followed by remarriage is adultery. (Jesus then speaks about his love for little children and their innocence.)

[If the "Shorter Form" is used, the indented text in brackets is omitted.]

℣. The Lord be with you. ℞. **And with your spirit.**
✠ A reading from the holy Gospel according to Mark.
℞. **Glory to you, O Lord.**

THE Pharisees approached Jesus and asked, "Is it lawful for a husband to divorce his wife?" They were testing him. He said to them in reply, "What did Moses command you?" They replied, "Moses permitted a husband to write a bill of divorce and dismiss her." But Jesus told them, "Because of the hardness of your hearts he wrote you this commandment. But from the beginning of creation, *God made them male and female. For this reason a man shall leave his father and mother and be joined to his wife, and the two shall become one flesh.* So they are no longer two but one flesh. Therefore what God has joined together, no human being must separate." In the house the disciples again questioned Jesus about this. He said to them, "Whoever divorces his wife and marries another commits adultery against her; and if she divorces her husband and marries another, she commits adultery."

[And people were bringing children to him that he might touch them, but the disciples rebuked them. When Jesus saw this he became indignant and said to them,"Let the children come to me; do not prevent them, for the kingdom of God belongs to such as these. Amen, I say to you, whoever does not accept the kingdom of God like a child will not enter it." Then he embraced them and blessed them, placing his hands on them.]

The Gospel of the Lord. ℟. **Praise to you, Lord Jesus Christ.**   ➙ No. 15, p. 18

PRAYER OVER THE OFFERINGS   [Sanctifying Work]

Accept, O Lord, we pray,
the sacrifices instituted by your commands
and, through the sacred mysteries,
which we celebrate with dutiful service,
graciously complete the sanctifying work
by which you are pleased to redeem us.
Through Christ our Lord.
℟. **Amen.**   ➙ No. 21, p. 22 (Pref. P 29-36)

COMMUNION ANT. Lam 3:25   [Hope in the Lord]

The Lord is good to those who hope in him, to the soul that seeks him. ↓

OR Cf. 1 Cor 10:17   [One Bread, One Body]

Though many, we are one bread, one body, for we all partake of the one Bread and one Chalice. ↓

PRAYER AFTER COMMUNION   [Nourished by Sacrament]

Grant us, almighty God,
that we may be refreshed and nourished
by the Sacrament which we have received,

so as to be transformed into what we consume.
Through Christ our Lord.
℟. **Amen.**   → No. 30, p. 77

Optional Solemn Blessings, p. 97, and Prayers over the People, p. 105

———————

*"Sell what you have, and give to the poor . . .
then come, follow me."*

OCTOBER 10

28th SUNDAY IN ORDINARY TIME

ENTRANCE ANT. Ps 130 (129):3-4   [A Forgiving God]

**If you, O Lord, should mark iniquities, Lord, who
could stand? But with you is found forgiveness, O God
of Israel.**   → No. 2, p. 10

COLLECT   [Good Works]

May your grace, O Lord, we pray,
at all times go before us and follow after
and make us always determined
to carry out good works.
Through our Lord Jesus Christ, your Son,

who lives and reigns with you in the unity of the Holy
  Spirit,
one God, for ever and ever. ℟. **Amen.** ↓

FIRST READING Wis 7:7-11   [Riches of Wisdom]

**To what can Wisdom be compared in value? She is above
all desires because in her all good things are found—
countless riches.**

A reading from the Book of Wisdom

I PRAYED, and prudence was given me;
  I pleaded, and the spirit of wisdom came to me.
I preferred her to scepter and throne,
and deemed riches nothing in comparison with her,
    nor did I liken any priceless gem to her;
because all gold, in view of her, is a little sand,
    and before her, silver is to be accounted mire.
Beyond health and comeliness I loved her,
and I chose to have her rather than the light,
    because the splendor of her never yields to sleep.
Yet all good things together came to me in her com-
    pany,
    and countless riches at her hands.
The word of the Lord. ℟. **Thanks be to God.** ↓

RESPONSORIAL PSALM Ps 90   [Filled with God's Love]

℟. **Fill us with your love, O Lord, and we will sing for joy!**

Teach us to number our days aright,
  that we may gain wisdom of heart.
Return, O LORD! How long?
  Have pity on your servants!—℟.

Fill us at daybreak with your kindness,
  that we may shout for joy and gladness all our days.

Make us glad, for the days when you afflicted us,
for the years when we saw evil.—Ṛ.

Let your work be seen by your servants
and your glory by their children;
and may the gracious care of the LORD our God be
ours;
prosper the work of our hands for us!
Prosper the work of our hands!—Ṛ. ↓

SECOND READING Heb 4:12-13   [God's Living Word]

God's word is penetrating and sharp. Nothing is hidden
from God, and all must render an account to him.

A reading from the Letter to the Hebrews

BROTHERS and sisters: Indeed the word of God is
living and effective, sharper than any two-edged
sword, penetrating even between soul and spirit, joints
and marrow, and able to discern reflections and
thoughts of the heart. No creature is concealed from
him, but everything is naked and exposed to the eyes
of him to whom we must render an account.—The
word of the Lord. Ṛ. **Thanks be to God.** ↓

ALLELUIA Mt 5:3   [Poor in Spirit]

Ṛ. **Alleluia, alleluia.**
Blessed are the poor in spirit,
for theirs is the kingdom of heaven.
Ṛ. **Alleluia, alleluia.** ↓

GOSPEL Mk 10:17-30 or 10:17-27   [All for God]

A rich man asks Jesus what he must do to be saved. Jesus
answers—keep the commandments. The man says that he
does. One thing more, then, Jesus lovingly continues—
sell what you have and give to the poor. The man left. Jesus
added how hard it is for a rich person to get to heaven.

*[If the "Shorter Form" is used, the indented text in brackets is
omitted.]*

℣. The Lord be with you. ℟. **And with your spirit.**

✠ A reading from the holy Gospel according to Mark.
℟. **Glory to you, O Lord.**

A S Jesus was setting out on a journey, a man ran
up, knelt down before him, and asked him, "Good
teacher, what must I do to inherit eternal life?" Jesus
answered him, "Why do you call me good? No one is good
but God alone. You know the commandments: *You shall
not kill; you shall not commit adultery; you shall not
steal; you shall not bear false witness; you shall not
defraud; honor your father and your mother.*" He replied
and said to him, "Teacher, all of these I have observed
from my youth." Jesus, looking at him, loved him and said
to him, "You are lacking in one thing. Go, sell what you
have, and give to the poor and you will have treasure in
heaven; then come, follow me." At that statement his face
fell, and he went away sad, for he had many possessions.

Jesus looked around and said to his disciples, "How
hard it is for those who have wealth to enter the kingdom
of God!" The disciples were amazed at his words. So
Jesus again said to them in reply, "Children, how hard it
is to enter the kingdom of God! It is easier for a camel to
pass through the eye of a needle than for one who is rich
to enter the kingdom of God." They were exceedingly
astonished and said among themselves, "Then who can
be saved?" Jesus looked at them and said, "For human
beings it is impossible, but not for God. All things are possible for God."

[Peter began to say to him, "We have given up everything and followed you." Jesus said, "Amen, I say to
you, there is no one who has given up house or
brothers or sisters or mother or father or children or
lands for my sake and for the sake of the gospel who
will not receive a hundred times more now in this
present age: houses and brothers and sisters and

mothers and children and lands, with persecutions,
and eternal life in the age to come."]

The Gospel of the Lord. R̸. **Praise to you, Lord Jesus
Christ.**   → No. 15, p. 18

PRAYER OVER THE OFFERINGS   [Devotedness]

Accept, O Lord, the prayers of your faithful
with the sacrificial offerings,
that, through these acts of devotedness,
we may pass over to the glory of heaven.
Through Christ our Lord.

R̸. **Amen.**   → No. 21, p. 22 (Pref. P 29-36)

COMMUNION ANT. Cf. Ps 34 (33):11   [God's Providence]

**The rich suffer want and go hungry, but those who
seek the Lord lack no blessing. ↓**

OR 1 Jn 3:2   [Vision of God]

**When the Lord appears, we shall be like him, for we
shall see him as he is. ↓**

PRAYER AFTER COMMUNION   [Christ's Divine Nature]

We entreat your majesty most humbly, O Lord,
that, as you feed us with the nourishment
which comes from the most holy Body and Blood of
    your Son,
so you may make us sharers of his divine nature.
Who lives and reigns for ever and ever.

R̸. **Amen.**   → No. 30, p. 77

Optional Solemn Blessings, p. 97, and Prayers over the People, p. 105

"To sit at my right or at my left is not mine to give."

OCTOBER 17

29th SUNDAY IN ORDINARY TIME

ENTRANCE ANT. Cf. Ps 17 (16):6, 8   [Refuge in God]

To you I call; for you will surely heed me, O God; turn
your ear to me; hear my words. Guard me as the apple
of your eye; in the shadow of your wings protect me.

→ No. 2, p. 10

COLLECT   [Sincerity of Heart]

Almighty ever-living God,
grant that we may always conform our will to yours
and serve your majesty in sincerity of heart.
Through our Lord Jesus Christ, your Son,
who lives and reigns with you in the unity of the Holy
    Spirit,
one God, for ever and ever. ℟. **Amen.** ↓

FIRST READING Is 53:10-11   [The Servant of Yahweh]

The suffering servant speaks of his life as a sin offering
that his people may prosper enjoying a long life. Through
his suffering he will bear the guilt of many.

536

A reading from the Book of the Prophet Isaiah

THE LORD was pleased
to crush him in infirmity.
If he gives his life as an offering for sin,
he shall see his descendants in a long life,
and the will of the LORD shall be accomplished
through him.

Because of his affliction
he shall see the light in fullness of days;
through his suffering, my servant shall justify many,
and their guilt he shall bear.
The word of the Lord. ℟. **Thanks be to God.** ↓

RESPONSORIAL PSALM Ps 33   [Trust in God]

℟. Lord, let your mercy be on us, as we place our trust in you.

Upright is the word of the LORD,
and all his works are trustworthy.
He loves justice and right;
of the kindness of the LORD the earth is full.—℟.

See, the eyes of the LORD are upon those who fear him,
upon those who hope for his kindness,
to deliver them from death
and preserve them in spite of famine.—℟.

Our soul waits for the LORD,
who is our help and our shield.
May your kindness, O LORD, be upon us,
who have put our hope in you.—℟. ↓

SECOND READING Heb 4:14-16   [Jesus Our High Priest]

Jesus Christ, the Son of God, is the high priest who shares all our weaknesses, except sin. His mercy comes to all who seek it.

A reading from the Letter to the Hebrews

BROTHERS and sisters: Since we have a great high priest who has passed through the heavens, Jesus, the Son of God, let us hold fast to our confession. For we do not have a high priest who is unable to sympathize with our weaknesses, but one who has similarly been tested in every way, yet without sin. So let us confidently approach the throne of grace to receive mercy and to find grace for timely help.—The word of the Lord. ℟. **Thanks be to God.** ↓

ALLELUIA Mk 10:45   [Divine Ransom]

℟. **Alleluia, alleluia.**
The Son of Man came to serve
and to give his life as a ransom for many.
℟. **Alleluia, alleluia.** ↓

GOSPEL Mk 10:35-45 or 10:42-45   [Greatness in Serving]

James and John request a special honor in the kingdom of heaven. Jesus reminds them and the other ten that anyone who aspires to greatness must be prepared to serve first.

[If the "Shorter Form" is used, the indented text in brackets is omitted.]

℣. The Lord be with you. ℟. **And with your spirit.**
✝ A reading from the holy Gospel according to Mark.
℟. **Glory to you, O Lord.**

[JAMES and John, the sons of Zebedee, came to Jesus and said to him, "Teacher, we want you to do for us whatever we ask of you." He replied, "What do you wish me to do for you?"

They answered him, "Grant that in your glory we may sit one at your right and the other at your left." Jesus said to them, "You do not know what you are asking. Can you drink the cup that I drink or be baptized with the baptism with which I am baptized?" They said to him, "We can." Jesus said to them, "The cup that I drink, you will drink, and with the baptism with which I am baptized, you will be baptized; but to sit at my right or at my left is not mine to give but is for those for whom it has been prepared." When the ten heard this, they became indignant at James and John.]

Jesus summoned the Twelve* and said to them, "You know that those who are recognized as rulers over the Gentiles lord it over them, and their great ones make their authority over them felt. But it shall not be so among you. Rather, whoever wishes to be great among you will be your servant; whoever wishes to be first among you will be the slave of all. For the Son of Man did not come to be served but to serve and to give his life as a ransom for many."—The Gospel of the Lord. ℟. **Praise to you, Lord Jesus Christ.**   ➙ No. 15, p. 18

PRAYER OVER THE OFFERINGS   [Respect Gifts]

Grant us, Lord, we pray,
a sincere respect for your gifts,
that, through the purifying action of your grace,
we may be cleansed by the very mysteries we serve.
Through Christ our Lord.
℟. **Amen.**   ➙ No. 21, p. 22 (Pref. P 29-36)

COMMUNION ANT. Cf. Ps 33 (32):18-19 [Divine Protection]
Behold, the eyes of the Lord are on those who fear him, who hope in his merciful love, to rescue their souls from death, to keep them alive in famine. ↓

---

* Only the Shorter Form has "the Twelve."

OR Mk 10:45   [Christ Our Ransom]
The Son of Man has come to give his life as a ransom for many. ↓

PRAYER AFTER COMMUNION   [Eternal Gifts]
Grant, O Lord, we pray,
that, benefiting from participation in heavenly things,
we may be helped by what you give in this present age
and prepared for the gifts that are eternal.
Through Christ our Lord.
℟. **Amen.**   → No. 30, p. 77

Optional Solemn Blessings, p. 97, and Prayers over the People, p. 105

"Jesus, son of David, have pity on me."

OCTOBER 24
30th SUNDAY IN ORDINARY TIME

ENTRANCE ANT. Cf. Ps 105 (104):3-4   [Seek the Lord]
Let the hearts that seek the Lord rejoice; turn to the Lord and his strength; constantly seek his face.
                                      → No. 2, p. 10

COLLECT [Increase Virtues]

Almighty ever-living God,
increase our faith, hope and charity,
and make us love what you command,
so that we may merit what you promise.
Through our Lord Jesus Christ, your Son,
who lives and reigns with you in the unity of the Holy
    Spirit,
one God, for ever and ever. ℟. **Amen.** ↓

FIRST READING Jer 31:7-9 [God's Deliverance]

Jeremiah's hymn opens with joy for God has bestowed salvation on his people. He has delivered his people and will
guide and bless them so none will go astray.

A reading from the Book of the Prophet Jeremiah

T HUS says the LORD:
    Shout with joy for Jacob,
    exult at the head of the nations;
        proclaim your praise and say:
The LORD has delivered his people,
    the remnant of Israel.
Behold, I will bring them back
    from the land of the north;
I will gather them from the ends of the world
    with the blind and the lame in their midst,
the mothers and those with child;
    they shall return as an immense throng.
They departed in tears,
    but I will console them and guide them;
I will lead them to brooks of water,
    on a level road, so that none shall stumble.
For I am a father to Israel,
    Ephraim is my first-born.
The word of the Lord. ℟. **Thanks be to God.** ↓

RESPONSORIAL PSALM Ps 126   [God's Mighty Works]

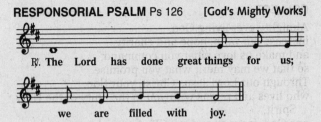

℟. The Lord has done great things for us;
we are filled with joy.

When the LORD brought back the captives of Zion,
    we were like men dreaming.
Then our mouth was filled with laughter,
    and our tongue with rejoicing.—℟.

Then they said among the nations,
    "The LORD has done great things for them."
The LORD has done great things for us;
    we are glad indeed.—℟.

Restore our fortunes, O LORD,
    like the torrents in the southern desert.
Those that sow in tears
    shall reap rejoicing.—℟.

Although they go forth weeping,
    carrying the seed to be sown,
they shall come back rejoicing,
    carrying their sheaves.—℟. ↓

SECOND READING Heb 5:1-6   [Christ the Mediator]

Every high priest is designated by God. He is selected from
among the people to be their mediator with God. No one
takes this honor by himself. •

A reading from the Letter to the Hebrews

BROTHERS and sisters: Every high priest is taken
from among men and made their representative
before God, to offer gifts and sacrifices for sins. He is

able to deal patiently with the ignorant and erring, for he himself is beset by weakness and so, for this reason, must make sin offerings for himself as well as for the people. No one takes this honor upon himself but only when called by God, just as Aaron was. In the same way, it was not Christ who glorified himself in becoming high priest, but rather the one who said to him:

> You are my son:
> this day I have begotten you;

just as he says in another place:

> You are a priest forever
> according to the order of Melchizedek.

The word of the Lord. ℟. **Thanks be to God.** ↓

ALLELUIA Cf. 2 Tm 1:10   [Divine Life]

℟. **Alleluia, alleluia.**
Our Savior Jesus Christ destroyed death
and brought life to light through his Gospel.
℟. **Alleluia, alleluia.** ↓

GOSPEL Mk 10:46-52   [Healing of a Blind Man]

Bartimaeus, a blind man, hearing Jesus called out loudly, "Jesus, son of David, have pity on me!" Jesus summoned him and, seeing his faith, cured him. Bartimaeus followed Jesus.

℣. The Lord be with you. ℟. **And with your spirit.**
✤ A reading from the holy Gospel according to Mark.
℟. **Glory to you, O Lord.**

A S Jesus was leaving Jericho with his disciples and a sizable crowd, Bartimaeus, a blind man, the son of Timaeus, sat by the roadside begging. On hearing that it was Jesus of Nazareth, he began to cry out and say, "Jesus, son of David, have pity on me." And many rebuked him, telling him to be silent. But he kept calling out all the more, "Son of David, have pity on me." Jesus stopped and said, "Call him." So they called the blind man,

saying to him, "Take courage; get up, Jesus is calling you."
He threw aside his cloak, sprang up, and came to Jesus.
Jesus said to him in reply, "What do you want me to do for
you?" The blind man replied to him, "Master, I want to
see." Jesus told him, "Go your way; your faith has saved
you." Immediately he received his sight and followed
him on the way.—The Gospel of the Lord. ℟. **Praise to
you, Lord Jesus Christ.**   → No. 15, p. 18

PRAYER OVER THE OFFERINGS   [Glorifying God]

Look, we pray, O Lord,
on the offerings we make to your majesty,
that whatever is done by us in your service
may be directed above all to your glory.
Through Christ our Lord.
℟. **Amen.**   → No. 21, p. 22 (Pref. P 29-36)

COMMUNION ANT. Cf. Ps 20 (19):6   [Saving Help]

**We will ring out our joy at your saving help and exult
in the name of our God. ↓**

OR Eph 5:2   [Christ's Offering for Us]

**Christ loved us and gave himself up for us, as a fra-
grant offering to God. ↓**

PRAYER AFTER COMMUNION   [Celebrate in Signs]

May your Sacraments, O Lord, we pray,
perfect in us what lies within them,
that what we now celebrate in signs
we may one day possess in truth.
Through Christ our Lord.
℟. **Amen.**   → No. 30, p. 77

Optional Solemn Blessings, p. 97, and Prayers over the People, p. 105

"You shall love your neighbor as yourself."

OCTOBER 31

31st SUNDAY IN ORDINARY TIME

ENTRANCE ANT. Cf. Ps 38 (37):22-23

[Call for God's Help]

Forsake me not, O Lord, my God; be not far from me!
Make haste and come to my help, O Lord, my strong
salvation! ➔ No. 2, p. 10

COLLECT [Praiseworthy Service]

Almighty and merciful God,
by whose gift your faithful offer you
right and praiseworthy service,
grant, we pray,
that we may hasten without stumbling
to receive the things you have promised.
Through our Lord Jesus Christ, your Son,
who lives and reigns with you in the unity of the Holy
    Spirit,
one God, for ever and ever. ℟. **Amen.** ↓

545

FIRST READING Dt 6:2-6   [Keeping the Commandments]

> Moses instructs the people to hold fast to the commandments of the Lord. In this way they shall love God and they will prosper in the Lord's favor.

A reading from the Book of Deuteronomy

MOSES spoke to the people, saying: "Fear the LORD, your God, and keep, throughout the days of your lives, all his statutes and commandments which I enjoin on you, and thus have long life. Hear then, Israel, and be careful to observe them, that you may grow and prosper the more, in keeping with the promise of the LORD, the God of your fathers, to give you a land flowing with milk and honey.

"Hear, O Israel! The LORD is our God, the LORD alone! Therefore, you shall love the LORD, your God, with all your heart, and with all your soul, and with all your strength. Take to heart these words which I enjoin on you today."—The word of the Lord. ℟. **Thanks be to God.** ↓

RESPONSORIAL PSALM Ps 18   [God Our Helper]

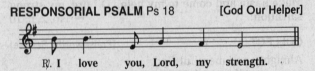

℟. I love you, Lord, my strength.

I love you, O LORD, my strength,
　O LORD, my rock, my fortress, my deliverer.—℟.

My God, my rock of refuge,
　my shield, the horn of my salvation, my stronghold!
Praised be the LORD, I exclaim,
　and I am safe from my enemies.—℟.

The LORD lives! And blessed be my rock!
　Extolled be God my savior,
you who gave great victories to your king
　and showed kindness to your anointed.—℟. ↓

SECOND READING Heb 7:23-28   [Jesus the High Priest]

Jesus has a priesthood that will not pass away. He is a high priest holy, innocent, undefiled, separated from sinners and higher than the heavens. He offered one sacrifice for sin.

A reading from the Letter to the Hebrews

BROTHERS and sisters: The levitical priests were many because they were prevented by death from remaining in office, but Jesus, because he remains forever, has a priesthood that does not pass away. Therefore, he is always able to save those who approach God through him, since he lives forever to make intercession for them.

It was fitting that we should have such a high priest: holy, innocent, undefiled, separated from sinners, higher than the heavens. He has no need, as did the high priests, to offer sacrifice day after day, first for his own sins and then for those of the people; he did that once for all when he offered himself. For the law appoints men subject to weakness to be high priests, but the word of the oath, which was taken after the law, appoints a son, who has been made perfect forever.—The word of the Lord. ℟. **Thanks be to God.** ↓

ALLELUIA Jn 14:23   [Love in Practice]

℟. **Alleluia, alleluia.**
Whoever loves me will keep my word, says the Lord;
and my Father will love him and we will come to him.
℟. **Alleluia, alleluia.** ↓

GOSPEL Mk 12:28-34   [Love for God and Neighbor]

Jesus describes the first commandment—the total love for God—and the second—love for neighbor.

℣. The Lord be with you. ℟. **And with your spirit.**
✛ A reading from the holy Gospel according to Mark.
℟. **Glory to you, O Lord.**

ONE of the scribes came to Jesus and asked him, "Which is the first of all the commandments?" Jesus replied, "The first is this: *Hear, O Israel! The Lord our God is Lord alone! You shall love the Lord your God with all your heart, with all your soul, with all your mind, and with all your strength.* The second is this: *You shall love your neighbor as yourself.* There is no other commandment greater than these." The scribe said to him, "Well said, teacher. You are right in saying, 'He is One and there is no other than he.' And 'to love him with all your heart, with all your understanding, with all your strength, and to love your neighbor as yourself' is worth more than all burnt offerings and sacrifices." And when Jesus saw that he answered with understanding, he said to him, "You are not far from the kingdom of God." And no one dared to ask him any more questions.—The Gospel of the Lord.

℟. **Praise to you, Lord Jesus Christ.**   → No. 15, p. 18

PRAYER OVER THE OFFERINGS   [God's Mercy]

May these sacrificial offerings, O Lord,
become for you a pure oblation,
and for us a holy outpouring of your mercy.
Through Christ our Lord.

℟. **Amen.**   → No. 21, p. 22 (Pref. P 29-36)

COMMUNION ANT. Cf. Ps 16 (15):11   [Joy]

You will show me the path of life, the fullness of joy in your presence, O Lord. ↓

OR Jn 6:58   [Life]

Just as the living Father sent me and I have life because of the Father, so whoever feeds on me shall have life because of me, says the Lord. ↓

PRAYER AFTER COMMUNION   [Renewal]

May the working of your power, O Lord,
increase in us, we pray,
so that, renewed by these heavenly Sacraments,
we may be prepared by your gift
for receiving what they promise.
Through Christ our Lord.
R̹. **Amen.**   → No. 30, p. 77

Optional Solemn Blessings, p. 97, and Prayers Over the People, p. 105

"Blessed are the clean of heart, for they will see God."

NOVEMBER 1

ALL SAINTS

Solemnity

ENTRANCE ANT.   [Honoring All the Saints]

Let us all rejoice in the Lord, as we celebrate the feast
day in honor of all the Saints, at whose festival the
Angels rejoice and praise the Son of God. → No. 2, p. 10

COLLECT   [Reconciliation]

Almighty ever-living God,
by whose gift we venerate in one celebration
the merits of all the Saints,
bestow on us, we pray,
through the prayers of so many intercessors,
an abundance of the reconciliation with you
for which we earnestly long.
Through our Lord Jesus Christ, your Son,
who lives and reigns with you in the unity of the Holy
    Spirit,
one God, for ever and ever.
℟. **Amen.** ↓

FIRST READING Rv 7:2-4, 9-14   [A Huge Crowd of Saints]

The elect give thanks to God and the Lamb who saved them. The whole court of heaven joins the acclamation of the saints.

A reading from the Book of Revelation

I, JOHN, saw another angel come up from the East,
holding the seal of the living God. He cried out in
a loud voice to the four angels who were given power
to damage the land and the sea, "Do not damage the
land or the sea or the trees until we put the seal on the
foreheads of the servants of our God." I heard the number of those who had been marked with the seal, one
hundred and forty-four thousand marked from every
tribe of the children of Israel.

After this I had a vision of a great multitude, which
no one could count, from every nation, race, people,
and tongue. They stood before the throne and before
the Lamb, wearing white robes and holding palm
branches in their hands. They cried out in a loud voice:
    "Salvation comes from our God, who is seated on the
        throne,
      and from the Lamb."

All the angels stood around the throne and around the elders and the four living creatures. They prostrated themselves before the throne, worshiped God, and exclaimed:

"Amen. Blessing and glory, wisdom and thanksgiving,
honor, power, and might
be to our God forever and ever. Amen."

Then one of the elders spoke up and said to me, "Who are these wearing white robes, and where did they come from?" I said to him, "My lord, you are the one who knows."He said to me,"These are the ones who have survived the time of great distress; they have washed their robes and made them white in the Blood of the Lamb."— The word of the Lord. ℟. **Thanks be to God.** ↓

RESPONSORIAL PSALM Ps 24 [Longing To See God]

℟. **Lord, this is the people that longs to see your face.**

The LORD's are the earth and its fullness;
the world and those who dwell in it.
For he founded it upon the seas
and established it upon the rivers.—℟.

Who can ascend the mountain of the LORD?
or who may stand in his holy place?
One whose hands are sinless, whose heart is clean,
who desires not what is vain.—℟.

He shall receive a blessing from the LORD,
a reward from God his savior.
Such is the race that seeks for him,
that seeks the face of the God of Jacob.—℟. ↓

SECOND READING 1 Jn 3:1-3   [We Shall See God]

God's gift of love has been the gift of His only Son as Savior of the world. It is this gift that has made it possible for us to be called the children of God.

A reading from the first Letter of Saint John

BELOVED: See what love the Father has bestowed on us that we may be called the children of God. Yet so we are. The reason the world does not know us is that it did not know him. Beloved, we are God's children now; what we shall be has not yet been revealed. We do know that when it is revealed we shall be like him, for we shall see him as he is. Everyone who has this hope based on him makes himself pure, as he is pure.—The word of the Lord. ℟. **Thanks be to God.** ↓

ALLELUIA Mt 11:28   [Rest in the Lord]

℟. **Alleluia, alleluia.**
Come to me, all you who labor and are burdened,
and I will give you rest, says the Lord.
℟. **Alleluia, alleluia.** ↓

GOSPEL Mt 5:1-12a   [The Beatitudes]

Jesus is meant to be the new Moses proclaiming the new revelation on a new Mount Sinai. This is the proclamation of the reign, or the "Good News." Blessings are pronounced on those who do not share the values of the world.

℣. The Lord be with you. ℟. **And with your spirit.**
✝ A reading from the holy Gospel according to Matthew.
℟. **Glory to you, O Lord.**

WHEN Jesus saw the crowds, he went up the mountain, and after he had sat down, his disciples came to him. He began to teach them, saying:
   "Blessed are the poor in spirit,
      for theirs is the Kingdom of heaven.

Blessed are they who mourn,
  for they will be comforted.
Blessed are the meek,
  for they will inherit the land.
Blessed are they who hunger and thirst for righ-
    teousness,
  for they will be satisfied.
Blessed are the merciful,
  for they will be shown mercy.
Blessed are the clean of heart,
  for they will see God.
Blessed are the peacemakers,
  for they will be called children of God.
Blessed are they who are persecuted for the sake of
    righteousness,
  for theirs is the Kingdom of heaven.
Blessed are you when they insult you and persecute
you and utter every kind of evil against you falsely
because of me. Rejoice and be glad, for your reward
will be great in heaven."—The Gospel of the Lord.
℟. **Praise to you, Lord Jesus Christ.**   → No. 15, p. 18

PRAYER OVER THE OFFERINGS

[The Saints' Concern for Us]

May these offerings we bring in honor of all the Saints
be pleasing to you, O Lord,
and grant that, just as we believe the Saints
to be already assured of immortality,
so we may experience their concern for our salvation.
Through Christ our Lord. ℟. **Amen.** ↓

PREFACE (P 71)   [Strength and Example]

℣. The Lord be with you. ℟. **And with your spirit.**
℣. Lift up your hearts. ℟. **We lift them up to the Lord.**
℣. Let us give thanks to the Lord our God. ℟. **It is right
and just.**

It is truly right and just, our duty and our salvation,
always and everywhere to give you thanks,
Lord, holy Father, almighty and eternal God.

For today by your gift we celebrate the festival of your
city,
the heavenly Jerusalem, our mother,
where the great array of our brothers and sisters
already gives you eternal praise.

Towards her, we eagerly hasten
as pilgrims advancing by faith,
rejoicing in the glory bestowed upon those exalted
members of the Church
through whom you give us, in our frailty, both strength
and good example.

And so, we glorify you with the multitude of Saints
and Angels,
as with one voice of praise we acclaim: ➜ No. 23, p. 23

COMMUNION ANT. Mt 5:8-10 [The Saints: Children of God]

**Blessed are the clean of heart, for they shall see God.
Blessed are the peacemakers, for they shall be called
children of God. Blessed are they who are persecuted
for the sake of righteousness, for theirs is the
Kingdom of Heaven.** ↓

PRAYER AFTER COMMUNION   [Heavenly Homeland]

As we adore you, O God, who alone are holy
and wonderful in all your Saints,
we implore your grace,
so that, coming to perfect holiness in the fullness of
your love,
we may pass from this pilgrim table
to the banquet of our heavenly homeland.
Through Christ our Lord.
℟. **Amen.**   ➜ No. 30, p. 77

Optional Solemn Blessings, p. 97, and Prayers over the People, p. 105

"They [gave] from their surplus wealth, but she . . . has contributed all she had, her whole livelihood."

NOVEMBER 7

32nd SUNDAY IN ORDINARY TIME

ENTRANCE ANT. Cf. Ps 88 (87):3   **[Answer to Prayer]**

Let my prayer come into your presence. Incline your ear to my cry for help, O Lord.   ➨ No. 2, p. 10

COLLECT   **[Freedom of Heart]**

Almighty and merciful God,
graciously keep from us all adversity,
so that, unhindered in mind and body alike,
we may pursue in freedom of heart
the things that are yours.
Through our Lord Jesus Christ, your Son,
who lives and reigns with you in the unity of the Holy
    Spirit,
one God, for ever and ever. ℞. **Amen.** ↓

FIRST READING 1 Kgs 17:10-16   [Food from God]

Elijah asks a poor widow for food and water. Regardless of
her dire want, she baked a cake for him. The Lord rewarded her and her son with oil and food for a year.

A reading from the first Book of Kings

IN those days, Elijah the prophet went to Zarephath.
As he arrived at the entrance of the city, a widow
was gathering sticks there; he called out to her, "Please
bring me a small cupful of water to drink." She left to
get it, and he called out after her, "Please bring along a
bit of bread." She answered, "As the LORD, your God,
lives, I have nothing baked; there is only a handful of
flour in my jar and a little oil in my jug. Just now I was
collecting a couple of sticks, to go in and prepare
something for myself and my son; when we have eaten
it, we shall die." Elijah said to her, "Do not be afraid. Go
and do as you propose. But first make me a little cake
and bring it to me. Then you can prepare something for
yourself and your son. For the LORD, the God of Israel,
says, 'The jar of flour shall not go empty, nor the jug of
oil run dry, until the day when the LORD sends rain
upon the earth.' " She left and did as Elijah had said.
She was able to eat for a year, and he and her son as
well; the jar of flour did not go empty, nor the jug of oil
run dry, as the LORD had foretold through Elijah.—The
word of the Lord. ℟. **Thanks be to God.** ↓

RESPONSORIAL PSALM Ps 146   [The Lord Feeds the Hungry]

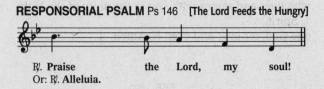

℟. **Praise**   the   Lord,   my   **soul!**
Or: ℟. **Alleluia.**

The LORD keeps faith forever,
    secures justice for the oppressed,
    gives food to the hungry.
The LORD sets captives free.—R̸.

The LORD gives sight to the blind;
    the LORD raises up those who were bowed down.
The LORD loves the just;
    the LORD protects strangers.—R̸.

The fatherless and the widow he sustains,
    but the way of the wicked he thwarts.
The LORD shall reign forever;
    your God, O Zion, through all generations. Alle-
    luia.—R̸. ↓

SECOND READING Heb 9:24-28   [Christ's Sacrifice for Sin]

**Christ entered into heaven to appear before God, not for
sacrifice again, but to take away sin by his sacrifice. Christ
will not die again but he will come to bring about salvation for those who wait for him.**

A reading from the Letter to the Hebrews

CHRIST did not enter into a sanctuary made by
hands, a copy of the true one, but heaven itself, that
he might now appear before God on our behalf. Not that
he might offer himself repeatedly, as the high priest
enters each year into the sanctuary with blood that is not
his own; if that were so, he would have had to suffer
repeatedly from the foundation of the world. But now
once for all he has appeared at the end of the ages to
take away sin by his sacrifice. Just as it is appointed that
human beings die once, and after this the judgment, so
also Christ, offered once to take away the sins of many,
will appear a second time, not to take away sin but to
bring salvation to those who eagerly await him.—The
word of the Lord. R̸. **Thanks be to God.** ↓

ALLELUIA Mt 5:3   [Kingdom of the Poor]

℟. **Alleluia, alleluia.**
Blessed are the poor in spirit,
for theirs is the kingdom of heaven.
℟. **Alleluia, alleluia.** ↓

GOSPEL Mk 12:38-44 or 12:41-44   [Almsgiving]

Jesus exposes the scribes who have betrayed their office.
The wealthy contribute much to the collection from their
surplus but the two coins from the widow are of more
value before God.

*[If the "Shorter Form" is used, the indented text in brackets is
omitted.]*

℣. The Lord be with you. ℟. **And with your spirit.**
✠ A reading from the holy Gospel according to Mark.
℟. **Glory to you, O Lord.**

[IN the course of his teaching Jesus said to
the crowds, "Beware of the scribes, who like
to go around in long robes and accept greetings
in the marketplaces, seats of honor in syna-
gogues, and places of honor at banquets. They
devour the houses of widows and, as a pretext,
recite lengthy prayers. They will receive a very
severe condemnation."]

[He] [*Shorter Form:* Jesus] sat down opposite the
treasury and observed how the crowd put money into
the treasury. Many rich people put in large sums. A
poor widow also came and put in two small coins
worth a few cents. Calling his disciples to himself, he
said to them, "Amen, I say to you, this poor widow put
in more than all the other contributors to the treasury.
For they have all contributed from their surplus
wealth, but she, from her poverty, has contributed all
she had, her whole livelihood."—The Gospel of the
Lord. ℟. **Praise to you, Lord Jesus Christ.**

→ No. 15, p. 18

PRAYER OVER THE OFFERINGS   [Celebrating the Passion]

Look with favor, we pray, O Lord,
upon the sacrificial gifts offered here,
that, celebrating in mystery the Passion of your Son,
we may honor it with loving devotion.
Through Christ our Lord.
℟. **Amen.**   ➜ No. 21, p. 22 (Pref. P 29-36)

COMMUNION ANT. Cf. Ps 23 (22):1-2 [The Lord Our Shepherd]

**The Lord is my shepherd; there is nothing I shall
want. Fresh and green are the pastures where he gives
me repose, near restful waters he leads me.** ↓

OR Cf. Lk 24:35   [Jesus in the Eucharist]

**The disciples recognized the Lord Jesus in the break-
ing of bread.** ↓

PRAYER AFTER COMMUNION   [Outpouring of the Spirit]

Nourished by this sacred gift, O Lord,
we give you thanks and beseech your mercy,
that, by the pouring forth of your Spirit,
the grace of integrity may endure
in those your heavenly power has entered.
Through Christ our Lord.
℟. **Amen.**   ➜ No. 30, p. 77

Optional Solemn Blessings, p. 97, and Prayers over the People, p. 105

"The sun will be darkened.... And then they will see 'the Son of Man....'"

NOVEMBER 14

33rd SUNDAY IN ORDINARY TIME

ENTRANCE ANT. Jer 29:11, 12, 14   [God Hears Us]

The Lord said: I think thoughts of peace and not of affliction. You will call upon me, and I will answer you, and I will lead back your captives from every place.

→ No. 2, p. 10

COLLECT   [Glad Devotion]

Grant us, we pray, O Lord our God,
the constant gladness of being devoted to you,
for it is full and lasting happiness
to serve with constancy
the author of all that is good.
Through our Lord Jesus Christ, your Son,
who lives and reigns with you in the unity of the Holy
    Spirit,
one God, for ever and ever.
℟. **Amen.** ↓

560

FIRST READING Dn 12:1-3   [The Last Judgment]

Daniel describes events that will occur at the end of the world. It will be a time of distress, but the just will live forever in glory while others shall endure horror and disgrace.

A reading from the Book of the Prophet Daniel

IN those days, I, Daniel,
   heard this word of the Lord:
"At that time there shall arise
   Michael, the great prince,
   guardian of your people;
it shall be a time unsurpassed in distress
   since nations began until that time.
At that time your people shall escape,
   everyone who is found written in the book.

"Many of those who sleep in the dust of the earth shall
      awake;
   some shall live forever,
   others shall be an everlasting horror and disgrace.

"But the wise shall shine brightly
   like the splendor of the firmament,
and those who lead the many to justice
   shall be like the stars forever."
The word of the Lord. ℟. **Thanks be to God.** ↓

RESPONSORIAL PSALM Ps 16   [God Our Hope]

℟. You   are   my in - her - i - tance, O   Lord!

O LORD, my allotted portion and my cup,
   you it is who hold fast my lot.
I set the LORD ever before me;
   with him at my right hand I shall not be disturbed.
      —℟.

Therefore my heart is glad and my soul rejoices,
    my body, too, abides in confidence;
because you will not abandon my soul to the nether-
    world,
    nor will you suffer your faithful one to undergo cor-
    ruption.

℟. **You are my inheritance, O Lord!**

You will show me the path to life,
    fullness of joys in your presence,
    the delights at your right hand forever.—℟. ↓

SECOND READING Heb 10:11-14, 18   [Jesus in Glory]

Jesus, unlike the other priests, offered only one sacrifice for sin and took his place forever at God's right hand. He has perfected those who are being sanctified.

A reading from the Letter to the Hebrews

BROTHERS and sisters: Every priest stands daily at his ministry, offering frequently those same sacrifices that can never take away sins. But this one offered one sacrifice for sins, and took his seat forever at the right hand of God; now he waits until his enemies are made his footstool. For by one offering he has made perfect forever those who are being consecrated.

Where there is forgiveness of these, there is no longer offering for sin.—The word of the Lord. ℟. **Thanks be to God.** ↓

ALLELUIA Lk 21:36   [Be Vigilant]

℟. **Alleluia, alleluia.**

Be vigilant at all times
and pray that you have the strength to stand before the
    Son of Man.

℟. **Alleluia, alleluia.** ↓

GOSPEL Mk 13:24-32   [The Last Judgment]

Jesus tells about the end of the world—the darkening of
the sun, moon and stars. Then the Son of Man will come
in glory. Learn from the signs of the fig tree. No one knows
the exact time of this happening.

℣. The Lord be with you. ℟. **And with your spirit.**
✝ A reading from the holy Gospel according to Mark.
℟. **Glory to you, O Lord.**

JESUS said to his disciples: "In those days after that
tribulation the sun will be darkened, and the moon
will not give its light, and the stars will be falling from
the sky, and the powers in the heavens will be shaken.

"And then they will see 'the Son of Man coming in
the clouds' with great power and glory, and then he
will send out the angels and gather his elect from the
four winds, from the end of the earth to the end of the
sky.

"Learn a lesson from the fig tree. When its branch
becomes tender and sprouts leaves, you know that
summer is near. In the same way, when you see these
things happening, know that he is near, at the gates.
Amen, I say to you, this generation will not pass away
until all these things have taken place. Heaven and
earth will pass away, but my words will not pass away.

"But of that day or hour, no one knows, neither the
angels in heaven, nor the Son, but only the Father."—
The Gospel of the Lord. ℟. **Praise to you, Lord Jesus
Christ.**   → No. 15, p. 18

PRAYER OVER THE OFFERINGS   [Everlasting Happiness]

Grant, O Lord, we pray,
that what we offer in the sight of your majesty
may obtain for us the grace of being devoted to you
and gain us the prize of everlasting happiness.
Through Christ our Lord.
℟. **Amen.**   → No. 21, p. 22 (Pref. P 29-36)

COMMUNION ANT. Ps 73 (72):28   [Hope in God]

To be near God is my happiness, to place my hope in God the Lord. ↓

OR Mk 11:23-24   [Believing Prayer]

Amen, I say to you: Whatever you ask in prayer, believe that you will receive, and it shall be given to you, says the Lord. ↓

PRAYER AFTER COMMUNION   [Growth in Charity]

We have partaken of the gifts of this sacred mystery,
humbly imploring, O Lord,
that what your Son commanded us to do
in memory of him
may bring us growth in charity.
Through Christ our Lord.

℟. **Amen.**   → No. 30, p. 77

Optional Solemn Blessings, p. 97, and Prayers over the People, p. 105

"My kingdom does not belong to this world."

NOVEMBER 21

Last Sunday in Ordinary Time

OUR LORD JESUS CHRIST, KING OF THE UNIVERSE

Solemnity

ENTRANCE ANT. Rev 5:12; 1:6   [Christ's Glory]
How worthy is the Lamb who was slain, to receive power and divinity, and wisdom and strength and honor. To him belong glory and power for ever and ever.   → No. 2, p. 10

COLLECT   [King of the Universe]
Almighty ever-living God,
whose will is to restore all things
in your beloved Son, the King of the universe,
grant, we pray,
that the whole creation, set free from slavery,
may render your majesty service
and ceaselessly proclaim your praise.
Through our Lord Jesus Christ, your Son,

who lives and reigns with you in the unity of the Holy
Spirit,
one God, for ever and ever. ℟. **Amen.** ↓

FIRST READING Dn 7:13-14 [Everlasting Kingship]

**Daniel foresees the coming of the Son of Man. He receives
all honor and glory. All peoples of every nation serve him.
His kingship shall last forever.**

A reading from the Book of the Prophet Daniel

AS the visions during the night continued, I saw
one like a Son of man coming,
on the clouds of heaven;
when he reached the Ancient One
and was presented before him,
the one like a Son of man received dominion, glory,
and kingship;
all peoples, nations, and languages serve him.
His dominion is an everlasting dominion
that shall not be taken away,
his kingship shall not be destroyed.
The word of the Lord. ℟. **Thanks be to God.** ↓

RESPONSORIAL PSALM Ps 93 [The Lord Is King]

℟. **The Lord is king; he is robed in maj - es - ty.**

The LORD is king, in splendor robed;
robed is the LORD and girt about with strength.—℟.

And he has made the world firm,
not to be moved.
Your throne stands firm from of old;
from everlasting you are, O LORD.—℟.

Your decrees are worthy of trust indeed;
holiness befits your house,
O LORD, for length of days.—℟. ↓

SECOND READING Rv 1:5-8   [The Alpha and the Omega]

> By the shedding of his blood, Jesus has made us a royal
> nation of priests to serve God. The Lord God is the Alpha
> and Omega—the beginning and the end. He is Almighty.

A reading from the Book of Revelation

JESUS Christ is the faithful witness, the firstborn of
the dead and ruler of the kings of the earth. To him
who loves us and has freed us from our sins by his
blood, who has made us into a kingdom, priests for his
God and Father, to him be glory and power forever and
ever. Amen.
  Behold, he is coming amid the clouds,
      and every eye will see him,
      even those who pierced him.
  All the peoples of the earth will lament him.
      Yes. Amen.
"I am the Alpha and the Omega," says the Lord God, "the
one who is and who was and who is to come, the
almighty."—The word of the Lord. ℟. **Thanks be to God.** ↓

ALLELUIA Mk 11:9, 10   [Son of David]

℟. **Alleluia, alleluia.**
Blessed is he who comes in the name of the Lord!
Blessed is the kingdom of our father David that is to
  come!
℟. **Alleluia, alleluia.** ↓

GOSPEL Jn 18:33b-37   [Christ's Kingdom]

> Before Pilate, Jesus admits that he is a king but that his
> kingdom is not of this world. Jesus says that he came into
> the world to testify to the truth.

℣. The Lord be with you. ℟. **And with your spirit.**
✛ A reading from the holy Gospel according to John.
℟. **Glory to you, O Lord.**

PILATE said to Jesus, "Are you the King of the
Jews?" Jesus answered, "Do you say this on your

own or have others told you about me?" Pilate answered, "I am not a Jew, am I? Your own nation and the chief priests handed you over to me. What have you done?" Jesus answered, "My kingdom does not belong to this world. If my kingdom did belong to this world, my attendants would be fighting to keep me from being handed over to the Jews. But as it is, my kingdom is not here." So Pilate said to him, "Then you are a king?" Jesus answered, "You say I am a king. For this I was born and for this I came into the world, to testify to the truth. Everyone who belongs to the truth listens to my voice."—The Gospel of the Lord. ℞.
Praise to you, Lord Jesus Christ.   ➔ No. 15, p. 18

PRAYER OVER THE OFFERINGS   [Unity and Peace]

As we offer you, O Lord, the sacrifice
by which the human race is reconciled to you,
we humbly pray
that your Son himself may bestow on all nations
the gifts of unity and peace.
Through Christ our Lord.
℞. **Amen.** ↓

PREFACE (P 51)   [Marks of Christ's Kingdom]

℣. The Lord be with you. ℞. **And with your spirit.**
℣. Lift up your hearts. ℞. **We lift them up to the Lord.**
℣. Let us give thanks to the Lord our God. ℞. **It is right and just.**

It is truly right and just, our duty and our salvation,
always and everywhere to give you thanks,
Lord, holy Father, almighty and eternal God.

For you anointed your Only Begotten Son,
our Lord Jesus Christ, with the oil of gladness
as eternal Priest and King of all creation,
so that, by offering himself on the altar of the Cross
as a spotless sacrifice to bring us peace,

he might accomplish the mysteries of human redemption
and, making all created things subject to his rule,
he might present to the immensity of your majesty
an eternal and universal kingdom,
a kingdom of truth and life,
a kingdom of holiness and grace,
a kingdom of justice, love and peace.

And so, with Angels and Archangels,
with Thrones and Dominions,
and with all the hosts and Powers of heaven,
we sing the hymn of your glory,
as without end we acclaim: → No. 23, p. 23

COMMUNION ANT. Ps 29 (28):10-11   [Blessing of Peace]
**The Lord sits as King for ever. The Lord will bless his
people with peace.** ↓

PRAYER AFTER COMMUNION   [Christ's Eternal Kingdom]

Having received the food of immortality,
we ask, O Lord,
that, glorying in obedience
to the commands of Christ, the King of the universe,
we may live with him eternally in his heavenly
   Kingdom.
Who lives and reigns for ever and ever.
℟. **Amen.**   → No. 30, p. 77

Optional Solemn Blessings, p. 97, and Prayers over the People, p. 105

PASTORAL HELPS

- **Christ's Presence in Liturgical Celebrations**

- **The Liturgical Year and the History of Salvation**

CHRIST'S PRESENCE IN
LITURGICAL CELEBRATIONS
Christ Is Personally Present to Us

WE know of two types of presence—local and personal. The first is a simple accident of space and involves no interrelation between the things that are close to one another or even touch. The second is a substantial presence of heart, mind, and will. This is the only true presence for conscious beings in our experience. It is the only way in which the union of hearts and minds takes place.

The Liturgy makes Christ personally present to us. Furthermore, Christ's Presence in the Liturgy is not a static thing, an object of adoration. It is a living achievement in which we cooperate and in which we actively share. To attain the salvation wrought by God in Christ we must enter into the event of Jesus' sacrificial Death and Glorification, which breaks the bonds of time and is accessible to all ages. We do this by participating fully, consciously, and actively in liturgical celebrations of the Church.

Generally speaking, there are four liturgical presences of Christ and each is a different mode of his presence for a specific purpose in regard to us. A brief look at them may make it possible for us to share more fully in the benefits of this astonishing gift of Christ's presence among us.

Christ's Presence in the Assembly

On any given Sunday (or weekday for that matter), a group of persons come together to perform the sacred actions of Christian worship in a particular place. At first they are barely aware of one another; then they begin to act in unison: they rise, sing, perform actions, pray, and utter responses. They welcome the presiding member of the gathering (the priest who acts in the person of Christ) as indispensable for what they are doing, they listen to him, and they give their assent to the prayer that he makes in the name of all.

This is the Christian Assembly. It is rooted in the profoundly human reality of "togetherness" and in the words of Christ: "Where two or three are gathered together in my name, I am in their midst" (Mt 18:20).

The Assembly is the overwhelming manifestation and realization-in-action of the unity of the Body of Christ, the oneness of the baptized. It is the covenant-celebration of the mission entrusted by God to his people to Christianize the world. The Liturgy that flows from the Assembly is a series of prayerful and self-sustaining actions of a faith-community. Members of the Assembly are more than simply consumers, clients, or patients. They are the Church, which is the fundamental doer, actor, and minister of the Liturgy.

Out of the Assembly come the priest who presides, the deacon who ministers to him, the acolytes who assist him, the lectors who proclaim God's Word, the extraordinary ministers who administer Christ's Body and Blood (to those physically present as well as to those who make up its extension because o their inability to be present), the choristers who create the mood of the celebration, and various others.

In the celebrant's greeting, we discern the Presence of the Risen Lord among us. As we accomplish the Eucharistic Sacrifice, which is a prayer (and indeed the Greatest Prayer), Jesus prays with us. In the words of St. Augustine, "He prays for us and in us, and is prayed to by us: he prays for us as our Priest and in us as our Head. As our God, he is prayed to by us." Thus, Jesus is among us as our Friend and Intercessor with the Father.

Christ's Presence in His Priest or Minister

Christ is present in liturgical services in the Priest or Minister who celebrates. At Mass he is present in the Priest who offers the Holy Sacrifice "in the person of Christ," that is, "in specific sacramental identification with the eternal High Priest, who is the Author and principal Subject of this Sacrifice of his, a sacrifice in which, in truth, nobody can take his place" (John Paul II).

Christ is the sole Priest. He alone accomplishes the full communion of human beings with God. He is not only a possible way—he is the Way. He brings not only a truth—he is the Truth. He is not only a living being—he is the Life. All this is summed up in the phrase one Mediator.

"Whoever hears you hears me" (Lk 10:16). In mysterious fashion, the presence of the Lord is manifested also by the one who is called to preside at our Eucharist. Even though he is one of us, he has been chosen to become the sign of the Other. The priest is not the one who presides at our Eucharist; he is the sign of Christ who presides. The priest is a sign of Christ, Head of the Church, and at the same time a sign of the union of the Body with its Head.

In every Sacrament, Christ is also present in his Minister. Through actions and words that "signify" his Presence and his actions, he communicates to us the intention of salvation that he pursues in the world, and that he is in the process of achieving it in us here and now.

The priest consecrates and offers the sacrifice in the name of Christ; he (or a minister) baptizes, confirms, absolves, anoints the sick in the name of Christ. But through him it is Christ who is re-presented, made present anew.

Thus, Jesus is among us as our Representative and Companion who pleads our cause before the Father.

Christ's Presence in His Word

The Word of God acts in many ways—e.g., through private Bible reading and through people. However, it is especially in the Liturgy that the Word is present and active.

In the Liturgy of the Word, the speaker is the Crucified and Risen Christ, who is both the content and the key to the understanding of the Old and New Testament. In him the Father has said everything to us and given everything to us.

The reading from the Old Testament (usually the Prophets) looks forward to Christ the Messiah—bringing Christ before us. The reading from the New Testament (usually from the apostles) looks back to Christ the Lord—bringing Christ in our midst.

No doubt it is "Christ himself who speaks while the Scriptures are read in the Church" (Vatican II: *Constitution on the Sacred Liturgy*, no. 7). But in the Gospel he speaks to us in a way that is clearer, more personal, more decisive, and more enriching that in the other texts.

The Gospel is the high point of the Liturgy of the Word, because in it the Good News of Christ is preached by the

Risen Lord. It is Christ living and present among us who continues to speak to us as he calls us to faith and conversion. He is as present to us as he was to the people who gathered to hear him along the roads of the Holy Land. He comes to us as our Teacher who leads us to all truth.

It is our task to discern the saving event of Christ's Presence among us and God's intervention in our lives that flow out of the reading. More important, we must embrace Christ's Word with an open heart and mind and respond in positive fashion to it. In this task our faith is paramount. It will help us to respond to Christ who leads us to the One who is all Truth.

Christ's Presence in the Eucharist

The last way in which Christ is present in liturgical celebrations is in the Eucharist under the signs of Bread and Wine. This is known as the Presence of Christ par excellence, his Real Presence. One of the reasons for this is that it is the only one that remains. The Bread and Wine remain the Body and Blood, Soul and Divinity of Christ as long as they last after they are consecrated.

In the Eucharistic celebration, Christ is present in a way that is absolutely special: as Priest and Victim, offering himself in a sacrifice of covenant and thanksgiving, recapitulating and appropriating his whole People to make this People in turn priest and victim of the unique Sacrifice. He comes as our God who unites us to himself and to one another.

This presence is active, dynamic, substantial, and permanent. When Communion is over, the Hosts that remain continue to realize Christ's presence among us!

This is the most important presence of Christ and is intended to be the means for our close union with our brothers and sisters who share that Presence with us. It provides our entrance into the Sacred Banquet in which the living Memory of Christ's Passion is recalled, our souls are filled with grace, and we receive a pledge of future glory.

The Eucharist is the vehicle by which Christ comes to us daily in the Spirit. It is the vehicle that effects a transformation in Christians and in the world that is wrought by the Risen Christ.

THE LITURGICAL YEAR
AND THE HISTORY OF SALVATION

1. THE LITURGICAL YEAR

EVERY Sunday the Church keeps the memory of our Lord's Paschal Mystery. She sanctifies time, consecrates it to God, and as it were inserts us into the History of Salvation. Within the cycle of a year she unfolds the whole mystery of Christ—from his foreshadowings in the Old Testament to his majestic Life and Work in the New Testament.

Thus, the feasts of the Liturgical Year are first of all celebrations of the History of Salvation. The mysteries of our Salvation are to be honored not as something past but as something present, for while the act itself (e.g., Christ's birth, death, resurrection, ascension, and the descent of the Holy Spirit) is past, its effects are present. Each feast puts before our mind the sign of some hidden sacred reality, which must be applied to us. We should celebrate the mysteries of our Salvation as happening now to us and we should undergo their mystical effect with an open heart. The best way to do so is by an active participation in Public Worship, aided by the Missal.

We can also be aided by the following summary of the major events of the History of Salvation.

2. ABRAHAM

a) The time around 1850 B.C. was a turning point in the long history of human beings. Almighty God interfered in the course of things and spoke to a man called Abraham. This man lived in what we call now the Fertile Crescent, i.e., the fertile countries along the Tigris and Euphrates rivers, the Jordan river and the Nile

577

river, that surround the Syrian desert as a crescent. God gave the gift of faith to a simple Bedouin, Abraham, who surrendered himself and his family entirely to God. Note that God blessed Abraham, promised to give the land of Canaan to his descendants, made a covenant (alliance) with him and wanted Abraham's faith to be sealed with a sign—circumcision (see Rom 4:11). This is the first establishment of the Kingdom of God on this earth. Read: Gen 11:27—12:9; Gen 17:1-14.

b) It is St. Paul who explains this simple beginning of God's dealings with humanity. Read: Gal 3:16, 26-29, 7-9; Rom 4:18-25. The Church considers Abraham the Father of all the faithful.

c) During the time that the Kingdom of God was restricted to Abraham's carnal offspring, initiation into it was achieved by the sign of circumcision. Now that it is open to all, through Christ's Death and Resurrection, Baptism and Confirmation are the signs (sacraments) of initiation into God's people on earth. Read: Acts 15:1-12; Col 2:11-14.

3. PASSOVER AND EXODUS

a) "Abraham was the father of Isaac, and Isaac the father of Jacob, and Jacob the father of Judah and his brothers" (Mt 1:2). The clan of Jacob emigrated to Egypt where it later fell into slavery. However, God did not forget his chosen people. He bestowed a leader upon the people of Israel (Moses) who led them out of slavery in Egypt. This is called the Exodus. Read: Gen 37; 41:37-46; 46:1-7, 28-34; Ex 1:1-14; 2:1-21; 3:1-14; 11; 12; 14:10-31.

b) God's people were saved from bondage and evil by the Passover sacrifice and its Sacrificial Repast—which foreshadowed the perfect Sacrifice of Jesus

Christ on the Cross. Because Jesus was man, he could offer a sacrifice. Because he was also God, his Sacrifice symbolized an infinitely perfect obedience and self-surrender and was worthy of God the Father. We are saved from evil because of the blood of our Passover Lamb, Jesus Christ. We partake in this Sacrifice, made present to us under the signs of bread and wine, and eat the Sacrificial Repast. Read: Heb 10:4-10; Mk 14:12-16, 22-24; 1 Cor 5:6-8.

4. GOD'S PROTECTION

a) Israel, God's people, went through the Red Sea and obtained their freedom from slavery in Egypt. Under the leadership of Moses they wandered in the desert for forty years and hoped to enter the Promised Land. Whatever they needed in the desert—water, meat, and bread—they received through the prayer of Moses. Read: Ex 16:4-15, 31-35; 17:1-7.

b) We, who are the new people of God, obtained our freedom from the bondage of Satan by going through the water of Baptism (best symbolized in the ancient Church by immersion!). Under the leadership of Christ the Church passes through the desert of life, hoping to enter the Promised Land: heaven. All that the people need in order to reach their supreme goal is given through Christ, our Lord. Read: 1 Cor 10:1-11; 2 Cor 5:1-10; Jn 6:48-71.

5. THE COVENANT

a) Moses ascended Mount Sinai as the mediator between God and the people. It was on this mountain that God proclaimed the Ten Commandments. The Covenant of God with Abraham was then four hundred years old (see Gen 17:1-8). It is a perpetual Covenant, unfolded gradually and consummated with the blood of sacrifice, which reaches its final perfection in its renewed form on Calvary. Read: Ex 19:1-8, 16-25; 20:1-17; 24:4-8.

b) The Mediator of the New Covenant is Jesus Christ. It is established on Calvary with all peoples of the world. The New Covenant is consummated with the Sacrifice of Christ's Precious Blood. Read: Heb 3:1-6; 8:6-13; Lk 22:14-20.

6. FIRST FULFILLMENT OF GOD'S PROMISE

God promised Abraham to give the land of Canaan to his descendants (Gen 12:7). God began to fulfill his promise when the Jews crossed the river Jordan at Jericho under the leadership of Joshua. He realized it under the kingship of David and of Solomon. This great kingdom, ever more idealized in Jewish history, was actually the Kingdom of God. The king was merely his representative and servant (2 Sam 7:5). Since the kings were anointed to be king (2 Sam 5:3) they were called: "The anointed of Yahweh," which means in Hebrew: "Mashiah." Hence the Bible speaks of the "Messiah" or "Christ" (from the Greek), being the king of the great Kingdom of God to come. But this first fulfillment of God's promise contained a further promise, namely, of the Universal Kingdom of God, the Church. God gradually revealed that David's kingdom merely prefigured this great Kingdom to come. Read: 2 Sam 5:1-5; 7:1-17 (esp. 12-16); Ps 71:1-17; Lk 1:31-33; Mk 1:14-15; Mt 9:35-38; Lk 22:24-30; Jn 18:33-38.

7. THE EXILE (BABYLONIAN CAPTIVITY)

a) Israel knew that all the blessings and promises of God depended on faithfulness to the Covenant. But Israel was not faithful. God sent prophets to remind his people of the Covenant. He threatened them and finally had to punish them. Israel was carried away into exile. Read: 1 Kings 19:1-4; 21; Am 3; Isa 1:1-4; 5:1-7; Jer 2:4-7; 6:16-19; 15:5-6; Bar 6:1-6.

b) It was in the exile of Babylon that God's people started praying again. We should pray the psalms of God's chosen people and make them our prayer. Exile and punishment may be seen as separation from God, when we have sinned. We are now: Israel, House of Jacob, House of Judah, Zion or Jerusalem. Read: Ps 136:1-6; 78; 41; 125; 135:1-9, 26.

8. GOD'S PLAN OF SALVATION

a) The wise men of Israel, moved by the Holy Spirit (Gen 1:1—2:7) tell us that God created everything. To make "everything" more understandable for the people of their time, they divided it up in six portions, calling them "days," in order to suggest that the Jews had six days to work and were supposed to rest on the Sabbath. Compare this story about creation with the lesson about it by St. Paul to the Athenians. Read: Gen 1:1—2:7; Acts 17:22-34.

b) They give us God's plan: Human beings would share in God's own life. They would be only a little less than the angels (Ps 8:6). They would live in happiness without pain, frustration, hard labor, or sickness and without dying would be admitted to see God in heaven. But this plan could not be realized, because Adam ate from the tree of knowledge of good and evil (committed sin). The Bible speaks of: "sin of the world" or simply: "sin." This is called "original sin"—the sinful condition in which all of us are born because of the sins of our first parents and everybody's sin. Read: Gen 1:26-30; 2:8-25.

c) God chose a people for himself. He began with Abraham. Patiently, he revealed his plans more clearly and finally established the Kingdom of God through Christ. God did not give up his original plan. He restored all things in Jesus. Read: Eph 1:3-10.

9. PREPARATION

a) The punishment of the exile was the punishment of a loving Father. The prophet Ezekiel, who was with the exiled Jews in Babylon, taught them these things. This punishment was to cleanse the people from evil and to prepare them gradually for the coming of the Universal Kingdom of God with the true "Anointed," Jesus Christ. Read: Ezek 36:24-28, 33-38.

b) In the past centuries before the coming of Christ, the pious Jews, called "The Holy Remnant" or sometimes "The Poor of Yahweh," fostered that waiting and desire for the Kingdom of God. They knew their Bible and prayed. Their prayer should be our prayer during our celebration of Advent. Read: Gen 3:14-15; Isa 7:14; 9:1-7; 11:1-9; 40:1-11; 53:1-7; Ps 21; Isa 45:8.

c) John the Baptist is the last of the prophets in the time of preparation. He introduced the Promised Messiah to his contemporaries. Read: Mt 3.

10. THE KINGDOM OF GOD IS AT HAND

a) When Jesus of Nazareth began preaching and establishing the Kingdom of God, he taught plainly: "I have come, not to abolish [the law and the prophets], but to fulfill them" (Mt 5:17). The kingdom of David was only a first fulfillment of God's promise to Abraham. It contained a further promise, which has been fulfilled in the Kingdom of the Anointed of Yahweh par excellence: Christ Jesus. Read: Mk 1:14-22; Mt 5:17-20; 4:23-25; Jn 1:35-51.

b) Christ Jesus explained that it was he of whom the prophets had spoken (see Jn 1:45) and he worked many miracles to manifest the glory and power of God in him. Read: Lk 4:14-22; Mt 11:16 and Isa 35:5 and 61:1; Lk 18:31-34; 24:13-35 (esp. 25-27); Jn 2:1-12 (esp. 11); 11:1-44 (esp. 42); 12:37-43.

c) With both plain words and parables Jesus explained the nature of the Kingdom and what it means to us. It is a universal Kingdom for all people of faith, who are henceforth the real children of Abraham (see Gal 3:7). It is a people cleansed from iniquity (see Eph 5:25-27) and sharing God's life as originally planned by him (see No. 8b). Read: Mt 22:1-4; 21:33-43; Jn 10:11-16; 15:1-11; 3:1-6; Mt 13.

d) Jesus established a hierarchy of bishops to rule the Kingdom, to teach and to distribute God's blessings in his name, while he resides in heaven, sitting at God's right hand, i.e., as Man sharing power with God, being King and High Priest, interceding for us at God's throne (see Heb 7:25). Read: Mt 28:16-20; Lk 10:1-16 (esp. 16); Jn 20:19-23; Mt 16:13-20; Jn 21:15-17; 1 Cor 11:23-26 (esp. 24).

e) The gradually more perfect realization of the Kingdom in every person follows the universal law of birth and growth: Through pain and death to life everlasting! But it is worthwhile to give up everything to gain it. Read: Jn 12:20-26; Mt 10:16-20; Lk 22:15-30; 12:22-34; 18:18-30; 24:25-27.

11. THE UNIVERSAL CHURCH

The History of our Salvation began with Abraham, reached a peak in the Death and Resurrection of our Lord and became complete with the descent of the Holy Spirit. But it goes on. Christ leads the Church through the Holy Spirit (see Jn 14:16 and Mt 10:20). He continues to teach us and to bless us through holy Signs, the Sacraments. And our grateful answer to God by good behavior is possible only with the help of Christ. Read: Acts 8:26-40; 8:14-17; 2:42-47; 2 Tim 1:6-9; Eph 5:22-33; Rom 8:26.

12. THE FINAL FULFILLMENT

When Christ Jesus established the Kingdom of God, the promise to Abraham was fulfilled. God's original plan was restored in human beings. Sin and evil were defeated. Human beings shared in God's life. But like David's kingdom (see No. 6) this first fulfillment contains a promise, namely, the glorious Kingdom of God in the future world. This will be realized when Jesus will surrender the Kingdom to the Father and God will be all in all. Read: Mt 25:33-46; 1 Cor 15:22-28; Rev 21:1-4; Titus 2:11-15; Mt 6:10.

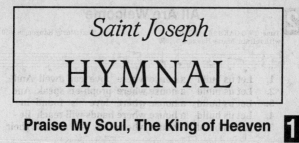

Saint Joseph
HYMNAL

Praise My Soul, The King of Heaven **1**

F. Lyte

John Goss

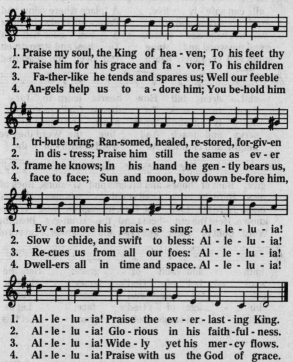

1. Praise my soul, the King of hea - ven; To his feet thy
2. Praise him for his grace and fa - vor; To his children
3. Fa-ther-like he tends and spares us; Well our feeble
4. An-gels help us to a - dore him; You be-hold him

1. tri-bute bring; Ran-somed, healed, re-stored, for-giv-en
2. in dis - tress; Praise him still the same as ev - er
3. frame he knows; In his hand he gen - tly bears us;
4. face to face; Sun and moon, bow down be-fore him,

1. Ev - er more his prais - es sing: Al - le - lu - ia!
2. Slow to chide, and swift to bless: Al - le - lu - ia!
3. Re-cues us from all our foes: Al - le - lu - ia!
4. Dwell-ers all in time and space. Al - le - lu - ia!

1. Al - le - lu - ia! Praise the ev - er-last - ing King.
2. Al - le - lu - ia! Glo - rious in his faith-ful - ness.
3. Al - le - lu - ia! Wide - ly yet his mer - cy flows.
4. Al - le - lu - ia! Praise with us the God of grace.

585

All Are Welcome

2

Tune: TWO OAKS 9 6 8 6 8 7 10
with refrain; Marty Haugen, b. 1950

Text: Marty Haugen, b. 1950

1. Let us build a house where love can dwell And
2. Let us build a house where proph-ets speak, And
3. Let us build a house where love is found In
4. Let us build a house where hands will reach Be -
5. Let us build a house where all are named, Their

all can safe - ly live, A place where saints and
words are strong and true, Where all God's chil-dren
wa - ter, wine and wheat: A ban - quet hall on
yond the wood and stone To heal and strength-en,
songs and vi - sions heard And loved and treas-ured,

chil - dren tell How hearts learn to for -
dare to seek To dream God's reign a -
ho - ly ground, Where peace and jus - tice
serve and teach, And live the Word they've
taught and claimed As words with - in the

give. Built of hopes and dreams and vi - sions, Rock of
new. Here the cross shall stand as wit-ness And as
meet. Here the love of God, through Je - sus, Is re-
known. Here the out - cast and the stran-ger Bear the
Word. Built of tears and cries and laugh-ter, Prayers of

faith and vault of grace; Here the
sym - bol of God's grace; Here as
vealed in time and space; As we
im - age of God's face; Let us
faith and songs of grace, Let this

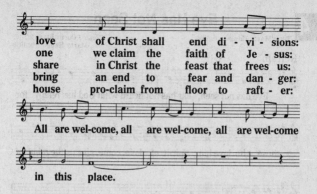

love   of Christ shall   end di - vi - sions:
one   we claim the   faith of   Je - sus:
share   in Christ the   feast that frees us:
bring   an end to   fear and   dan - ger:
house   pro-claim from   floor to   raft - er:

All are wel-come, all   are wel-come, all   are wel-come

in this   place.

Praise to the Lord

3

1. Praise to the Lord,
   The almighty, the King of creation;
   O my soul, praise him,
   For he is our health and salvation;
   Hear the great throng,
   Joyous with praises and song,
   Sounding in glad adoration.

2. Praise to the Lord,
   Who doth prosper thy way and defend thee;
   Surely his goodness
   And mercy shall ever attend thee;
   Ponder anew
   What the almighty can do,
   Who with his love doth befriend thee.

3. Praise to the Lord,
   O let all that is in me adore him!
   All that hath breath join
   In our praises now to adore him!
   Let the "Amen"
   Sung by all people again
   Sound as we worship before him. Amen.

Eye Has Not Seen

4

Tune: Marty Haugen, b. 1950

Text: 1 Corinthians 2:9-10;
Marty Haugen, b. 1950

Refrain

Eye has not seen, ear has not heard what God has read-y for those who love him; Spir-it of love, come, give us the mind of Je - sus, teach us the wis-dom of God.

Verses 1-3

1. When pain and sor-row weigh us down, be near to us, O Lord, for - give the weak - ness of our faith, and bear us up with-in your peace-ful word.

2. Our lives are but a sin-gle breath, we flow-er and we fade, yet all our days are in your hands, so we re-turn in love what love has made.

3. To those who see with eyes of faith, the Lord is ev - er near, re - flect-ed in the fac - es of all the poor and low-ly of the world.

D.C.

Verse 4

4. We sing a mys-t'ry from the past in halls where saints have

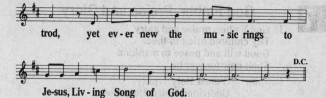

trod, yet ev-er new the mu-sic rings to

D.C.

Je-sus, Liv-ing Song of God.

Praise God from Whom All Blessings Flow 5

1. Praise God, from whom all blessings flow;
   Praise him, all creatures here below;
   Praise him above, ye heav'nly host:
   Praise Father, Son, and Holy Ghost.

2. All people that on earth do dwell,
   Sing to the Lord with cheerful voice;
   Him serve with mirth, his praise forth tell,
   Come ye before him and rejoice.

3. Know that the Lord is God indeed;
   Without our aid he did us make;
   We are his flock, he doth us feed,
   And for his sheep he doth us take.

4. O enter then his gates with praise,
   Approach with joy his courts unto;
   Praise, laud, and bless his name always,
   For it is seemly so to do. Amen.

Faith of Our Fathers 6

1. Faith of our fathers! living still,
   In spite of dungeon, fire, and sword;
   O how our hearts beat high with joy,
   Whene'er we hear that glorious word!

   Refrain: Faith of our fathers! holy faith,
   We will be true to thee till death.

2. Faith of our fathers! We will love
   Both friend and foe in all our strife,
   And preach thee too, as love knows how,
   By kindly words and virtuous life.

3. Faith of our fathers! Mary's prayers
   Shall keep our country close to thee;
   And through the truth that comes from God,
   O we shall prosper and be free.

589

7   # God Father, Praise and Glory

1. God Father, praise and glory
   Thy children bring to thee.
   Good will and peace to mankind
   Shall now forever be.

Refrain: O most Holy Trinity,
                 Undivided Unity; Holy God,
                 Mighty God, God immortal be adored.

2. And thou, Lord Coeternal.
   God's sole begotten Son;
   O Jesus, King anointed,
   Who hast redemption won.—*Refrain*

3. O Holy Ghost, Creator.
   Thou gift of God most high;
   Life, love and sacred Unction
   Our weakness thou supply.—*Refrain*

8   # Praise the Lord of Heaven

Praise the Lord of Heaven,
Praise Him in the height.
Praise Him all ye angels,
Praise Him stars and light;
Praise Him skies and waters
    which above the skies
When His word commanded,
Mighty did arise,

Praise Him man and maiden,
Princes and all kings,
Praise Him hills and mountains,
All created things;
Heav'n and earth He fashioned
    mighty oceans raised;
This day and forever
His name shall be praised.

9   # Holy, Holy, Holy

1. Holy, holy, holy! Lord God almighty.
   Early in the morning our song shall rise to thee:
   Holy, holy, holy! Merciful and mighty,
   God in three persons, blessed Trinity.

2. Holy, holy, holy! Lord God almighty.
   All thy works shall praise thy name in earth and sky
       and sea;
   Holy, holy, holy! Merciful and mighty,
   God in three persons, blessed Trinity.

3. Holy, holy, holy! All thy saints adore thee,
   Praising thee in glory, with thee to ever be;
   Cherubim and Seraphim, falling down before thee,
   Which wert and art and evermore shall be.

590

Now Thank We All Our God

10

1. Now thank we all our God,
   With heart and hands and voices,
   Who wondrous things hath done,
   In whom the world rejoices;
   Who from our mother's arms
   Hath blessed us on our way
   With countless gifts of love,
   And still is ours today.

2. All praise and thanks to God,
   The Father now be given,
   The Son, and him who reigns
   With them in highest heaven,
   The one eternal God
   Whom earth and heav'n adore;
   For thus it was, is now,
   And shall be ever more.

The Church's One Foundation

11

1
The Church's one foundation
Is Jesus Christ her Lord.
She is his new creation,
By water and the Word;
From heav'n he came and sought her,
To be his holy bride;
With his own blood he bought her,
And for her life he died.

2
Elect from ev'ry nation,
Yet one o'er all the earth.
Her charter of salvation,
One Lord, one faith, one birth;
One holy Name she blesses,
Partakes one holy food;
And to one hope she presses,
With ev'ry grace endued.

3
Mid toil and tribulation,
And tumult of her war.
She waits the consummation
Of peace for evermore;
Till with the vision glorious
Her loving eyes are blest,
And the great Church victorious
Shall be the Church at rest.

12 Awake, Awake and Greet the New Morn

Tune: REJOICE, REJOICE, 9 8 9 8 8 7 8 9;
Marty Haugen, b. 1950

Text: Marty Haugen, b. 1950

1. A - wake! a - wake, and greet the new morn, For
2. To us, to all in sor - row and fear, Em -
3. In dark - est night his com - ing shall be, When
4. Re - joice, re - joice, take heart in the night, Though

an - gels her-ald its dawn-ing, Sing out your joy, for
man - u - el comes a - sing-ing, His hum-ble song is
all the world is de - spair-ing, As morn-ing light so
dark the win - ter and cheer-less, The ris - ing sun shall

now* he is born, Be - hold! the Child of our long - ing.
qui - et and near, Yet fills the earth with its ring - ing;
qui - et and free, So warm and gen - tle and car - ing.
crown you with light, Be strong and lov - ing and fear - less;

Come as a ba - by weak and poor, To bring all hearts to-
Mu - sic to heal the bro-ken soul And hymns of lov - ing
Then shall the music break forth in song, The lame shall leap in
Love be our song and love our prayer, And love our end - less

geth - er, He o - pens wide the heav'n - ly door And
kind - ness, The thun - der of his an - thems roll To
won - der, The weak be raised a - bove the strong, And
sto - ry, May God fill ev - 'ry day we share, And

lives now in - side us for ev - er.
shat - ter all ha - tred and blind - ness.
weap - ons be bro - ken a - sun - der.
bring us at last in - to glo - ry.

* During Advent: "soon"

Canticle of the Sun

Tune: Marty Haugen, b. 1950

Text: Marty Haugen, b. 1950

Refrain

The heav-ens are tell-ing the glo-ry of God,

and all cre-a-tion is shout-ing for joy. Come,

dance in the for-est, come, play in the field, and

sing, sing to the glo-ry of the Lord.

Verses

1. Praise for the sun, the bring-er of day, He car-ries the
2. Praise for the wind that blows through the trees, The seas' might-y
3. Praise for the rain that wa-ters our fields, And bless-es our
4. Praise for the fire who gives us his light, The warmth of the
5. Praise for the earth who makes life to grow, The crea-tures you

light of the Lord in his rays; The moon and the stars who
storms ⁊ the gen-tl-est breeze; They blow where they will, they
crops ⁊ so all the earth yields; From death un-to life her
sun ⁊ to bright-en our night; He danc-es with joy, his
made ⁊ to let your life show; The flow-ers and trees that

D.C.

light up the way Un-to your throne.
blow where they please To please the Lord.
mys-'try re-vealed Springs forth in joy.
help us to know The heart of love.
pres-ence re-vealed To lead us home.

14 We Praise Thee, O God, Our Redeemer

Ps 26:12
Tr. Julia B. Cady

E. Kremser

1. We praise Thee, O God, our Re-
deem-er, Cre - a - tor, In grate-ful de-
vo - tion our trib - ute we bring; We
lay it be -fore Thee, we kneel and a-
dore Thee, We bless Thy ho - ly name, glad
prais - es we sing.

2. We wor - ship Thee, God of our
fa - thers, we bless Thee; Thro' trou - ble and
tem - pest our Guide hast Thou been; When
per - ils o'er - take us, es - cape Thou wilt
make us, And with Thy help, O Lord, our
bat - tles we win.

3. With voic - es u - nit - ed our
prais - es we of - fer, To Thee, great Je -
ho - vah, glad an - thems we raise. Thy
strong arm will guide us, our God is be -
side us, To Thee, our great Re-deem - er for -
ev - er be praise. A - men.

Rejoice, the Lord Is King

15

C. Wesley, alt.

J. Darwall, 1770

1. Re - joice, the Lord is King! Your Lord and King a-
2. The Lord, the Sav - ior reigns, The God of truth and
3. His king-dom can - not fail; He rules o'er earth and

1. dore! Let all give thanks and sing, And tri-umph
2. love, When he had purged our stains, He took his
3. heav'n; The King of vic - t'ry hail, all praise to

Refrain

1. ev - er more. Lift up your heart! Lift
2. seat a - bove.
3. Christ be giv'n.

up your voice! Re - joice! a-gain I say re - joice!

We Gather Together

16

(Same Melody as Hymn No. 14)

1. We gather together to ask the Lord's blessing;
   He chastens and hastens his will to make known;
   The wicked oppressing now cease from distressing;
   Sing praises to his name; he forgets not his own.

2. Beside us to guide us, our God with us joining,
   Ordaining, maintaining his kingdom divine;
   So from the beginning the fight we were winning;
   Thou Lord, wast at our side: all glory be thine.

3. We all do extol thee, thou leader triumphant,
   And pray that thou still our defender wilt be.
   Let thy congregation escape tribulation:
   Thy name be ever praised! O Lord, make us free!

17

Come All You People

Tune: Alexander Gondo;
arr. by John L. Bell, b. 1949

Text: Alexander Gondo

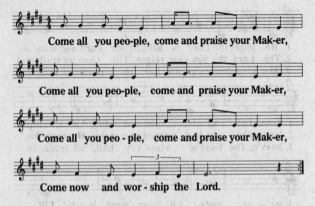

Come all you peo-ple, come and praise your Mak-er,

Come all you peo-ple, come and praise your Mak-er,

Come all you peo - ple, come and praise your Mak-er,

Come now and wor - ship the Lord.

18

To Jesus Christ, Our Sovereign King

1. To Jesus Christ, our sov'reign King,
   Who is the world's Salvation,
   All praise and homage do we bring
   And thanks and adoration.

2. Your reign extend, O King benign,
   To ev'ry land and nation;
   For in your kingdom, Lord divine,
   Alone we find salvation.

3. To you and to your Church, great King,
   We pledge our heart's oblation;
   Until before your throne we sing
   In endless jubilation.

   Refrain:
   **Christ Jesus, Victor! Christ Jesus, Ruler!
   Christ Jesus, Lord and Redeemer!**

Crown Him with Many Crowns

1. Crown him with many crowns,
   The Lamb upon his throne;
   Hark how the heav'nly anthem drowns
   All music but its own;

   Awake my soul, and sing
   Of him who died for thee,
   And hail him as thy matchless King
   Through all eternity.

2. Crown him of lords the Lord,
   Who over all doth reign,
   Who once on earth, the incarnate Word,
   For ransomed sinners slain.

   Now lives in realms of light,
   Where saints with angels sing
   Their songs before him day and night,
   Their God, Redeemer, King.

O Perfect Love

1. O perfect Love, all human thought transcending.
   Lowly we kneel in prayer before thy throne,
   That theirs may be the love that knows no ending,
   Whom thou for evermore dost join in one.

2. O perfect Life, be thou their full assurance
   Of tender charity and steadfast faith,
   Of patient hope, and quiet, brave endurance,
   With child-like trust that fears not pain nor death.

On Jordan's Bank

1. On Jordan's bank the Baptist's cry
   Announces that the Lord is nigh,
   Awake and hearken, for he brings
   Glad tidings of the King of Kings.

2. Then cleansed be ev'ry breast from sin;
   Make straight the way of God within,
   Oh, let us all our hearts prepare
   For Christ to come and enter there.

Gather Us In

Tune: GATHER US IN, Irreg.,
Marty Haugen, b. 1950

Text: Marty Haugen, b. 1950

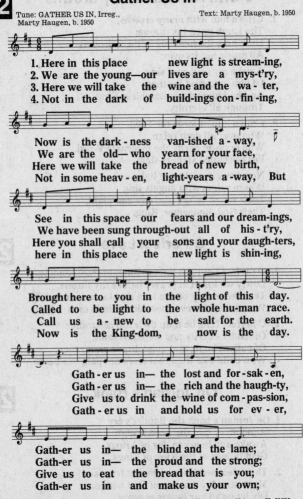

1. Here in this place   new light is stream-ing,
2. We are the young—our   lives are a mys-t'ry,
3. Here we will take   the   wine and the wa - ter,
4. Not in the dark   of   build-ings con-fin-ing,

Now is the dark - ness   van-ished a - way,
We are the old— who   yearn for your face,
Here we will take the   bread of new birth,
Not in some heav - en,   light-years a -way,   But

See in this space our   fears and our dream-ings,
We have been sung through-out all of his-t'ry,
Here you shall call   your   sons and your daugh-ters,
here in this place   the   new light is shin-ing,

Brought here to you in   the   light of this   day.
Called to be light to   the   whole hu-man   race.
Call us a - new to   be   salt for the   earth.
Now is the King-dom,   now is the   day.

Gath-er us in— the lost and for-sak-en,
Gath-er us in— the rich and the haugh-ty,
Give us to drink the wine of com - pas-sion,
Gath-er us in   and hold us for ev - er,

Gath-er us in— the blind and the lame;
Gath-er us in— the proud and the strong;
Give us to eat   the bread that is you;
Gath-er us in   and make us your own;

Call to us now, and we shall a - wak - en,
Give us a heart so meek and so low - ly,
Nour-ish us well, and teach us to fash-ion
Gath-er us in— all peo-ples to - geth - er,

We shall a-rise at the sound of our name.
Give us the cour-age to en - ter the song.
Lives that are ho-ly and hearts that are true.
Fire of love in our flesh and our bone.

Confitemini Domino / Come and Fill

23

Tune: Jacques Berthier, 1923-1994

Text: Psalm 137,
Give thanks to the Lord for he is good;
Taizé Community, 1982

Ostinato Refrain

Con - fi - te - mi - ni   Do - mi - no
Come and fill our hearts   with your peace.

quo - ni - am   bo-nus. Con - fi - te - mi - ni
You a - lone, O Lord, are ho - ly. Come and fill our hearts

Do - mi - no,   Al - le - lu - ia!
with your peace,   Al - le - lu - ia!

O Come, O Come, Emmanuel

John M. Neal, Tr.   Melody adapted by T. Helmore

O come, O come, Emmanuel,
And ransom captive Israel,
That mourns in lowly exile here,
Until the Son of God appear.

Refrain: Rejoice! Rejoice! O Israel,
To thee shall come Emmanuel.

25

Come, Thou Long Expected Jesus

1. Come, thou long expected Jesus,
Born to set thy people free;
From our sins and fears release us,
Let us find our rest in thee.

2. Israel's strength and consolation,
Hope of all the earth thou art;
Dear desire of every nation,
Joy of every longing heart.

3. Born thy people to deliver,
Born a child and yet a king.
Born to reign in us for ever,
Now thy gracious kingdom bring.

26

O Come Little Children

O come little children, O come one and all
Draw near to the crib here in Bethlehem's stall
And see what a bright ray of heaven's delight,
Our Father has sent on this thrice holy night.

He lies there, O children, on hay and straw,
Dear Mary and Joseph regard HIm with awe,
The shepherds, adoring, how humbly in pray'r
Angelical choirs with song rend the air.

O children bend low and adore Him today,
O lift up your hands like the shepherds, and pray
Sing joyfully children, with hearts full of love
In jubilant song join the angels above.

O Come, All Ye Faithful

1. O come, all ye faithful, joyful and triumphant,
   O come ye, O come ye to Bethlehem;
   Come and behold Him born, the King of angels.

   Refrain:
   O come, let us adore Him,
   O come, let us adore Him,
   O come, let us adore Him, Christ the Lord.

2. Sing choirs of angels, Sing in exultation.
   Sing all ye citizens of Heav'n above;
   Glory to God, Glory to the highest.—*Refrain*

3. Yea, Lord, we greet thee, born this happy morning,
   Jesus to thee be all glory giv'n;
   Word of the Father, now in flesh appearing.—*Refrain*

The First Noel

1. The first Noel the angel did say,
   Was to certain poor shepherds in fields as they lay;
   In fields where they lay keeping their sheep
   On a cold winter's night that was so deep.

   Refrain:
   Noel, Noel, Noel, Noel,
   Born is the King of Israel.

2. They looked up and saw a star,
   Shining in the east, beyond them far,
   And to the earth it gave great light,
   And so it continued both day and night.—*Refrain*

3. This star drew nigh to the northwest,
   O'er Bethlehem it took its rest,
   And there it did stop and stay,
   Right over the place where Jesus lay.—*Refrain*

4. Then entered in those wise men three,
   Full reverently upon their knee,
   And offered there, in his presence,
   Their gold and myrrh and frankincense.—*Refrain*

A Child Is Born in Bethlehem
Three Magi Kings

Carlton

1. A Child is born in Beth-le-hem, al-
2. Though found with-in a man-ger poor, al-
3. O let us sing in one ac-cord, al-

1. Three Ma-gi Kings came from a-far, al-
2. Their pre-cious gifts to Him they bring, al-

1. le - lu - ia;   O come, re-joice Je - ru -
2. le - lu - ia;   His King-dom shall for - e'er
3. le - lu - ia;   And bless, for - ev - er Christ

1. le - lu - ia;   Led by a light, the Christ-
2. le - lu - ia;   An of-f'ring to the In -

1. sa - lem,   al - le - lu - ia, al - le - lu - ia.
2. en - dure,   al - le - lu - ia, al - le - lu - ia.
3. the Lord,   al - le - lu - ia, al - le - lu - ia.

1. mas star,   al - le - lu - ia, al - le - lu - ia.
2. fant King,   al - le - lu - ia, al - le - lu - ia.

Responsory: All

Let grate - ful hearts now sing,   A song
of joy and ho - ly praise to Christ the new-born King.

Silent Night

Silent night, holy night!
All is calm, all is bright.
'Round yon Virgin Mother and Child,
Holy Infant so tender and mild:
Sleep in heavenly peace,
Sleep in heavenly peace.

Silent night, holy night!
Shepherds quake at the sight!
Glories stream from heaven afar,
Heav'nly hosts sing Alleluia:
Christ, the Savior is born,
Christ, the Savior is born!

3. Silent night, holy night!
   Son of God, love's pure light.
   Radiant beams from thy holy face,
   With the dawn of redeeming grace,
   Jesus, Lord, at thy birth,
   Jesus, Lord, at thy birth.

Hark! The Herald Angels Sing

1. Hark! The herald angels sing.
   "Glory to the new-born King.
   Peace on earth, and mercy mild
   God and sinners reconciled."
   Joyful all ye nations rise,
   Join the triumph of the skies.
   With th' angelic host proclaim,
   "Christ is born in Bethlehem."

   Refrain:
   Hark! The herald angels sing,
   "Glory to the new-born King."

2. Christ, by highest heaven adored,
   Christ, the everlasting Lord.
   Late in time behold Him come,
   Off-spring of a virgin's womb.
   Veiled in flesh, the God-head see;
   Hail th' incarnate Deity!
   Pleased as Man with men to appear,
   Jesus, our Immanuel here!—*Refrain*

O Sing a Joyous Carol

1. O sing a joyous carol
Unto the Holy Child,
And praise with gladsome
   voices
His mother undefiled.
Our gladsome voices greeting
Shall hail our Infant King;
And our sweet Lady listens
When joyful voices sing.

2. Who is there meekly lying
In yonder stable poor?
Dear children, it is Jesus;
He bids you now adore.
Who is there kneeling by him
In virgin beauty fair?
It is our Mother Mary,
She bids you all draw near.

Good Christian Men Rejoice

Tr. John Mason Neale

1. Good Chris-tian men, re - joice —— With
2. Good Chris-tian men, re - joice —— With
3. Good Chris-tian men, re - joice —— With

1. heart and soul and voice; —— Give ye heed to
2. heart and soul and voice; —— Now ye hear of
3. heart and soul and voice; —— Now ye need not

1. what we say: Je - sus Christ is born to - day!
2. end-less bliss: Je - sus Christ was born for this!
3. fear the grave: Je - sus Christ was born to save!

1. Ox and ass be - fore him bow, And he is
2. He has oped the heav - n'ly door, And man is
3. Calls you one and calls you all To gain his

1. in the man - ger now. Christ is born
2. bless - ed ev - er - more. Christ was born
3. Ev - er - last - ing hall. Christ was born

1. to - day! —— Christ is born to - day!
2. for this! —— Christ was born for this!
3. to save! —— Christ was born to save!

604

Angels We Have Heard on High

34

1. Angels we have heard on high,
   Sweetly singing o'er the plains,
   And the mountains in reply
   Echoing their joyous strains.

   Refrain: Gloria in excelsis Deo. (Repeat)

2. Shepherds, why this jubilee,
   Why your rapturous song prolong?
   What the gladsome tidings be
   Which inspire your heav'nly song?—*Refrain*

3. Come to Bethlehem and see
   Him whose birth the angels sing;
   Come, adore on bended knee
   Christ the Lord, the new-born King.—*Refrain*

Away in a Manger

35

1. Away in a manger, no crib for his bed,
   The little Lord Jesus laid down his sweet head.
   The stars in the bright sky looked down where he lay,
   The little Lord Jesus asleep on the hay.

2. The cattle are lowing, the baby awakes,
   But little Lord Jesus no crying he makes.
   I love thee, Lord Jesus! Look down from the sky,
   And stay by my side until morning is nigh.

3. Be near me Lord Jesus, I ask thee to stay
   Close by me forever, and love me I pray.
   Bless all the dear children in thy tender care,
   And fit us for heaven to live with thee there.

O Little Town of Bethlehem

36

O little town of Bethlehem,
How still we see thee lie!
Above the deep and dreamless sleep
The silent stars go by;
Yet in the dark streets shineth
The everlasting Light;
The hopes and fears of all the years
Are met in thee tonight.

For Christ is born of Mary,
And gathered all above,
While mortals sleep, the angels keep
Their watch of wondering love.
O morning stars, together
Proclaim the holy birth!
And praising sing to God the King
And peace to men on earth.

O holy Child of Bethlehem!
Descend on us we pray;
Cast out our sin, and enter in,
Be born in us today.
We hear the Christmas angels,
The great glad tidings tell;
O come to us, abide with us,
Our Lord Emmanuel.

37

What Child Is This?

What child is this, who laid to rest,
On Mary's lap is sleeping?
Whom angels greet with anthems sweet,
While shepherds watch are keeping?

Refrain:
This, this is Christ the King,
Whom shepherds guard and angels sing;
Haste, haste to bring him laud,
The Babe, the Son of Mary.

Why lies he in such mean estate
Where ox and ass are feeding?
Good Christian fear, for sinners here
The silent Word is pleading.—*Refrain*

So bring him incense, gold, and myrrh,
Come peasant, king to own him,
The King of kings salvation brings,
Let loving hearts enthrone him.—*Refrain*

We Three Kings

1. We three kings of Orient are
   Bearing gifts we traverse afar,
   Field and fountain, moor and mountain,
   Following yonder star.

   Refrain:
   O Star of wonder, Star of night,
   Star with royal beauty bright,
   Westward leading, still proceeding,
   Guide us to thy perfect light.

2. Born a king on Bethlehem's plain,
   Gold I bring to crown Him again,
   King forever, ceasing never,
   Over us all to reign.—*Refrain*

3. Frankincense to offer have I
   Incense owns a Deity high,
   Prayer and praising, all men raising,
   Worship Him, God most High.—*Refrain*

4. Myrrh is mine, its bitter perfume
   Breathes a life of gathering gloom:
   Sorrowing, sighing, bleeding, dying,
   Sealed in the stone-cold tomb.—*Refrain*

5. Glorious now behold Him arise,
   King and God and Sacrifice,
   Alleluia, Alleluia,
   Earth to the heavens replies.—*Refrain*

Holy God, We Praise Thy Name

1. Holy God, we praise Thy Name!
   Lord of all, we bow before Thee!
   All on earth Thy sceptre claim,
   All in heaven above adore Thee.
   Infinite Thy vast domain,
   Everlasting is Thy reign. *Repeat last two lines*

2. Hark! the loud celestial hymn,
   Angel choirs above are raising;
   Cherubim and seraphim,
   In unceasing chorus praising,
   Fill the heavens with sweet accord;
   Holy, holy, holy Lord! *Repeat last two lines*

40 Lord, Who throughout These 40 Days

1. Lord, who throughout these forty days
For us did fast and pray,
Teach us with you to mourn our sins,
And close by you to stay.

2. And through these days of penitence,
And through your Passiontide,
Yea, evermore, in life and death,
Jesus! with us abide.

3. Abide with us, that so, this life
Of suff'ring over past,
An Easter of unending joy
We may attain at last. Amen.

41 When I Behold the Wondrous Cross

1. When I behold the won-drous cross
2. For-bid it, Lord, that I should boast,
3. See from his head, his hands, his feet,
4. Were all the realms of na-ture mine,

1. On which the prince of glo-ry died,
2. Save in the death of Christ, my God;
3. What grief and love flow min-gled down;
4. It would be off-'ring far too small;

1. My rich-est gain I count but loss,
2. The vain things that at-tract me most,
3. Did e'er such love that sor-row meet,
4. Love so a-maz-ing, so di-vine,

1. And pour con-tempt on all my pride.
2. I sac-ri-fice them to his blood.
3. Or thorns com-pose so rich a crown?
4. De-mands my soul, my life, my all.

Jesus, Remember Me

Tune: Jacques Berthier, 1923-1994

Text: Luke 23:42
Taizé Community, 1981

Ostinato Refrain

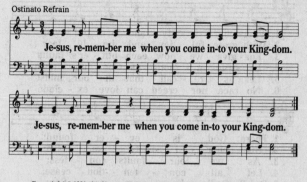

Je-sus, re-mem-ber me when you come in-to your King-dom.

Je-sus, re-mem-ber me when you come in-to your King-dom.

O Sacred Head Surrounded

1. O sacred Head surrounded
   By crown of piercing thorn!
   O bleeding Head, so wounded,
   Reviled, and put to scorn!
   Death's pallid hue comes ov'r you,
   The glow of life decays,
   Yet angel hosts adore you,
   And tremble as they gaze.

2. I see your strength and vigor
   All fading in the strife,
   And death with cruel rigor,
   Bereaving you of life.
   O agony and dying!
   O love to sinners free!
   Jesus, all grace supplying,
   O turn your face on me.

Where Charity and Love Prevail

1. Where char - i - ty and love pre - vail
2. With grate - ful joy and ho - ly fear
3. For - give we now each oth - er's faults
4. Let strife a - mong us be un - known,
5. Let us re - call that in our midst
6. No race nor creed can love ex - clude

1. There God is ev - er found;
2. His char - i - ty we learn;
3. As we our faults con - fess;
4. Let all con - ten - tion cease;
5. Dwells God's be - got - ten Son;
6. If hon - ored be God's Name;

1. Brought here to - geth - er by Christ's love
2. Let us with heart and mind and soul
3. And let us love each oth - er well
4. Be his the glo - ry that we seek,
5. As mem - bers of his Bod - y joined
6. Our broth - er - hood em - brac - es all

1. By love are we thus bound.
2. Now love him in re - turn.
3. In Chris - tian ho - li - ness.
4. Be ours his ho - ly peace.
5. We are in him made one.
6. Whose Fa - ther is the same.

O Faithful Cross

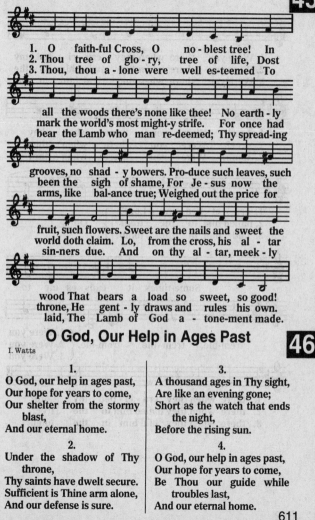

1. O faith-ful Cross, O no - blest tree! In
2. Thou tree of glo - ry, tree of life, Dost
3. Thou, thou a - lone were well es-teemed To

all the woods there's none like thee! No earth - ly
mark the world's most might-y strife. For once had
bear the Lamb who man re-deemed; Thy spread-ing

grooves, no shad - y bowers. Pro-duce such leaves, such
been the sigh of shame, For Je - sus now the
arms, like bal-ance true; Weighed out the price for

fruit, such flowers. Sweet are the nails and sweet the
world doth claim. Lo, from the cross, his al - tar
sin-ners due. And on thy al - tar, meek - ly

wood That bears a load so sweet, so good!
throne, He gent - ly draws and rules his own.
laid, The Lamb of God a - tone-ment made.

O God, Our Help in Ages Past

I. Watts

1.
O God, our help in ages past,
Our hope for years to come,
Our shelter from the stormy
blast,
And our eternal home.

2.
Under the shadow of Thy
throne,
Thy saints have dwelt secure.
Sufficient is Thine arm alone,
And our defense is sure.

3.
A thousand ages in Thy sight,
Are like an evening gone;
Short as the watch that ends
the night,
Before the rising sun.

4.
O God, our help in ages past,
Our hope for years to come,
Be Thou our guide while
troubles last,
And our eternal home.

611

Were You There

1. Were you there when they cru - ci - fied my
2. Were you there when they nailed him to the
3. Were you there when they laid him in the

1. Lord? Were you there when they
2. tree? Were you there when they
3. tomb? Were you there when they

1. cru - ci - fied my Lord?
2. nailed him to the tree?
3. laid him in the tomb? Oh _____

Some-times it caus-es me to

trem-ble, trem-ble trem-ble.
1. Were you
2. Were you
3. Were you

1. there when they cru - ci - fied my Lord?
2. there when they nailed him to the tree?
3. there when they laid him in the tomb?

At the Cross Her Station Keeping

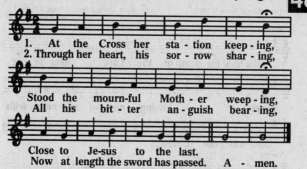

1. At the Cross her sta-tion keep-ing,
2. Through her heart, his sor-row shar-ing,

Stood the mourn-ful Moth-er weep-ing,
All his bit-ter an-guish bear-ing,

Close to Je-sus to the last.
Now at length the sword has passed. A-men.

3. Oh, how sad and sore distressed
Was that Mother highly blessed
Of the sole begotten One!

4. Christ above in torment hangs,
She beneath beholds the pangs
Of her dying, glorious Son.

5. Is there one who would not weep
'Whelmed in miseries so deep
Christ's dear Mother to behold?

6. Can the human heart refrain
From partaking in her pain,
In that mother's pain untold?

7. Bruised, derided, cursed, defiled,
She beheld her tender Child,
All with bloody scourges rent.

8. For the sins of His own nation
Saw Him hang in desolation
Till His spirit forth He sent.

9. O sweet Mother! fount of love,
Touch my spirit from above,
Make my heart with yours accord.

10. Make me feel as you have felt.
Make my soul to glow and melt
With the love of Christ, my Lord.

11. Holy Mother, pierce me through,
In my heart each wound renew
Of my Savior crucified.

12. Let me share with you His pain,
Who for all our sins was slain,
Who for me in torments died.

13. Let me mingle tears with you
Mourning Him Who mourned for me,
All the days that I may live.

14. By the Cross with you to stay,
There with you to weep and pray,
Is all I ask of you to give.

15. Virgin of all virgins blest!
Listen to my fond request.
Let me share your grief divine.

16. Let me, to my latest breath
In my body bear the death
Of that dying Son of yours.

17. Wounded with His every wound,
Steep my soul till it has swooned
In His very blood away.

18. Be to me, O Virgin, nigh,
Lest in flames I burn and die,
In His awful judgment day.

19. Christ, when You shall call me hence
Be Your Mother my defense.
Be Your Cross my victory.

20. While my body here decays,
May my soul Your goodness praise
Safe in heaven eternally.
Amen. Alleluia.

49 Now We Remain

Tune: David Haas, b. 1957

Text: Corinthians, 1 John, 2 Timothy;
David Haas, b. 1957

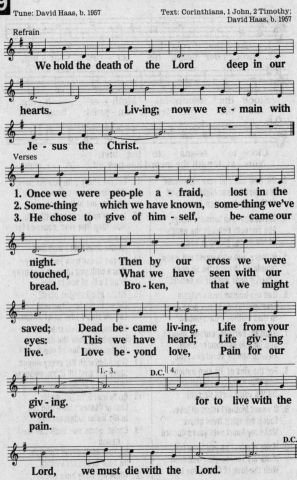

Refrain

We hold the death of the Lord deep in our hearts. Living; now we remain with Jesus the Christ.

Verses

1. Once we were people a-fraid, lost in the night. Then by our cross we were saved; Dead became living, Life from your giving.

2. Some-thing which we have known, some-thing we've touched, What we have seen with our eyes: This we have heard; Life giving word.

3. He chose to give of himself, became our bread. Broken, that we might live. Love beyond love, Pain for our pain.

for to live with the Lord, we must die with the Lord.

O Lord, Hear My Prayer

Tune: Jacques Berthier, 1923-1994
Ostinato Chorale

Text: Psalm 102
Taizé Community, 1982

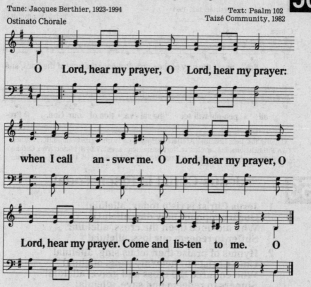

O Lord, hear my prayer, O Lord, hear my prayer:

when I call an-swer me. O Lord, hear my prayer, O

Lord, hear my prayer. Come and lis-ten to me. O

Stay Here and Keep Watch

Tune: Jacques Berthier, 1923-1994

Text: from Matthew 26;
Taizé Community

Stay here and keep watch with me. The hour has come.

Stay here and keep watch with me. Watch and pray.

52 Prepare the Way of the Lord

Tune: Jaques Berthier, 1923-1994

Text: Luke 3:4, 6;
Taizé Community

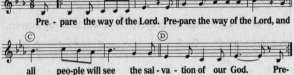

Canon

(A) (B)
Pre - pare the way of the Lord. Pre-pare the way of the Lord, and

(C) (D)
all peo-ple will see the sal - va - tion of our God. Pre-

53 Jesus Christ Is Risen Today

1. Jesus Christ is ris'n today, alleluia!
   Our triumphant holy day, alleluia!
   Who did once upon the cross, alleluia!
   Suffer to redeem our loss, alleluia!

2. Hymns of praise then let us sing, alleluia!
   Unto Christ our heav'nly King, alleluia!
   Who endured the cross and grave, alleluia!
   Sinners to redeem and save, alleluia!

3. Sing we to our God above, alleluia!
   Praise eternal as his love, alleluia!
   Praise him, all ye heav'nly host, alleluia!
   Father, Son and Holy Ghost, alleluia!

54 At the Lamb's High Feast We Sing

1. At the Lamb's high feast we sing
   Praise to our victor'ous King,
   Who has washed us in the tide
   Flowing from his pierced side;
   Praise we him whose love divine
   Gives the guests his Blood for wine,
   Gives his Body for the feast,
   Love the Victim, Love the Priest.

2. When the Paschal blood is poured,
   Death's dark Angel sheathes his sword;
   Israel's hosts triumphant go
   Through the wave that drowns the foe.

Christ, the Lamb whose Blood was shed,
Paschal victim, Paschal bread;
With sincerity and love
Eat we Manna from above.

Christ the Lord Is Risen Today

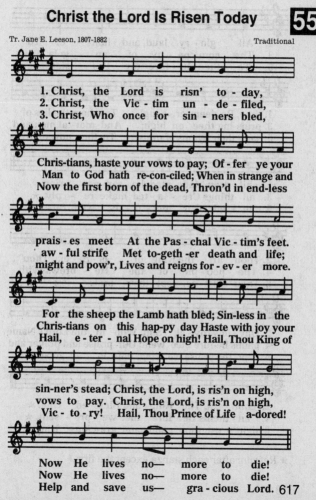

Tr. Jane E. Leeson, 1807-1882

Traditional

1. Christ, the Lord is risn' to-day,
2. Christ, the Vic-tim un-de-filed,
3. Christ, Who once for sin-ners bled,

Chris-tians, haste your vows to pay; Of-fer ye your
Man to God hath re-con-ciled; When in strange and
Now the first born of the dead, Thron'd in end-less

prais-es meet At the Pas-chal Vic-tim's feet.
aw-ful strife Met to-geth-er death and life;
might and pow'r, Lives and reigns for-ev-er more.

For the sheep the Lamb hath bled; Sin-less in the
Chris-tians on this hap-py day Haste with joy your
Hail, e-ter-nal Hope on high! Hail, Thou King of

sin-ner's stead; Christ, the Lord, is ris'n on high,
vows to pay. Christ, the Lord, is ris'n on high,
Vic-to-ry! Hail, Thou Prince of Life a-dored!

Now He lives no— more to die!
Now He lives no— more to die!
Help and save us— gra-cious Lord. 617

56 All Glory, Laud, and Honor

Tr. John Mason Neale, 1851   Melchior Teschner, pub. 1615

1. All glo-ry, laud, and hon-or To
3. The com-pa-ny of an-gels Are
5. To thee be-fore thy Pas-sion They

1. thee, Re-deem-er, King!   To whom the lips of
3. prais-ing thee on high;   And mor-tal men and
5. sang their hymns of praise: To thee, now nigh ex-

1. chil-dren Made glad ho-san-nas ring.
3. all things Cre-a-ted make re-ply. ★
5. alt-ed, Our mel-o-dy we raise. ★

2. Thou art the King of Is-ra-el, Thou
4. The peo-ple of the He-brews With
6. Thou didst ac-cept their prais-es: Ac-

2. Dav-id's roy-al Son, Who in the Lord's Name
4. palms be-fore thee went: Our praise and prayer and
6 cept the praise we bring, Who in all good de-

2. com-est, The King and Bless-ed One. ★
4. an-thems Be-fore thee we pre-sent. ★
6 light-est, thou good and gra-cious King. ★

★ *Refrain:* after each stanza except the first.

618

The Strife Is O'er

Alleluia! Alleluia! Alleluia!

1. The strife is o'er, the battle done!
   The victory of life is won!
   The song of triumph has begun! Alleluia!

2. The powers of death have done their worst,
   But Christ their legions has dispersed;
   Let shouts of holy joy outburst! Alleluia!

3. The three sad days are quickly sped,
   He rises glor'ous from the dead;
   All glory to our risen Head! Alleluia!

4. He closed the yawning gates of hell;
   The bars from heaven's high portals fell;
   Let hymns of praise His triumph tell! Alleluia!

O Sons and Daughters, Let Us Sing!

Alleluia! Alleluia! Alleluia!

1. O sons and daughters, let us sing!
   The King of heav'n, the glorious King,
   Today is ris'n and triumphing. Alleluia!

2. On Easter morn, at break of day,
   The faithful women went their way
   To seek the tomb where Jesus lay. Alleluia!

3. An angel clad in white they see,
   Who sat and spoke unto the three,
   "Your Lord doth go to Galilee." Alleluia!

4. On this most holy day of days,
   To you our hearts and voice we raise,
   In laud and jubilee and praise. Alleluia!

5. Glory to Father and to Son,
   Who has for us the vict'ry won
   And Holy Ghost; blest Three in One. Alleluia!

Christ the Lord Is Risen Again

1. Christ the Lord is ris'n a - gain!
2. He who gave for us his life,
3. He who bore all pain and loss

Christ has bro - ken ev - 'ry chain!
Who for us en - dured the strife,
Com - fort - less up - on the Cross,

Hark, the an - gels shout for joy,
Is our Pas - chal Lamb to - day!
Lives in glo - ry now on high,

Sing - ing ev - er more on high,
We too sing for joy and say,
Pleads for us and hears our cry,

Al - le - lu - ia. Al - le - lu -

ia. Al - le - lu - ia.

Creator Spirit, Lord of Grace

Creator Spirit, Lord of Grace,
Make thou our hearts thy dwelling place;
And, with thy might celestial, aid
The souls of those whom thou hast made.

O to our souls thy light impart,
And give thy love to every heart;
Turn all our weakness into might,
O thou the source of life and light.

Send Us Your Spirit

Tune: David Haas, b. 1957
acc. by Jeanne Cotter, b. 1964

Text: David Haas, b. 1957

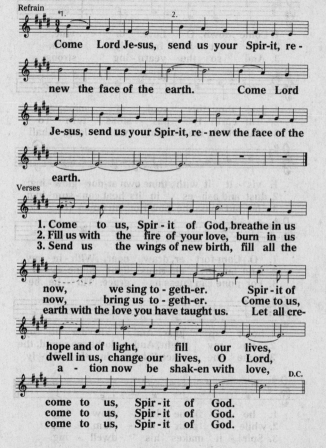

Refrain

*1. 2.

Come Lord Je-sus, send us your Spir-it, renew the face of the earth. Come Lord
Je-sus, send us your Spir-it, re-new the face of the
earth.

Verses

1. Come to us, Spir-it of God, breathe in us
2. Fill us with the fire of your love, burn in us
3. Send us the wings of new birth, fill all the

now, we sing to-geth-er. Spir-it of
now, bring us to-geth-er. Come to us,
earth with the love you have taught us. Let all cre-

hope and of light, fill our lives,
dwell in us, change our lives, O Lord,
a - tion now be shak-en with love,

D.C.

come to us, Spir-it of God.
come to us, Spir-it of God.
come to us, Spir-it of God.

*May be sung in canon.

Come Down, O Love Divine

1. Come down, O Love divine,
2. O let it freely burn,
3. And so the yearning strong,

1. Seek thou this soul of mine, And
2. Till earth-ly pas - sions turn To
3. With which the soul will long, Shall

1. vis - it it with thine own ar-dor glow-ing;
2. dust and ash-es in its heat con - sum-ing;
3. far out-pass the pow'r of hu-man tell-ing;

1. O Com-fort - er, draw near, With - in my
2. And let thy glo-rious light Shine ev - er
3. For none can guess its grace, Till he be-

1. heart ap - pear, And kin - dle it, thy
2. on my sight, And clothe me round, the
3. come the place Where - in the Ho - ly

1. ho - ly flame be - stow - ing.
2. while my path il - lum - ing.
3. Spir - it makes his dwell - ing.

Come, Holy Ghost, Creator Blest

1. Come, Holy Ghost, Creator blest,
   And in our hearts take up thy rest;
   Come with thy grace and heav'nly aid
   To fill the hearts which thou hast made,
   To fill the hearts which thou hast made.

2. O Comforter, to thee we cry,
   Thou heav'nly gift of God most high;
   Thou fount of life and fire of love
   And sweet anointing from above,
   And sweet anointing from above.

3. Praise we the Father, and the Son,
   And the blest Spirit with them one;
   And may the Son on us bestow
   The gifts that from the Spirit flow,
   The gifts that from the Spirit flow.

O God of Loveliness

1. O God of loveliness, O Lord of Heav'n above,
   How worthy to possess my heart's devoted love!
   So sweet Thy Countenance, so gracious to behold,
   That one, and only glance to me were bliss untold.

2. Thou are blest Three in One, yet undivided still;
   Thou art that One alone whose love my heart can fill,
   The heav'ns and earth below, were fashioned by Thy
       Word;
   How amiable art Thou, my ever dearest Lord!

3. O loveliness supreme, and beauty infinite
   O everflowing Stream, and Ocean of delight;
   O life by which I live, my truest life above,
   To You alone I give my undivided love.

Psalm 23: Shepherd Me, O God

Music: Marty Haugen   Text: Psalm 23; Marty Haugen

Refrain

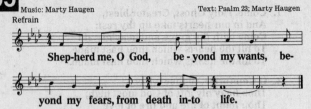

Shep-herd me, O God, be-yond my wants, be-yond my fears, from death in-to life.

Verses

1. God is my shepherd, so nothing shall I want,
   I rest in the meadows of faithfulness and love,
   I walk by the quiet waters of peace.

2. Gently you raise me and heal my weary soul,
   you lead me by pathways of righteousness and truth,
   my spirit shall sing the music of your name.

3. Though I should wander the valley of death,
   I fear no evil, for you are at my side, your rod and your staff,
   my comfort and my hope.

4. Surely your kindness and mercy follow me all the days
   of my life;
   I will dwell in the house of my God for evermore.

Eat This Bread

Tune: Jacques Berthier, 1923-1994   Text: John 6; adapt. by Robert J. Batastini, b. 1942
and the Taizé Community

Refrain

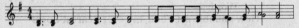

Eat this bread, drink this cup, come to him and nev-er be hun-gry.

Eat this bread, drink this cup, trust in him and you will not thirst.

When Morning Gilds the Skies

E. Caswall, Tr.   Traditional

1. When morn - ing gilds the skies   My
2. Be this, while life is   mine,   My
3. To   God, the Word, on   high   The
4. Let   earth's wide cir - cle round   In

1. heart a - wak - ing cries;   May Je - sus Christ be
2. cant - i - cle di - vine;   May Je - sus Christ be
3. hosts of an - gels cry;   May Je - sus Christ be
4. joy - ful song re - sound;   May Je - sus Christ be

1. praised!   A - like at work and   prayer   To
2. praised!   Be   our e - ter - nal   song, Through
3. praised!   Let   na - tions too up - raise   Their
4. praised!   Let   air, and sea, and   sky, Through

1. Je - sus   I   re - pair: May Je - sus Christ be
2. all   the   a - ges long.   May Je - sus Christ be
3. voice in hymns of   praise: May Je - sus Christ be
4. depth and height re - ply   May Je - sus Christ be

1. praised!   May Je - sus Christ be   praised!
2. praised!   May Je - sus Christ be   praised!
3. praised!   May Je - sus Christ be   praised!
4. praised!   May Je - sus Christ be   praised!

68 Loving Shepherd of Your Sheep

1. Lov - ing Shep - herd of your sheep,
2. Lov - ing Shep - herd you did give,
3. Lov - ing Shep - herd ev - er near,

Keep us Lord in safe - ty keep;
Your own life that we might live;
Teach us still your voice to hear;

Noth - ing can your pow'r with - stand,
May we love you day by day,
Suf - fer not our steps to stray

None can pluck us from your hand.
Glad - ly your sweet Will o - bey.
From the straight and nar - row way.

Good Shep - herd, shield us.
Good Shep - herd, shield us.
Good Shep - herd, shield us.

69 In the Lord's Atoning Grief

1. In the Lord's atoning grief
   Be our rest and sweet relief;
   Deep within our hearts we'll store
   Those dear pains and wrongs he bore.

2. Thorns and cross and nail and spear,
   Wounds that faithful hearts revere,
   Vinegar and gall and reed
   And the pang his soul that freed.

3. Crucified we thee adore,
   Thee with all our hearts implore;
   With the saints our soul unite,
   In the realms of heav'nly light.

Taste and See

Tune: James E. Moore, Jr., b. 1951

Text: Psalm 34;
James E. Moore, Jr., b. 1951

Refrain

Taste and see, taste and see the good-ness of the
Lord. O taste and see, taste and see the
good-ness of the Lord, of the Lord.

Verses

1. I will bless the Lord at all times.
2. Glo-ri-fy the Lord with me,
3. Wor-ship the Lord, all you peo-ple.

Praise shall al-ways be on my lips;
To-geth-er let us all praise God's name.
You'll want for noth-ing if you ask.

my soul shall glo-ry in the Lord
I called the Lord who an-swered me;
Taste and see that the Lord is good;

D.C.

for God has been so good to me.
from all my tou-bles I was set free.
in God we need put all our trust.

71

Song of the Body of Christ / Canción del Cuerpo de Cristo

Tune: NO KE ANO' AHI, Irreg.,
Hawaiian traditional,
arr. by David Haas, b. 1957

Text: David Haas, b. 1957
Spanish translation by Donna Peña, b. 1955,
and Ronald F. Krisman, b. 1946

Refrain

We come to share our sto-ry we
Hoy ve-ni-mos a con-tar nues-tra_his-to-ria, com-par-

come to break the bread, We come to
tien-do_el pan ce-les-tial. Hoy ve-ni-mos jun-tos

know our ris-ing from the dead.
a ce-le-brar tu mis-te-rio pas-cual.

Verses

1. We come as your peo-ple, we
2. We are called to heal the bro-ken, to be
3. Bread of life and cup of prom-ise, in this
4. You will lead and we shall fol-low, you will
5. We will live and sing: your prais-es, "Al le-

come as your own, u-nit-ed with each
hope for the poor, we are called to feed the
meal we all are one. In our dy-ing and our
be the breath of life; liv-ing wa-ter, we are
lu-ia" is our song. May we live in love and

D.C.

oth-er, love finds a home.
hun-gry at our door.
ris-ing, may your king-dom come.
thirst-ing for your light.
peace our whole life long.

628

1. Hoy ve - ni - mos por-que so - mos tu pue - blo, re - na -
2. A sa - nar al en - fer - mo nos lla - mas, al an -
3. Pan de vi - da y san-gre de la a-lian - za, haz-nos
4. Nos guia-rás y te se-gui - re - mos. Nues-tro a-
5. Vi - vi - re - mos can-tan - do "A - lo - ja." "A - le -

ci - dos por tu per - dón, re - u - ni - dos
sio-so, tu es-pe-ran - za tra - er, y al ham - brien - to,
u - no en es-ta co-mu - nión. Que tu rei - no
lien - to vi-tal tú se - rás. Nues-tra luz en el
lu - ya" es nues-tra can-ción. Que vi - va - mos por

D.C.

en tu a - mor, y de un co-ra - zón.
nues - tro a-li - men - to o - fre - cer.
ven - ga en nues - tra trans - for-ma - ción.
dí-a y en la no - che bri - lla - rás.
siem - pre en paz y fra-ter - na u - nión.

Ubi Caritas

72

Tune: Jacques Berthier 1923-1994   Text: 1 Corinthians 13:2-8

Refrain

U - bi ca - ri - tas et a - mor,
Live in char - i - ty and stead - fast love,

u - bi ca - ri - tas De - us i - bi est.
live in char - i - ty; God will dwell with you.

I Am the Bread of Life

Tune: BREAD OF LIFE, Irreg with refrain;
Suzanne Toolan, SM, b. 1927.

Text: John 6;
Suzanne Toolan, SM, b. 1927

1. ___ I am the Bread of life. You who
2. The bread that__ I will give is my
3. Un - less_____ you eat of the
4. ___ I am the Res - ur - rec - tion,___
5. Yes, Lord,_____ I be - lieve that___

1. ___ Yo soy el pan de vi - da. El que
2. El pan que__ yo da - ré____ es mi
3. ___ Mien - tras no co-mas el___
4. ___ Yo soy la re - su - rrec - ción.___
5. ___ Sí, Se - ñor, yo cre - o que___

come to me shall not hun - ger;___ and who be-
flesh for the life of the world, _____ and if you
flesh of the Son of Man_____ and___
I _____ am the life._____ If you be -
you_____ are the Christ,_____ the____

vie - ne_a mí no ten-drá ham - bre.____ El que
cuer - po___ vi - da del mun - do,__ y el que
cuer-po del hi-jo del hom-bre, ___ y___
Yo_____ soy la vi - da._____ El que
tú e - res el Cris - to, _____ El____

lieve in me shall not thirst._____ No one can come to
eat of this bread, _____ you shall__ live for
drink_____ of his blood, and drink___ of his
lieve _____ in___ me,_____ e - ven_ though you
Son___ of__ God,___ Who___ has___

cree_en mí no ten-drá sed._____ Na - die__ vie - ne_a
co - ma__ de mi car-ne_____ ten-drá__ vi - da_e-
be - bas _ de su san-gre y be-bas__ de su
cree_____ en_____ mí,_____ aun-que__ mu - rie-
Hi - jo de Dios,___ que vi - no al

me   un - less   the___ Fa - ther   beck-ons.
ev - er,_____   you   shall__live   for   ev - er.
blood,   you shall   not have life   with - in   you.
die,_____   you   shall__live   for   ev - er.
come   in - to_____the_____   world.___
mí - na,_____   mien - tras el Pa - dre   lla - me.
ter - na,_____   ten - drá___   vi - da e - ter - na.
san - gre,   no ten - drá___   vi - da   en ti.
ra,_____   ten - drá vi - da   e - ter - na.
mun - do_____   pa-ra sal-var-nos.

And I will raise you up,   and I will
Yo   le re - su - ci - ta - ré,   Yo lo re -

raise   you up,   and I will raise   you
su - ci - ta - ré,   Yo lo re - su - ci - ta -

up   on   the   last   day.
ré   el   dí - a   de_El.

O Lord, I Am Not Worthy   74

1. O Lord, I am not worthy,
   That thou should come to me,
   But speak the word of comfort
   My spirit healed shall be.

2. And humbly I'll receive thee,
   The bridegroom of my soul,
   No more by sin to grieve thee
   Or fly thy sweet control.

3. O Sacrament most holy,
   O Sacrament divine,
   All praise and all thanksgiving
   Be every moment thine.

75

The Summons

Tune: KELVINGROVE, 7 6 7 6 777 6;
Scottish traditional; arr. by John L. Bell, b. 1949

Text: John L. Bell, b. 1949;

1. Will you come and fol - low me If I but call your name? Will you go where you don't know And nev - er be the same? Will you let my love be shown, Will you let my name be known, Will you let my life be grown In you and you in me?

2. Will you leave your - self be - hind If I but call your name? Will you care for cruel and kind And nev - er be the same? Will you risk the hos - tile stare Should your life at - tract or scare? Will you let me an - swer prayer In you and you in me?

3. Will you let the blind - ed see If I but call your name? Will you set the pris - 'ners free And nev - er be the same? Will you kiss the lep - er clean, And do such as this un - seen, And ad - mit to what I mean In you and you in me?

4. Will you love the 'you' you hide If I but call your name? Will you quell the fear in - side And nev - er be the same? Will you use the faith you've found To re - shape the world a - round, Through my sight and touch and sound In you and you in me?

632

You Are Mine

Tune: David Haas, b. 1957   Text: David Haas, b. 1957

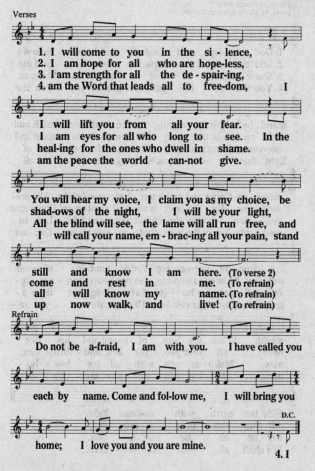

Verses

1. I will come to you in the si - lence,
2. I am hope for all who are hope-less,
3. I am strength for all the de - spair-ing,
4. am the Word that leads all to free-dom,

I will lift you from all your fear.
I am eyes for all who long to see. In the
heal-ing for the ones who dwell in shame.
am the peace the world can-not give.

You will hear my voice, I claim you as my choice, be
shad-ows of the night, I will be your light,
All the blind will see, the lame will all run free, and
I will call your name, em - brac-ing all your pain, stand

still and know I am here. (To verse 2)
come and rest in me. (To refrain)
all will know my name. (To refrain)
up now walk, and live! (To refrain)

Refrain

Do not be a-fraid, I am with you. I have called you

each by name. Come and fol-low me, I will bring you

home; I love you and you are mine.

4. I

77 God of Day and God of Darkness

Tune: BEACH SPRING, 8 7 8 7 D;
The Sacred Harp, 1844;
harm. by Marty Haugen, b. 1950

Text: Marty Haugen, b. 1950;

1. God of day and God of dark - ness, Now we
2. Still the na - tions curse the dark - ness, Still the
3. Show us Christ in one an - oth - er, Make us
4. You shall be the path that guides us, You the

stand be - fore the night; As the shad - ows stretch and
rich op - press the poor; Still the earth is bruised and
ser - vants strong and true; Give us all your love of
light that in us burns; Shin-ing deep with - in all

deep - en, Come and make our dark-ness bright. All cre-
brok - en By the ones who still want more. Come and
jus - tice So we do what you would do. Let us
peo - ple, Yours the love that we must learn, For our

a - tion still is groan-ing For the dawn-ing of your
wake us from our sleep-ing, So our hearts can - not ig-
call all peo-ple ho - ly, Let us pledge our lives a-
hearts shall wan-der rest-less 'Til they safe to you re-

might, When the Sun of peace and jus - tice
nore all your peo - ple lost and bro - ken,
new, Make us one with all the low - ly,
turn; Find - ing you in one an - oth - er,

Fills the earth with ra-diant light.
All your chil - dren at our door.
Let us all be one in you.
We shall all your face dis - cern.

We Walk by Faith

Tune: SHANTI, CM;
Marty Haugen, b. 1950

Text: Henry Alford, 1810-1871, alt.

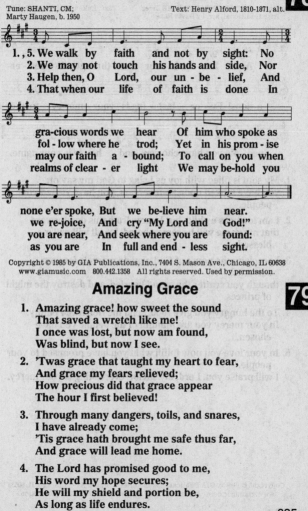

1., 5. We walk by faith and not by sight: No
2. We may not touch his hands and side, Nor
3. Help then, O Lord, our un-be-lief, And
4. That when our life of faith is done In

gra-cious words we hear Of him who spoke as
fol-low where he trod; Yet in his prom-ise
may our faith a-bound; To call on you when
realms of clear-er light We may be-hold you

none e'er spoke, But we be-lieve him near.
we re-joice, And cry "My Lord and God!"
you are near, And seek where you are found:
as you are In full and end-less sight.

Amazing Grace

1. Amazing grace! how sweet the sound
   That saved a wretch like me!
   I once was lost, but now am found,
   Was blind, but now I see.

2. 'Twas grace that taught my heart to fear,
   And grace my fears relieved;
   How precious did that grace appear
   The hour I first believed!

3. Through many dangers, toils, and snares,
   I have already come;
   'Tis grace hath brought me safe thus far,
   And grace will lead me home.

4. The Lord has promised good to me,
   His word my hope secures;
   He will my shield and portion be,
   As long as life endures.

Holy Is Your Name / Luke 1:46-55

Music: WILD MOUNTAIN THYME, Irreg.   Text: Luke 1:46-55, David Haas
Irish traditional; arr. by David Haas

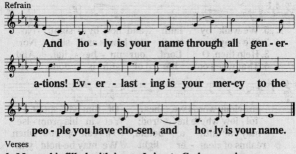

Refrain

And ho-ly is your name through all gen-er-a-tions! Ev-er-last-ing is your mer-cy to the peo-ple you have cho-sen, and ho-ly is your name.

Verses

1. My soul is filled with joy as I sing to God my savior:
   you have looked upon your servant, you have visited your
   people.

2. I am lowly as a child, but I know from this day forward
   that my name will be remembered, for all will call me
   blessed.

3. I proclaim the pow'r of God, you do marvels for your
   servants;
   though you scatter the proud hearted, and destroy the might
   of princes.

4. To the hungry you give food, send the rich away empty.
   In your mercy you are mindful of the people you have
   chosen.

5. In your love you now fulfill what you have promised to your
   people.
   I will praise you, Lord, my savior, everlasting is your mercy.

Sing My Tongue the Savior's Glory

1. Sing my tongue, the Savior's glory,
   Of his flesh the mystr'y sing;
   Of the Blood all price exceeding,
   Shed by our immortal King,
   Destined for the world's redemption,
   From a noble womb to spring.

2. Of a pure and spotless Virgin
   Born for us on earth below,
   He, as Man, with man conversing,
   Stayed, the seeds of truth to sow;
   Then he closed in solemn order
   Wondrously his life of woe.

3. On the night of that Last Supper,
   Seated with his chosen band,
   He the Paschal victim eating,
   First fulfills the Law's command;
   Then as food to his Apostles
   Gives himself with his own hand.

4. Word made flesh the bread of nature
   By his word to Flesh he turns;
   Wine into his blood he changes
   What though sense no change discerns?
   Only be the heart in earnest,
   Faith her lesson quickly learns.

   (Tantum ergo)

5. Down in adoration falling
   Lo! the sacred Host we hail,
   Lo! o'er ancient forms departing,
   Newer rites of grace prevail;
   Faith for all defects supplying,
   Where the feeble senses fail.

6. To the Everlasting Father,
   And the Son who reigns on high,
   With the Holy Ghost proceeding
   Forth from each eternally
   Be salvation, honor, blessing,
   Might, and endless majesty. Amen.

Immaculate Mary

82

1. Immaculate Mary, thy praises we sing,
   Who reignest in splendor with Jesus, our King.

   Refrain:
   Ave, ave, ave, Maria! Ave, ave, Maria!

2. In heaven, the blessed thy glory proclaim,
   On earth, we thy children invoke thy fair name.
   —*Refrain*

3. Thy name is our power, thy virtues our light,
   Thy love is our comfort, thy pleading our might.
   —*Refrain*

4. We pray for our mother, the Church upon earth,
   And bless, dearest Lady, the land of our birth.
   —*Refrain*

Hail, Holy Queen Enthroned Above

83

1. Hall, holy Queen enthroned above, O Maria!
   Hail, Mother of mercy and of love, O Maria!

   Refrain:
   Triumph, ail ye cherubim,
   Sing with us, ye seraphim,
   Heav'n and earth resound the hymn.
   Salve; salve, salve Regina.

2. Our life, our sweetness here below, O Maria!
   Our hope in sorrow and in woe, O Maria!
   —*Refrain*

3. To thee we cry, poor sons of Eve, O Maria!
   To thee we sigh, we mourn, we grieve, O Maria!
   —*Refrain*

4. Turn, then, most gracious Advocate, O Maria!
   Toward us thine eyes compassionate, O Maria!
   —*Refrain*

5. When this our exile's time is o'er, O Maria!
   Show us thy Son for evermore, O Maria!
   —*Refrain*

For All the Saints

William W. How
R. Vaughan Williams, 1872-1958

Moderately, in unison

1. For all the saints,
   who from their labors
   rest,
   Who Thee by faith
   before the world con-
   fessed,
   Thy Name, O Jesus, be
   for ever blest.
   Alleluia, alleluia!

2. O blest communion!
   fellowship divine!
   We feebly struggle,
   they in glory shine;
   Yet all are one in Thee,
   for all are Thine.
   Alleluia, alleluia!

3. From earth's wide
   bounds,
   from ocean's farthest
   coast,
   Through gates of pearl
   streams
   in the countless host,
   Singing to Father, Son
   and Holy Ghost.
   Alleluia, alleluia!

America

1.
My country, 'tis of thee,
Sweet land of liberty,
Of thee I sing;
Land where my fathers died,
Land of the pilgrim's pride
From ev'ry mountainside
Let freedom ring.

2.
My native country, thee,
Land of the noble free,
Thy name I love;
I love thy rocks and rills,
Thy woods and templed hills;
My heart with rapture thrills
Like that above.

America the Beautiful

1. O beautiful for spacious skies,
   For amber wave of grain,
   For purple mountain majesties
   Above the fruited plain.
   America! America! God shed his grace on thee.
   And crown thy good with brotherhood
   From sea to shining sea.

2. O beautiful for pilgrim feet
   Whose stern impassioned stress
   A thoroughfare for freedom beat
   Across the wilderness.
   America! America! God mend thy ev'ry flaw,
   Confirm thy soul in self control,
   Thy liberty in law.

Ye Watchers and Ye Holy Ones

Athelstan Riley, 1858-1945

Cologne, 1623

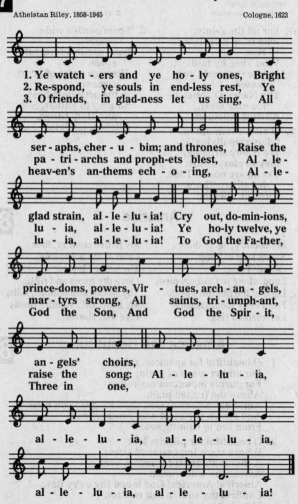

1. Ye watch - ers and ye ho - ly ones, Bright ser - aphs, cher - u - bim; and thrones, Raise the glad strain, al - le - lu - ia! Cry out, do-min-ions, prince-doms, powers, Vir - tues, arch - an - gels, an - gels' choirs, raise the song: Al - le - lu - ia, al - le - lu - ia, al - le - lu - ia, al - le - lu - ia!

2. Re-spond, ye souls in end-less rest, Ye pa - tri - archs and proph-ets blest, Al - le - lu - ia, al - le - lu - ia! Ye ho-ly twelve, ye mar - tyrs strong, All saints, tri - umph-ant, raise the song:

3. O friends, in glad-ness let us sing, All heav-en's an-thems ech - o - ing, Al - le - lu - ia, al - le - lu - ia! To God the Fa-ther, God the Son, And God the Spir - it, Three in one,

HYMN INDEX

TREASURY OF PRAYERS

MORNING PRAYERS

Most holy and adorable Trinity, one God in three Persons, I praise you and give you thanks for all the favors you have bestowed upon me. Your goodness has preserved me until now. I offer you my whole being and in particular all my thoughts, words and deeds, together with all the trials I may undergo this day. Give them your blessing. May your Divine Love animate them and may they serve your greater glory.

I make this morning offering in union with the Divine intentions of Jesus Christ who offers himself daily in the holy Sacrifice of the Mass, and in union with Mary, his Virgin Mother and our Mother, who was always the faithful handmaid of the Lord.

Glory be to the Father, and to the Son, and to the Holy Spirit. Amen.

Prayer for Divine Guidance through the Day

Partial indulgence (No. 21) *

Lord, God Almighty, you have brought us safely to the beginning of this day. Defend us today by your mighty power, that we may not fall into any sin, but that all our words may so proceed and all our thoughts and actions be so directed, as to be always just in your sight. Through Christ our Lord. Amen.

* The indulgences quoted in this Missal are taken from the 1968 Vatican edition of the "Enchiridion Indulgentiarum" (published by Catholic Book Publishing Corp.).

Partial indulgence (No. 1)

Direct, we beg you, O Lord, our actions by your holy inspirations, and carry them on by your gracious assistance, that every prayer and work of ours may begin always with you, and through you be happily ended. Amen.

NIGHT PRAYERS

I adore you, my God, and thank you for having created me, for having made me a Christian and preserved me this day. I love you with all my heart and I am sorry for having sinned against you, because you are infinite Love and infinite Goodness. Protect me during my rest and may your love be always with me. Amen.

Eternal Father, I offer you the Precious Blood of Jesus Christ in atonement for my sins and for all the intentions of our Holy Church.

Holy Spirit, Love of the Father and the Son, purify my heart and fill it with the fire of your Love, so that I may be a chaste Temple of the Holy Trinity and be always pleasing to you in all things. Amen.

Plea for Divine Help

Partial indulgence (No. 24)

Hear us, Lord, holy Father, almighty and eternal God; and graciously send your holy angel from heaven to watch over, to cherish, to protect, to abide with, and to defend all who dwell in this house. Through Christ our Lord. Amen.

PRAYERS BEFORE HOLY COMMUNION

Act of Faith

Lord Jesus Christ, I firmly believe that you are present in this Blessed Sacrament as true God and true Man, with your Body and Blood, Soul and Divinity. My Redeemer and my Judge, I adore your Divine Majesty together with the angels and saints. I believe, O Lord; increase my faith.

Act of Hope

Good Jesus, in you alone I place all my hope. You are my salvation and my strength, the Source of all good. Through your mercy, through your Passion and Death, I hope to obtain the pardon of my sins, the grace of final perseverance and a happy eternity.

Act of Love

Jesus, my God, I love you with my whole heart and above all things, because you are the one supreme Good and an infinitely perfect Being. You have given your life for me, a poor sinner, and in your mercy you have even offered yourself as food for my soul. My God, I love you. Inflame my heart so that I may love you more.

Act of Contrition

O my Savior, I am truly sorry for having offended you because you are infinitely good and sin displeases you. I detest all the sins of my life and I desire to atone for them. Through the merits of your Precious Blood, wash from my soul all stain of sin, so that, cleansed in body and soul, I may worthily approach the Most Holy Sacrament of the Altar.

PRAYERS AFTER HOLY COMMUNION

Act of Faith

Jesus, I firmly believe that you are present within me as God and Man, to enrich my soul with graces and to fill my heart with the happiness of the blessed. I believe that you are Christ, the Son of the living God!

Act of Adoration

With deepest humility, I adore you, my Lord and God; you have made my soul your dwelling place. I adore you as my Creator from whose hands I came and with whom I am to be happy forever.

Act of Love

Dear Jesus, I love you with my whole heart, my whole soul, and with all my strength. May the love of your own Sacred Heart fill my soul and purify it so that I may die to the world for love of you, as you died on the Cross for love of me. My God, you are all mine; grant that I may be all yours in time and in eternity.

Act of Thanksgiving

From the depths of my heart I thank you, dear Lord, for your infinite kindness in coming to me. How good you are to me! With your most holy Mother and all the angels, I praise your mercy and generosity toward me, a poor sinner. I thank you for nourishing my soul with your Sacred Body and Precious Blood. I will try to show my gratitude to you in the Sacrament of your love, by obedience to your holy commandments, by fidelity to my duties, by kindness to my neighbor and by an earnest endeavor to become more like you in my daily conduct.

Act of Offering

Jesus, you have given yourself to me, now let me give myself to you; I give you my body, that it may be chaste and pure. I give you my soul, that it may be free from sin. I give you my heart, that it may always love you. I give you every thought, word, and deed of my life, and I offer all for your honor and glory.

Prayer to Christ the King

O Christ Jesus, I acknowledge you King of the universe. All that has been created has been made for you. Exercise upon me all your rights. I renew my baptismal promises, renouncing Satan and all his works and pomps. I promise to live a good Christian life and to do all in my power to procure the triumph of the rights of God and your Church.

Divine Heart of Jesus, I offer you my poor actions in order to obtain that all hearts may acknowledge your sacred Royalty, and that thus the reign of your peace may be established throughout the universe. Amen.

Indulgenced Prayer before a Crucifix

Look down upon me, good and gentle Jesus, while before your face I humbly kneel, and with a burning soul pray and beseech you to fix deep in my heart lively sentiments of faith, hope and charity, true contrition for my sins, and a firm purpose of amendment, while I contemplate with great love and tender pity your five wounds, pondering over them within me, calling to mind the words which David, your prophet, said of you, my good Jesus: "They have pierced my hands and my feet; they have numbered all my bones" (Ps 22:17-18).

A *plenary indulgence* is granted on each Friday of Lent and Passiontide to the faithful, who after Communion piously recite the above prayer before an image of Christ crucified; on other days of the year the indulgence is partial. *(No. 22)*

Prayer to Mary

O Jesus living in Mary, come and live in your servants, in the spirit of your holiness, in the fullness of your power, in the perfection of your ways, in the truth of your mysteries. Reign in us over all adverse powers by your Holy Spirit, and for the glory of the Father. Amen.

Anima Christi

Partial indulgence (No. 10)

> Soul of Christ, sanctify me.
> Body of Christ, save me.
> Blood of Christ, inebriate me.
> Water from the side of Christ, wash me.
> Passion of Christ, strengthen me.
> O good Jesus, hear me.
> Within your wounds hide me.
> Separated from you let me never be.
> From the malignant enemy, defend me.
> At the hour of death, call me.
> And close to you bid me.
> That with your saints I may be
> Praising you, for all eternity. Amen.

THE SCRIPTURAL WAY OF THE CROSS

The Way of the Cross is a devotion in which we accompany, in spirit, our Blessed Lord in his sorrowful journey to Calvary, and devoutly meditate on his suffering and death.

A plenary indulgence *is granted to those who make the Way of the Cross. (No. 63)*

1. Jesus Is Condemned to Death—God so loved the world that he gave his only-begotten Son to save it (Jn 3:16).

2. Jesus Bears His Cross—If anyone wishes to come after me, let him deny himself, and take up his cross daily (Lk 9:23).

3. Jesus Falls the First Time—The Lord laid upon him the guilt of us all (Is 53:6).

4. Jesus Meets His Mother—Come, all you who pass by the way, look and see whether there is any suffering like my suffering (Lam 1:13).

5. Jesus Is Helped by Simon—As long as you did it for one of these, the least of my brethren, you did it for me (Mt 25:40).

6. Veronica Wipes the Face of Jesus—He who sees me, sees also the Father (Jn 14:9).

7. Jesus Falls a Second Time—Come to me, all you who labor, and are burdened, and I will give you rest (Mt 11:28).

8. Jesus Speaks to the Women—Daughters of Jerusalem, do not weep for me, but weep for yourselves and for your children (Lk 23:2).

9. Jesus Falls a Third Time—Everyone who exalts himself shall be humbled, and he who humbles himself shall be exalted (Lk 14:11).

10. Jesus Is Stripped of His Garments—Every one of you who does not renounce all that he possesses cannot be my disciple (Lk 14:33).

11. Jesus Is Nailed to the Cross—I have come down from heaven, not to do my own will, but the will of him who sent me (Jn 6:38).

12. Jesus Dies on the Cross—He humbled himself, becoming obedient to death, even to death on a cross. Therefore God has exalted him (Phil 2:8-9).

13. Jesus Is Taken Down from the Cross—Did not the Christ have to suffer those things before entering into his glory? (Lk 24:26).

14. Jesus Is Placed in the Tomb—Unless the grain of wheat falls into the ground and dies, it remains alone. But if it dies, it brings forth much fruit (Jn 12:24-25).

STATIONS
of the
CROSS

1. Jesus Is Condemned to Death

O Jesus, help me to appreciate Your sanctifying grace more and more.

2. Jesus Bears His Cross

O Jesus, You chose to die for me. Help me to love You always with all my heart.

3. Jesus Falls the First Time

O Jesus, make me strong to conquer my wicked passions, and to rise quickly from sin.

4. Jesus Meets His Mother

O Jesus, grant me a tender love for Your Mother, who offered You for love of me.

STATIONS
of the
CROSS

5. Jesus Is Helped by Simon

O Jesus, like Simon lead me ever closer to You through my daily crosses and trials.

6. Jesus and Veronica

O Jesus, imprint Your image on my heart that I may be faithful to You all my life.

7. Jesus Falls a Second Time

O Jesus, I repent for having offended You. Grant me forgiveness of all my sins.

8. Jesus Speaks to the Women

O Jesus, grant me tears of compassion for Your sufferings and of sorrow for my sins.

STATIONS
of the
CROSS

9. Jesus Falls a Third Time

O Jesus, let me never yield to despair. Let me come to You in hardship and spiritual distress.

10. He Is Stripped of His Garments

O Jesus, let me sacrifice all my attachments rather than imperil the divine life of my soul.

11. Jesus Is Nailed to the Cross

O Jesus, strengthen my faith and increase my love for You. Help me to accept my crosses.

12. Jesus Dies on the Cross

O Jesus, I thank You for making me a child of God. Help me to forgive others.

STATIONS
of the
CROSS

13. Jesus Is Taken Down from the Cross

O Jesus, through the intercession of Your holy Mother, let me be pleasing to You.

14. Jesus Is Laid in the Tomb

O Jesus, strengthen my will to live for You on earth and bring me to eternal bliss in heaven.

Prayer after the Stations

JESUS, You became an example of humility, obedience and patience, and preceded me on the way of life bearing Your Cross. Grant that, inflamed with Your love, I may cheerfully take upon myself the sweet yoke of Your Gospel together with the mortification of the Cross and follow You as a true disciple so that I may be united with You in heaven. Amen.

The Five Joyful Mysteries

Said on Mondays and Saturdays [except during Lent], and the Sundays from Advent to Lent.

3. The Nativity
For the spirit of poverty.

1. The Annunciation
For the love of humility.

4. The Presentation
For the virtue of obedience.

2. The Visitation
For charity toward my neighbor.

5. Finding in the Temple
For the virtue of piety.

1. The Baptism of Jesus
For living my Baptismal Promises.

The Five

Luminous

Mysteries *

Said on Thursdays [except during Lent].
*Added to the Mysteries of the Rosary by Pope John Paul II in his Apostolic Letter of October 16, 2002, entitled *The Rosary of the Virgin Mary.**

2. The Wedding at Cana
For doing whatever Jesus says.

4. The Transfiguration
Becoming a New Person in Christ.

3. Proclamation of the Kingdom
For seeking God's forgiveness.

5. Institution of the Eucharist
For active participation at Mass.

The Five Sorrowful Mysteries

Said on Tuesdays and Fridays throughout the year, and every day from Ash Wednesday until Easter.

3. Crowning with Thorns
For moral courage.

1. Agony in the Garden
For true contrition.

4. Carrying of the Cross
For the virtue of patience.

2. Scourging at the Pillar
For the virtue of purity.

5. The Crucifixion
For final perseverance.

The Five Glorious Mysteries

Said on Wednesdays [except during Lent], and the Sundays from Easter to Advent.

1. The Resurrection
For the virtue of faith.

2. The Ascension
For the virtue of hope.

4. Assumption of the BVM
For devotion to Mary.

3. Descent of the Holy Spirit
For love of God.

5. Crowning of the BVM
For eternal happiness.

PRAYER TO ST. JOSEPH

O Blessed St. Joseph, loving father and faithful guardian of Jesus, and devoted spouse of the Mother of God, I beg you to offer God the Father his divine Son, bathed in blood on the Cross. Through the holy Name of Jesus obtain for us from the Father the favor we implore.

FOR THE SICK

Father, your Son accepted our sufferings to teach us the virtue of patience in human illness. Hear the prayers we offer for our sick brothers and sisters. May all who suffer pain, illness or disease realize that they are chosen to be saints, and know that they are joined to Christ in his suffering for the salvation of the world, who lives and reigns with you and the Holy Spirit, one God, for ever and ever.

FOR RELIGIOUS VOCATIONS

Father, you call all who believe in you to grow perfect in love by following in the footsteps of Christ your Son. May those whom you have chosen to serve you as religious provide by their way of life a convincing sign of your kingdom for the Church and the whole world.

PRAYER FOR CIVIL AUTHORITIES

Almighty and everlasting God, You direct the powers and laws of all nations; mercifully regard those who rule over us, that, by Your protecting right hand, the integrity of religion and the security of each country might prevail everywhere on earth. Through Christ our Lord. Amen.

PRAYER FOR HEALTH

O Sacred Heart of Jesus, I come to ask of Your infinite mercy the gift of health and strength that I may serve You more faithfully and love You more sincerely than in the past. I wish to be well and strong if this be Your good pleasure and for Your greater glory. Filled with high resolves and determined to perform my tasks most perfectly for love of You, I wish to be enabled to go back to my duties.

PRAYER FOR PEACE AND JOY

Jesus, I want to rejoice in You always. You are near. Let me have no anxiety, but in every concern by prayer and supplication with thanksgiving I wish to let my petitions be made known in my communing with God.

May the peace of God, which surpasses all understanding, guard my heart and my thoughts in You.

PRAYER TO KNOW GOD'S WILL

God the Father of our Lord Jesus Christ, the Author of glory, grant me spiritual wisdom and revelation. Enlighten the eyes of my mind with a deep knowledge of You and Your holy will. May I understand of what nature is the hope to which You call me, what is the wealth of the splendor of Your inheritance among the Saints, and what is the surpassing greatness of Your power toward me.

PRAYER FOR ETERNAL REST

Eternal rest grant unto them, O Lord, and let perpetual light shine upon them. May the souls of the faithful departed, through the mercy of God, rest in peace. Amen.

MAJOR PRACTICES

THE LITURGICAL YEAR

The Liturgical Year is the succession of Times and Feasts of the Church celebrated annually from Advent to Advent.

As presently constituted, the Liturgical Year has the following Times (divisions):

Advent: Beginning on the Sunday closest to November 30 (the Feast of St. Andrew), this period of preparation for the Nativity of the Lord extends over four Sundays.

Christmas Time: This Time begins with the Vigil Masses for the Solemnity of the Nativity of the Lord [Christmas] and concludes on the Feast of the Baptism of the Lord. The period from the end of Christmas Time until the beginning of Lent is included in Ordinary Time (see below).

Lent: The penitential season of Lent begins on Ash Wednesday and ends on Holy Thursday before the Mass of the Lord's Supper that evening. The final week, Holy Week, concludes with the Sacred Paschal Triduum, which takes place from the evening of Holy Thursday to the evening of Easter Sunday.

Easter Time: This Time spans a 50-day period, from the Solemnity of Easter to Pentecost. Its central theme is the Resurrection of Christ together with our resurrection from sin to the new life of grace.

Ordinary Time: This Time comprises the other 33 or 34 weeks of the Liturgical Year. It includes not only the period between the end of Christmas Time and the beginning of Lent but all Sundays and weekdays after Pentecost until the beginning of Advent. It is "ordinary" only by comparison, because the great Feasts of our Lord are prepared for and specially celebrated other times of the year.

Feasts: The first Christians knew only one Feast, Easter, the Feast of our Lord's Resurrection. But this they celebrated all the time, whenever they gathered for the Eucharist. In the Eucharistic celebration, every day and especially every Sunday became for them a little Easter. Easter, in fact, is the center in which all Mysteries of our Redemption merge.

Eventually, however, the Church began to celebrate many of these mysteries in their own right, with Feasts of their own, especially the Birth of our Lord, His Life and Death as well as His Resurrection and Glorification, and also the sending of the Holy Spirit and His work of grace in the soul. Gradually added were Feasts of the Blessed Mother Mary and the Saints.

The Liturgical Year, therefore, has had a long history of development. As early as the year 700, however, the Roman Liturgical Year was essentially as it is today, with two major cycles, Christmas with its Advent and Easter with its Lent, plus the Sundays in between.

HOLYDAYS OF OBLIGATION
Holydays in the United States

Solemnity of Mary, the Holy Mother
of God .... January 1
Ascension of the Lord .... 40 days after Easter or
Sunday after the 6th Sunday of Easter
Assumption of the Blessed Virgin Mary .... August 15
All Saints .... November 1
Immaculate Conception of the Blessed
Virgin Mary .... December 8
Nativity of the Lord [Christmas] .... December 25

SPIRITUAL WORKS OF MERCY

1. To admonish the sinner (correct those who need it).
2. To instruct the ignorant (teach the ignorant).
3. To counsel the doubtful (give advice to those who need it).
4. To comfort the sorrowful (comfort those who suffer).
5. To bear wrongs patiently (be patient with others).
6. To forgive all injuries (forgive others who hurt you).
7. To pray for the living and the dead (pray for others).

CORPORAL WORKS OF MERCY

1. To feed the hungry.
2. To give drink to the thirsty.
3. To clothe the naked.
4. To visit the imprisoned.
5. To shelter the homeless.
6. To visit the sick.
7. To bury the dead.

THE TEN COMMANDMENTS

1. I, the Lord, am your God. You shall not have other gods besides Me.
2. You shall not take the name of the Lord, your God, in vain.
3. Remember to keep holy the Sabbath day.
4. Honor your father and your mother.
5. You shall not kill.
6. You shall not commit adultery.
7. You shall not steal.
8. You shall not bear false witness against your neighbor.
9. You shall not covet your neighbor's wife.
10. You shall not covet your neighbor's goods.

PRECEPTS OF THE CHURCH
(Traditional Form)

1. To participate at Mass on all Sundays and Holydays of Obligation.
2. To fast and to abstain on the days appointed.
3. To confess our sins at least once a year.
4. To receive Holy Communion during Easter Time.
5. To contribute to the support of the Church.
6. To observe the laws of the Church concerning marriage.

GUIDELINES FOR THE RECEPTION
OF COMMUNION

For Catholics

As Catholics, we fully participate in the celebration of the Eucharist when we receive Holy Communion. We are encouraged to receive Communion devoutly and frequently. In order to be properly disposed to receive Communion, participants should not be conscious of grave sin and normally should have fasted for one hour. A person who is conscious of grave sin is not to receive the Body and Blood of the Lord without prior sacramental confession except for a grave reason where there is no opportunity for confession. In this case, the person is to be mindful of the obligation to make an act of perfect contrition, including the intention of confessing as soon as possible (*Code of Canon Law, canon 916*). A frequent reception of the Sacrament of Penance is encouraged for all.

For Fellow Christians

We welcome our fellow Christians to this celebration of the Eucharist as our brothers and sisters. We pray that our common baptism and the action of the Holy Spirit in this Eucharist will draw us closer to one another and begin to dispel the sad divisions that separate us. We pray that these will lessen and finally disappear, in keeping with Christ's prayer for us "that they may all be one" (John 17:21).

Because Catholics believe that the celebration of the Eucharist is a sign of the reality of the oneness of faith, life, and worship, members of those churches with whom we are not yet fully united are ordinarily not admitted to Holy Communion. Eucharistic sharing in exceptional circumstances by other Christians requires permission according to the directives of the diocesan bishop and the provisions of canon law (*canon 844 § 4*). Members of the Orthodox Churches, the Assyrian Church of the East, and the Polish National Catholic Church are urged to respect the discipline of their own Churches. According to Roman Catholic discipline, the Code of Canon Law does not object to the reception of Communion by Christians of these Churches (*canon 844 § 3*).

For Those Not Receiving Holy Communion

All who are not receiving Holy Communion are encouraged to express in their hearts a prayerful desire for unity with the Lord Jesus and with one another.

For Non-Christians

We also welcome to this celebration those who do not share our faith in Jesus Christ. While we cannot admit them to Holy Communion, we ask them to offer their prayers for the peace and the unity of the human family.

RITE OF PENANCE
(Extracted from the Rite of Penance)

Texts for the Penitent

The penitent should prepare for the celebration of the sacrament by prayer, reading of Scripture, and silent reflection. The penitent should think over and should regret all sins since the last celebration of the sacrament.

RECEPTION OF THE PENITENT

The penitent enters the confessional or other place set aside for the celebration of the sacrament of penance. After the welcoming of the priest, the penitent makes the sign of the cross saying:

In the name of the Father, and of the Son, and of the Holy Spirit. Amen.

The penitent is invited to have trust in God and replies:

Amen.

READING OF THE WORD OF GOD

The penitent then listens to a text of Scripture which tells about God's mercy and calls man to conversion.

CONFESSION OF SINS AND ACCEPTANCE OF SATISFACTION

The penitent speaks to the priest in a normal, conversational fashion. The penitent tells when he or she last celebrated the sacrament and then confesses his or her sins. The penitent then listens to any advice the priest may give and accepts the satisfaction from the priest. The penitent should ask any appropriate questions.

PRAYER OF THE PENITENT AND ABSOLUTION

Prayer

Before the absolution is given, the penitent expresses sorrow for sins in these or similar words:

**My God,
I am sorry for my sins with all my heart.
In choosing to do wrong
and failing to do good,
I have sinned against you
whom I should love above all things.
I firmly intend, with your help,
to do penance,
to sin no more,
and to avoid whatever leads me to sin.
Our Savior Jesus Christ
suffered and died for us.
In his name, my God, have mercy.**

OR:

> Remember that your compassion, O LORD,
> and your love are from of old.
> In your kindness remember me,
> because of your goodness, O LORD.

OR:

> Thoroughly wash me from my guilt
> and of my sin cleanse me.
> For I acknowledge my offense,
> and my sin is before me always.

OR:

> Father, I have sinned [. . .] against you.
> I no longer deserve to be called your son.
> Be merciful to me a sinner.

OR:

> Father of mercy,
> like the prodigal son
> I return to you and say:
> "I have sinned against you
> and am no longer worthy to be called your son."
> Christ Jesus, Savior of the world,
> I pray with the repentant thief
> to whom you promised Paradise:
> "Lord, remember me in your kingdom."
> Holy Spirit, fountain of love,
> I call on you with trust:
> "Purify my heart,
> and help me to walk as a child of light."

OR:

> Lord Jesus,
> you opened the eyes of the blind,
> healed the sick,
> forgave the sinful woman,
> and after Peter's denial confirmed him in your love.
> Listen to my prayer:
> forgive all my sins,
> renew your love in my heart,
> help me to live in perfect unity with my fellow Christians
> that I may proclaim your saving power to all the world.

OR:

> Lord Jesus,
> you chose to be called the friend of sinners.
> By your saving death and resurrection
> free me from my sins.
> May your peace take root in my heart

and bring forth a harvest
of love, holiness, and truth.

OR:

Lord Jesus Christ,
you are the Lamb of God;
you take away the sins of the world.
Through the grace of the Holy Spirit
restore me to friendship with your Father,
cleanse me from every stain of sin
in the blood you shed for me,
and raise me to new life
for the glory of your name.

OR:

Lord God,
in your goodness have mercy on me:
do not look on my sins,
but take away all my guilt.
Create in me a clean heart
and renew within me an upright spirit.

OR:

Lord Jesus, Son of God,
have mercy on me, a sinner.

ABSOLUTION

*If the penitent is not kneeling, he or she bows his or her head
as the priest extends his hands (or at least extends his right
hand).*

God, the Father of mercies,
through the death and resurrection of his Son
has reconciled the world to himself
and sent the Holy Spirit among us
for the forgiveness of sins;
through the ministry of the Church
may God give you pardon and peace,
and I absolve you from your sins
in the name of the Father, and of the Son, ✠
and of the Holy Spirit. Amen.

PROCLAMATION OF PRAISE OF GOD AND DISMISSAL

Penitent and priest give praise to God.

Priest: Give thanks to the Lord, for he is good.
Penitent: His mercy endures for ever.

Then the penitent is dismissed by the priest.

Form of Examination of Conscience

This suggested form for an examination of conscience should be completed and adapted to meet the needs of different individuals and to follow local usages.

In an examination of conscience, before the sacrament of penance, each individual should ask himself these questions in particular:

1. What is my attitude to the sacrament of penance? Do I sincerely want to be set free from sin, to turn again to God, to begin a new life, and to enter into a deeper friendship with God? Or do I look on it as a burden, to be undertaken as seldom as possible?

2. Did I forget to mention, or deliberately conceal, any grave sins in past confessions?

3. Did I perform the penance I was given? Did I make reparation for any injury to others? Have I tried to put into practice any resolution to lead a better life in keeping with the Gospel?

Each individual should examine his life in the light of God's word.

I. The Lord says: "You shall love the Lord your God with your whole heart."

1. Is my heart set on God, so that I really love him above all things and am faithful to his commandments, as a son loves his father? Or am I more concerned about the things of this world? Have I a right intention in what I do?

2. God spoke to us in his Son. Is my faith in God firm and secure? Am I wholehearted in accepting the Church's teaching? Have I been careful to grow in my understanding of the faith, to hear God's word, to listen to instructions on the faith, to avoid dangers to faith? Have I been always strong and fearless in professing my faith in God and the Church? Have I been willing to be known as a Christian in private and public life?

3. Have I prayed morning and evening? When I pray, do I really raise my mind and heart to God or is it a matter of words only? Do I offer God my difficulties, my joys, and my sorrows? Do I turn to God in time of temptation?

4. Have I love and reverence for God's name? Have I offended him in blasphemy, swearing falsely, or taking his name in vain? Have I shown disrespect for the Blessed Virgin Mary and the saints?

5. Do I keep Sundays and feast days holy by taking a full part, with attention and devotion, in the liturgy, and especially in the Mass? Have I fulfilled the precept of annual confession and of communion during the Easter season?

6. Are there false gods that I worship by giving them greater attention and deeper trust than I give to God: money, superstition, spiritism, or other occult practices?

II. The Lord says: "Love one another as I have loved you."

1. Have I a genuine love for my neighbors? Or do I use them for my own ends, or do to them what I would not want done to myself? Have I given grave scandal by my words or actions?

2. In my family life, have I contributed to the well-being and happiness of the rest of the family by patience and genuine love? Have I been obedient to parents, showing them proper respect and giving them help in their spiritual and material needs? Have I been careful to give a Christian upbringing to my children, and to help them by good example and by exercising authority as a parent? Have I been faithful to my husband/wife in my heart and in my relations with others?

3. Do I share my possessions with the less fortunate? Do I do my best to help the victims of oppression, misfortune, and poverty? Or do I look down on my neighbor, especially the poor, the sick, the elderly, strangers, and people of other races?

4. Does my life reflect the mission I received in confirmation? Do I share in the apostolic and charitable works of the Church and in the life of my parish? Have I helped to meet the needs of the Church and of the world and prayed for them: for unity in the Church, for the spread of the Gospel among the nations, for peace and justice, etc.?

5. Am I concerned for the good and prosperity of the human community in which I live, or do I spend my life caring only for myself? Do I share to the best of my ability in the work of promoting justice, morality, harmony, and love in human relations? Have I done my duty as a citizen? Have I paid my taxes?

6. In my work or profession am I just, hard-working, honest, serving society out of love for others? Have I paid a fair wage to my employees? Have I been faithful to my promises and contracts?

7. Have I obeyed legitimate authority and given it due respect?

8. If I am in a position of responsibility or authority, do I use this for my own advantage or for the good of others, in a spirit of service?

9. Have I been truthful and fair, or have I injured others by deceit, calumny, detraction, rash judgment, or violation of a secret?

10. Have I done violence to others by damage to life or limb, reputation, honor, or material possessions? Have I involved them in loss? Have I been responsible for advising an abortion or procuring one?

Have I kept up hatred for others? Am I estranged from others through quarrels, enmity, insults, anger? Have I been guilty of refusing to testify to the innocence of another because of selfishness?

11. Have I stolen the property of others? Have I desired it unjustly and inordinately? Have I damaged it? Have I made restitution of other people's property and made good their loss?

12. If I have been injured, have I been ready to make peace for the love of Christ and to forgive, or do I harbor hatred and the desire for revenge?

III. Christ our Lord says: "Be perfect as your Father is perfect."

1. Where is my life really leading me? Is the hope of eternal life my inspiration? Have I tried to grow in the life of the Spirit through prayer, reading the word of God and meditating on it, receiving the sacraments, self-denial? Have I been anxious to control my vices, my bad inclinations and passions, e.g., envy, love of food and drink? Have I been proud and boastful, thinking myself better in the sight of God and despising others as less important than myself? Have I imposed my own will on others, without respecting their freedom and rights?

2. What use have I made of time, of health and strength, of the gifts God has given to me to be used like the talents in the Gospel? Do I use them to become more perfect every day? Or have I been lazy and too much given to leisure?

3. Have I been patient in accepting the sorrows and disappointments of life? How have I performed mortification so as to "fill up what is wanting to the sufferings of Christ"? Have I kept the precept of fasting and abstinence?

4. Have I kept my senses and my whole body pure and chaste as a temple of the Holy Spirit consecrated for resurrection and glory, and as a sign of God's faithful love for men and women, a sign that is seen most perfectly in the sacrament of matrimony? Have I dishonored my body by fornication, impurity, unworthy conversation or thoughts, evil desires or actions? Have I given in to sensuality? Have I indulged in reading, conversation, shows, and entertainments that offend against Christian and human decency? Have I encouraged others to sin by my own failure to maintain these standards? Have I been faithful to the moral law in my married life?

5. Have I gone against my conscience out of fear or hypocrisy?

6. Have I always tried to act in the true freedom of the sons of God according to the law of the Spirit, or am I the slave of forces within me?